Aerospace Power in the Twenty-First Century

A Basic Primer

Clayton K. S. Chun

United States Air Force Academy
in cooperation with
Air University Press

Colorado Springs, Colorado
and
Maxwell Air Force Base, Alabama

July 2001

Library of Congress Cataloging-in-Publication Data

Chun, Clayton K. S.
    Aerospace power in the twenty-first century : a basic primer / Clayton K.S. Chun.
      p. cm.
    Includes index.
    ISBN 1-58566-091-4
      1. Air power. 2. Space warfare. 3. Air power—History—20th century. 4. Astronautics, Military. 5. United States. Air Force. 6. Military doctrine—United States. I. Title.

UG630 .C52 2001
358.4'00973—dc21

                                                                                                           2001034104

First Printing June 2001
Second Printing July 2002

Disclaimer

Opinions, conclusions, and recommendations expressed or implied within are solely those of the author and do not necessarily represent the views of the United States Air Force Academy, the United States Air Force, the Department of Defense, or any other US government agency. Cleared for public release: distribution unlimited.

Contents

Chapter		Page
	DISCLAIMER	ii
	FOREWORD	xi
	ABOUT THE AUTHOR	xiii
	PREFACE	xv
1	Aerospace Concepts and Definitions	1
	Aerospace Power Defined	1
	Characteristics of Aerospace Power	4
	Aerospace Power in War	14
	What Aerospace Forces Can Accomplish . . .	23
	The Aerospace Environment	27
	Aerospace Elements	29
	Summary	33
2	Aerospace Power Theory	35
	What Is Theory?	35
	What Should Aerospace Power Theory Do? . .	37
	Giulio Douhet: The First Airpower Theorist . .	39
	Billy Mitchell: America's First Airpower Theorist	45
	Sir Hugh Trenchard: An Independent Air Force for Britain	50
	Jack Slessor: Support for Ground Forces . . .	53
	Claire Chennault: Pursuit-Aviation Enthusiast	56
	William A. Moffett: Father of Naval Aviation . .	59
	Alexander P. de Seversky: Airpower Advocate	63
	John Warden: The Five-Ring Model	66
	Space Power Theory	69
	Summary	72

Chapter		Page
3	**Functions and Capabilities of Aerospace Power: Air and Space Superiority/Strategic Attack**	75
	Air and Space Superiority: The First Order of Business	77
	The Battle of Britain: The Luftwaffe's Failure to Control the Skies	79
	Total Air Domination: The Six-Day War	86
	Air Superiority and Operation Overlord	92
	Defeating the Enemy through Strategic Attack	99
	Japan's Hawaii Operation	100
	Slamming Saddam: Operation Desert Storm	108
	The Eighth Air Force in the Combined Bomber Offensive, 1943–45	119
4	**Functions and Capabilities of Aerospace Power: Interdiction/Close Air Support**	131
	Interdiction: Striking the Enemy Before He Can Attack	131
	Operation Strangle: Korea, 1951	133
	The Easter Offensive: Airpower Halts the North Vietnamese	139
	Interdiction at Sea: The Battle of the Bismarck Sea	145
	Supporting the Troops with Close Air Support	151
	Airpower Fails at Kasserine Pass	153
	Gunships for Close Air Support in Vietnam	159
	Close Air Support in the Korean War: A Navy and Marine Corps View	165
5	**Functions and Capabilities of Aerospace Power: Rapid Mobility/Space and Information**	175
	Mobility Operations: Moving Manpower, Munitions, and Machines	175
	Failure at Stalingrad: Air Supply Falls Flat	177

Chapter	Page

Transporting an Army: Operation Desert Shield	184
Airlift Saves Berlin: Operation Vittles	190
Space and Information: The Enabler of Operations	196
Finding a Needle in a Haystack: The Great Scud Hunt	198
Corona: The First Space-Reconnaissance System	205
Information Averts a Nuclear Showdown: Cuba, 1962	210

6 Functions and Capabilities of Aerospace Power: Airpower Unleashed 221
    At the End of Empire: The 1982 Falklands War in the Air 222
    Eighty-Five to Zero: Israel's Bekaa Valley Campaign 240
    Stopping the Luftwaffe Cold: The Soviet Tactical Air Effort in World War II 251
    Summary 260

7 Planning for Aerospace Operations 263
    Air Campaign Planning Concepts 264
    A Framework for Air Campaign Planning . . . 270
    Researching the Combat Environment 270
    Determining Air and Space Objectives 272
    Determining Centers of Gravity 275
    Determining Air and Space Strategy 276
    Putting the Campaign Together 278
    Air Campaign Planning Concerns 279
    Air Campaign Planning: National Implications 283

8 Taking Off into the Wild Blue Yonder 289
    Strategic or Ground-Operations Support? . . 291
    Unmanned Aerial Vehicles and the Future of Aerial Warfare 295

Chapter	Page
The Advancement of Space Forces: An Independent Force?	297
Building a Mobile Force	301
Information: The Key to Victory	305
Technological Solutions for an Unknown World	310
Fighting Jointly	317
Summary	319
GLOSSARY	323
INDEX	327

Illustrations

Figure		
1	Warden's Basic Five-Ring Model Used in Desert Storm	68
2	Egypt	87
3	Overlord Theater of Operations	96
4	Pacific Area	102
5	Desert Storm Theater of Operations	109
6	Korean Conflict	134
7	New Guinea	147
8	Tunisia	156
9	Southeast Asia	162
10	The Eastern Front	180
11	Berlin Airlift	193
12	Cuba	212

Figure		Page
13	Argentina and the Falkland Islands (Islas Malvinas)	223
14	West Falkland and East Falkland	224
15	Lebanon and the Bekaa Valley	242

Photo

	Page
C-5 cargo aircraft	2
Global Positioning System satellite	5
C-17 enhances global mobility	6
Peacekeeper ICBM	8
Tomahawk cruise missile	9
Titan III	10
B-17 destroyed at Hickam Field	13
B-17 bombing a ball-bearing plant	16
P-47s in World War II	17
Aircraft provide a wide variety of capabilities	18
Air Force B-66 Destroyer leads F-105 Thunderchiefs	19
Destroyed MiG-25 during Operation Desert Storm	21
F-15 air superiority fighter	22
Minuteman III ICBM	24
Precision-guided attacks	25
Navy F-18s	28
Logistics is one of the keys to airpower	31

Photo	Page
World War I German aviator	41
Trench warfare in World War I	42
Destroyed German city in World War II	44
Brig Gen William "Billy" Mitchell	47
Carrier aviation supports operations in Kosovo	60
Eddie Rickenbacker	78
Bombing of Britain	84
MiG-21	89
American troops invade Normandy	98
Air raid Pearl Harbor	105
USS *Arizona* burning at Pearl Harbor	107
Army Apache attack helicopters	113
Cruise missile launched from a B-52	114
F-111 strike aircraft	115
F-117 aircraft over Iraq	116
Destroyed Scud missile storage facilities	117
Destroyed Iraqi aircraft shelters	118
B-17 bomber attacks Focke-Wulf plant	121
Adolph Hitler inspects bomb damage	125
US Navy fighter in the Korean War	132
B-29 bombers over Korea	136
F-4E fighter	140

Photo	Page
A-10s providing CAS in Kosovo	152
Erwin Rommel, the Desert Fox	154
AC-47 gunship in the Vietnam War	161
CAS from Navy Corsairs in the Korean War	169
Air mobility in World War II	176
German forces in the Soviet Union in World War II	179
Civilian airliners support deployment of troops in Operation Desert Shield	184
C-47s provide invaluable service during Berlin airlift	192
Scud missile that failed to reach its target	199
Defense Support Program satellite	201
Patriot missile battery	203
F-15E	204
Minuteman ICBM force	209
Nuclear warhead bunker at San Cristóbal, Cuba	215
HMS *Broadsword*	232
F-16s providing air superiority	267
B-29 bombers destroy Chosen oil refinery	268
AWACS aircraft	282
Damage from air interdiction mission	283
B-2 refueling	286
Predator UAV	296

Photo	Page
Communications satellites	300
C-17s transport combat equipment and personnel	303
Space power in the field	307
B-2 Spirit bomber	314

Foreword

Developing future aerospace leaders is the key to ensuring the national security of the country. Such development is based on a firm understanding of the theory, principles, and applications of aerospace power. Without this foundation, aerospace and military leaders would have a difficult time deploying and using air and space forces in today's dynamic world. With the end of the Cold War, the United States military has been challenged by a series of world events that have forced aerospace leaders to apply air and space power in many innovative ways. They have had to focus on and question many previously held beliefs about air and space power. Future leaders will need to be well grounded in the capabilities and limitations of aerospace power to envision how to plan, operate, and build aerospace capabilities.

Dr. Chun's *Aerospace Power in the Twenty-First Century: A Basic Primer* is a great start towards understanding the importance of aerospace power and its ability to conduct modern warfare. Aerospace power is continually changing because of new technology, threats, and air and space theories. However, many basic principles about aerospace power have stood the test of time and warfare. This book provides the reader with many of these time-tested ideas for consideration and reflection. Although *Aerospace Power in the Twenty-First Century* was written for future officers, individuals desiring a broad overview of aerospace power are invited to read, share, and discuss many of the ideas and thoughts presented here. Officers from other services will find that this introduction to air and space forces will give them a good grasp of aerospace power. More experienced aerospace leaders can use this book to revisit many of the issues that have affected air and space forces in the past and that might affect them in the future. Air Force officers will discover that *Aerospace Power in the Twenty-First Century* is a very timely and reflective resource for their professional libraries.

JOHN R. DALLAGER, Lieutenant General
Superintendent
United States Air Force Academy

About the Author

Dr. Clayton K. S. Chun, a 1978 graduate of the University of California, Berkeley, holds an MA in economics from the University of California, Santa Barbara; an MS in systems management from the University of Southern California; and a PhD in public policy analysis from the RAND Graduate School. He is professor of economics at the United States Army War College, Carlisle Barracks, Pennsylvania, where he is an instructor for the Department of National Security and Strategy, teaching "War, National Policy, and Strategy" and courses on national security economics. He successfully completed a career as an Air Force officer, having held several staff and command positions with the Office of the Secretary of the Air Force, the Air Staff, Air University's School of Advanced Airpower Studies, Headquarters Pacific Air Forces, as well as space and missile assignments. In his last assignment, Dr. Chun held positions as deputy group commander of the 34th Education Group and commander of the 34th Education Squadron at the United States Air Force Academy.

Clayton K. S. Chun

Preface

Addressed either to the novice or any individual who wants to understand the rudimentary aspects of aerospace power, this book exposes readers to relevant aerospace capabilities, theories, applications, operational planning, and key issues. Theories and applications of aerospace power are not limited to the United States Air Force but apply to aerospace forces in general. Although the Air Force has forces and capabilities that include a very wide range of activities, other air and space forces reflect several of these same capabilities and many unique ones. Understanding how these forces operate can help both students who are new to aerospace power and individuals familiar with ground and maritime forces appreciate the strengths and weaknesses of air and space forces.

The book introduces the reader to definitions and concepts of aerospace power. Material in chapter 1 provides a set of definitions, characteristics, and concepts for readers. Aerospace power is defined in terms of how it contributes to the successful conduct of war through an evaluation of its ability to operate under a set of principles of war. A discussion of the environment and elements of aerospace power concludes the chapter.

Chapter 2 gives the reader a survey of major air and space theories. A study of any academic subject calls for a good theoretical foundation to explain and predict actions. Diverse theories address the application of aerospace power. Some of them view airpower as a force that can replace other military capabilities. Some stress the integration of airpower into existing forces, while others maintain that air and space assets should provide greater support to other forces. Several theories were written just after the introduction of the airplane. Others are more contemporary views that look at airpower and space power through the prism of experience gained from conflicts and advancements in capabilities that illustrate the value of air and space systems. Theory provides a forum to debate many issues. How one defines the use, organization, and structure of military forces frequently depends upon leadership's beliefs and theories. A solid grounding in aerospace theory provides a good start for understanding the use of aircraft and space systems.

With a grounding in theory, a student can then consider the application of aerospace power. Chapters 3–6 concentrate on aerospace power's functions and capabilities, which have been tested in war and peace. These chapters explain each function and then provide three short case studies for illustration, discussion, and further study. Instead of looking only at successes, the chapters also include failed efforts. Instructors using this text may wish to compare a failure to a success. Studying failures often allows students to evaluate why actions were not successful and to ponder what they could have done to correct the situation. These case studies allow for a discussion of the issues and problems that each commander faces in achieving certain goals or confronting particular situations.

Instructors can use the case studies to stimulate discussion or to allow students to make their own evaluations. Further, I do not mean to imply that these studies represent the only examples of aerospace functions. To give the reader a more encompassing view of aerospace power, they include experiences from sister services and foreign military services. Instructors may wish to use contemporary case studies or issues to supplement or replace the ones provided to illustrate issues facing current aerospace forces. In the future, I hope to revise the studies to include more humanitarian missions and other deployments throughout the world.

Learning about the capabilities of aerospace forces is important, but students should also have some acquaintance with a frequently ignored aspect of aerospace power—air campaign planning. Chapter 7 concentrates on the process of planning for the appropriate use of aerospace power—one of the most important responsibilities of a military commander. Readers may not require exposure to such planning in great detail, but acquiring a general knowledge of the deployment of air and space forces can help shape their thoughts on objectives, conditions, and alternative solutions. Instructors and students might use this rudimentary focus on planning to evaluate the previous chapters' case studies in terms of how they may have avoided failure or improved the application and operation of air or space forces.

Chapter 8 discusses some key issues that aerospace leaders face today and will face in the future. Many of them involve new technology and innovation. Aerospace power was built and thrives upon advanced technology, which, together with the process of innovation, allows air and space forces to create new options and opportunities to enhance capabilities or solve problems. New war-fighting capabilities, organizations, relationships with other military forces, and additional issues depend upon advanced technology and the way aerospace leaders handle its application.

Gaining a good understanding of aerospace power theory, doctrine, and strategy requires a continual review of current events. Unfortunately, many books and articles on aerospace power assume the reader already has knowledge about these issues and concepts. If the development of aerospace and joint leaders is to improve, candidates in precommissioning agencies, as well as new and junior officers, need a firm foundation in the principles and theories of aerospace power. My goal in preparing this text is to provide this basic knowledge. These few chapters should give readers a general understanding of the primary missions and capabilities of aerospace power.

Preparing this text has been a career-long objective. Too many times I have seen Air Force officers view themselves only as technicians or specialists, not as Air Force officers. I strongly believe that the service and nation deserve more; however, Air Force officers need to be airpower and space power advocates—not zealots. Becoming proficient in one's chosen career field or specialty is admirable and necessary. Indeed, to become true military professionals and to become the most effective aerospace and joint team members and future leaders, officers must understand the strengths and weaknesses of applying air and space forces. This knowledge can only improve their ability to lead and make decisions in their specialties. This concern is exacerbated by the present trend towards reduced resources and increased deployments.

I wish to thank several individuals and organizations for supporting me in this effort. Fellow members of the 34th Education Group and 34th Education Squadron at the United

States Air Force Academy helped motivate me in preparing and writing this book. In particular I want to express my thanks to Col Thomas A. Drohan, Dr. Charles Krupnick, Ms. Delores Karolick, Lt Col John R. Higgs, Maj Larry Walker, and many others. Additionally, Dr. Dan Mortensen of Air University's College of Aerospace Doctrine, Research and Education inspired and encouraged me to complete this work over the years. Special thanks go to the staff of the Department of Defense Media Center at March Air Reserve Base, California, for the photographs that richly illustrate the subjects discussed. Finally, I would like to thank Dr. Marvin Bassett and the fine staff at Air University Press for making this book a reality. The research grant that I received—the McDermott Award for Research Excellence at the United States Air Force Academy—provided financial support. My family, however, is the real inspiration for completing this primer. My wife Cheryl and sons Douglas and Raymond patiently endured many missed weekends and evenings as I researched and wrote on airpower and space power. I could not have completed this project without their support.

CLAYTON K. S. CHUN
US Army War College
Carlisle, Pennsylvania

Chapter 1

Aerospace Concepts and Definitions

Aerospace power means several things to many people. Some military members might identify aircraft with aerospace power. Others might see aerospace power as the integration of aircraft and space systems. Aerospace power is a relative newcomer to warfare compared to land or naval power. However, nations have used aircraft for military and commercial purposes over the past 100 years. This is only a small slice in the history of warfare compared to land and naval warfare. Aerospace power has dramatically changed over the years and has produced several distinct capabilities that have changed the face of warfare. Future aerospace leaders require a solid foundation or understanding of the purpose, characteristics, theory, and functions of air and space power to effectively employ aerospace power in war. Before one can study this dynamic subject, one needs to understand some basic definitions, concepts, and beliefs regarding aerospace power.

Aerospace Power Defined

Over the past century, aircraft have been used in modern military operations ranging from global war to peacekeeping. This wide capability has led to much discussion among advocates and critics of aerospace power. Defining aerospace power over the last few years has been a challenge for large land-based air forces as well as smaller forces. The rapid growth in air and space technology has added more capabilities to air and space forces over the years. Supersonic speeds, stealth capability, and rapid mobility are a few of the many capabilities incorporated into airpower in the past. Space systems have also shown their worth with their ability to enhance terrestrial events involving communications, weather, navigation, early warning, and intelligence, as well as their ability to provide other key information for a war fighter. The concept of "information warfare" and its ties to space systems and mod-

C-5 cargo aircraft can provide combat or humanitarian missions on short notice.

ern information technology is also changing the face of aerospace power.

Modern aerospace power includes many functions and capabilities. A definition of aerospace power will help frame the discussion of this elusive subject and give the reader a foundation to address many of the timely and timeless issues facing students of air and space power theory, doctrine, strategy, and operations. Aerospace power includes air, space, and the integration of air and space power. Operations in air and space have led to many discussions about the resources, value, strategies, and ideas about the newest form of warfare. People who have attempted to write a definition of airpower through the years have wrestled with making it an all-inclusive yet succinct expression for this continually evolving concept. In 1925 William "Billy" Mitchell, an early advocate of aerial bombardment, gave one of the earliest definitions of airpower: "the ability to do something in or through the air, and as the air covers the whole world, aircraft are able to go anywhere on the planet."[1] The "ability to do something" brings to mind a strength or power to influence events. Mitchell's definition makes no distinction between military and civilian exploitation of the air. Other definitions are more focused on military operations and the distinction of the type of object that travels or manipulates air operations. For example, the Royal Air Force (RAF) defines airpower as "the use, or denial of the use, of the air or space for military purposes, by or to vehicles capable of sustained and controlled flight beyond the area and the range of the immediate surface conflict."[2] This view provides a more distinct definition of airpower's limits and capabilities. The RAF's airpower view specifies the level, instruments, and priorities for airpower. This definition adds the dimension of denying air *and* space access to a foe and restricts the discussion of airpower to vehicles that can operate beyond the immediate battlefield, excluding bullets in flight or artillery shells. If Mitchell's definition is broad, then the RAF view may be too limited. However, they share a common theme of exploiting the environment above Earth's surface through the operation of a vehicle. This debate about airpower has plagued students for years.

Advances in commercial air transportation, satellite communications, and information applications have added new dimensions to Mitchell's definition of airpower. These capabilities are key to military aerospace power's future and need to be addressed in a definition. Aerospace power, as opposed to airpower only, might be better defined as "the exploitation of the environment above Earth's surface by aerospace vehicles or devices to conduct operations in support of national objectives." This definition adds the air and space environment to the debate and reflects the growing importance of space, as does the RAF definition. Additionally, like Mitchell's definition, it includes military and civilian use of air and space. Commercial air and space operations are areas of growing technological and financial strength for many corporations. Aerospace power is a unique form of military and commercial power that can help a country achieve numerous national objectives. Unfortunately, this definition of aerospace power is fleeting since technology alters the face of aerospace power. However, this is the challenge of studying, developing, and applying aerospace power. The nature and use of aerospace power are limited only by the imagination of its leaders and, more importantly, the men and women who support its operation. This study of aerospace power concentrates on its military application. Although commercial aerospace power is vital to the international and domestic economy, the use or threatened use of military forces has a more immediate and crucial role among national security concerns. The definition of aerospace power is only a start in one's study of the value of air and space systems. One also needs to understand characteristics that underlie the use of this expanding military power.

Characteristics of Aerospace Power

Aircraft and space systems have many advantages that can support military operations in many unique ways. One of their greatest advantages is the *flexibility* to operate in many types of operations, purposes, theaters, and environments. Aerospace power's inherent flexibility allows it to plan an attack on a foe in one area, quickly respond to another threat in another area, or return to a base different than the one from which it took off. In the 1960s, during the Vietnam War, US Air Force (USAF) North American F-100 Super Saber and US Navy McDonnell Douglas A-4 Skyhawk aircraft might plan a mission against enemy bridges for a particular day. During the course of the day and while the planes were en route to their targets, a friendly ground unit might come under fire from a superior-sized enemy guerilla force. The F-100 and A-4 aircraft could swiftly change their mission to support the friendly ground unit by dropping their munitions on the guerillas. The aircraft could then return to their respective bases or aircraft carriers, rearm, attack the original target, or again support the ground forces. These air forces could also have simply diverted a portion of their aircraft to attack the guerilla force and simultaneously attack the bridges. The flexibility of aircraft provided the commander a number of options to use this force in innovative ways.

An aerospace force gives the commander many alternatives and options that aircraft and space systems can support in most situations that involve military forces. This force application may range from lethal use of weapons, to reconnaissance, to sending aircraft to drop food supplies. While these air and space forces can be used in many situations, they can also be used in unison to accomplish a single mission.

AEROSPACE CONCEPTS AND DEFINITIONS

Global Positioning System satellite providing navigation support—an illustration of space power

In many military situations, a commander may not have sufficient resources to meet all requirements. The commander must prioritize missions among limited assets. Aerospace forces can swiftly *concentrate* their efforts against a single target or series of targets. The speed, range, and flexibility of aerospace forces give a commander the unique ability to provide an overwhelming force against a foe in one instance and move swiftly against another enemy position within minutes. During Operation Desert Storm, coalition air forces struck diverse targets, including ground forces, air defenses, industrial sites, nuclear/biological weapons, oil, and leadership. Target coordination among aircraft units concerning when an attack should start or who should strike the target requires precise timing and planning. For example, coalition air forces conducted over 23,430 missions against ground forces during Operations Desert Shield/Desert Storm. Limited aircraft and munitions, attack on enemy air defenses, reconnaissance, timing of attacks, and damage assessments are all issues requiring resolution by a centralized command to ensure that the proper missions are conducted, without duplication, and that an adequate response is made. However, since aerospace operations must be flexible, lower-echelon commanders must have the ability to quickly change a planned course of action or react to unforeseen situations. These subordinate commanders must have the flexibility to conduct operations. They should have the ability to modify their plans to use their forces in an appropriate manner.

The introduction of aircraft and space systems has added a critical element to modern military activities—specifically, speed. Mountains, rivers, and difficult terrain can significantly slow down a ground force. Ground-force movements might be measured in tens of miles per day. Naval forces may travel faster. Open ocean travel might be measured in hundreds of miles per day. Aircraft and space systems can reach speeds several magnitudes above those of ground and naval forces. Speed allows aircraft and space systems to conduct several missions

The C-17 enhances global mobility for the United States.

during the same period it takes ground and possibly naval forces to accomplish a single mission. A corollary of the speed characteristic is aerospace power's responsiveness to situations. Aerospace forces can also react faster to rapidly changing situations than can many other military forces. A timely response to a dangerous situation may save an army or provide humanitarian relief.

Aircraft and spacecraft not only can travel faster than a ship or a truck, but also they can cover greater distances and operate over longer *ranges*. Before the introduction of aircraft, military operations were normally localized to a limited area. Railroads increased the options of fighting over continental distances during the American Civil War. Aircraft revolutionized global conflict. During World War II, US Army Air Forces (AAF) and RAF bomber units were able to fly hundreds of miles to strike targets in Germany on a daily basis. The AAF was also able to bomb Japan from Pacific bases hundreds of miles away during day and night operations. Later, the invention of intercontinental ballistic missiles (ICBM) and jet bombers (with refueling support) allowed nations to attack targets continents away—literally exhibiting a global capability. Advances in space systems may push ranges farther into Earth orbits to actions in deep space or even to other planets.

Increased speed and range provide more alternatives and opportunities, which allow a commander better *freedom of action* to conduct operations. This freedom of action allows an air force to select a mission over a range of operations. A commander's operations are greatly expanded among a multitude of targets that may be attacked. Conversely, land forces generally need to attack enemy forces one at a time on a front. This limitation may significantly slow down ground operations and, ultimately, an entire campaign. Although great advances in technology and maneuver strategies have tempered this observation over time, aerospace forces have a broader selection of targets that they may attack. Similarly, naval vessels can travel the seven seas to attack many targets, but they are limited to coastal targets and ships in range of their gunfire and antiship missiles. Longer-range shipboard and submarine missiles are improving naval force projections.[3]

Peacekeeper ICBM

Another characteristic of aerospace power is its ability to provide a *global perspective*. Ground forces normally have a perspective based on the opposing front lines. Naval forces are also limited to operating mostly along the horizon. Although modern technology has allowed ground and naval forces to extend their vision beyond the horizon, it cannot compare to

AEROSPACE CONCEPTS AND DEFINITIONS

Tomahawk cruise missile from the USS *Missouri* conducts an attack during Operation Desert Storm.

the perspective of aerospace assets. Satellites can provide countrywide imagery in a matter of minutes and global coverage of a foe's military actions. This coverage could include not only air and space operations, but also several ground theaters and areas where naval forces sail in geographically separated theaters.

Aerospace power can also affect the *tempo and timing* of situations. A commander can use aerospace forces to strike enemy positions and invoke a reaction from the foe or shape his reaction. If a commander wants to shape a foe's reaction,

The Titan III can carry satellites into orbit.

he will need split-second coordination of actions and decisions to counteract the actions taken by the opposing forces. The fast tempo of aerospace operations also requires rapid decision making. Quick timing, freedom of action, and flexibility of forces to take action require accurate information. A future aerospace leader must be able to gather, analyze, and synthesize information into effective life-and-death decisions. Aircraft commanders may face situations in which they choose between conducting their planned missions or supporting another action. They must make their decision by weighing their assigned mission's objectives against what they might gain from pursuing an alternative requirement.

Aerospace power also puts fewer friendly forces at risk of casualties, except for incidents of friendly fire. Casualties are a natural outcome of conflict, and modern technology has increased the lethality of weapons, resulting in the possibility of massive casualties. The *casualty reduction* of friendly deaths and wounds is a paramount consideration in the planning

AEROSPACE CONCEPTS AND DEFINITIONS

and coordination of combat operations. In combat, aircraft and spacecraft, whether manned or unmanned, expose fewer human lives to danger than do comparable land and naval force applications for the same mission. Casualty reduction and increased lethality from modern aerospace weapons give a commander a powerful combination to strike an enemy when timely attacks are vital and when other military forces are not available.

Although aerospace forces have many strengths, they also have some limitations. A student of aerospace power should consider these strengths and weaknesses in the application of air and space forces. Similarly, a military planner should do the same with land and naval forces. Aerospace, land, and naval forces are like tools used by a commander. Each tool is designed and used for a specific task. Selecting only one tool for all jobs may get the job done, but it may not be as effective or efficient as using the tools in combination. Whenever a commander uses these "tools," he or she should consider all strengths and weaknesses of military power and select the right combination of forces. The study of the limitations of aerospace power is a start to understanding how to maximize the use of aircraft or space systems over many situations that aerospace leaders will face in the future.

Aircraft and space systems were developed from and rely primarily on high technology that requires *significant resources.* New materials, propulsion systems, guidance systems, satellites, and other complex devices rely on significant research and development in many areas for their existence. These efforts require funding, scientific resources, industrial production, and other assets that have alternative uses. A nation needs to make a conscious decision to expend these limited, valuable resources to expand or maintain aerospace capabilities. If the nation cannot or is not willing to do so, it risks having a technologically obsolete force—a situation that may endanger its military forces and, ultimately, the nation. The resource requirement puts aerospace forces at odds with land and naval forces for competition with limited funding or personnel.

Each pound of equipment or weapon that an aerospace vehicle must carry requires an appropriate amount of propulsion and support. The capacity of an aircraft or rocket carrying a payload is limited because of size or weight. Aircraft can transport only a limited number of passengers, supplies, or armored vehicles. A booster rocket can carry a limited number of pounds with a limited size into low earth orbit. Relative to ships, railroads, or a truck convoy, aerospace systems have *limited payloads*. Once aircraft drop their munitions on a target, they must return to base and fight another day. Normally, these aircraft do not conduct other activities after accomplishing their primary mission. Ships can carry several tanks from one continent to another, albeit at a slower speed, compared to a jet transport, which can carry two armored vehicles at most.

Aircraft and space systems can patrol areas around the world. However, unlike ground forces, they *cannot occupy territory*. Peacekeeping operations that rely on a local police or constabulary force require a ground presence to arrest criminals or conduct many types of law-enforcement duties. Aircraft can observe some activities and can take some actions but are not a pure substitute for the presence of soldiers enforcing a treaty on the ground. New technology that includes pilotless, long-duration vehicles and space systems can allow surveillance of surface activities, but weather, enemy deception and camouflage, and other actions can limit these capabilities. Currently, aircraft usually stay in one geographic area for a limited time. Even with aerial refueling, aircraft must eventually return to their bases for repairs, replenishment of supplies, or crew rest. Satellites may have geosynchronous orbits that provide a relatively stationary orbit to provide "coverage" over a particular region, but it is usually limited to equatorial regions around the globe and still does not put forces on the ground.

Aerospace forces operate above Earth's surface, but they are still *reliant on ground support*. Aircraft cannot stay in the air indefinitely. Crews need to be replaced, maintenance must be conducted at bases, munitions and fuel must be supplied to planes, and services from other support systems must be provided to aircraft. Aircraft are tied to Earth's surface, and their bases or aircraft carriers make these systems vulnerable to attack. Space systems also rely on ground launch, support, and control. A foe does not have to attack a satellite directly; he can disable or destroy the satellite's ground-control station or interfere with its communications link to effectively neutralize its capabilities.

Space assets have limited mobility and may have less flexibility than aircraft, soldiers, or naval vessels. Satellites operate under the laws of orbital mechanics and travel along predictable paths. Once they are in orbit, changes in position are made with limited onboard fuel to power their propulsion systems. Refueling these satellites is neither easy nor inexpensive. Unless one absolutely needs these satellites to move, their orbital paths are usually not changed. Essentially, they have a limited capability to change orbits. Additionally, a nation may have reduced imagery coverage because of an intelligence satellite's peculiar orbit and may require another satellite or other asset to support the same mission. Surface forces might move out of a satellite's path or camouflage themselves before they are detected and then conduct their assigned mission.

Aircraft and spacecraft are very *fragile*. Speed, range, and weight considerations require airframe or satellite body con-

B-17 destroyed at Hickam Field during the Pearl Harbor attack. The Hawaiian Air Force was severely damaged during the attack.

struction that uses lightweight materials, which may affect survivability. Unlike a tank or ship, an aircraft's fuselage might be manufactured with aluminum or other materials that provide sufficient structural strength for flight but do little to protect it against a missile or shell. Damage from enemy attacks or even a bird hitting the Plexiglas canopy might force the aircraft to abandon its mission or even destroy the vehicle. Aircraft and spacecraft might not be able to sustain operations under significant air or space defenses.

These strengths and limitations should allow one to assess, in a general manner, where the use of aerospace forces is appropriate. Depending on the environment, condition of the force, and the political objective desired, aerospace power might or might not contribute significantly to a conflict. Applying inappropriate resources to a situation is not only wasteful, but also subjects aircrews or other personnel to needless risks. Aircraft and spacecraft give a commander many alternatives to exercise against an adversary. The appropriate application of aerospace power depends upon a decision maker's pitting the strengths of his or her aircraft and space systems against the weaknesses of the enemy. Additionally, the commander needs to limit the exposure of aerospace forces' limitations while minimizing the strengths of the enemy.

Aerospace Power in War

Aerospace power's strengths and weaknesses are important in combat planning. How one employs these forces is also an important issue. The elements that make aerospace power work together allow a nation to use a combination of lethal capabilities in war. Throughout the history of warfare, several individuals have identified ideas and concepts about war and the means by which leaders apply their military forces. These "principles" help one to understand the application of military forces and the ways one can think about fighting a war and using aerospace power. Although there is no universal agreement upon a list of these principles of war, the study and time-tested use of these ideas can help one address many issues facing a decision maker in times of war. One should neither substitute these principles for critical thinking nor ignore them as just an irrelevant "history lesson." Successful generals do not follow these principles as a simple checklist but apply them as appropriate, considering the situation. Using them is more an art than a science, and a particular situation may call for using all or some of the principles—or just one. Solving aerospace power problems requires imagination and initiative rather than a slavish devotion to following a list of principles.

Col J. F. C. Fuller developed a set of principles of war in 1925. Fuller, a Royal Army officer, compiled many of these military thoughts in *The Foundations of the Science of War*. Although he was an expert in armored warfare, his list of principles of war gives us a point of departure to discuss war in general and the way these principles might apply to aerospace power. Many of the lessons from successes in war underscore Fuller's principles of war, and one can learn about the potential application of aerospace power by reviewing these situations. These principles include objective, offensive, mass, economy of force, maneuver, unity of command, security, surprise, and simplicity.[4]

The most important principle of war is *objective*, which provides a focus or goal that all aerospace forces are trying to achieve for a situation. A concise and coherent objective allows a commander to concentrate his or her efforts on solving a particular problem or series of problems. If a commander can adequately identify an objective, his or her subordinates can better define and clarify their role and effort in any operation. An objective allows individuals to better prepare themselves to accomplish the commander's aims. For example, in World War II the AAF and RAF in Europe conducted a sustained bombing campaign against Nazi Germany's industrial and military targets. The Combined Bomber Offensive's objective was to reduce the war-making capability of the Third Reich. Bombing missions were planned to systematically cripple the ability of Germany to make armaments and thereby reduce its ability to support military operations. A commander's objective should also satisfy any higher-level political or military objective. Defining "what you have to do" (objective) will

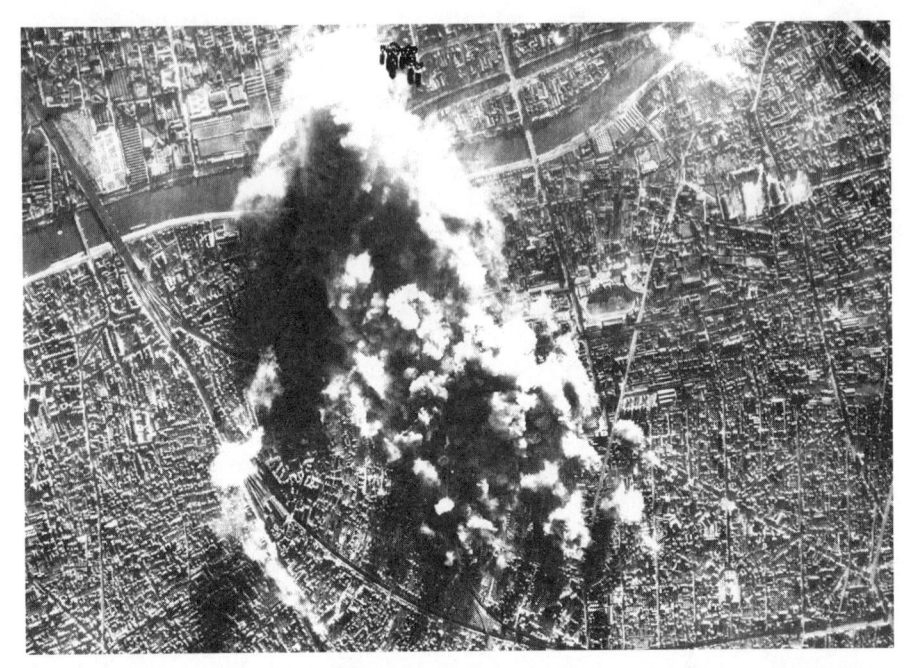

Destruction from above. During the Combined Bomber Offensive in 1943, a B-17 bombs a ball-bearing plant and aircraft-engine repair depot near Paris, France.

help the commander solve the problem of how to accomplish the mission.

Winning a war also takes initiative and action. Military forces often need to be more proactive than reactive in many situations. Nations take *offensive* actions to defeat an enemy or eject him from their borders. Maintaining a defensive stance just limits the country to maintain its status quo, and the best it can do is "not lose." Offensive operations allow a nation to shape an environment and strike a foe before he has a chance to attack. Aerospace forces are well suited to take offensive actions due to their speed, range, ability to concentrate, and perspective. The Israeli Defense Forces/Air Force (IDF/AF) was able to clearly demonstrate the value of offensive air operations during its Six-Day War against Egypt, Syria, and Jordan in June 1967. Israeli jets conducted a surprise, massive ground attack against the Egyptian air force that rendered it incapable of further military capability. The Israelis then eliminated the Syrian and Jordanian air forces. Without air support, Arab ground forces were left open to attack by IDF/AF planes and armored units. The IDF/AF shaped the battlefield so that Israeli surface forces could conduct offensive ground action to overcome a larger Arab ground force.

If a nation takes the offensive in a conflict, it may have the option of attacking with fewer forces along a broad front or assaulting the enemy on a narrower front with all its forces. The probability of a successful breakthrough on the front is increased if the nation can *mass* its forces against a decisive point along the front. Forces using mass can concentrate their capability against an enemy's weaknesses. Mass allows a nation to deliver a devastating blow to an enemy, both physically and psychologically. On 24 December 1944, bombers and fighters of the AAF and RAF conducted a coordinated attack against supply lines, bridges, troop concentrations, rail lines, and airfields, and supported Allied ground operations along the Ardennes front (also known as the Battle of the Bulge). Over 2,300 aircraft missions helped push German forces out of the Bulge and inflicted great damage on enemy ground forces. Allied aircraft were able to concentrate and attack German forces that had a significant impact on the battlefield.

In World War II, P-47s performed a number of missions, such as air superiority, interdiction, and close air support.

Although a commander needs to use mass and conduct an attack with decisive force, military forces are usually resource-constrained. Air forces do not have an inexhaustible supply of aircraft, pilots, munitions, or other support. Commanders need to provide a sufficient number of resources for a military force so that it can accomplish its mission. The selection of a minimum of resources to satisfy mission requirements—*economy of force*—is a challenge for a planning staff, especially if it is faced with several important military operations. If too many resources are devoted to a mission, the excess resources cannot be employed to accomplish some other mission.

For example, during the Vietnam War, the USAF was assigned to destroy the Than Hoa Bridge on 3 April 1965. A large "strike" package of 79 Republic F-105 Thunderchiefs dropped 638 750-pound bombs and fired 298 rockets but failed to destroy the bridge. Five aircraft were lost in the attack. The bridge was a target of many missions throughout the war. In 1972 the USAF was finally able to destroy the span by using 16 F-4 Phantoms equipped with advanced Paveway laser-guided bombs, thus eliminating the need for large numbers of aircraft. Technology allowed the USAF to reduce the

Aircraft provide a wide variety of capabilities that allow commanders to effectively select resources for combat and noncombat missions.

An Air Force B-66 Destroyer leads F-105 Thunderchiefs in an attack over North Vietnam in 1966. The F-105 bore the brunt of many attacks in the Vietnam War.

number of munitions and aircraft used to destroy the bridge and effectively accomplish the mission. The F-4s used 24 guided munitions and 48 unguided bombs to destroy the bridge. The USAF estimated that the damage from the mission was equivalent to using 2,400 unguided bombs.[5]

Military forces can cause a foe to move or position himself in a less effective manner to conduct his operations. A nation's military force can use *maneuver* to create favorable conditions on the battlefield for exploitation—including the capability to attack, retreat, or further shape the battlefield. Aerospace forces can use their speed and range to position themselves to influence the movement of enemy forces or support the movement of soldiers to a critical area on a battlefield. Such movement could block an enemy's advance or put friendly forces in an optimal position to attack. An example of stopping an enemy's advance occurred during Desert Shield/Desert Storm, when the United States moved more than 526,277 tons of cargo and over 499,627 passengers by aircraft. The rapid transport of troops, supplies, and weapons helped stop the possible invasion of Saudi Arabia by Iraq. The rapid movement of combat-ready forces into Saudi Arabia allowed the nation to take several alternative courses of action, while limiting those of Iraq.

The conduct of military operations is a very complex situation that requires timely planning and intense coordination of effort. If the operation involves joint aerospace, land, and naval forces, there is a distinct possibility of miscommunication, contradictory plans, and actions that are mistakenly disregarded. An effective method to avoid many of these shortcomings is to appoint a single commander who is in charge of all operations to ensure *unity of command*. Commanders with singular authority and appropriate decision-making capability provide better coordination and planning. Failure to achieve unity of command can result in counterproductive efforts. Air operations in the Vietnam War were divided among several commanders. The control of air operations was divided among the USAF, Navy, Army (helicopters), and Marine Corps, as well as various major commands within the four services. This organization produced a fragmented command and control (C^2) of air resources.

Aerospace systems are extremely fragile devices. Enemy ground forces can attack aircraft on the ground, where they are vulnerable to small-arms fire. Carefully planned air attacks may be displaced if a foe is tipped off about any impending actions. Military forces require *security* to protect their assets and avoid giving the enemy any unintended advantages. Airfield protection has been an important prerequisite to make airpower available for action and to give a commander maximum support to conduct operations. During the Vietnam War, Vietcong guerillas were able to conduct harassing attacks to disrupt aircraft ground-support activities and destroy aircraft. Although these raids did not affect the outcome of the war, future incidents involving nuclear, biological, and chemical (NBC) weapons may significantly affect the availability and operation of aircraft. Surface-to-surface ballistic missile at-

AEROSPACE CONCEPTS AND DEFINITIONS

Destroyed MiG-25 during Operation Desert Storm. Achieving air superiority can also come from defeating aircraft on the ground.

tacks using conventional munitions may leave a runway unusable or may severely damage parked aircraft.

Enemy forces that are prepared and can benefit from defensive weapons are more difficult to defeat than unprepared forces that are attacked in open terrain. The chance of success for an offensive action against the enemy is increased greatly if a military force can attain *surprise*—the mirror image of security. A military force conducting a surprise operation takes advantage of selecting the time, location, and type of action it can take against an adversary. The enemy has no ability to react immediately to an action taken against him. Air raids are classic examples of surprise. If the military force can avoid detection from surveillance before its attack, then it may significantly improve the probability of conducting a successful surprise attack. Such an attack may catch aircraft on the airfield or outside of hangars, air defenses unprepared for action, or protective revetments vulnerable to immediate destruction. In May 1981, the IDF/AF attacked an Iraqi nuclear reactor at Osirak. Operation Babylon's objective was to de-

F-15 air superiority fighter

stroy Iraq's growing nuclear weapons program. Several McDonnell Douglas F-15 Eagle and General Dynamics F-16 Fighting Falcon aircraft avoided radar detection and enemy fighters before conducting their operation. The attack was a complete surprise, and the reactor was destroyed, pushing back Iraq's nuclear capability several years.

The final principle of war is *simplicity*. Complicated plans and actions may unintentionally create additional problems for a military force. An overly complex plan may cause mistakes or prevent actions and thus endanger the entire plan's success. Keeping a plan or operation simple allows a commander to use his or her forces in a flexible manner so as to effectively counter an adversary's reactions to the plan. Clear, concise, and understandable plans promote better coordination and understanding of the operation. For example, conducting an aerial photoreconnaissance mission of a particular battle-damaged target is easier to plan and execute than conducting total surveillance of an area and then looking for battle-damaged targets. In the former case, intelligence analysts need only focus on a single target. In the latter, the same intelligence analysts need to find the target and then determine its battle damage.

The principles of war provide many issues to consider during the application of military forces. Aerospace power highlights many of these principles. Although following them gives commanders a better understanding of how they might increase their chances of achieving success on the battlefield, these principles will never guarantee victory. There is no formula for their correct application. Their application depends on many variables that can significantly affect the actions of friendly and enemy forces. Understanding the ideas and importance of these principles of war provides fledgling commanders a first step towards using aerospace forces.

What Aerospace Forces Can Accomplish

Aerospace forces, like land and naval assets, accomplish several purposes in conflict and in peace. The introduction of the aircraft and space systems has provided revolutionary changes to a nation's ability to fight. The versatility of aerospace forces allows a national leader to pursue many alternatives to solve a country's problems in war. One needs to understand specific missions that aircraft and spacecraft can accomplish or support before he or she employs them. Aerospace forces can conduct deterrence, compellence, denial, coercion, decapitation, and humanitarian missions.

The most important objective accomplished by aerospace forces is their deterrent mission. *Deterrence*, whether in a nuclear or conventional conflict, discourages a nation or party from taking certain actions. During the Cold War, the United States created a force of nuclear-armed bombers and missiles capable of surviving a nuclear attack and subsequently inflicting significant damage on the attacking nation. Aerospace forces provided bombers, ICBMs, early warning satellites, defensive capabilities, communications, and reconnaissance forces that gave the nation 24-hour, combat-ready forces to retaliate against an enemy or to react quickly to a situation. These forces made a potential enemy think twice before launching a preemptive nuclear or conventional strike against the United States. The

America's nuclear deterrent power rests partly on the Minuteman III ICBM.

speed, range, and flexibility of aerospace forces also give them a decided advantage in achieving conventional deterrent value. Aircraft that are ready to bomb targets at a moment's notice also help stop another nation from taking certain actions because of the fear of a swift, decisive reaction. Aircraft can demonstrate deterrent value by providing a visible display of combat power if they fly near an enemy's border or conduct training exercises in plain sight of an adversary.

AEROSPACE CONCEPTS AND DEFINITIONS

Similarly, a nation could use the threat of destruction to *compel* another nation, organization, or group of people to take an action. Compellence is not about retaliation or compensation. A nation can take actions to threaten another country. These actions may be offensive or provocative in nature. For example, a nation might threaten to begin military operations unless it receives territorial concessions from a neighbor within a specified time frame. If the nation does not comply, national leaders could initiate a bombing or invasion attempt.

Unfortunately, nations sometimes are not deterred from conducting combat operations or taking some other undesirable course of action. If combat should occur, then aerospace forces can *deny* an armed force or nation the ability to conduct those actions. Deterrence actions involve changing the mind-set of a potential adversary. Denial actions include physical attacks upon the adversary's military or other appropriate targets to stop or reverse an action. For example, during Desert Storm, coalition air forces attacked Iraqi transportation, supply, industrial, and other targets that supported enemy forces to reduce their military capabilities. Successful missions against

Precision-guided attacks can stop the flow of supplies and reduce the enemy's combat power.

ground-transportation targets such as roads, bridges, and railroads helped slow down Iraqi ground-force movements and reduced the enemy's ability to fight because the flow of supplies and troop reinforcements was reduced to a trickle.

Once combat operations start, aerospace forces can *coerce* an offending nation or party to take a certain course of action. Coercion involves the use of force to punish the transgressions of a foe in hopes of altering a nation's will. Although coercion may use attacks on physical targets, its main goal is to change the behavior of a nation, organization, or group of people through psychological means. However, a significant issue regarding coercion is the problem of escalation. What if the target organization or enemy does not cooperate? Does the coercive power increase the level of attack? Is there a ceiling to the escalation of force? In 1999 the North Atlantic Treaty Organization (NATO) conducted an air campaign, Operation Allied Force, against Serbian forces in Kosovo and Yugoslavia. These NATO air forces attacked several key leadership and command centers in the hopes of forcing Serbian national leaders to accept conditions to end the conflict and stop operations. NATO air forces also attacked a number of other targets that affected the living conditions of the Serbian populace. This action may have added internal pressure on the Serbian leaders to accede to NATO's demands by creating public dissension among the Serbian populace and reducing the country's war-making capacity.

Another mission that aerospace forces can readily accomplish is *decapitation*. Aerospace forces deliver lethal, precision weapons at great speeds and range that make them weapons of choice to isolate top enemy leadership from its sources of power (i.e., its military and population). A single jet bomber might destroy a telecommunications center, thus preventing the enemy leader from transmitting vital commands to his forces and his nation's citizens. The objective of decapitation is to separate the "brain" (national leader) from the "body" (nation) so that the body is paralyzed and cannot take effective action. Because the body might not be able to function sufficiently to exist, it may no longer remain a threat.

Finally, aerospace power is not always involved in conflict but may take *humanitarian actions*. Aerospace power can rapidly deliver aid to nations that suffer natural disasters such as earthquakes, fires, or floods. Aircraft can swiftly deliver critical food and shelter when hours literally count in life-threatening situations. Commanders can use aircraft to fly over contested areas and provide quick, precision delivery of supplies and material. On 24 June 1948, the Soviet Union blockaded all road, rail, and waterways into Berlin to make allied forces abandon the city. No food or supplies were allowed into the city. A tense standoff between Soviet and allied military forces threatened to escalate into another world war. Instead, allied air forces conducted Operation Vittles (the Berlin airlift), which used aircraft to carry 2.3 million tons of food, coal, and supplies to keep the citizens of Berlin alive. The Soviet Union saw that Berlin would not fold and ended the blockade on 12 May 1949.

Aerospace forces can accomplish a wide variety of operations, including taking actions to prevent war by deterring a potential enemy from conducting military operations. The flexibility attributed to the inherent nature of aerospace power allows a nation to use a single aircraft to produce effects that once were achieved only by millions of soldiers. One plane might destroy a nuclear-weapons production plant and thereby end a nation's ability to threaten a wide region of the world, or that plane itself might use a nuclear weapon. Conversely, many aircraft might staunch the flow of an enemy invasion force attacking a helpless neighbor or conduct operations to ensure that friendly ground forces invade an enemy. Aerospace power also gives the nation a very effective tool to provide humanitarian aid around the world. This capability is being called upon more often than in the past because of the result of ethnic conflicts, enhanced ability to conduct such operations, greater awareness of deadly situations, and frequent growth of humanitarian missions around the world.

The Aerospace Environment

Aerospace assets conduct their missions in a unique environment. Air and space forces operate in the third dimension—the area above Earth's surface. The air and space environments are quite different. Aircraft fly due to aerodynamic lift. Spacecraft manipulate orbital mechanics to operate in the vacuum of space. Although these environments significantly differ, both can affect land and naval operations. Land and naval forces generally influence operations on their own environments. Land forces confront and occupy opposing land forces but usually have limited effects on naval and aerospace forces. Similarly, naval forces primarily conduct actions against foes on the ocean's surface and subsurface areas. The Navy does have a strike capability against land targets. Aerospace forces can directly act against both land and naval forces. More importantly, aerospace forces can move quickly within the atmosphere or space, concentrate, and then operate against either land or naval forces—or both.

Advancing technology increases the future promise of vehicles that may one day routinely operate in air and space environments. Altitude, range, and speed limitations hampered early propeller aircraft. Later, jet aircraft extended the operating characteristics to high altitudes and supersonic speeds. Dur-

Navy F-18s

ing the 1950s and 1960s, rockets and spacecraft extended aerospace's reach into the cosmos. Today, the space shuttle launches into space like a rocket, deploys satellites in space, and then returns to Earth like an airplane. Tomorrow, aerospace planes may operate at hypersonic speeds in space while taking off and landing on Earth like airplanes. The gap between air and space vehicles may greatly narrow with these developments.

Aerospace Elements

Aerospace power relies on both vehicles and other elements to accomplish its missions. The elements that create aerospace power include an aerospace industry, people, support systems, equipment, and rational direction. The strength of a nation's economy and its political will are key to the development and maintenance of aerospace power, but this is true of any military force as well. A country must have sufficient economic strength to provide adequate financial, technological, and productive capacity to enable the government to expertly operate aerospace forces. The economic strength of a nation sets the pace for developing military forces and directly affects its national security. Aerospace power also depends on the willingness of the nation's populace to permit use of their resources for building, maintaining, and applying aerospace power. Without the backing of a nation's population, aerospace power may be limited in scope and use.

Aerospace power owes many of its capabilities to technological advances, which often require complex electronics, information systems, propulsion, life support, munitions, and other devices. Engineers, scientists, computer experts, technicians, and extensive capital investment in facilities and equipment make these innovations possible. The aerospace industry not only provides equipment repair, but also gives the nation the ability to produce new aircraft or spacecraft. Individual nations may create their own aerospace industry, or they may use the services of another nation's industrial capacity by importing many of these products. Today, many nations do not depend upon domestic aerospace industrial strength to produce aircraft or space systems. For example, the United States arguably must depend on foreign industry to provide computer chips, raw materials, and other imported products to ensure the manufacture of many military aerospace components. In the future, growth in economic globalization will increase foreign interdependence for industrial products.

Piloting an aircraft is a complex task. Maintaining an aerospace force also requires the existence of a technology base. People must fly, maintain, and operate the support systems that keep a nation's aerospace power working around the clock. These people must have the sufficient motivation, education, and training to keep aircraft and space systems in operable condition. A nation's military must keep the people who are involved in maintaining aerospace power motivated to continue working in the aerospace industry or as a part of the military aerospace force. If there is little or no motivation for people to support the aerospace force, a nation may become trapped in an expensive and ultimately ineffective force due to low experience levels. The nation must also maintain a sound educational system to instill the proper levels of knowledge to produce engineers, technicians, and people capable of operating and maintaining advanced technology or exploiting it. Finally, the aerospace force must have facilities and programs to train people in specific methods of operating and maintaining the equipment and systems of the aerospace force. These training programs must be able to expand and adapt to changes in situations or threats.

Aircraft and satellites cannot operate by themselves. Although a crew can fly an aircraft, it relies on a number of diverse, complex support systems while in the air and on the ground. A crew may require assistance from satellite navigation systems to get data on locations. The crew also needs a communications network to relay critical information about landing instructions, weather, and other key data necessary to operate the plane. Ground-support operations also include air traffic control, maintenance, supply, and facilities that include maintenance hangars and runways. Similarly, space systems also require much ground support that includes communications, data processing, satellite-control facilities, and launchpads. Aerospace power is not just about platforms. Typically, many individuals still concentrate on the end result of aerospace power—aircraft and spacecraft—when they think about this form of military activity. Technologically advanced aerospace systems require extensive support from specialists with a wide range of expertise. Flight surgeons provide medical support for crews; aircraft-maintenance personnel ensure that vital repairs are made to aircraft; and satellite-control personnel make sure that proper orbital adjustments are made to maintain peak efficiency and effectiveness for the system.

A nation may have all the physical elements necessary to organize and function as an aerospace force, but it is useless unless it is given direction. A nation could use its aerospace force for independent military actions, such as nuclear deterrence. Conversely, the country could use this aerospace force as a supporting resource for its ground forces or as an equal partner to all of its sister services. Before the nation decides to

Logistics is one of the keys to airpower.

use its aerospace force in a particular manner, it needs to provide direction and guidance on how it will use this capability to better prepare and employ its forces. Without solid direction to shape and provide a common set of beliefs about aerospace power, these forces might not provide optimal service to the nation. The country might acquire unnecessary aircraft and space systems that might not give it the appropriate forces to win a war of national survival. Guidance issued to aerospace forces might come from national objectives, strategy, beliefs, experience, theory, and other sources. Developing the guidance and plans to build, shape, and operate an aerospace force is one of the most challenging issues facing leaders. Unknown threats, resource constraints, and other dynamic factors create much uncertainty about future guidance to build the aerospace force of the future.

Aerospace industry, people, support systems, and guidance all help aircraft and space systems stay in operation. However, one of the most important factors in aerospace power revolves around the equipment available for use. Aircraft are composed of several systems, including propulsion, communications, guidance, airframe, electronic devices, radar, and munitions. These systems are further composed of subsystems and components, which must work together to allow the aircraft to operate. Space systems—which operate without the benefit of being easily repaired, unless retrieved by another space system or recovered upon reentry for reuse—must rely on existing onboard components. At a minimum, the equipment must have advanced capabilities and be reliable, maintainable, and cost-effective.

Aerospace power is not just about aircraft or orbiting satellites. The key components of an aerospace industry—people, support systems, guidance, and equipment—all contribute to a nation's ability to conduct operations above Earth's surface. Although a nation may be able to operate an aerospace force without one or more of these elements in the short run, the ability of that country to exploit air or space in the future will be limited. The complexity of flying or launching a vehicle into low earth orbit requires considerable energy, time, and resources. The coordination and integration of these efforts are one of the challenges a nation faces if it wishes to use aerospace power.

Summary

Aerospace power, like other forms of military power, has unique characteristics, definitions, strengths, and weaknesses. Understanding these characteristics in relation to other military forces and the principles of war should help the reader appreciate how aircraft and space systems can support military operations today and in the future. The concepts of aerospace power provide a foundation that allows one to evaluate how aerospace power should be used in military and humanitarian situations. This function gives one the tools to solve problems that involve these forces. The planning and operation of these complex military capabilities require a common understanding about aerospace power.

Students of aerospace power face a continual challenge. Technological change, shifting threats, the application of air and space forces, and other dynamic events have modified people's thoughts about aerospace power through the years. Early airpower advocates struggled to define what role aircraft should play in future wars through a vision limited by existing technology and theories of the day. Some military officers charged that aircraft played a pivotal role that would end a conflict through long-range bombardment. Others thought aircraft would better serve a ground commander as flying artillery. The emergence of nuclear weapons, ballistic missiles, and space systems has added to the aerospace power debate through the years. In the future, newly discovered technologies and capabilities will undoubtedly change viewpoints on the role of aerospace power. However, the basic concepts discussed in this chapter should help guide the discussion of these issues. Aerospace power theories, doctrines, and strategies will be revised over time, but the basic concepts and ideas should enhance one's ability to apply new capabilities to the future of aerospace power.

Notes

1. William Mitchell, *Winged Defense: The Development and Possibilities of Modern Air Power—Economic and Military* (New York: Dover, 1988), 3–4.

2. Philip Towle, "The Distinctive Characteristics of Air Power," in *The Dynamics of Air Power,* ed. Group Capt Andrew Lambert and Arthur C. Williamson (Bracknell: RAF Staff College, 1996), 3.

3. Submarine-launched ballistic missiles have provided an intercontinental nuclear-attack capability since the 1960s.

4. The United States Air Force developed a set of principles of war, based on Fuller's set, and applied it to aerospace power. This list is incorporated into Air Force Doctrine Document (AFDD) 1, *Air Force Basic Doctrine,* 1 September 1997, 11–21.

5. Eduard Mark, *Aerial Interdiction: Air Power and the Land Battle in Three American Wars* (Washington, D.C.: Center for Air Force History, 1994), 387.

Chapter 2

Aerospace Power Theory

Aerospace power can support a nation and military commander in different ways. It can perform bombardment missions against an enemy's industrial base, support ground forces by attacking supply lines, or rapidly move armored forces around the globe. The optimal use of aerospace power depends on many factors: available forces, objectives, enemy military capabilities, established plans, principles and concepts of operations, and an appropriate theory. Several individuals have advocated that nations use their aircraft and space systems to support or win wars in particular ways. These theories have shaped the face of airpower in the past and continue to do so in the present. Perhaps they will also guide future aerospace power in several important organizational, force-structure, planning, and operational areas. This chapter identifies the fundamental theories that have had the greatest impact upon aerospace power today.

This chapter first defines what a theory is and why it is important. This definition should help one compare theories as well as decide whether the theory seems reasonable and is applicable today and for the future. The chapter then discusses the work of several key theorists. Ideas and concepts dealing with aerospace power are based on individual experience, beliefs, prediction, and contemporary technology. A reader should note that these theories evolved as events changed over time. The study of theory helps frame and make relevant how aerospace power can be employed, developed, and built. More importantly, these theories may provide insight into solving a nation's future military problems.

What Is Theory?

For decades, airpower thinkers have developed, written, and debated their ideas on the role and impact of aircraft on war. These enterprising visionaries developed theories on the application of early aircraft that have had a great impact on developing a force. Military space theory is still in its infancy. However, military commanders are beginning to view military space forces as a vital element of present and future combat operations. Before one can study these theories, one needs to understand what a theory is and how it can be used in the study of aerospace power.

Theory provides a foundation for a field of study. A theory can help an individual explain a state of nature, define or establish a set of beliefs about a subject, provide knowledge about the principles of a subject, and predict a future condition. A person can use theory to explain how a particular function works. This explanation may provide basic facts or a model that provides one an interpretation of the events and actions taken throughout a process.[1] Theory guides individuals towards a common understanding of a subject because it should define and relay a set of beliefs that people can agree upon, discuss, and debate. A theory can also set forth observations about the nature of the subject. The principles of war, as earlier discussed, were not proven "facts" or laws; they were merely a series of ideas expressed by individuals about lessons from combat experience and beliefs. Finally, a theory should predict or explain how a future condition, situation, or outcome might change, given the application of certain beliefs or ideas about a subject. This aspect of a theory allows the individual to say, "If one uses this idea, then this will happen."

If this is a definition of theory one can use, then where does theory come from? A person may create a theory through several diverse avenues. Observations from actual events allow one to draw some correlation to the cause and effect of events. This gives an individual a rudimentary basis to make some conclusions about the nature of an event if one uses a particular function in a certain way. For example, in economics one might observe the conditions of supply and demand. If demand for a product is greater than the supply, the price for the item would rise, and shortages of the good or service might result. Additionally, the increased price might induce firms to produce more of the good or service.

A series of events provides a better foundation for drawing conclusions than does a single observation. Over time, situations with different conditions may help individuals refine their theory and make it more resilient and universal in scope. Individuals may also form theories through experimentation. A controlled experiment using observed tests might allow one to vary the use of actions on similar situations and then measure the differences in their final results. This measurement requires a careful experimental design. The difference in effects might help one develop a theory based on these results. A theory may also come from a person's set of beliefs. A potential theory might develop from an individual's thoughts, perceived logic, beliefs, or reflections about a subject. For example, a theory's development can also come from a combination of these sources. Observation may lead to a series of experiments that results in a belief about a subject. Theory becomes the foundation for the discussion and development of aerospace forces. Individuals and organizations have sought to develop air forces based on theory. The adoption of theory by military leaders as a framework to develop forces demonstrates its relevance for present and future use. Theory is always changing and evolving due to dynamic conditions and will require the attention of future leaders for its application.

What Should Aerospace Power Theory Do?

Aerospace power theories should add to the field of study, as is the case in any other discipline, such as economics, political science, mathematics, or engineering. Aerospace power theory is another resource for military leaders to develop a set of plans for combat, build a fleet of aircraft and spacecraft, train people, and think about how their aerospace forces will fight in the future. Aerospace theories may include a complete theory on all aspects of aerospace operations or a single segment, like strategic-bombardment theory. Regardless of the level of theory, a discussion of how the element of aerospace power is defined in terms of its role in military operations, its basic propositions, and its effects on the battlefield is paramount.

A complete aerospace power theory should address what aircraft and space systems can contribute to military operations and how a commander should employ those forces in combat. The theory, at a minimum, should address the issue by predicting "if one employs airpower or space power under these conditions, then the result will be . . . ," given the proper use of force. More importantly, the theory should discuss how aerospace power will get certain results and explain why the results were achieved. The theory's author can also demonstrate the difference in capabilities between different military forces such as naval or land forces. This discussion allows a reader to assess the relationship between aerospace power and other military forces' abilities to conduct the same operation and its impact on the future battlefield. The proposed theory becomes an integral part of a commander's assessment to compare, contrast, and select the best forces to accomplish a mission.

"Traditional" aerospace theory has been based on aircraft. There are few recognized theories on space power. Perhaps the need to produce a theory has not kept pace with the technological and operational growth in space power. Conversely, after World War I, several airpower theorists created and openly discussed their theories. Several highly public debates took place on the implications of these theories. Those debates ranged from the accepted role of airpower in relation to ground and naval forces to the moral value of using bombers against civilian targets. Airpower theory also was used to justify an independent role and organization for air forces from other forces. These theories also helped national and military leaders plan future campaigns against anticipated antagonists in the looming global conflict of World War II. The acquisition, training of forces, and deployment of military aircraft were predicated on these campaign plans, which mirrored the leading airpower theories of the day. The United States built its land-based air forces around the long-range strategic bomber.[2] Other nations, like Germany, followed a different path by developing an air force designed to support ground forces. After the war, the United States geared much of its air force to support nuclear operations. Airpower theory had an influential grip on the development and capabilities of fighting forces. In the future, revolutionary ideas and theories about space power may result in new organizations, methods of fighting, and relations among services, as well as determine the number of resources available to apply in the next war.

Giulio Douhet: The First Airpower Theorist

Gen Giulio Douhet developed one of the first and most influential airpower theories. Douhet, an Italian army officer, was highly influenced by Italy's airpower experience during its colonial era and World War I. Although not a pilot, Douhet took command of an airplane battalion in the Italian army in 1912. His airpower theory was explained in *The Command of the Air*, written in 1921 and revised in 1927. Douhet's ideas greatly affected the thoughts of leaders of the United States Army Air Corps. Ultimately, his thoughts were extensively studied and modified by the Air Corps's prestigious Air Corps Tactical School (ACTS), whose graduates became the leaders of the future United States Air Force. Their experience in the school significantly affected many key decisions during and after World War II. ACTS was the intellectual center for the fledgling Air Corps and significantly influenced the Air Corps and AAF for many years.

Douhet's main thesis was that airpower, through carefully planned long-range bombardment, could devastate a nation and render the use of a ground war moot. An important prerequisite of Douhet's theory was the command of the air, or what is known today as air superiority. A nation's aircraft had to be able to attack at will and deny an enemy's air force the capability to conduct similar attacks. The air force had to either destroy or disable its enemy's ability to fly in order to secure access to bombing targets. Similarly, the enemy could not bomb a friendly nation if it did not control access to the air. A nation's aircraft could attack enemy planes in the air, on the ground, or in "production centers." However, attacking aircraft on the ground was Douhet's preferred method of controlling the air. Land and naval forces were still a necessary part of war since conquered nations needed to be occupied or sea-lanes of communications patrolled. The primacy of land and naval forces was challenged while airpower ascended into a dominant role. Douhet believed that only an "adequate aerial force," without need of land or naval weapons, could destroy an enemy's air force.[3] Before aircraft could conduct operations, a nation needed to gain command of the air; this was so important that Douhet equated its attainment as a first step towards maintaining the national defense.

After achieving command of the air, an air force could bomb an enemy's vital centers of government, industry, and population. Hindering a nation's ability to wage war is important. Douhet made no distinction between combatants and noncombatants. The total mobilization of whole nations' populations, economies, industries, and societies to fight in World War I illustrated the difficulty of discriminating among a soldier on the front, a production worker manufacturing small arms, or a banker financing the war effort. A weak link in the total mobilization effort was civilian morale. The linkage between civilian morale and ending a conflict was the key to Douhet's theory of airpower.

Unlike the soldier on the front, steeled by combat, civilian morale was fragile and very unstable. If a nation could bomb production centers, cities, homes, and other areas where civilians congregated, then their morale would soon ebb. The disenchanted civilians would demonstrate against the war and force their government to capitulate. In order to hasten the destruction of civilian morale, Douhet advocated that an air force use any means to inflict damage upon the enemy. This included the possible use of explosive, incendiary, and poison-gas weapons. Douhet thought that a combination of those weapons would create a synergistic effect that would deepen the drop in civilian morale. Germany's first attempts to use primitive strategic bombers and zeppelins against London inspired Douhet concerning the possibilities of winning a war by breaking a populace's will. The German raids against Britain produced no conclusive evidence about shattering the enemy's will. Additionally, Douhet's advocacy of a massive first strike against the enemy underscored his support for the offensive use of airpower. The newly developed aircraft's speed and range would allow the nation's air force to conduct massive bombardment campaigns and render ground and naval forces useless. The aircraft's speed and the height at which it flew also made defense against an offensive aerial attack difficult.

AEROSPACE POWER THEORY

World War I German aviator drops a bomb over the western front. Bombing would later become a contentious issue among theorists.

Douhet's ideas were developed in the context of the horrors suffered in World War I. On 1 July 1916, the British army suffered 20,000 deaths and 40,000 wounded during the Battle of the Somme. German losses were over 6,000 killed and wounded. The 10-month Battle of Verdun ended with over 377,000 French and 337,000 German deaths. Aerial bombardment of cities with relatively fewer, albeit civilian, deaths would be more humane than the slaughter in the trenches. Douhet reasoned that aerial warfare, under the command of an airman, was less destructive than previous modes of combat. Aircraft put under the command of ground or naval forces

41

Trench warfare in World War I

would merely act in secondary roles, like reconnaissance, and not take full advantage of their capabilities. The full potential of aerial warfare would not be realized; only the horrors of trench warfare would remain. Airpower had to have an independent role in future wars and not be subordinated to either the army or navy. An independent air force organized to conduct long-range bombardment at a moment's notice was the only answer.

The air force needed only two types of aircraft: "battleplanes" and reconnaissance aircraft. Douhet believed that an air force should be composed mostly of battleplanes, which would have sufficient self-defense armaments to protect themselves from enemy aircraft attack. These aircraft could act as defensive fighters and bombers but were designed primarily for bombing missions. There was no need for a specialized interceptor or attack aircraft with the deployment of the battleplane, which could attack from any direction against an enemy. The expansiveness of the air made ground and aerial defense against bombing missions nearly impossible for a defender to detect, plan, or execute. Seeking air-to-air combat was pointless for the stronger or weaker air force. Reconnaissance aircraft were used to gather information to "keep from being surprised by the enemy."[4] Speed was the best weapon of these aircraft, which could detect enemy preparations for war and provide information that would later be transformed into targets for the battleplanes. However, the main type of aircraft that an independent air force should adopt was clearly the battleplane; all others were merely ancillary aircraft that detracted from the main purpose of the air force—strategic bombardment.

Douhet's theory on airpower can be summed up by his statement "To conquer the command of the air means victory: to be beaten in the air means defeat and acceptance of whatever terms the enemy may be pleased to impose."[5] Although much has been written about Douhet's thoughts on breaking the will and morale of civilian populations via bombardment, command of the air was the key to the destruction of cities. In Douhet's eyes, the command of the air allowed the air force to accomplish total victory against the enemy relatively quickly, compared to the ponderous land campaigns of the time. Today, the prospect of bombing innocent civilians is repulsive, but we have adopted the idea that an independent air force should attack targets of national significance, not just civilians. Douhet speculated that a hypothetical aerial attack conducted in a single day on "governing bodies, banks, [and] other public services" might plunge Rome's population into a state of terror.[6] This is the effect Douhet believed might end the war. The air force could create more problems for a city if it also destroyed or disabled rails, as well as telegraph, telephone, and radio communications. Douhet's list of possible targets was the first recognition of what an air force bombardment campaign should attack to affect the well-being of a nation.

These ideas—an independent air force's winning a war through the exclusive use of airpower and establishing command of the air—would soon attract many adherents and advocates of airpower. Early aviation technology allowed Douhet to peek into the future and develop his ideas about aerial warfare. Airpower was in its infancy, and as technology advanced, airpower advocates promoted many of Douhet's themes. Some of

Destruction of a German city in World War II breaks the will of the people. Douhet's hypothesis is tested.

his ideas would be proven in combat during World War II; others resulted in tragic consequences for opposing forces and enemy populations during the war.

Douhet's theory on airpower had several limitations. Aside from the use of poison gas and incendiary weapons, Douhet advocated a war against civilians to break the will of a population. He also made several assumptions that may not be reasonable today. Douhet saw the public's morale as fragile and susceptible to being swiftly broken by aerial bombardment. As a result, he reasoned that the demoralized population would pressure the government to end the war—assuming that the government listens to the population. But totalitarian or autocratic regimes might not listen. Additionally, populations are quite resilient to military attacks. Many cases in military history record that when some cities were put under siege, as occurred in the American Civil War, the population's will did not crumble. Another potential problem is the assumption that the airplane or battleplane will break through enemy defenses unscathed and defeat the nation. Douhet did not anticipate high technology's refinement of defensive weapons, such as high-speed aircraft interceptors, radar, or antiaircraft missiles. Arguably, Douhet's theory works on nations that have large cities or industrial targets. Would his ideas be appropriate for a war against an insurgency with guerilla forces or an agrarian society? There was almost universal agreement that a nation could be defeated by airpower. Little provision existed for a nation's size or type of conflict since war, in Douhet's eyes, was total.

Despite these limitations, Giulio Douhet did write the first comprehensive airpower theory that helped give others the inspiration to develop their own theories. His theory was a starting place for many airmen to attempt to build an independent air force, carved out of their land and naval services. General Douhet provided the push to define and legitimize national air forces—a movement that carried into the post–World War II era.

Billy Mitchell:
America's First Airpower Theorist

William "Billy" Mitchell was a combat-experienced aviator in the US Army who wrote about the use of airpower and its future application in war. He was the son of a US senator and joined the Army during the Spanish-American War. Mitchell was an ardent airpower zealot who commanded American combat aviation on the western front during World War I. He later became assistant director of the Army's Air Service after the war. Mitchell's name made many newspapers' headlines when he used Air Service bombers to demonstrate that these aircraft could sink captured German battleships. These experiments showed that the battleship was not invulnerable to air attacks and that aircraft could adequately defend the coasts as effectively as Army coastal-defense artillery units or the Navy. He continued to press his case within the Army and with the public. Mitchell was later court-martialed and resigned as a result of his vehement advocacy of an independent role for airpower and charges he made that naval officers were criminally responsible for an airship disaster.

Mitchell was not an originator of new ideas. Instead, he borrowed heavily from existing concepts (e.g., those of Douhet and others) and his experiences from World War I. He was adamant about the independence of an air force and the central command of air assets by an airman. Mitchell believed that an autonomous air force, coequal in status to the Army and Navy, could conduct long-range bombardment against vital centers of an enemy without attacking its land or naval forces. Additionally, he thought that an airman must command the independent air force, that only "air-minded" countries could fully support an air force, and that all aviation resources, including naval aircraft, should be controlled by this independent air force. The country should organize the three separate services into a unified department of defense. Mitchell believed that airpower would dominate both land and naval forces. Although Mitchell's ideas sound similar to Douhet's, he differed greatly from the Italian general in several areas.

Mitchell believed in using aerial, long-range bombardment against an opposing nation's industry and infrastructure. Unlike Douhet, Mitchell abhorred direct attacks against civilians in any form. US Army aviators eschewed the concept of attacking defenseless women and children as politically unpalatable and did not fully support Douhet's ideas.[7] Instead, Mitchell thought attacks against the war-making capability of a nation were more effective. These targets included industry, agriculture, and infrastructure (e.g., roads, rails, bridges, waterways, and other vital centers). Attacking these targets required precision bombardment in order to destroy factories

AEROSPACE POWER THEORY

Brig Gen William "Billy" Mitchell, an early airpower advocate in the US Army Air Corps

and avoid civilian casualties. Mitchell thought the bombing of a nation's "nerve centers" early in the conflict would significantly disrupt the country.[8] Instead of applying Douhet's thesis that war was won by breaking the will of the people, Mitchell tried to hinder the enemy's war-making capability by attacking vital centers of command and industry. The destruction of a nation's direct war-making capability would stop the enemy's ability to conduct operations. Although Mitchell believed that air forces could attack an enemy's homeland, he still supported the idea that land and naval forces would also contribute to an enemy's defeat. Armies and navies were still targets to be destroyed, and the airplane would enable a nation to do this at a lower cost and faster speed.

Mitchell did, however, champion the idea of gaining control of the air, like Douhet. Mitchell agreed with Douhet's theory that gaining control of the air was the first objective for any air force. An air force attempting to gain superiority over an enemy's air forces would do so primarily by conducting air battles against enemy air forces. Mitchell believed that "the only effective defense against aerial attack is to whip the enemy's air forces in air battles."[9] This differed greatly from Douhet's concept that control of the air be achieved primarily by attacking enemy aircraft on the ground. Additionally, the ability to gain control of the air would require specialized fighter aircraft instead of battleplanes. Mitchell also advocated that an air force build a mixture of aircraft that included bomber, pursuit (fighter), attack (to support ground troops), and observation (reconnaissance) planes. In 1921, Mitchell estimated that this "balanced" force would be composed of about 60 percent pursuit, 20 percent bomber, and 20 percent attack aircraft—hardly a force dominated by strategic bombers. Mitchell's perception of force structure appears more balanced and capable of a multitude of missions for a nation. The long-range bomber was still the primary aircraft type, despite the acknowledgement of attack, pursuit, and observation planes. Bombers would deliver a knockout punch to an enemy's war-making capability. Pursuit aircraft could help defend the nation against bombing attacks. For the United States, the bomber had to traverse oceans to strike naval vessels at sea or attack European targets. Douhet's Italian battleplanes would conduct their bombardment missions over shorter ranges than would American aircraft.

After gaining control of the air, Mitchell's air force could attack a nation's vital centers or other targets such as troop formations and supplies. Any remaining enemy aircraft would be occupied with defending their country from bombardment missions. Since two oceans protected the United States, long-range bombers could easily attack enemy battle fleets. In July 1921, Mitchell successfully demonstrated the ability of aircraft to sink battleships when his planes sank the German battleship *Ostfriesland* and other vessels with 2,000-pound bombs. The sinking of this heavily armored dreadnought signaled a new age for naval and aerial warfare. This dramatic show of airpower dominance over a naval vessel once thought invulnerable provided a national demonstration of airpower and started a debate about the value of aircraft.

Mitchell's ideas were instrumental in orienting future American airpower towards bombardment and creating an independent force from the Army and Navy. However, like Douhet, Mitchell also made several assumptions about airpower that would later be challenged under combat and practical experience, while others would be validated. Offensive combat air operations were the keys to success. The bomber would get through to the enemy's vital centers, contingent upon a friendly force's ability to win the critical air battles that would determine control of the air. Mitchell thought that air defenses were not as far evolved as bombers, which allowed offensive combat operations to dominate aerial warfare. Antiaircraft artillery (AAA) and pursuit aircraft were not as technologically advanced, in his opinion, and the bomber appeared to rule the skies. If bombers could get through, then enemy forces could also do the same to friendly cities and industry. Additionally, advances in technology that made the bomber supreme were not seriously considered for the single-engined fighter.

Mitchell did bring many defense issues to the public for debate. Aircraft were pitted against naval battleships for the mission of defending the United States. Mitchell sought a public forum on airpower issues rather than restricting himself to a military audience, as did Douhet. Defense budgets were shrinking during the interwar years in the United States, and services were competing for every defense dollar. Mitchell's bombing experiments exposed the vulnerabilities and potential obsolescence of naval vessels to aircraft attack. These experiments inspired Mitchell to embrace the idea that airpower would dominate both land and naval warfare in the future. The creation of an independent air force from the Army also ruffled many feathers in that service. Many US Army leaders envisioned aircraft protecting ground units from enemy bomber forces and supporting ground operations—not conducting an independent bombing role. All of these ideas would be tested in World War II. Mitchell did not live long enough to see bombers' domination of the AAF during World War II or to see the creation of his cherished independent air force in 1947.

Sir Hugh Trenchard: An Independent Air Force for Britain

Marshal of the Royal Air Force Sir Hugh Trenchard was a driving force within the RAF. Although he was not initially an advocate of an independent air force or long-range bombardment, he later defended the RAF as a separate service from the army and navy. Trenchard was the head of the RAF, and his ideas about what the service should be would ultimately influence the RAF's performance during World War II. While Douhet and Mitchell wrote about their theories in books and articles, Trenchard used his position to advocate his theories in staff papers and lectures. Head of the Royal Flying Corps in France during World War I, he later commanded the Independent Air Force (later the RAF) in 1918. This separate air force was created to protect the homeland from the threat of German aerial attacks.

Trenchard believed wholeheartedly in the concept that airpower's strength lay in its ability to conduct offensive operations. Additionally, he thought that an enemy nation might capitulate if a bomber force could destroy the will of its population through attacks on vital industrial and communications targets. Trenchard embraced the idea that the demoralized population would rise up against its government and force it to surrender. Trenchard's theme about crushing an adversary's will through bombing sounds like Douhet's beliefs—indeed, evidence exists to indicate that Douhet did influence Trenchard's ideas.[10] Also, the chief of the RAF firmly advocated that control of the air was a prerequisite to all air operations. Finally, he believed that such air-controlling air forces could be "substituted" for more expensive army units. Trenchard's idea of substitution met with success in its application in colonial Britain.

The notion that an offensive air force was paramount also supported his idea of strategic bombardment. The strategic effect of causing the enemy's population to lose its will and causing industrial capacity to suffer was justification for maintaining a coequal service, separate from the Royal Army and Royal Navy. Trenchard did not advocate the targeting of civilians per se; rather, he intended to attack industrial targets and infrastructure while limiting collateral damage.[11] He believed that the "moral effect of bombing stands to the material in a proportion of 20 to 1" in terms of the effectiveness of an aerial-bombardment campaign.[12] That is, the effect of bombing on a population's will was more substantial than the physical damage it caused. Breaking the will of the people would come from indirect attacks against a nation's production centers—not against their homes. Trenchard's approach could break the will of the people via factory workers who suffered from attacks on industrial targets. Curiously, Trenchard thought that the air raids against England by Germany actually raised British morale.[13] He also advocated the use of night bombing to deny the enemy any relief. Continuous bombing would complement daytime attacks and ultimately reduce losses from air defenses.

Like Douhet or Mitchell, Trenchard also thought that gaining control of the air had to occur before any other air operation could take place. Trenchard's combat experience concerning the lack of success in destroying enemy airfields led him to the idea of air battles. The Independent Air Force devoted over 40 percent of its air strikes to attacks on German airfields in World War I.[14] Once control of the air was achieved, the RAF could accomplish several missions. An independent RAF could conduct strategic bombing missions to break the will of the people; it could support ground units against enemy troop formations; or it might attack enemy supply and transportation resources. Trenchard did not advocate that the sole purpose of independent air operations was strategic bombardment. He never lost sight of cooperation with ground forces. Before its independence, the Royal Flying Corps heavily supported ground operations, and Trenchard did not abandon this concept.

During the 1920s and 1930s, British military budgets were slashed for economic reasons during the global depression. Great Britain's military still had to defend a vast empire stretching from Africa to the Americas. Maintaining troops and naval forces in those colonies was expensive, especially to a military stretched thin to cover global commitments. Trenchard introduced the concept of substitution or air control to remedy the situation. Essentially, aircraft in combination with mobile army units could attack rebel base camps or forces threatening colonial status. The RAF could bombard villages, crops, enemy base camps, or any other targets, usually after a warning was given to the population. Air forces were to act as police at a lower cost than an occupying army would incur. However, mountainous geography or guerilla forces, able to blend into the local populace, proved difficult for air control to handle. But air control could and did work in several locations. In 1921, five RAF squadrons replaced 33 Royal Army and colonial battalions. The cost of keeping an equivalent military capability fell from an annual outlay of £20 million to only £2 million.[15] Not only was the expense reduced, but also casualties were lowered—and the RAF squadrons proved more mobile than ground forces. The RAF also pacified Somaliland at an expenditure of £77,000, compared to an estimated expense of £6 million—the equivalent of two army divisions. These concepts were the beginning of using air forces as expeditionary forces that could independently conduct operations far from home to satisfy national political objectives.

Whereas Douhet only wrote about his theories and Mitchell brought public attention to the airpower debate, Sir Hugh Trenchard actually applied airpower theory. Trenchard was able to develop doctrine, plan force structure, and groom future RAF leaders schooled in the beliefs of strategic bombing.

One of Trenchard's greatest achievements was keeping the RAF intact as an independent service. Defense budget cuts forced all services to defend themselves against reductions in roles and missions. Trenchard succeeded in keeping the RAF intact, albeit at a reduced size. Not only did Trenchard believe in many of the ideas advocated by Douhet and Mitchell, he made them more practical. He added the ideas of night bombing, air control, and destruction of the enemy's will through attacks on industry and infrastructure to the growing debate about airpower.

Jack Slessor: Support for Ground Forces

John "Jack" Slessor was a subordinate of Sir Hugh Trenchard. He would later become chief of the Air Staff for the RAF from 1950 to 1953. Slessor entered the Royal Flying Corps as a pilot and later prepared the RAF for World War II. Slessor shared many ideas that Trenchard believed, and he advanced several new thoughts regarding air support to ground forces. He was able to see several of his ideas put into action during his tenure as commander in chief of the Mediterranean Allied Air Forces in 1944, during some of the most bitter ground combat in Italy. Slessor's contribution to airpower theory in regard to attacking enemy forces behind the immediate battlefield was a revelation to many airmen. His assignment as an instructor at the Army Staff College at Camberley from 1931 to 1934 affected his views. He later published a book based on his lectures at the Army Staff College entitled *Airpower and Armies* and advocated a role for airpower to support ground operations.

Slessor believed in many of the popular airpower theories of the day, especially Trenchard's, including the notion that strategic bombardment was the primary role of an air force and that control of the air was a prerequisite for all air operations. However, his Camberley experience made him ponder how airpower might support land operations. Unlike his contemporaries who saw the horrors of trench warfare, Slessor was exposed to many technological marvels being discussed at the Army Staff College—specifically, the tank. Perhaps the old concept of trench warfare would be relegated to the dustbin of history. If armored and mobile ground forces could sweep through a nation, could they alter the face of warfare—as airpower was about to do?

While Trenchard supported the concept of damaging the will of a population through attacks on industry, Slessor held a view much like Mitchell's. Slessor's strategic-bombardment campaign would concentrate on attacking important distribution points, industries, communications, and other targets to shut down industrial and war-making capabilities. Not all of the industrial capabilities need be destroyed—only key industries that would force the collapse of certain production. Timing and proper targeting (Slessor was vague about which targets) against a nation's industry were just as effective as and more efficient than a war of annihilation.

What marks Slessor from Douhet, Trenchard, and Mitchell is his concern about support to ground operations. His *Airpower and Armies* addresses issues about how airpower could support British land forces in an expeditionary ground campaign. Slessor was not advocating the use of close air support (CAS)—direct attacks against enemy forces engaged in combat with friendly forces. Instead, he preferred interdiction—the destruction of enemy supply and troop reinforcement to the battlefront. Slessor thought of attacks on supply lines that would curtail the reinforcement of equipment, ammunition, and consumable goods as a means of choking off the fighting capability of a foe's ground forces. These actions would reduce the fighting capability of the enemy and increase the chance of his defeat by ground forces. Control of the air would allow air forces to strike rail, canal, road, and other forms of transportation during daylight. Cooperation between air and ground forces would allow the nation to better succeed against the enemy—the first seeds of joint planning and execution of a campaign.

Jack Slessor did foresee occasions in which air forces needed to conduct CAS missions. He provided three conditions that air forces and armies needed to achieve to maximize their chances of success for these tactical missions. First, the air force had to attain control of the air. This control was, at a minimum, local or over the battlefield area. Preferably, the air force would control the air over the whole theater of operations. Second, joint coordination between air and ground forces was essential in order to plan missions, ensure that timing of attacks was carefully coordinated, and reduce careless execution that might result in friendly casualties from these air attacks. CAS missions required more coordination and interservice cooperation than interdiction strikes against enemy supply lines.[16] Third, a commander might use CAS missions in three ways: to support a breakthrough against the enemy's front lines, help pursue retreating enemy forces, or counterattack an enemy's attempt to conduct his own breakthrough against positions held by friendly forces.[17] Airpower's role in support of ground operations was better served in interdiction than in CAS. The latter was more reactive, and one could avoid attacks on friendly forces if the ability of enemy forces to conduct such attacks was eliminated through interdiction.

Slessor's experience in the Italian campaign during World War II provided him firsthand observations of the effects of airpower on a disciplined, entrenched German ground force. He made several interesting observations in "The Effect of Airpower in a Land Offensive," his report of 18 June 1944. The Italian campaign was fought over mountainous terrain that allowed German forces to build defenses and let them have access to several rail and road systems capable of resupplying frontline forces. He observed that airpower could not independently defeat a "highly organized and disciplined army, even when the army is virtually without air support of its own." Further, air missions cannot "entirely prevent the movement of strategic reserves to the battlefront" and isolate the enemy. However, airpower can "make it impossible" for a determined ground force to mount a prolonged defense against a ground offensive. Airpower could also turn a retreat by these organized forces into a rout, and this would "eliminate an entire army as an effective fighting force."[18] Slessor's view was that airpower, not land forces, significantly reduced the fighting capability of the German forces in Italy. This allowed the Allied forces to grind down German forces and expel them from the battlefield. His thoughts on interdiction, first developed at Camberley, proved their worth.

Jack Slessor was an airpower visionary. He advanced the ideas of using airpower to support ground and joint operations between army and air forces but also saw the value of strategic bombardment against a nation's war-fighting capability. Slessor also was the first airpower theorist to recognize that joint cooperation and coordination were necessary among air and ground forces in order to succeed with CAS and interdiction. Slessor provided a more practical and balanced view of airpower than did Douhet, Mitchell, or Trenchard, Slessor's mentor.

Claire Chennault: Pursuit-Aviation Enthusiast

Throughout the 1920s and 1930s, the ideas of Douhet, Mitchell, Trenchard, and Slessor were discussed by many military-aviation advocates. Strategic bombardment was a keystone to all of their airpower theories. Bombers would get through air defenses to deliver their deadly cargoes and destroy a nation almost single-handedly with impunity. Nowhere was this theory adopted more vigorously than in the United States. The Army Air Corps established the Tactical School in 1920 at Langley Field, Virginia, to evaluate all aspects of air tactics, strategy, and doctrine. The school would later move in 1931 to Maxwell Field, Alabama, and change its name to the Air Corps Tactical School, where the faculty and students concentrated on developing a strategic-bombardment strategy—the industrial-web theory. The ACTS industrial-web theory revolved around the use of daylight high-altitude precision attack on a selected number of targets that, if successfully conducted, would collapse a nation's industry. These selected industries would shut down the "web." Daylight precision bombing was required because of the limited number of bombers available. Air Corps bombers needed to attack these targets more efficiently and effectively instead of using the mass bomber force envisioned by Douhet. Mitchell's influence upon the Air Corps was institutionalized within ACTS. But one man, Claire Chennault, criticized these ideas.

Chennault was an unabashed supporter of pursuit aircraft. As an ACTS instructor, Captain Chennault questioned the invulnerability of strategic bombers from modern air defenses. Bomber advocates assumed that an air defense force had little chance of detecting attacking bombers as well as bombers capable of defending themselves against interceptors. Chennault challenged these assumptions. His main thesis was that an air defense system needed to have a sufficient communications and detection system created in depth with high-speed fighters. This system could then successfully intercept and thwart a bomber attack. Bomber enthusiasts believed that long-range attacks were limited only by an aircraft's range since air defenses were ineffective. Chennault approached the problem from a different angle: bomber effectiveness was limited to its ability to avoid destruction by pursuit aircraft. Chennault was influenced by a series of antiaircraft exercises conducted in 1933 at Fort Knox, Kentucky.

Chennault helped organize and plan the Fort Knox exercises, which involved the use of an early warning system composed of civilian observers, communications, and centralized fighter-control centers to detect incoming enemy bombers and direct pursuit aircraft to disrupt them. Chennault accused the Air Corps's bomber advocates or "bomber boys" of rigging the exercise to understate the pursuit aircraft's capabilities. He alleged that the defenders were forced to use obsolete pursuit planes against the Air Corps's latest, fastest bombers. Chennault also accused Air Corps officials of denying the establishment of air-warning sites near the targets.[19] He stressed that the Air Corps needed to develop a high-speed interceptor, improve fighter training, and develop an early warning system. The Fort Knox exercises supported Chennault's ideas. If pursuit aircraft had sufficient warning, timely detection, and territory, then the bomber could be intercepted. Pursuit aircraft required timely preparations to take off, as well as guidance and information about their targets. This requirement made long-distance detection imperative, with continual updates on target location, speed, and direction. Only a well-designed-and-operated early warning system could deliver such information. Chennault also advanced the concept of using a mobile early warning system. Unlike the situation in smaller countries such as England and Italy, the size of the United States might make total continental air defense coverage too expensive. Army operators could activate the warning system in locations that faced an immediate threat and provide additional support to those areas. Curiously, Chennault did not strongly advocate the use of pursuit escorts to defend against interceptors. Perhaps his lack of support for an escort role was based on his emphasis on offensive actions for pursuit aircraft.

Chennault began to formulate a contrary view to the bomber school of thought at ACTS, posing questions in five areas:

1. Should an air force be wholly of the bombardment type?
2. Should fighter types predominate?
3. Should an air force be "balanced" as to types?
4. Of what value are ground defenses against air attack?
5. Can fighters intercept and defeat raiders with any degree of certainty?[20]

These questions were a serious attempt to debate the merits of developing a force fielded heavily with bombers. Most of the previous airpower theories were written without experience or experimentation—only speculation. Chennault's Fort Knox exercises did lend a voice to argue for aerial interception and the potential vulnerabilities of bombers against modern fighters. Although in 1930, ACTS advocated using pursuit escort aircraft to ward off enemy fighters from attacking bombers, this changed to a doctrine of bombers not requiring any pursuit support. The advanced technology of high-speed, multiengine bombers allowed these aircraft to outperform any fighters. Unfortunately, the bomber advocates did not realize that technology might enable the construction of equal or superior high-speed interceptors and accurate detection systems.

Claire Chennault opened a debate about the control of the air or air superiority. Douhet believed that his battleplanes could win the command of the air by bombing airplanes on the ground at airfields. Mitchell advocated winning the skies through air battles. Chennault's defensive pursuit aircraft might place both ideas under more scrutiny. Pursuit aircraft might deny control of the air without actually winning air superiority and threatening bomber operations. Pursuit aircraft's primary role was to control the air by shooting down enemy airplanes. This early air superiority theory challenged Douhet and many theorists at ACTS. Chennault also believed that pursuit aircraft were capable of missions other than interception.

Pursuit aircraft could also attack enemy airfields. They were flexible enough to operate under many conditions and could be used in several areas to meet military requirements,[21] thus allowing a commander to use airpower as a weapon of opportunity. Chennault stressed that pursuit aircraft could be used in either defensive or offensive roles. Mass pursuit aircraft could provide a potent force to deliver devastating attacks against enemy bombers, which would not reach their targets intact, regardless of what Douhet thought.

Claire Chennault's ideas would eventually be proven correct in combat in World War II. An early warning system with a well-trained and armed fighter force defeated a modern German bomber force during the Battle of Britain. Similarly, unescorted bomber attacks on Germany resulted in massive casualties for Allied bomber aircrews trying to fly against German interceptors. Only after the AAF started to use escort fighters did bomber operations become more effective, reducing losses significantly. Chennault's own experience in China with the world-renowned American Volunteer Group—the Flying Tigers—from 1941 to 1942 underscored the value of effectively using pursuit aircraft against enemy bomber forces and the flexibility of pursuit aircraft to conduct a variety of missions. The debate about aircraft types that dominated debates in the 1930s is still the subject of headline news today.

William A. Moffett: Father of Naval Aviation

Rear Adm William A. Moffett, US Navy, was a contemporary airpower supporter and innovator during the highly public debates between William Mitchell and the Air Corps. Moffett's concern was to apply the newly developed airpower to naval operations. Douhet, Mitchell, and other airpower theorists concentrated on land-based airpower. In contrast, Admiral Moffett applied the airplane to warfare at sea; this involved airships, land-based search airplanes, seaplanes, and the newly emerging aircraft carriers. Moffett's advocacy of aircraft carriers and carrier aviation was most influential on airpower, resulting in a debate rivaling the infighting within the US Army on the future of aircraft. The Navy was divided between aviation advocates like Moffett and supporters of the battleship. Although Moffett did not create a theory of aerial warfare, as did Douhet or Mitchell, he did have a vision of extending the striking power of the Navy through the use of aircraft to change naval warfare forever. During World War II, Moffett's persistence paid off handsomely for the United States and its Allies with carrier aviation. Mobile airpower, from the invasions of North Africa to the island-hopping campaigns in the Pacific, proved the power of the airplane at sea. Moffett also demonstrated the value of the airplane over the battleship, when aircraft attacking ships consistently demonstrated their superiority during Pearl Harbor, Coral Sea, Midway, the Mariana Islands, and other battles.

Use of the battleship and capital ship dominated naval thought in the 1920s. The battleship supporters or "gun club" viewed command of the sea as the main objective and believed the

In a demonstration of airpower at sea, carrier aviation supports operations in Kosovo in 1999. Admiral Moffett's dream is attained.

battleship would win the day by sweeping the sea of enemy ships in large naval battles. Aircraft were most useful but only for spotting the enemy fleet and directing naval gunfire against targets. These aircraft were critical to ensuring that the fleet could sink enemies before being fired upon. Control of the air was important to keeping friendly spotting planes airborne and keeping enemy fleet aircraft out of the air.

Moffett, a onetime battleship captain himself, was a graduate of the naval aviation observer courses—he was not a pilot. However, Moffett did embrace aviation as the future for the Navy. In 1921 he became the head of a new naval bureau, the Bureau of Aeronautics, which was responsible for all procurement, training, technical, and other issues regarding naval aviation. The bureau even established a naval air factory to build its own aircraft. Like Trenchard, he was in a position to apply his ideas to an organization, but this time it involved naval aviation to the fleet. Unlike Mitchell and Trenchard, Moffett did not try to gain an independent role for aviation. Instead, naval aviation would better serve the fleet by integrating its power into the Navy. Naval aviation would only strengthen the fleet's ability to seize command of the sea.[22]

Moffett's view of carrier-based aircraft significantly differed from that of his battleship-supporting contemporaries. Gun-club supporters saw aircraft as a source of limited reconnaissance, spotting for naval gunfire, protection of the battleship fleet from enemy aircraft, and antisubmarine operations. These battleship supporters believed that carrier aircraft could help win a major naval engagement by attacking an adversary's ships and slowing them down until friendly battleships could engage them in battle. Moffett thought that a large naval-aviation force launched from an aircraft carrier could successfully conduct an offensive to defeat an enemy fleet, independent of the battleship.[23] He had witnessed Mitchell's successful bombing experiments on the *Ostfriesland*. Moffett thought that the Navy should not rely on a fleet composed mostly of battleships, should at least consider protection of the fleet by aircraft, and should use these aircraft for long-range strike operations. More importantly, aircraft could sink heavy ships, and the Navy could exploit this new technology. Moffett believed that aircraft carriers would be the cornerstone of the future for naval aviation.[24] Aircraft carriers were needed to allow naval aviation to concentrate a mass of aerial assets to strike at the heart of the enemy fleet—the battleship.[25] Moffett supported the idea that the Navy was the first line of defense and that aircraft carriers would extend this line, bearing the brunt of the nation's defense.

He developed his ideas on a carrier task force in conjunction with surface-force advocates. Using his position at the Bureau of Aeronautics, he was able to develop long-range patrol aircraft for coastal defense (as opposed to Mitchell's position of using Air Corps bombers) and to push through the purchase of aircraft carriers and their introduction in fleet exercises in 1925. As a result, Adm William Sims, a proponent of battleship superiority and an influential gun-club member, was convinced by Moffett of the carrier's value. By 1929 Moffett saw the fruits of his labor blossom when the USS *Lexington* and USS *Saratoga,* the US Navy's first modern carriers, were deployed with the fleet. The introduction of these carriers was aided by Moffett's insistence that the speed and size of these ships would allow aerial operations to continue if land bases were denied to the United States. The naval-limitation agreements among Great Britain, the United States, Japan, and others during the 1920s were geared towards battleships during this discussion. Moffett was able to convince Congress to convert the *Lexington* and *Saratoga* to carriers and avoid violating the 1922 Washington Naval Limitation Treaty ceilings on battleship strength by using this conversion. Japan's construction of land bases on islands it received after World War I would see American aircraft carriers take the war to these islands and the Japanese homeland later in World War II.

William Moffett was able to integrate airpower into a force structure that capitalized on the airplane's superior range, speed, flexibility, and lethality. Naval-aviation advocates like Moffett avoided many of the acrimonious debates within their organization that dogged Mitchell, his supporters, and the Air Corps leaders. Aircraft operations were seen by Moffett as a way to take a battle to the enemy. He stated that "the air fleet of an enemy will never get within striking distance of our coasts as long as our aircraft carriers are able to carry the preponderance of airpower to sea."[26] Instead of Mitchell's views that Air Corps bombers could take the war to an enemy's industry and interior infrastructure, Moffett advocated the power of aircraft carriers to deny this ability to an enemy by striking at his borders and his fleet.

Alexander P. de Seversky: Airpower Advocate

Alexander de Seversky was an unabashed airpower proponent who helped shaped the USAF during and after World War II. He was a Russian fighter ace in World War I, engineer and founder of the Seversky Aircraft Corporation, Air Corps reserve officer, and airpower theorist. Although de Seversky did not have many original ideas, he refined a number of Mitchell's ideas and brought them to the American public's attention. De Seversky's ideas were popularized during World War II in a Walt Disney animated movie *Victory through Airpower* (named after his first book) that educated the public and AAF personnel about airpower's value to the Allied war effort.[27] Unfortunately, many of his views were openly biased against the Navy and were more propaganda than fact. He also held a personal grudge against Gen Henry "Hap" Arnold, commander of the AAF, because of a perceived slight from Arnold over direction of the Seversky Aircraft Company. These views limited his influence among many naval and several AAF officers during the war. However, de Seversky's drive to educate the American public about the great value airpower offered to defend the United States was invaluable in creating the USAF.

De Seversky insisted that airpower was quickly becoming the decisive weapon for modern warfare. Airpower alone could not win a war. But aircraft would provide devastating blows against an enemy's industrial capacity and "blockade" or paralyze his government. The reduction or curtailment of supply lines, communications, and transportation by aerial blockade could severely hamper a nation due to airpower's ability to strike at any point—at sea or against that nation, as well as its colonies or allies. Armies and navies would provide forces for occupation and "possession" of the enemy's territory.[28] Both Douhet's claims that airpower could win a war through destroying the will of the people and Mitchell's contention about defeating the enemy's ability to conduct war were keys for de Seversky. He believed that the proper application of airpower could halt the effective and efficient running of an enemy's government (i.e., induce paralysis). But World War II events did not prove Douhet's or Mitchell's theories to be fully correct. The Luftwaffe's strategic bombing campaign against Britain in 1940, albeit limited due to the RAF fighter defenders, did not destroy the will of the people or stop the British war capability—neither did it paralyze the government. De Seversky believed that the Luftwaffe failed to paralyze the British because strategic bombardment first requires control of the air—something the Luftwaffe clearly failed to achieve. Additionally, strategic bombing requires the "correct" choice of targets, sufficient bombing capacity, and continuity of effort.[29] The Luftwaffe failed to meet these conditions; if Germany had accomplished these goals, the British government would have been paralyzed, leaving the island ripe for invasion. United States airpower would do better by avoiding the mistakes of the Luftwaffe through improved weapons and planning.

The effectiveness of strategic bombardment depended on the objective of the air campaign. Bombardment could accomplish several objectives: strike a population, hit industry, or attack enemy forces. Each nation had a unique set of "vital centers" that could contribute to meeting these objectives. A commander needed to have a clear objective for airpower to strike. The commander then needed to assess the targets that were essential in a bombing campaign. De Seversky did not attempt to define what these targets were; he merely parroted much of the prevailing AAF thought: destroy all industrial infrastructure and crush the enemy's ability to conduct war.[30] However, he believed that any war was really a total war. Destruction of the nation was the goal of airpower, and he proposed a strategy of "extermination."[31]

De Seversky thought that airpower's primary value lay in its strategic offensive power. Long-range bombers could strike targets within an enemy's country or attack enemy forces far from American-held bases. Unlike surface forces that had to attack enemy forces from the adversary's outermost defensive perimeter, aircraft could bypass these forces and strike independently of surface forces. Any diversion from this use of strategic offensive bombardment was a waste of valuable resources. Tactical support of ground or naval operations fell in this category.

Control of the air was not only necessary for success in a strategic-bombing campaign, but also was the key to the success of surface combat. Without air superiority, surface forces were at the mercy of enemy air forces. De Seversky stated that "no land or sea operations are possible without first assuming control of the air above."[32] Pursuit aircraft were necessary to accomplish this goal. The only effective means of destroying airpower was airpower. In de Seversky's opinion, AAA and other ground defenses were not effective against aircraft. Without adequate aircraft able to attack incoming bombers, the latter could strike targets far out at sea or inland. Armies and navies were vulnerable to air attack and needed protection. A corollary to de Seversky's observation was that the Navy's inability to conduct a strategic offensive would lead to its replacement by airpower because of surface vulnerability to air attack.[33] Airpower made nations once thought invulnerable to attack subject to massive aerial bombardment. America needed to develop a large air force rather than devote resources to an outmoded navy and army.

De Seversky had a profound effect on the postwar air force. Airpower advocates looked at the destruction, both physical and psychological, wrought on Germany, Italy, and Japan. Certainly, airpower had contributed to much of the disintegration of the Axis powers, but it did not obviate the need for a ground invasion of Europe or occupation of Japan. Even the atomic bombing of Japan did not lessen the impact that a Russian ground invasion of occupied Manchuria and the threatened invasion of the Japanese home island by Allied forces had on the final Japanese surrender. Airpower alone did not win the war, but it was a decisive element of the war. Bombers and missiles armed with atomic bombs could provide an intercontinental strike capability against the Soviet Union during the Cold War. These weapons were capable of rendering a near-fatal blow to a massive Soviet war machine. The Army and Navy would be reduced to the secondary role of mopping-up operations after airpower had delivered a staggering punch.

In the Cold War, the rise of American strategic airpower was a reflection of many of de Seversky's views. Strategic bombardment—from both aircraft and missiles—replaced the traditional emphasis on ground and naval forces as defenders of the nation. Airpower's transition to a premiere fighting force equal to its surface siblings finally occurred after decades of debate and action.

John Warden: The Five-Ring Model

Col John Warden, USAF, retired, developed a theory of strategic attack on a nation based on inflicting paralysis through the use of airpower. Warden planned an initial air campaign, "Instant Thunder," to attack Iraq during Operation Desert Storm. The plan was later modified for use in the conflict. Colonel Warden had written a National War College thesis on air campaign planning that served as a basis for his thoughts on attacking an enemy. His views have been modified over the years to define particular sets of targets that can be attacked to create a paralyzing effect throughout a nation.

Warden believes that an enemy nation has certain centers of gravity (COG) that can create vulnerabilities to its security. One can classify these national COGs within a series of systems. In Warden's opinion, successful attack on a hierarchy of these systems can significantly contribute to the nation's downfall. Airpower can speed the destruction of the nation by attacking targets in a parallel manner (simultaneously) instead of employing traditional surface combat that attacks targets one at a time or serially. Technology allows the precision attack of one aircraft against targets that once required fleets of aircraft. These advances allow commanders to attack several targets at once instead of using all of their forces to attack one system at a time. Parallel attacks prevent an enemy from conducting military operations that may affect friendly forces. Additionally, after a nation's air forces gain air superiority, they can conduct strategic-bombardment campaigns or support surface forces. This gives air forces the freedom to attack a number of targets among these systems.

Warden's objective was to affect the mind of the enemy's leadership or the system of the enemy as a whole. While Douhet thought that attacks on a population would break the nation's will to resist, Warden disagreed, maintaining that one could not successfully target human behavior and that the accuracy of changes was not sufficiently predictable to ensure victory. However, physical attacks on military and industrial targets that were properly linked to political objectives would provide a better opportunity to defeat a nation.

An enemy's "system of systems" is composed of five areas or "rings." This five-ring model was used against Iraq (fig. 1). Warden later admitted that each nation has unique COGs that may cause a commander to view other countries with different rings.[34] These COGs provide air campaign planners a priority for basing their actions. The most important system or ring is leadership, which occupies the center position within a series of five concentric rings. Leadership or command is critical as a first target because important decisions, direction, and coordination come from leadership. Disabling or destroying this ring would separate the "brain" from the enemy's "body." This action is intended to leave the enemy nation without guidance. For example, the leadership ring might include an enemy's top national decision-making bodies, key C^2 organizations, and communications systems.

Other rings include organic essentials, infrastructure, population, and fielded forces. Organic essentials are facilities or processes that a nation requires for its existence. In the case of Iraq, these would include oil and petroleum processing, electricity, weapons of mass destruction, and nuclear processing plants. Infrastructure includes a nation's transportation capability. Hindering the efficient flow of goods and services limits the country's ability to conduct business and military operations. Targets include roads, rails, harbors, and airports. Warden did not advocate direct, indiscriminate attacks against the civilian population and felt it morally reprehensible to do so. However, if pressure were applied through the population to affect an adversary's government, then this pressure might support the successful conclusion of the conflict. Enemy morale might be lowered by continuous, around-the-clock attack on a number of targets that would disrupt the normal, day-to-

Rings labeled from outer to inner: Fielded Forces, Population, Infrastructure, Organic Essentials, Leadership.

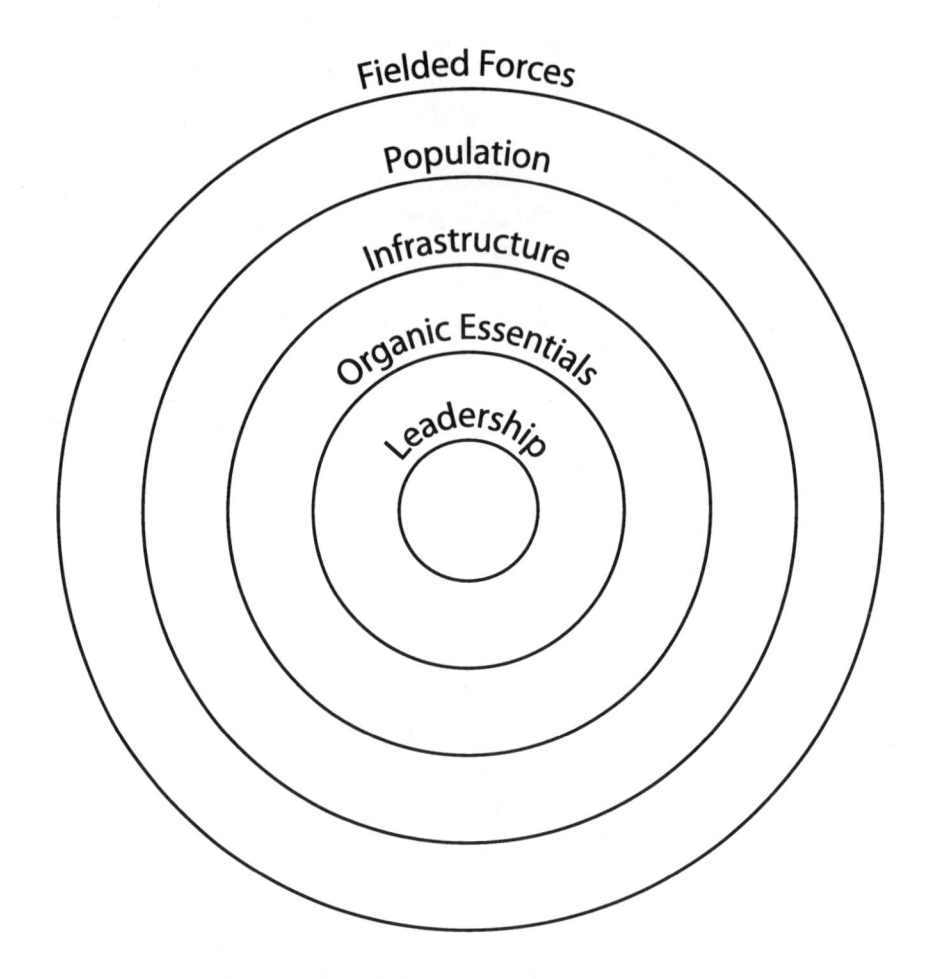

Figure 1. Warden's Basic Five-Ring Model Used in Desert Storm
(Adapted from Col John A. Warden III, "The Enemy as a System," *Airpower Journal* 9, no. 1 [Spring 1995]: 47)

day lives of ordinary people. Fielded forces, the last ring, are the traditional military forces that armies and navies attack. The fielded forces of an enemy have been viewed in the past as the most vital ring. But Warden thought that these forces were merely tools for the enemy to reach a particular end. If they were incapable of conducting operations because of air attacks on the other rings, then they would become less capable of achieving an enemy's political objectives. Warden proposed that one should attack from the innermost ring out. That is, the first ring to be struck is leadership, and the last is fielded forces. Airpower allows a commander to hit all or selected rings in a parallel attack. The flexibility of air forces gives them the particular advantage of striking enemy systems in many ways.

Warden's theory concentrated on strategic effects on the enemy force's systems as a whole. These attacks might not be directed solely against a foe's fielded forces but might oppose the political objectives of the nation. Technology has allowed airpower to realize many of the capabilities that early theorists (e.g., Douhet and Mitchell) could only dream or speculate about for the future. Warden's assumption about attacking an enemy based on his systems or organizations may work for clearly defined adversaries or operations. One wonders how Colonel Warden's theory might translate against guerilla forces or terrorists with unidentified COGs or rings.

Space Power Theory

Early airpower theorists found a readily available readership among veteran World War I aviators and others who flew missions or observed the actions of aerial combat. Unfortunately, military space activities, since their inception in the 1950s, have been shrouded in a cloak of secrecy. Although the United States had a highly visible manned and unmanned civilian space program, the classified nature of space surveillance, imagery, and other capabilities precluded a wide discussion of military space theory. Additionally, international desire and national policy to deweaponize space have also constrained the discussion of military space theory. Finally, the influence of commercial space activities has seriously complicated the military space picture. Nations that did not previously have access to space communications, imagery, and navigation now have the instantaneous benefit of using these assets without making the massive investment of resources or time required for a space program.

Recently, there has been more discussion about military space activities due to the rapid application of space technologies to aerial weapons and surface activities, as well as the explosion of commercial space usage. Unlike the theories of early airpower advocates, few military space theories provide a comprehensive treatment of manned and unmanned systems. Several authors have developed proposed space doctrines and policies. Doctrine is guidance, based on experience or beliefs, provided to commanders for the conduct of military operations. Doctrine is not theory; it does not provide a prediction or explanation of an action or state of nature. A space theory should address the issues of how and why military space resources accomplish national objectives.[35] However, there have been some attempts to develop a space power theory.

One theory about space power assumes that space is a natural extension of the air environment. Barring the physical differences between vehicles operating in the air compared to those operating in space, advocates of this idea believe that the same actions capable of being conducted in the air can be done in space. The only difference between air and space is that space vehicles will fly faster, further, and higher than aerial vehicles but will require more support. Strategic bombardment, space control, and other actions can be conducted at a higher altitude than existing aerial vehicles can attain.

Another theory views space like the ocean. Space vehicles provide a valuable resource that the nation needs to protect. Naval theorists, notably Alfred Thayer Mahan, maintained that a seafaring nation needs to control the sea-lanes of communications in peace—at least over sovereign territory—and during war. Sea control was necessary to ensure that nations could conduct free trade. Control also allows a nation to deny the same sea-lanes to a foe in war. Control of space is similar to control of the sea. One may view the United States as an emerging spacefaring nation, just as it was a seafaring nation in the early twentieth century. The change in environment is irrelevant since the concept is not dependent on geography. Military capabilities in space must be used to control space operations. A nation needs to control information produced by space assets, protect support facilities and space vehicles against attacks, and maintain a capability to deny or disable an adversary's space systems.[36] Increasingly, space is being used for lucrative commercial purposes such as telecommunications.

Control of this medium would be similar to control of sea-lanes of communications to enable nations to conduct trade or commerce.

A different approach stresses space systems' innate ability to provide continuous situational awareness of terrestrial activities and their value to a nation. Satellites can detect activities on Earth's surface and relay that information to air, land, and naval forces for action. Additionally, space is vital to all terrestrial activities—political, economic, and military. These observations indicate that space power is a precondition for control of the sea, land, or air.[37] This theory includes four conjectures. First, space assets become a necessary condition to enhance the war-fighting capabilities of air, land, and sea forces. Second, space forces can attack terrestrial forces directly and can also extend the damage inflicted by aerial and surface forces. Attacks from space on surface forces by space-to-ground missiles, reentry vehicles, or other weapons are extensions of high-altitude bombardment. Increased accuracy from space navigation and communications systems can also enhance the ability to conduct precision attacks against targets or identify previously unknown targets. Third, the nation must deprive enemies from attaining any advantage in space that they might use against it. Fourth, fragile, valuable, and scarce space assets must be protected. Space systems have become a decisive element to future warfare and are not intrinsically linked to airpower but are independently controlled.[38] Advocates of this theory foresee an independent space force, much like early airpower theorists predicted an independent air force in the 1920s.

Development of space theory is a fertile field. Today there are no weapons in space. However, this might change as the value of space becomes more apparent to nations that want to exploit space or deny its use to others. Space is still important because of its global access and ability to support terrestrial operations. Space-based communications, navigation, weather, early warning, surveillance, and other combat-support missions are critical for aerial, ground, and maritime military operations. The relationship among space, air, land, and naval power is vital to ensure that a nation uses its limited resources for the proper application of military force. Like the airpower theories of the 1920s and 1930s, space power theory is confined to a prediction of the future because of the limitations of available technology. Future aerospace leaders will grapple with many new issues and concerns, one of which will be to develop a space and, potentially, aerospace theory. Many of the issues discussed and debated by Douhet, Mitchell, Moffett, and others may provide a basis for developing a space theory that explains the purposes and means of projecting power to achieve objectives. Conversely, space forces operate in a unique environment that may require new technologies and specific methods to conduct operations. The challenge of defining the value, use, and future of air and space operations will require all the creativity and foresight of our future leaders.

Summary

Aerospace theory has changed through the years. The first theories addressed by Giulio Douhet were more akin to speculation based on beliefs than theory based on extensive combat experience. Later, ideas were tested in combat, or experiments were conducted to gather appropriate information on which to base a theory. Other airpower theorists revised their theories after a period of reflection. Ultimately, the theories of Douhet, Mitchell, Trenchard, and others provided a guiding hand to define how aerospace power should be used, and this affected the development and employment of air forces around the world. Theory clearly affected the development of the AAF before, during, and after World War II, culminating with the creation of an independent air force. The ideas of Mitchell and ACTS significantly influenced the decision to adopt strategic bombardment as a primary mission of air forces. After the war, the United States used these ideas to assemble a nuclear force of bombers and ICBMs to defend the nation.

Notes

1. A model is a representation of reality that explains an aspect of the real world, item, system, or process.
2. *Strategic* refers to activities directly affecting the national survival or the effective conduct of the overall war.

3. Giulio Douhet, *The Command of the Air*, trans. Dino Ferrari (1942; reprint, Washington, D.C.: Center for Air Force History, 1983), 29.

4. Ibid., 119.

5. Ibid., 28.

6. Ibid., 51.

7. Robert Frank Futrell, *Ideas, Concepts, Doctrine: Basic Thinking in the United States Air Force, 1907–1960*, vol. 1 (Maxwell AFB, Ala.: Air University Press, 1989), 39.

8. Johnny R. Jones, *William "Billy" Mitchell's Air Power* (Maxwell AFB, Ala.: Airpower Research Institute; College of Aerospace Doctrine, Research and Education, 1997), 9.

9. William Mitchell, *Winged Defense: The Development and Possibilities of Modern Air Power—Economic and Military* (New York: Dover, 1988), 199.

10. R. A. Mason, *Air Power: A Centennial Appraisal* (London: Brassey's, 1994), 44.

11. David R. Mets, *The Air Campaign: John Warden and the Classical Airpower Theorists* (Maxwell AFB, Ala.: Air University Press, 1999), 23.

12. John Terraine, *The Right of the Line: The Royal Air Force in the European War, 1939–1945* (Hertfordshire: Wordsworth Editions, 1997), 9.

13. John H. Morrow Jr., *The Great War in the Air: Military Aviation from 1909 to 1921* (Washington, D.C.: Smithsonian Institution Press, 1993), 322.

14. Col Phillip S. Meilinger, "Trenchard, Slessor, and Royal Air Force Doctrine before World War II," in *The Paths of Heaven: The Evolution of Airpower Theory*, ed. Col Phillip S. Meilinger (Maxwell AFB, Ala.: Air University Press, 1997), 52.

15. Alan Stephens, "The True Believers: Airpower between the Wars," in *The War in the Air, 1914–1994: The Proceedings of a Conference Held by the Royal Australian Air Force in Canberra, March 1994*, ed. Alan Stephens (Fairburn Base, Australia: RAAF Air Power Studies Centre, 1994), 51.

16. Interdiction operations include missions whose purpose is to destroy, neutralize, or delay the enemy's military potential before it affects the operations of friendly forces.

17. Meilinger, "Trenchard, Slessor," 65.

18. Terraine, 598.

19. James Tate, *The Army and Its Air Corps: Army Policy toward Aviation, 1919–1941* (Maxwell AFB, Ala.: Air University Press, 1998), 161.

20. Thomas H. Greer, *The Development of Air Doctrine in the Army Air Arm, 1917–1941* (Washington, D.C.: Office of Air Force History, 1985), 56.

21. Ibid., 62.

22. Dr. David R. Mets, "The Influence of Aviation on the Evolution of American Naval Thought," in *The Paths of Heaven*, 125.

23. Ibid., 127.

24. William F. Trimble, *Admiral William A. Moffett: Architect of Naval Aviation* (Washington, D.C.: Smithsonian Institution Press, 1994), 90.

25. William F. Trimble, *Wings for the Navy: A History of the Naval Aircraft Factory, 1917–1956* (Annapolis: Naval Institute Press, 1990), 162.

26. Archibald D. Turnbull and Clifford L. Lord, *History of United States Naval Aviation* (New York: Arno Press, 1972), 215.

27. David MacIsaac, "Voices from the Central Blue: The Airpower Theorists," in *Makers of Modern Strategy: From Machiavelli to the Nuclear Age*, ed. Peter Paret (Princeton, N.J.: Princeton University Press, 1986), 631.

28. Alexander P. de Seversky, *Victory through Airpower* (New York: Simon and Schuster, 1942), 346.

29. Ibid., 72.

30. Phillip Meilinger, "Proselytizer and Prophet: Alexander de Seversky and American Airpower," in *Airpower: Theory and Practice*, ed. John Gooch (London: Frank Cass, 1995), 19.

31. Michael S. Sherry, *The Rise of American Air Power: The Creation of Armageddon* (New Haven, Conn.: Yale University Press, 1987), 128.

32. De Seversky, 123.

33. Ibid., 125.

34. John Warden, "Planning to Win," in *Testing the Limits: The Proceedings of a Conference Held by the Royal Australian Air Force in Canberra*, ed. Shaun Clarke (Fairburn Base, Australia: RAAF Air Power Studies Centre, 1998), 87.

35. James E. Oberg, *Space Power Theory* (Colorado Springs, Colo.: US Air Force Academy, 1999), 11.

36. Ibid., 138.

37. Maj Robert D. Newberry, *Space Doctrine for the Twenty-first Century* (Maxwell AFB, Ala.: Air University Press, 1998), 22.

38. Ibid.

Chapter 3

Functions and Capabilities of Aerospace Power: Air and Space Superiority/Strategic Attack

Air and space power theorists, combat experience, beliefs, organizational structure, threats, and other factors have shaped the composition and application of aerospace forces around the world. These forces conduct several functions that can support other military forces or can be used to conduct independent operations. Many of these air and space capabilities and functions were discussed and debated extensively by Douhet, Mitchell, and others. Conversely, some aerospace capabilities were developed as a result of technology or combat needs. Regardless of their origin, air forces around the world can conduct different levels of these functions and capabilities, given the appropriate resources, motivation, and opportunity. Particular circumstances and situations may dictate the relative importance of these functions. Each military situation, objective, or environment can influence a commander's emphasis on particular selections and focus for his or her forces.

Several functions characterize aerospace power, as discussed in this chapter and in chapters 4–6. The first and foremost is aerospace superiority. Giulio Douhet identified command of the air as the first objective that an air force needs before it can accomplish any other action. An aerospace force can conduct both *air and space superiority* missions. *Strategic attack* operations allow a nation to use its aerospace forces to directly affect another nation's ability to conduct war or exist as a sovereign nation. This chapter addresses those two functions. Aerospace forces can also conduct operations to stem the flow of supplies and forces before they arrive at a battlefield *(interdiction)* or directly support combat forces in the field against the enemy *(close air support)*—both of which are discussed in chapter 4. Surface and aerospace forces also need extensive logistical support to conduct operations and may require *rapid mobility* of materiel, manpower, and other resources. Aerospace forces can rapidly transport resources from one continent to the next within hours and use mobility to shape the face of war. *Space and information* operations support the gathering and processing of information through systems such as satellites. Those two functions are the topics of chapter 5. Aerial reconnaissance also provides information for crucial combat and national-level decisions. These platforms and their support systems give a commander a unique perspective to assess enemy abilities, battlefield awareness, and combat results. A commander might exploit the flexibility of airpower by blending these functions and capabilities to support particular operations or campaigns so that the enemy feels the full force of *airpower unleashed,* addressed in chapter 6. An air force might not need to conduct an extensive air superiority campaign because its adversary has few aircraft or ground-based air defenses. But the air force may need much CAS to ensure that an amphibious landing succeeds against a massive surface force.

Discussion of these areas includes three case studies for each function. Air and space superiority, strategic attack, interdiction, CAS, mobility, and space and information provide a visible reminder of aerospace power. The case studies are intended to illustrate the particular function or show aerospace power's capabilities and their importance in combat or in achieving an assigned national objective. In each instance, the first case study represents a failed application of the particular function, followed by case studies of two successful applications. Each of these studies showcases aerospace power in different situations and conditions, some in ways never before imagined possible.

Many times, students are urged to closely follow successful applications of a principle or an idea. Future aerospace leaders must recognize that understanding the misapplication of air and space assets is equally important if they wish to avoid such mistakes and increase their chances of victory. A very valuable method for understanding the nature of aerospace power is to learn from mistakes and problems. The case studies that highlight the failure to achieve or conduct a particular function should serve as a good starting point for discussion of the successful application of aerospace power. Readers will find that evaluating and avoiding failure is just as useful as emulating success.

Air and Space Superiority: The First Order of Business

Air and space superiority is a prerequisite to all other aerospace functions and capabilities. This function allows a country's aerospace force to attack an enemy from air and space without fear of being attacked from forces above Earth's surface. Air and space superiority also allows a nation the freedom to attack a foe with aerial weapons. Air superiority can be achieved through offensive counterair (OCA), defensive counterair (DCA), and suppression of enemy air defenses (SEAD). OCA operations include attacks on enemy aircraft and airfields, normally on or over enemy territory. Air forces use DCA to defend their air assets against an enemy aerial assault near or over friendly territory. DCA missions can be used to deny an enemy force air superiority over a specific geographic area. An air force is proactive and uses its initiative to conduct OCA missions, while it reacts to enemy initiatives by conducting DCA missions. SEAD destroys, disables, or degrades a foe's surface air-defense systems. This mission normally includes attacks or the disabling of ground or airborne radar systems to avoid both detection and subsequent attack on friendly forces; destruction of surface-to-air missiles (SAM) and AAA; and the neutralization of command, control, and communications activities that direct weapons against friendly air forces. Space superiority includes offensive counterspace (OCS) and defensive counterspace (DCS) activities. OCS operations attempt to destroy or disable enemy space systems or the data produced by those systems through attacks on the space system itself, the information data link from the system to a ground station, or terrestrial support facilities. Space forces can also conduct DCS operations to protect friendly space assets or their support systems from attack. This includes the use of decoys, hardening systems against electronic or radiation damage, camouflage, maneuvering, and other defensive measures.

Eddie Rickenbacker, first American air ace, demonstrated early attempts to gain air superiority in World War I.

Air and space superiority results in dominance over a foe in the respective medium that allows the force the ability to conduct operations. Command of the air, like command of the sea, is a vital requirement to conduct operations with reduced losses and increased probability of success. But how can an aerospace power achieve air and space superiority? Why is attainment of air and space superiority vital to a campaign? What can an aerospace power accomplish with air and space superiority? Reading these case studies should allow one to understand the importance commanders place on aerospace forces' getting and maintaining superiority in air and space. Additionally, the claims of air and space superiority as the prime objective for aerospace power can also be tested. Douhet and Mitchell claimed that the first task of airpower was to attain command of the air. How did the Luftwaffe fare in its campaign against Britain without air superiority? Does this case study support the claims of Douhet and Mitchell?

The Battle of Britain:
The Luftwaffe's Failure to Control the Skies

The Battle of Britain was a critical air campaign fought from July to November 1940. The RAF and German Luftwaffe forces conducted the first major all-aircraft battle in history through this campaign. The Battle of Britain demonstrated the value of achieving air superiority to allow an air force to conduct a strategic-bombardment campaign. This battle also revealed the need for defensive operations to deny air superiority to an enemy and their effectiveness in stopping a bomber campaign. Later, when Eighth Air Force flew unescorted B-17 and B-24 raids over Western Europe, we would relearn the lessons of the Battle of Britain by paying a heavy price in destroyed planes and lost aircrews.

The *Wehrmacht*, the German armed forces, had accomplished a miracle of planning and operational execution to defeat Poland, France, and other Western nations with a combination of armored blitzkrieg attacks supported by the Luftwaffe. Great Britain's expeditionary force on the European continent had been dealt a stunning defeat at the hands of Germany and had retreated across the English Channel from Dunkirk. Britain was the only nation at war with Germany that threatened Adolf Hitler's attempt to conquer Europe. The *Wehrmacht* high command speculated that it could attack England directly or wage a war of attrition along "peripheral areas" in the Mediterranean. If the Germans decided to confront England directly, their options were to attack shipping and industry with naval power and airpower, bomb civilian populations by terror raids, or invade England.[1] On 16 July 1940, Hitler authorized Operation *Seelöwe* (Sea Lion), the invasion of England. Germany was poised to deliver a knockout blow to England by conducting a massive bombing campaign to eliminate the RAF as an effective force to oppose an invasion of Britain. A major assumption of this plan was that the Luftwaffe would attain air superiority.[2]

Hitler issued top-secret directive no. 17 on 1 August 1940, defining the objectives of the Luftwaffe's air campaign. *Reichsmarschall* Hermann Göring, Hitler's second in command and commander of the Luftwaffe, was directed to

1. Defeat the RAF by first attacking flying formations, ground organization, and supply lines. Secondary targets included aircraft and antiaircraft-equipment production facilities.
2. Attack harbors (after gaining air superiority) that engaged in food supplies and food-supply production in England.
3. Destroy enemy warships and merchant shipping. The air war was to take precedence over war at sea.
4. Support naval operations and Operation Sea Lion.
5. Conduct terror raids only with Hitler's express approval.[3]

Göring prepared his forces to conduct operations on 10 August 1940 or Eagle Day. The Luftwaffe's high command interpreted Hitler's directive as meaning first, achieve air superiority; second, support Operation Sea Lion by eliminating the Royal Navy and RAF bombers that threatened the invasion; third, destroy British harbors, imports, and supplies; and fourth, launch authorized retaliatory terror raids on the British.[4] These attacks did not specifically target fighter forces but the entire RAF. They would include strikes against the RAF's bomber and coastal commands. The Luftwaffe would eliminate the RAF as an effective fighting force, thus reducing the possibility of an attack on Germany and reducing British capability to oppose the German invasion.

The German invasion of England would require a coordinated Luftwaffe attack on RAF fighter planes, airfields, C^2, and aircraft factories. However, the Luftwaffe had been strained by supporting a continuous European campaign since 1 September 1939. Although the Luftwaffe stood victorious, it had lost thousands of aircraft and combat-experienced aircrews. The Battle for France, from May 1940 through June 1940, cost the Luftwaffe 1,428 aircraft destroyed and 488 damaged.[5] The Luftwaffe was designed to support ground operations, not conduct a sustained strategic-bombardment campaign against industry or enemy airfields. Future victories were contingent upon a rapid ground offensive and defeat of enemy armies. Luftwaffe aircraft were not designed to attack at long ranges or conduct operations independently from ground forces. German land forces would capture any airfields that the Luftwaffe needed in order to sustain combat operations and extend its range over the enemy. After smashing through Poland, the Netherlands, and France, the Luftwaffe's air-support force required major rest, rearmament, and reorganization. The Luftwaffe was also involved in the invasion of Norway.

The Luftwaffe's aircraft reflected its doctrine of supporting ground forces. Their largest bomber, the Heinkel He-111, was a twin-engined aircraft designed as a commercial transport. The He-111 was underpowered and lacked speed. Other German bombers were faster, such as the Junkers Ju-88 or Dornier Do-17, but they could carry only half the bomb load and had less defensive armament than the He-111. The Germans also used the Junkers Ju-87 dive-bomber, a relatively slow, short-ranged, small-bomb-capacity, and lightly armored aircraft that worked well in close support of the army but had little value in a strategic-bombardment campaign.

In 1940 the Luftwaffe had two main fighter aircraft—the Messerschmitt Bf-109 and Bf-110. The Bf-109 was a single-engined modern fighter that was a worthy adversary of RAF fighters. Unfortunately for the Luftwaffe, it did not have a long range, either to escort bombers or attack RAF aircraft deep in England. The Luftwaffe did build the twin-engined Bf-110 escort fighter, which had sufficient range to support long-range bomber missions. The Bf-110 suffered from low acceleration and a wide turning radius, which made it vulnerable to RAF fighters. Bf-110 pilots did have the advantage of heavy armament, and the aircraft could dive against RAF fighters and deliver a devastating punch. Often, Bf-110s would escort bombers, while Bf-109s defended the Bf-110 escorts. German fighter escorts for bombers were limited to southern England due to the Bf-109's internal fuel supply. Unfortunately for the Luftwaffe, the enemy's industrial strength (i.e., aircraft, antiaircraft defenses, and other military production facilities) was concentrated in central England—out of effective Bf-109 range. The RAF could deploy its forces out of range of the Bf-109 at any time, whenever fighter or aircraft losses became too costly, and could resume operations over southern England if Operation Sea Lion were launched.[6]

In World War I, the RAF had learned its lesson to defend the country from bomber and zeppelin attacks. The British developed a radio detection (radar) system and integrated it into a C^2 system that directed fighter aircraft to intercept incoming enemy aircraft. The Chain Home radar system could detect aircraft at 120 miles and could determine an enemy aircraft's altitude, while its shorter-range brother, the Chain Home Low system, could detect the presence of aircraft at only 50 miles. The combination of radar, C^2, a series of observers, and modern interceptor aircraft would have to defend England against the onslaught of the Luftwaffe. Claire Chennault's theory of how to employ pursuit aircraft would be tested in combat.

The RAF's two main fighter interceptors were the Supermarine Spitfire Mark I and the Hawker Hurricane Mark I. The Spitfire was equal to the Bf-109 in performance except for the fact that the Bf-109 was faster at most altitudes and could outclimb the Spitfire at altitudes up to 20,000 feet. The Spitfire was more maneuverable than any Luftwaffe aircraft at all altitudes—a key factor in fighter combat—and usually attacked escorting fighters like the Bf-109. The Hurricane was outclassed by the Bf-109 except in terms of low-altitude maneuverability, and the British fighter could outturn the Bf-109 at all altitudes. If the Hurricane had had a height advantage, it could have defeated the Bf-109. Hurricanes usually intercepted the bombers. Also, the Hurricane's very sturdy design allowed it to take massive damage and still fly. The Spitfire and Hurricane were more than a match for the Bf-109, Germany's best fighter, and were significantly better armed than the Luftwaffe bombers. The Bf-109s that escorted Luftwaffe bombers took about half an hour to reach London. RAF radar and ground controllers would take some time to identify the targets and scramble aircraft. Spitfires and Hurricanes needed about 10 minutes to reach altitude and additional time to maneuver into an attack position.[7] This meant that the RAF had very little time to intercept invading forces. RAF Fighter Command had 347 serviceable Hurricanes and 160 Spitfires available to fight 656 Bf-109s and 200 Bf-110s.[8] By 10 August 1940, the Luftwaffe had 2,550 serviceable planes, which included bomber, ground-attack, fighter, long-range reconnaissance, and other types of aircraft to use against the RAF and knock the British defenses out of commission to ensure a successful Operation Sea Lion.

The Luftwaffe's air campaign was conducted in several phases. The Germans launched *Kanalkampf*, an attempt to attack British shipping, harbors, and coastal targets. This phase lasted about six weeks, from 10 July to 7 August. Bf-109s dominated the Spitfires and Hurricanes. German bombers struck convoys and ports at will. The second phase was fought from 8 August to 23 August. This phase included *Adlerangriff* (Eagle Day), which the Luftwaffe launched on 13 August. Eagle Day's objective was to gain air superiority over the RAF. The Luftwaffe's goal was to crush Fighter Command's radar, operations centers, and communications, as well as dominate the Spitfires and Hurricanes. Fighter Command's only reasonable response was to hang on and not be destroyed. This phase quickly became a battle of attrition. Although the Luftwaffe had a numeric advantage over the RAF, its force structure was not designed to conduct an extended air campaign. British aircraft-production capability could replace destroyed Spitfires and Hurricanes; however, it could not produce enough pilots to fill empty cockpits due to combat losses. The third phase concentrated on Luftwaffe attacks on RAF airfields and key industrial facilities, which would force Fighter Command to commit to a massive air battle that would determine which country would rule the skies over England. The destruction of aircraft-production factories and airfields would eliminate not only RAF Fighter Command as an effective military force, but also the entire RAF. The last phase, 7 September to the end of October, concentrated on day-and-night bombing missions against London. The London bombing campaign was Hitler's response to the RAF's bombing of Berlin. This phase switched the military objective from gaining command of the air to terror bombing. This change of strategic direction ultimately cost the Luftwaffe the Battle of Britain and forced the cancellation of the invasion of England.

There are several reasons why the Luftwaffe was not able to achieve air superiority over the smaller RAF Fighter Command. The limited range of Bf-109 fighters forced Luftwaffe bomber forces to fly limited missions with the questionable Bf-110 escorts. As a result, the Luftwaffe became subject to massive bomber losses. Luftwaffe bomber attacks from Norway fared worse since they were sent into battle without Bf-110 escorts, which did not have the range to accompany the bombers. As bomber losses mounted, Göring ordered the Bf-109s to provide close escort for the bombers and not attack

Bombing of Britain

Spitfires or Hurricanes unless in defense of the bombers. This change in policy limited the Luftwaffe's capability to control the skies. Bf-109s escorting bombers to London had only 10 minutes of combat time over the bombers' targets. According to German fighter ace Adolf Galland, the limited range of the fighters was the decisive factor in the battle.[9] This change in tactics allowed the RAF to take the initiative in most combat situations. The Luftwaffe did not have enough Bf-109s to conduct both escort and attack missions against RAF fighters and airfields. Eventually, the RAF's Spitfires and Hurricanes denied air superiority to the Luftwaffe and were able to attack vulnerable bombers repeatedly. The Luftwaffe lost a total of 1,636 aircraft during the Battle of Britain, but, more importantly, it could never replace experienced aircrews.[10] The RAF lost about 915 aircraft.

The British radar, communications, and C^2 system were not disabled by Luftwaffe attacks. The value and necessity of gain-

AIR AND SPACE SUPERIORITY/STRATEGIC ATTACK

ing information about an aerial adversary was amply demonstrated in the Battle of Britain. RAF personnel were able to detect and counter Luftwaffe attacks by directing fighter aircraft to intercept aircraft. This capability provided a distinct advantage to RAF defensive forces.

The Luftwaffe also suffered from poor intelligence. German military intelligence consistently overstated RAF losses and understated German aircraft destroyed. Luftwaffe target information was too old, incomplete, or incorrect. German pilots often took off from their airfields to conduct missions without knowing about RAF battle losses or conditions of their targets. The British not only had radar, but also had captured a German encryption device that allowed them to decipher Luftwaffe battle plans. The system, Ultra, gave British leaders advanced warning on daily German objectives.

German aircraft and the organization of the Luftwaffe also affected the battle. Luftwaffe aircraft that successfully defeated the ground forces and obsolete air forces over Western Europe were not capable of a sustained, long-range battle of attrition against the RAF. The Luftwaffe's CAS air force was incapable of absorbing massive losses. Additionally, the bomber force was not trained, organized, or armed to conduct sustained industrial and airfield attacks.

One of the major mistakes in World War II was the Luftwaffe's switch from its strikes on RAF Fighter Command to a terror campaign against London. Fighter Command was near collapse due to fighter, pilot, and airfield losses. If the Luftwaffe had continued its campaign, Fighter Command would have folded and ceded both air superiority and victory to Germany. The shift away from efforts to gain air superiority was a fatal flaw of the Luftwaffe campaign. Also, the switch to a terror campaign provided the "miracle" to Britain and allowed it to recover and defeat the Luftwaffe.

The final factor, certainly not an insignificant one, was Fighter Command's outstanding performance. Spitfire and Hurricane aircraft proved an even match for the Bf-109 and the German air force. Pilot and ground crews maintained fighter operations during the four critical months of the battle. The RAF hung on to defend the nation and successfully denied command of the air to the Luftwaffe. This led to German cancellation of Operation Sea Lion and to Hitler's critical error of invading the Soviet Union. The fate of the war was altered over a question of air superiority.

Total Air Domination: The Six-Day War

The Israeli Six-Day War in June 1967 is a classic example of an air force gaining air superiority. The Israeli Defense Forces/Air Force used surprise, offensive tactics, mass, and other principles of war to conduct a preemptive strike against the Egyptian Air Force (EAF) and then a lightning air assault on the Syrian Arab Air Force (SAAF). Both attacks allowed the IDF/AF to reduce a larger air force to a pile of twisted metal amid burning airfields. This one-day strike was a knockout punch that let the IDF/AF achieve total air domination to bomb and strafe Arab ground forces unmercifully before Israeli armored forces mauled the survivors. Air superiority gave the IDF/AF freedom from attack since it destroyed EAF and SAAF fighters on the ground. Israel was also able to conduct bombing runs and achieve overall freedom to attack facilities, troops, roads, and other targets.

During the early 1960s, several Arab nations took actions to antagonize and harass Israel. In 1964 a meeting among officials from the governments of Egypt, Syria, Jordan, and Lebanon ended in agreement to divert water from the Jordan River and significantly reduce water for Israeli use. Israeli forces were able to destroy the water project after responding to a series of Syrian artillery shellings of Israeli military positions. There were also several cross-border raids by guerilla forces against Israeli settlements that resulted in retaliatory air and ground operations. In April 1967, Israeli air and ground forces also attacked the Golan Heights after Syrian artillery units shelled surrounding Israeli homes and farms. Israeli military forces began to mobilize for a possible attack on their nation because of the increased frequency of raids and confrontations. The Egyptian and Syrian governments also believed that Israel was poised to conduct a preemptive attack on their nations. The Egyptian government demanded that United Nations (UN) peacekeepers leave the Sinai desert, a buffer zone created between Israel and Egypt after the 1956 Suez War to avoid detection of Egyptian military preparations. With England and France, Israel had participated in a surprise attack on Egypt in 1956. At the end of the war, Egypt lost control of the Sinai peninsula. The Sinai was put under UN protection to preclude any aggressive moves by Egypt against Israel (fig. 2).

Egypt, Syria, and other Arab nations started to mobilize their military forces. Egyptian army units occupied positions in the Sinai and across the Israeli border. By 20 May, over 10,000 Egyptian troops and 1,000 tanks were on Israel's border.[11] Egypt also closed Israel's access to the Red Sea through the Strait of Tiran on 22 May. Arab countries started to send

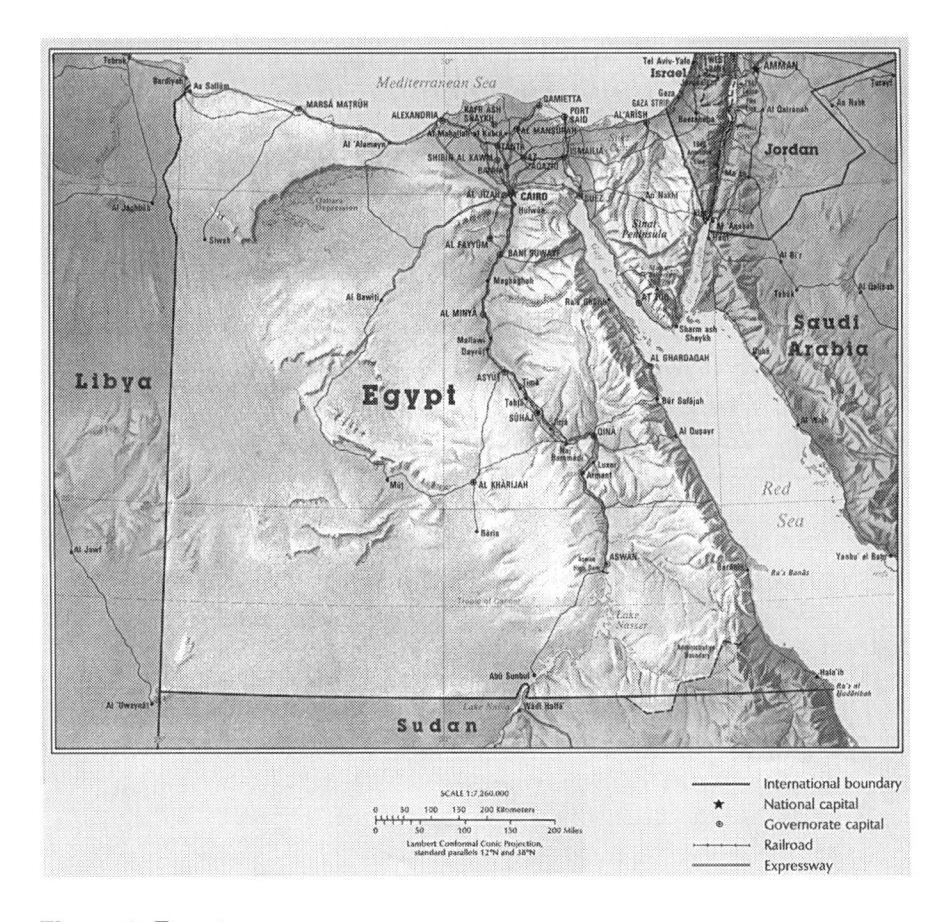

Figure 2. Egypt

ground units to ring Israel with a force of no fewer than 250,000 troops; 2,000 tanks; and over 700 aircraft. War seemed inevitable, and Arab military forces were prepared to cut Israel in two. Israel also prepared for action.

The Arab air forces were much larger than the IDF/AF on the eve of the Six-Day War. The EAF had a force of over 20,000 personnel and 450 combat aircraft. Soviet aircraft dominated the EAF arsenal, which included frontline MiG-21 Fishbed fighters, one of the most deadly interceptor aircraft in the world. The EAF also possessed Tu-16 Badger strategic bombers armed with air-to-surface missiles that threatened Israeli cities, industrial centers, and other targets. The Tu-16s could carry a payload of over 20,000 pounds. These bombers were the greatest threat to Israel since they could hit their targets within three minutes of entering Israeli early warning radar coverage and did not need to enter Israeli airspace to launch their missiles.[12] The Egyptian military also had Il-28 Beagle bombers that also had the range to strike Israeli targets. The EAF did suffer from poor reliability, a severe lack of trained pilots with combat experience, and doctrine based on that of the Soviet air force, which limited the EAF pilots' flexibility and initiative. SAAF, a smaller-scaled EAF without the Tu-16, had about 150 aircraft. The even smaller Jordanian and Iraqi air forces made up the bulk of the other forces.

IDF/AF forces had a much smaller force structure. Israeli air forces fielded about 245 combat aircraft. The Israelis had 72 Dassault Mirage IIICJ fighter-bombers, 18 Super Mystere B.2 fighter-bombers, 50 Mystere IV-A fighter-bombers, and several obsolete fighter-bombers and trainers pressed into service for combat use. The IDF/AF used multipurpose aircraft because of financial and manpower constraints. These aircraft needed to perform several functions adequately to defend the nation. The IDF/AF had to rely on superior strategy, training, and planning to make up for its lack of force structure. IDF/AF pilot training produced some of the world's finest air-to-air and air-to-ground attack pilots. Unfortunately, the numeric advantage of the Arab air forces required IDF/AF planners to look for new ways to neutralize the Arab advantage.

The IDF/AF planned to defeat the Arab air forces individually by a massive OCA operation. An air-to-air battle was not

The MiG-21 jet fighter was the nemesis of the US Air Force in the Vietnam War and of the IDF/AF in the Six-Day War of 1967.

feasible because of the Arabs' large force structure. Instead, IDF/AF planners would conduct a low-level, high-speed attack on EAF airfields first and then strike the SAAF. An initial attack on the EAF would eliminate the threat of the Tu-16s and defeat the larger of the two Arab main air forces. The IDF/AF would need a massive strike that would destroy almost all EAF aircraft on the ground and their runways without a requirement to repeat or sustain further operations against those targets. The IDF/AF commander, Maj Gen Mordechai Hod, decided not to attack the EAF and SAAF simultaneously since he was not assured of a decisive strike on both forces, due to his limited forces.[13] Hod ordered 12 aircraft held back to defend Israel. All remaining combat aircraft would strafe and bomb EAF airfields in a surprise attack.

This proposed attack had three main goals: achieve air superiority, destroy the Arab air forces as an effective offensive fighting force, and allow the IDF/AF to support ground operations after the destruction of the EAF and SAAF. The IDF/AF conducted routine training missions that it would later mimic on the day selected to conduct the surprise attack. These missions were designed to lull the EAF into a feeling that they were not the start of combat operations. Israeli fighter-bombers would carry air-to-ground munitions only—no air-to-air missiles—to maximize the destruction of enemy aircraft and airfields. These aircraft would fly at low levels to avoid Egyptian radar and air defense systems. After the attack on EAF forces, the IDF/AF would switch its efforts to the SAAF. Hod assumed that the SAAF would need at least two-and-a-half hours after the notification of the EAF strike to prepare and respond to the IDF/AF.

Planning called for the initial wave of IDF/AF fighter-bombers to reach their targets in the early morning during a period when EAF morning patrols were returning to base and there were few fighters in the air to oppose the IDF/AF. During this time, most EAF senior officers were commuting from their homes and bases and were not available to direct operations. Israeli forces had to make the most efficient use of forces—economy of force—and persist in their operations. This operation required rapid logistical support in terms of rearming and refueling combat planes. Instead of relying on a large number of aircraft, the IDF/AF would have to increase the tempo and number of missions per aircraft to conduct the campaign. The entire operation depended on surprise. Israel would have to conduct the air campaign under strict secrecy. A preemptive attack was key to trade force size for surprise. The IDF/AF, with approval of the Israeli prime minister and Cabinet, planned to begin the war at 0745 (0845 Cairo time) on 5 June 1967.[14]

Another clear, blue-sky morning greeted IDF/AF pilots as they took off from airfields throughout Israel. By 0700, 120 IDF/AF warplanes were winging their way to attack EAF airfields throughout Egypt. The aircraft flew out in three waves of 40 aircraft. One wave, composed of Mirage and Super Mysteres, flew west, out to the Mediterranean Sea, and then turned south to strike EAF airfields along the Sinai Canal. Other aircraft struck directly south from the Israeli border against airfields and targets in the Sinai. The last wave hit airfields along the Red Sea and interior of Egypt. The first wave was unopposed—a great strategic surprise that caught the EAF off guard and vulnerable to heavy damage.

Four aircraft from each wave were assigned to strafe and bomb each airfield. The four aircraft were scheduled to complete their airfield assault in 10 minutes. A follow-on attack by

AIR AND SPACE SUPERIORITY/STRATEGIC ATTACK

the next wave of jets was scheduled to strike other airfields 10 minutes after the initial wave. The third wave followed. IDF/AF aircraft returned to base, and ground crews refueled, rearmed, and repaired aircraft hit by AAA, all within 15 minutes of landing.[15] The Israelis were able to throw eight more waves of aircraft against the EAF for an additional 80 minutes of bombing.[16] There was a 10-minute pause after this blitz, followed by another eight waves of aircraft attacks. The EAF was devastated within three hours, with over 300 EAF aircraft destroyed or damaged. There were only a handful of EAF attempts to put aircraft into the sky to oppose the IDF/AF. One unsuccessful attempt was flown out of the Abu Sueir airfield. The EAF launched 20 MiG-21 interceptors that met 16 IDF/AF Mirage jets over the airfield. The EAF lost four MiG-21s to the IDF/AF in this engagement.

The successful strike against the EAF allowed the IDF/AF to turn its attention to the SAAF and the Royal Jordanian Air Force (RJAF). EAF aircraft and forces were unable to launch a counterattack against Israel. The SAAF and RJAF did manage to get aircraft into the air to strike Israeli targets, including airfields and an oil refinery. These Arab air attacks resulted in little significant damage, however. The IDF/AF responded with a heavier aerial attack against airfields in Syria and Jordan. Four SAAF airfields were hit, resulting in the destruction of about two-thirds of the SAAF aircraft. The RJAF was virtually demolished on the ground and ceased to be an effective fighting force for the rest of the war. All but one of its combat aircraft were destroyed in the attacks. The IDF/AF also struck Iraqi airfields.

At the end of the day, the RJAF was completely eliminated, the EAF was heavily damaged, and the SAAF would have to struggle to conduct a minimum of operations. The IDF/AF's preemptive attack had hit 25 airfields and destroyed hundreds of Arab aircraft. The IDF/AF claimed 240 EAF, 45 SAAF, 16 RJAF, and seven Iraqi aircraft destroyed on the ground and in the air.[17] The IDF/AF admitted to 19 aircraft lost. After these actions, the EAF and other Arab air forces were never a serious threat to Israel or its military forces throughout the Six-Day War. The EAF, SAAF, and Iraqi air force managed some limited missions against Israeli military forces, but these were conducted by exception. The IDF/AF was free to concentrate on supporting the army's ground operations and striking the enemy's ground forces.

Israel's bold use of preemptive bombing and strafing of airfields and aircraft on the first day of the war allowed the IDF/AF to achieve air superiority. The Arab air forces were not able to respond or take any actions against the IDF/AF. This allowed the IDF/AF the flexibility to continue attacks on airfields; support the eventual capture of much Arab territory by the Israeli army; and pummel retreating Arab ground forces. The IDF/AF gambled on the attack by using surprise and its highly trained fighter-pilot force to overcome the numeric strength of the Arab air forces. The attacks not only reduced the opposition forces facing the IDF/AF, but also severely shocked the Arab governments. The Arab military forces that were readying for a possible offensive were put on the defensive with a demoralized force. The character of the war for the Arabs swiftly changed to a conflict unplanned by the Cairo or Damascus governments. Instead of a swift victory for the Egyptians and Syrians, a one-day campaign, through air superiority, turned into a humiliating defeat. Israel's superior training, force employment, planning, initiative, and logistical support ruled the day for the IDF/AF.

The importance of air superiority was amply demonstrated in the Six-Day War. The attainment of air superiority gave Israel the opportunity to use a smaller air force to destroy forces much larger than its own. The value of air forces in a modern war was proven with a carefully planned campaign. Additionally, the IDF/AF revealed the value of airpower against ground forces without air superiority. If the IDF/AF had not gained command of the air, the Arab air forces might have inflicted more losses on the IDF/AF and created a war of attrition that would have lengthened the conflict and threatened the existence of Israel.

Air Superiority and Operation Overlord

The turning point of combat in the European theater of operations in World War II was the invasion of continental Europe, Operation Overlord, by Allied forces in Normandy, France, on

6 June 1944. The successful landing of American, British, and other Allied forces was the beginning of the end of the German *Wehrmacht's* domination of Western Europe. The long-awaited invasion required sufficient forces, logistics, and freedom from Luftwaffe attacks on the beaches, as well as the initial Allied footholds in France. The AAF's Eighth and Ninth Air Forces were to prepare the battlefield for Allied ground forces. The Eighth Air Force commander, Maj Gen James Doolittle, ordered his command to continue using its Boeing B-17 and Consolidated B-24 bombers to disrupt German industry and to use Republic P-47 and North American P-51 escort fighters to strangle Luftwaffe fighter resources.[18] AAF bomber and fighter units were to first focus on the *Wehrmacht's* overall combat capability and then concentrate on supporting ground commanders for Overlord and subsequent operations. Ninth Air Force was a "tactical" organization devoted to ground-support missions. The Ninth had one purpose: support operations for Overlord. Fighters from the Eighth and Ninth Air Forces—2,000 airplanes—and the Ninth's medium-bomber force were to conduct Operation Pointblank.

Operation Pointblank's goal was to make Overlord possible by destroying German military, industrial, and economic power, as well as the Germans' morale.[19] A combined offensive that involved AAF and RAF forces, starting in the spring of 1943, was used to destroy the Luftwaffe. These attacks would drain the Luftwaffe's resources from other fronts to protect the Reich and allow the Allies to pursue their plans to invade France.[20] Allied planners for Overlord envisioned airpower's playing a key role for the invasion's success. Luftwaffe fighter strength was rising fast, and if the Allies wanted to achieve air superiority, the Luftwaffe's fighter strength had to be sharply reduced. Continued attacks on the heart of Germany would cause munitions production to concentrate on more AAA and defensive fighters, not bombers or other ground offensive weapons. This would reduce Germany's ability to threaten American, British, and Soviet forces. Additionally, large bombing raids would force the Luftwaffe fighters to rise to defend German industries and allow the Allied fighters to engage the German air force in combat. RAF and AAF bombers were also used to hit airfields and aircraft-production facilities. The initial efforts of Pointblank were disappointing. German fighters shot down many AAF bombers as they attempted bombing runs over industrial targets over Europe in daylight.

The AAF upgraded its primary fighter escorts for the bombers by replacing its less capable Lockheed P-38 twin-engined fighters with the superior P-51 Mustang longer-range aircraft. The AAF also introduced long-range drop tanks that extended the range of all its fighters—P-38, P-47, and P-51. These modifications allowed the Eighth to oppose Luftwaffe air defenses on a more than equal footing, which helped reduce bomber losses. The bombers were also aided by a new H2X radar guidance system that would assist bombers in finding their targets—even in bad weather that would have forced a mission cancellation. On 20 February 1944, the Allies launched "Big Week," an attempt to destroy 12 key Luftwaffe aircraft-production facilities. AAF and RAF forces also smashed airfields, petroleum-storage facilities, key aircraft-component production sites (e.g., ball-bearing plants), and other targets. The Germans were forced to disperse their vulnerable industry, and that placed an immediate strain on Germany's overloaded transportation system. The German aircraft industry was able to produce at least twice as many fighter aircraft than in previous months because of dispersing, maximizing efficiencies, and significantly reducing production of other weapons. Fighter-aircraft production was only 1,300 aircraft per month in January; this increased to 1,600 planes by April and mushroomed to 3,000 by September.[21] The results of Big Week were still costly to Germany. The AAF and RAF dropped close to 19,000 tons of bombs and lost about 400 planes. The Luftwaffe lost 600 aircraft but, more importantly, sacrificed irreplaceable, experienced fighter pilots. Over 150 Luftwaffe fighters were lost in five days.[22] From January to June 1944, the Luftwaffe lost over 2,262 fighter pilots.[23] In May 1944, German fighter-pilot losses represented 25 percent of the entire force. By March 1944, the Luftwaffe had lost over 56 percent of its fighter force to air attacks. The Allied bombing campaign achieved its objective: crush the Luftwaffe, especially the fighter forces. Germany did not have the capacity to effectively challenge the RAF and AAF over Berlin, let alone the invasion area in faraway Normandy.

AIR AND SPACE SUPERIORITY/STRATEGIC ATTACK

The Eighth's bombers switched targets from mostly strategic industrial targets to additional support for the Overlord campaign. AAF bombers started to attack German airfields and the transportation systems throughout France. Bombers continued to hammer oil- and aircraft-production facilities. The Luftwaffe was stretched very thin. Experienced pilot replacements were dwindling, fuel to operate and train forces was running low, airfields were pushed further east to avoid AAF attacks, and Allied air strength was growing. The effective fighting force for the Luftwaffe was slowly changing to an ill-trained fighter defense force, which limited its ability to conduct operations. The RAF and AAF began to face Luftwaffe opposition that was only a shadow of what it had been a few months earlier. The Allies were winning the war of air superiority through a combination of attacking industry, disrupting airfields, and dominating the air through air-to-air victories. The RAF and AAF were using all means to gain air superiority.

Allied air forces began to concentrate their attacks on a number of targets as the proposed invasion date neared. The RAF and AAF struck transportation, materiel, troop concentrations, fortifications, and other targets that would directly hinder the invasion. AAF and RAF planners concentrated their efforts against Luftwaffe airfields within 150 miles of Caen, the major city closest to the Normandy beaches.[24] On 10 May, the Luftwaffe's radio and radar systems also came under an aerial onslaught to reduce the C^2 of enemy forces before the invasion.

Operation Overlord required complete mastery of the skies to allow the initial amphibious invasion forces to consolidate their positions on Normandy (fig. 3). The Allied Expeditionary Air Force was formed to support the invasion. It consisted of 173 fighter or fighter-bomber squadrons, 59 light or medium-bomber squadrons, and 50 support-aircraft squadrons. Fifteen squadrons supported coverage over the invasion fleet, 54 squadrons provided support over the beaches, 33 squadrons escorted bombers or conducted strafing missions in fighter sweeps, another 33 squadrons hit targets inland of the immediate invasion area, and 36 provided direct CAS to ground units.[25] Additionally, RAF Bomber Command and other AAF units would lend support. These forces totaled close to 12,000 aircraft.[26] American and British air forces were ready to dominate the skies over France by hunting for Luftwaffe fighters in Normandy. The Luftwaffe had only about 170 serviceable aircraft to oppose over 5,600 fighters.[27] Allied forces were able to fly a total of 14,674 sorties, or aircraft missions, over Normandy, with a loss of 113 aircraft, mostly due to ground fire.[28] The invasion was a success, due in great part to the lack of opposition air forces. The Luftwaffe was forced to stay on the ground, and very few Luftwaffe missions were flown against the invasion forces. By 10 June, RAF and AAF aircraft were operating from airfields in France, and that strengthened the Allied death grip on the Luftwaffe in France.

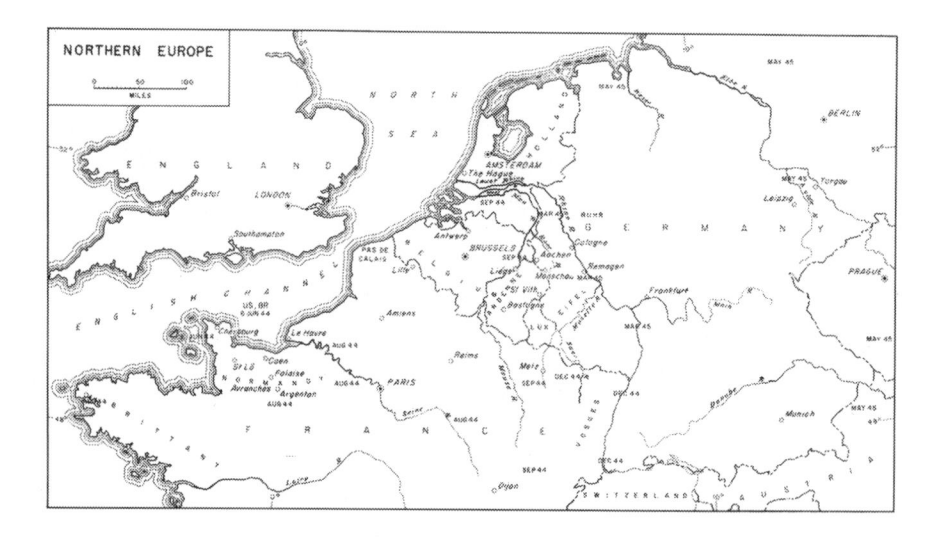

Figure 3. Overlord Theater of Operations

The Luftwaffe was ineffective in stopping the RAF and AAF from dominating the air over Normandy. *Generalfeldmarschall* Gerd von Rundstedt, commander of German forces in the west, including Normandy and the rest of France, believed Allied airpower was so dominating that his forces could do little to oppose the initial landings. On 20 June, Rundstedt wrote in his report "Experiences from the Invasion Battles of Normandy" that "within 2½ days, at a depth from the enemy bridgehead of about 65 miles, 29,000 enemy sorties were counted; of these, about 2,300 aircraft a day divebomb and strafe every movement on the ground, even a single soldier."[29] *Generalfeldmarschall* Erwin Rommel, commander of German forces in the Normandy area, was more direct in his assessment of Allied command of the air when he wrote, "The enemy's air superiority has a very grave effect on our movements. There's simply no answer to it."[30] German reinforcements and supplies were not able to provide effective replacements or move quickly to counter Allied actions. Allied air forces froze German forces in place and operated with minuscule Luftwaffe opposition.

The RAF and AAF would not be able to conduct this type of CAS to Army units and have the luxury of strafing "a single soldier" if it were not for air superiority over the Normandy beachhead and beyond. Although the Allies dominated the air, the ground forces still had to slug their way through a series of beach defenses and the formidable German Seventh and Fifteenth Armies. The American, British, and Canadian ground forces, involved in the initial invasion, needed every advantage possible to successfully conduct an amphibious invasion, consolidate, and break through German defenses to liberate France and drive on Germany. Allied air forces, free from enemy fighter opposition, attacked enemy rail lines and bridges two months before the invasion and all airfields 21 days before invading. If the Germans had had the ability to transport more troops and supplies into the Normandy area immediately after the invasion, then Allied forces would have faced much fiercer opposition. The Germans even may have been able to hold the invasion area to the thin strips of beaches and not allow a breakout to the interior of France. German forces were able to conduct significant counterattacks against British forces at Normandy. British and American forces were able to break out of the Normandy area only after a massive buildup of forces and an aerial bombardment campaign about a month and a half after the initial invasion. An effective Luftwaffe fighter force could have also stymied the invasion by interfering with Allied air-support missions and creating havoc among a series of critical preinvasion parachute landings at night.

The Allies' successful quest to obtain air superiority started well before the first American GI set foot on a French beach.

American troops invade Normandy, France, during Operation Overlord on D day, 6 June 1944.

Air superiority started with the Big Week campaign, moved to a massive campaign to destroy Luftwaffe airfields in France, and finally challenged any air opposition left over. Although the Luftwaffe still had several serviceable fighters in the Normandy area, the Allies were able to shoot down these planes and their reinforcements within 10 hours of the invasion.[31] The RAF and AAF had three possible strategies to achieve air superiority: dominate the local skies over the battlefield, attack aircraft production, or conduct operations to achieve control over a larger area by destroying airfields, support, and the supply system. The last strategy was attacking aircraft-production facilities that would reduce the Luftwaffe's ability to conduct air operations and destroy German fighter strength.[32]

The Allies conducted elements of all three strategies. They also introduced better fighter aircraft, such as the P-51, that had superior air-to-air capabilities compared to its predecessors, the P-38 and P-47. The P-51 was able to outfly and outfight its main opposition, the Focke-Wulf Fw-190 and Messerschmitt Bf-109 fighters. This concentrated aerial effort, which had the express purpose of knocking out the German air force, succeeded. These efforts mirrored many of the efforts of early airpower theorists. Douhet believed in striking airfields as a means of gaining command of the air. Mitchell thought that an air battle might allow the air force to gain air superiority. ACTS instructors thought that striking the industrial capability of a nation would slow a foe's war-making capability, which included air operations. This combination of actions denied the Luftwaffe the opportunity to challenge Allied airpower. Fortunately, the RAF and AAF were able to gain air superiority—a decisive measure in Normandy that put the Allies on the road to victory.

Defeating the Enemy through Strategic Attack

Douhet, Mitchell, and other early airpower theorists envisioned the defeat of an enemy through the destruction of targets that directly affected the conduct of the war. In the past, many military leaders identified strategic bombardment with attacks upon a nation's capital, industrial capacity, military headquarters, and similar targets. Although these targets are usually considered strategic, the objective and nature of strategic warfare have evolved to understanding the effect of the destruction or disruption of a target on the nation's ability to fight the war—not the target itself. The ACTS faculty and students identified particular targets that would cause a nation's industry to fail. The industrial-web theory was an early attempt to select particular key industries that would shutter a country's manufacturing capacity and its military capability. Similarly, aerospace leaders need to understand that the bombing of a single key target may eliminate the need to strike a whole structure of enemy targets.

Nuclear long-range bombers launched against the interior of a country characterized the notion of strategic attack by airpower during the Cold War. First, strategic attack is not limited to nuclear weapons only; precision conventional weapons can destroy targets and eliminate the nation's capability to function or reduce its military capability. Airpower does not necessarily need to destroy a target via nuclear warfare but perhaps merely disable or disrupt operations. Second, all types of aircraft can conduct a strategic attack. The key determination of whether a target is strategic or not is its impact on an enemy's war-making capability. Army helicopters that attack a critical communications or leadership target may have a larger strategic effect than a jet bomber that attacks an enemy ground unit. This distinction allows the smallest aircraft to have the potential to conduct a strategic attack and increases the flexibility that a commander can use to conduct a campaign. Third, strategic attack is not limited to attacks within the enemy nation. Air operations may be conducted against targets along the enemy's periphery. Also, a strategic attack may be directed against a nation's deployed space assets that may not be under direct control of the country. These conditions have altered the vision of strategic attack, and they provide a challenge to future aerospace leaders. Planning for strategic attack will require more information and analysis to determine the strategic effect of the attack—not just a determination of the vehicle or platform that will conduct it. Strategic attack may weaken an opponent so much that his surface forces may not offer strong resistance to friendly forces.

Japan's Hawaii Operation

Japan's Hawaii Operation was a bold surprise attack on US naval, air, and ground forces in 1941. The Japanese government had designs to expand its influence and territorial control throughout most of Southeast Asia. On 6 September 1941, the Japanese government made a decision to go to war against the United States. The Japanese army and navy general staffs began operational planning to conquer Malaya, Java, Borneo, the Bismarck Archipelago, the Netherlands East Indies, and the Philippines.[33] Capture of these areas would ensure ready access to raw materials. The United States had cut off exports of oil and other essential raw materials to Japan in response to Japanese actions in China. Japan's economy would disintegrate unless it could obtain access to resources. An obstacle in the way of the Japanese plans was the British, Dutch, and American military forces stationed in the Pacific. Although American forces in Hawaii were not located near Japan's targets in Southeast Asia, US Army and Navy forces could become formidable reinforcements if American forces in the Philippines were seized—or they might become the basis of a strike force against Japan.

The US Pacific Fleet represented a distinct threat to Japan's war plans. There was little chance of keeping the fleet from involvement if the Imperial Japanese military forces captured the Southeast Asian region. The Imperial Japanese Navy's (IJN) main goal in the Hawaii Operation was the destruction of the US Pacific Fleet—other targets would be considered secondary.[34] American naval power stationed at Pearl Harbor revolved around the battleship fleet and three aircraft carriers. If the Japanese could destroy the American Pacific Fleet and bases in the Philippines, Wake Island, and Guam, then the ability of the United States to respond to the Japanese seizure of Southeast Asia would be limited to attacks originating from the American west coast, thousands of miles away (fig. 4). A crippled US Navy would be forced to go on the defensive and allow the Japanese to consolidate and strengthen a Pacific perimeter if the Americans mounted a counterattack. The Americans would be forced to strip military forces from the Atlantic to reinforce the Pacific—an unpalatable option for the US Navy and Army, especially for the embattled British.

The Japanese Naval General Staff and Combined Fleet headquarters planned a carrier-based aircraft raid that would destroy the American naval forces in Pearl Harbor. After the elimination of this threat, the IJN and army could launch their plan to capture Southeast Asia. IJN planning was constrained by a larger political concern—ongoing negotiations between the Japanese and American governments to conclude a peaceful settlement to events in China and the economic sanctions placed on Japan. If these negotiations were successful, then the IJN would cancel the attack. If not, a declaration of war needed to be transmitted to the American government before the Pearl Harbor strike.

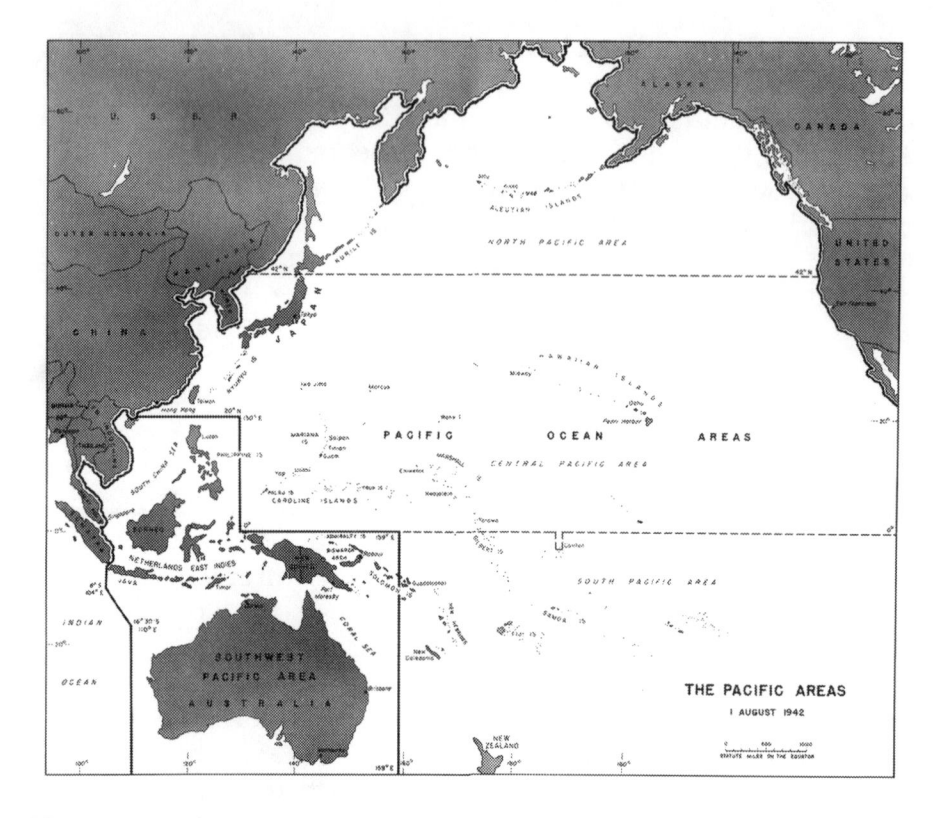

Figure 4. Pacific Area

The IJN would use 33 ships, including four heavy and two light aircraft carriers with approximately 360 combat planes for the Hawaii Operation. The attack fleet also contained 27 submarines to encircle the island of Oahu, the main Hawaiian island that was home to the bulk of American naval and military forces. IJN planners estimated that the attack had a 50 percent chance of success.[35] The submarines would increase the chance of sinking American naval vessels. Midget submarines would attempt to enter Pearl Harbor and attack ships. The attack was scheduled for 7 December (Hawaiian time)—a Sunday. A weekend attack would hopefully catch the Pacific Fleet by surprise. The IJN was receiving information on US fleet movements in and around Pearl Harbor from a spy in the Japanese Embassy in Honolulu. Two aircraft carriers, the

AIR AND SPACE SUPERIORITY/STRATEGIC ATTACK

Enterprise and *Lexington*, were known to operate in the area, but the third carrier—the *Saratoga*—was in dry-dock repair at San Diego. The aircraft carriers were the main targets of the IJN fleet.

Naval aviation had shown its value to Combined Fleet Adm Isoroku Yamamoto, the IJN commander in chief. Yamamoto had conceived of and advocated approval of the Hawaii Operation. Naval aviation had shown that, under combat conditions, it could sink ships. In May 1941, a Royal Navy carrier aircraft had significantly contributed to the sinking of the German navy's *Bismarck* with antiquated Swordfish torpedo biplanes. Earlier, on 11 November 1940, the Royal Navy had used 20 Swordfish aircraft to sink or disable three battleships of the Italian Fleet in the Gulf of Taranto. The Taranto attack knocked out much of the Italian naval effort in the Mediterranean during a crucial phase of the North Africa campaign. With the Italian Fleet disabled, the British were able to continue resupply of their forces in North Africa, support liberation efforts in the Balkans, and keep the Suez Canal open. The IJN would try to reproduce the same strategic effect against the United States with the attack on Pearl Harbor. The IJN would rely on small carrier aircraft to knock out the Pacific Fleet. Conversely, the prevailing Air Corps belief was that long-range bombers could conduct a strategic attack and sink a large ship, much like Mitchell had demonstrated with the *Ostfriesland*.

The IJN carrier-aircraft fleet was composed of three aircraft types. The Mitsubishi A6M2 Zero fighter plane, proven in combat over China, was faster and more maneuverable than any American fighter plane operating in Hawaii. Although it was faster than its rivals, it did not have self-sealing fuel tanks and was largely unarmored. These conditions would prove fatal to Japanese pilots later in the war. The IJN also used the Nakajima B5N2 Kate horizontal bomber and Aichi D3A1 Val dive-bomber. The Kate and Val aircraft were the main strike force used against the Pacific Fleet and in bombing runs against US Army airfields. The Zero aircraft were to provide bomber escort and strafe targets of opportunity.

American air defenses in the Pearl Harbor area included Army AAA, pursuit aircraft, and a radar system. Additionally, most naval vessels had AAA on board and aircraft based at US

Marine Corps and naval air stations on Oahu. In 1913 the War Department had established a large US Army presence—the Hawaiian Division, whose primary mission from 1920 to 1941 was to defend Pearl Harbor against "damage from naval or aerial bombardment."[36] Later, the chief of staff of the US Army, Gen George C. Marshall, directed the Hawaiian Division to protect the fleet as well as the Pearl Harbor facilities.

The US Army had two major and two minor airfields on Oahu. The two major air bases were Hickam Field and Wheeler Field. Hickam, located adjacent to Pearl Harbor, was a bomber base and headquarters of the Hawaiian Air Force. Wheeler Field, in the center of the island and next to a major Army base, Schofield Barracks, was home to the Hawaiian Air Force's fighter force. The mainstay of the Army Air Corps fighter force was the Curtiss P-40 B/C Tomahawk fighters. The P-40 would later shine in China as the primary fighter flying for Claire Chennault's Flying Tigers. However, the P-40 was obsolete by 1941. Air Corps pilots also flew a more antiquated fighter, the Curtiss P-36A. There were 55 P-40 B/C and 20 P-36A aircraft serviceable on 7 December 1941.[37] The two minor fields, Bellows and Haleiwa, contained a few fighter and observation aircraft. The Hawaiian Air Force also had 12 B-17D Flying Fortress bombers that were supposed to seek out and destroy an enemy fleet if Hawaii were attacked.[38]

The Hawaiian Division did operate an air warning system, but it was incomplete. The system was composed of five mobile SCR-270 long-range radar sets located in temporary locations and one set stationed on the northern tip of Oahu. The Army had received three fixed SCR-271 radar sets, but they were not installed at the time of the attack. The radar systems, land observers, and reconnaissance aircraft were linked to a centralized information center that was supposed to identify an air threat to Hawaii and send P-40 aircraft to intercept a foe within six minutes of detection.[39] The air warning system was also responsible for warning AAA units as well as Navy and Marine Corps aircraft. The system was still under development and was not ready to fully operate during the Pearl Harbor attack.

The IJN's success depended on complete surprise by the carrier aircraft. Avoiding the Hawaiian Air Force's fighters and

AIR AND SPACE SUPERIORITY/STRATEGIC ATTACK

the Hawaiian Division's radar systems was paramount. Fortunately for the Japanese, the US Army's air warning system was incomplete and did not provide its intended warning. IJN aircraft were to hit US Navy and Army targets in two waves. The first wave, composed of 183 aircraft, would strike Pearl Harbor, Hickam, Wheeler, and other airfields around Oahu. A midget submarine force was to enter Pearl Harbor and attack ships in conjunction with the air assault, but it accomplished little. A second wave would follow the first wave.

The attack on Pearl Harbor concentrated on "Battleship Row." The American carriers had left Pearl Harbor. The *Enterprise* was 200 miles from Pearl Harbor conducting training.[40] The *Lexington* was delivering Marine Corps aircraft to Wake Island. So the key objectives of the strategic attack were missing. The IJN did not have adequate intelligence that notified it of the missing carriers. The only forces left were battleships and other supporting naval vessels. Pearl Harbor did contain vital oil reserves, maintenance facilities, and a submarine base that

Air raid Pearl Harbor. Japan's use of carrier aircraft succeeded in sinking several battleships but did not cripple the US Pacific Fleet.

supported US Navy operations throughout the Pacific. If the IJN forces could destroy the oil and maintenance facilities, the US Pacific Fleet would have to withdraw many of its operations to the west coast. The submarine base was another lucrative strategic target. The Navy's submarine force received much credit for blockading the Japanese home islands and sinking many merchant and naval vessels after the Pearl Harbor attack, when the US Navy and Army could not strike the enemy.

At 0755, the first wave struck multiple targets in and around Pearl Harbor. An Army radar crew had detected the IJN carrier aircraft earlier, but the warning was not transmitted to the fighters at Wheeler Field. The first attack wave struck battleships and airfields with little opposition. The second wave hit Oahu with another 169 aircraft. The Japanese were able to sink four battleships, heavily damage five other battleships, and bomb or torpedo nine others. About 2,400 Americans were killed and 1,700 wounded in the attack. One hundred sixty-nine US aircraft were destroyed, and 150 were heavily damaged. The IJN carrier pilots successfully hit their targets with minimal losses—185 killed and one captured. Only 29 IJN planes failed to return to their aircraft carriers.

The Japanese strategic strike was a great success in employment. The Pacific Fleet's battleship forces were severely damaged, and all were put out of commission to various degrees. The IJN carrier air attacks knocked out US Army airfields and destroyed many aircraft. The Army's major losses were mainly in personnel, aircraft, and the shock of the attack. If the Japanese designed the attack to demoralize the American public so it would sue for peace, it actually had the reverse effect: the American public was now more inclined to fight a bitter conflict to assure Japan's defeat. The damage inflicted on American forces was lighter than first imagined. Although the battleship fleet was severely damaged, the all-important carrier fleet escaped unscathed in the attack. These carriers would later form the vanguard for the Pacific campaigns at Coral Sea and Midway. The Japanese also did not disable the Pearl Harbor shipyard maintenance and logistics capabilities. The loss of these facilities would have denied advance support for the eventual American campaign to recapture lost territory. The IJN also did not hit the oil-storage facilities near Pearl Harbor whose destruction would have seriously hindered all naval operations—more so than the loss of the battleships.[41] The combined Zero, Kate, and Val air assault also missed the submarine base. Submarine forces were the first naval vessels to strike back at Japan. The war record illustrated the importance of the US Navy's submarine fleet. Submarines would sink 1,113 merchant ships, with 65 probable kills, over the course of the war.[42] These actions greatly aided the strangling of Japan's industry, reduced food supplies, and crippled its war capability.

The Japanese strategic attack used only two waves of aircraft strikes. The Pacific Fleet was crippled, and the land-based bomber airfield at Hickam was smoldering. Several critics of the IJN did not understand why another wave of aircraft was not sent to demolish the remaining targets at Pearl Harbor. If the Japanese had launched more attacks, the destruction of the shipyard, oil facilities, and submarine base could have been accomplished. The Japanese did not ensure the

USS *Arizona* burning at Pearl Harbor

destruction of all key strategic targets. Adm Chuichi Nagumo, commander of the IJN Pearl Harbor task force, thought that another wave was unnecessary for several reasons. First, he believed that no additional significant damage could be inflicted on the Americans from the first two waves. Second, Nagumo thought the second wave had encountered stronger AAA fire, placing his aircraft in greater danger. Third, he also did not know what American naval and air forces were available for a counterattack against his carriers. Fourth, the Japanese task force was in range of American land-based bombers and in potential danger of attack.[43] The failure to take advantage of the American shock and losses doomed the chance of a dominant strategic attack by the Japanese. The IJN had achieved air superiority over Oahu by the destruction of the Hawaiian Air Force and the absence of the *Enterprise* and *Lexington*. Instead of devastating the Pacific Fleet, however, the IJN focused the attention of the American public on defeating the Axis powers.

Slamming Saddam: Operation Desert Storm

On 17 January 1991, coalition forces of the United States, Britain, France, and several other nations conducted a strategic attack against Iraqi targets. The targets included air defense systems, C^2 centers, leadership, suspected NBC weapons facilities, and military bases. The strategic campaign was designed to paralyze not only the Iraqi government of Saddam Hussein, but also his military forces that were occupying Kuwait. Hopefully, the American-led air campaign would significantly reduce the military capabilities and options that Saddam could employ against the coalition or hinder the eventual ground offensive to recapture Kuwait. Col John Warden originally proposed the concept of the strategic air campaign against Iraq. His proposal closely followed his theory on air campaigns.

A simmering dispute between Iraq and Kuwait over the ownership of oil resources exploded into open conflict. On 2 August 1990, the Iraqi Republican Guard crossed the Kuwaiti border and seized the country. The government of Kuwait, its citizens, and elements of the Kuwaiti military fled south to Saudi Arabia (fig. 5). The UN condemned the invasion and demanded

AIR AND SPACE SUPERIORITY/STRATEGIC ATTACK

an immediate withdrawal of Iraqi forces. The UN would later authorize the use of force to eject the Iraqis from Kuwait.

The United States responded quickly to a request by King Fahd of Saudi Arabia for aid to forestall a potential invasion of his country by Saddam Hussein. The loss of the oil fields of Kuwait was significant, but the additional loss of Saudi Arabian oil would be a disaster for the world's economies. President George Bush ordered the Army's 82d Airborne Division to deploy to Saudi Arabia. He also sent 48 Air Force McDonnell-Douglas F-15C/D Eagles from the 1st Fighter Wing to Saudi Arabia to defend Saudi airspace and deter further Iraqi ag-

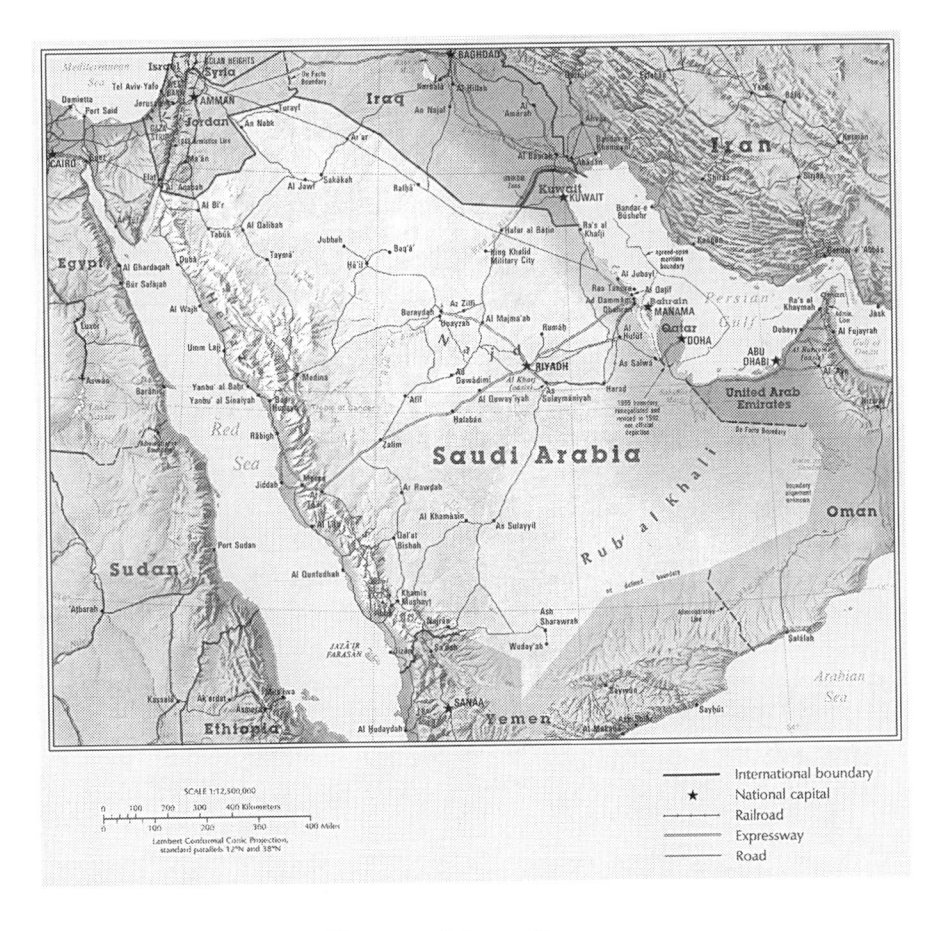

Figure 5. Desert Storm Theater of Operations

gression. The aircraft carrier USS *Eisenhower* and its battle group were rushed to the Persian Gulf. This was the start of Operation Desert Shield, the initial defense of Saudi Arabia and buildup of military forces to recapture Kuwait.

Bush's initial political objectives included the following:

- [Obtain the] immediate, complete, and unconditional withdrawal of Iraqi forces from Kuwait.
- Restore Kuwait's legitimate government.
- Maintain security and stability of Saudi Arabia and the Persian Gulf.
- Ensure the safety and protection of the lives of American citizens abroad.[44]

The American military needed to define these political objectives in terms of military ones. Lt Gen Charles Horner, senior USAF officer on the staff of Central Command (responsible for American military operations in the Persian Gulf), received a more well-defined set of military objectives from Bush:

- Force Iraq out of Kuwait.
- Destroy NBC capability (five-to-10-year setback).
- Minimize loss of life.
- Minimize civilian casualties.[45]

Horner was responsible for planning, organizing, and conducting the air campaign to accomplish these military objectives. Colonel Warden, head of Checkmate, an air-planning organization at the Pentagon, immediately started to develop an air plan to defeat Iraq and accomplish Bush's national objectives. Checkmate's plan, Instant Thunder, was designed to exploit Iraqi vulnerabilities and attack high-valued targets. Warden thought airpower alone could win the war and force the Iraqis out of Kuwait with minimal casualties.[46] Horner rejected Warden's plan, persuading the overall commander of Central Command, Gen Norman Schwarzkopf, to accept a four-phased offensive campaign:

- Phase 1: Strategic air campaign against Iraq.
- Phase 2: Air campaign against Iraqi air defenses in Kuwait.

AIR AND SPACE SUPERIORITY/STRATEGIC ATTACK

- Phase 3: Attrition of Iraqi ground-combat power to neutralize Iraq's deployed ground forces and isolate the Kuwait battlefield.
- Phase 4: Ground attack to eject Iraqi forces from Kuwait.[47]

Air forces could conduct the first two phases and support the last two. Warden's modified Instant Thunder campaign would be conducted in Phase 1. The strategic air campaign would concentrate on political-military leadership that would target command, control, and communications capabilities. The goal of the strategic air campaign was to isolate and handicap the ability of the Iraqi government to operate its military force. Additionally, the air campaign would destroy NBC warfare capability. Coalition air forces were also charged with eliminating the Iraqis' ability to conduct offensive military operations, as well as destroying support facilities and ballistic missile launchers. The strategic attack would also aim for electric power, oil refineries, key bridges, and rail lines.[48] There were over 350 strategic targets identified for the campaign. Air planners estimated that the strategic air campaign would last about a week. However, before the air campaign could become effective, air superiority would be needed in order to accomplish the initial attacks and subsequent air operations. Air operations against targets that controlled or operated Iraqi air defense radar, SAM sites, AAA, and fighter-interceptors would also be conducted on the first day of the campaign.

The Iraqi air force had just finished a 10-year war of attrition against Iran. The Iraqis had a mixed force of 750 to 800 fixed-wing, mostly Soviet and French, aircraft that was organized, trained, and operated under Soviet doctrine and guidance.[49] This force included 405 fighter-interceptors, including the top-of-the-line MiG-29. The Iraqi air force was the sixth largest in the world; however, most of its aircraft were obsolete, and its personnel were ill prepared for combat and oriented towards the defense of particular locations—not the overall country. The Iraqi Air Defense Command did have airborne radar, ground-based surveillance radar, and a number of French and Soviet SAM systems. These systems, like the air-breathing portion of the Iraqi air force, did not possess state-of-the-art equipment, and many personnel lacked training. Saddam Hussein's air defense forces included 7,000 AAA pieces, located at 970 sites, and over 16,000 SAMs, most of them defending Baghdad.[50] These forces also relied heavily on centralized command centers that would become lucrative targets to the coalition air forces, which had significant intelligence about the French-supplied aircraft and air defenses. Since France was a part of the UN effort to oust Iraq, it supplied valuable data about the Iraqi air defense capabilities. Although the Iraqi air force posed little danger to the coalition forces, it could hinder Desert Storm, the military campaign against Iraq.

The coalition air forces were composed of 11 national forces. United States air forces dominated the coalition effort. USAF, Navy, and Marine Corps aircraft made up 76 percent of all airframes,[51] including reconnaissance aircraft, fighters, bombers, transports, and other warplanes. The United States also provided space surveillance, early warning, communications, navigation, and early warning satellites that contributed greatly throughout all military operations during Desert Shield/Storm. The Phase 1 strategic air campaign would use all types of aircraft, including fighters, bombers, reconnaissance, tanker, electronic warfare, surveillance, special operations, and others to conduct the attack. All services contributed to the attack on Iraqi radar systems, as did US Army helicopters.

Phase 1 began a day earlier than the scheduled attack on Iraqi soil. The main attack was scheduled to begin on 17 January. On 16 January 1991, seven USAF Boeing B-52G bombers from Barksdale Air Force Base (AFB), Louisiana, were launched on a 14,000-mile round-trip mission to deliver 35 conventionally armed air launched cruise missiles. The US Navy also launched 52 Tomahawk cruise missiles from the battleships *Wisconsin* and *Missouri* and the cruiser *San Jacinto*.[52] Horner also coordinated an initial attack on air defense radar systems by USAF MH-53J Pave Low and Army AH-64 Apache attack helicopters. The helicopter assault would allow coalition aircraft to strike targets within Iraq without being detected; this would reduce the SAM and AAA directed against the strike force. Other aircraft, like the F-4G, EA-6B, and EF-111A, also supported SEAD missions. A coordinated attack required detailed planning to include combat air patrols

Airpower in Desert Storm. Army Apache attack helicopters provided CAS for ground forces.

(CAP), tanker support, timing of the cruise missile launching, sequence of attacks on targets, recovery efforts, and search and rescue capabilities.

After the air defense radar systems were destroyed, waves of aircraft entered Iraqi airspace to deliver a massive strike. Lockheed F-117A stealth strike aircraft, F-15E Strike Eagle fighter-bombers, B-52 bombers, RAF and Royal Saudi Air Force Tornado GR-1 ground-attack aircraft, General Dynamics F-111 Aardvark fighter-bombers, carrier-based A-6 Intruder bombers, and several types of support aircraft launched multiple raids along the southern border of Iraq and Kuwait. Coalition aircraft also launched attacks from Turkey. These aircraft struck the Iraqis' Kari air defense C^2 network, Scud tactical ballistic missile sites, storage and production facilities, communications lines, electricity, presidential office complex, Baath Party headquarters, airfields, weapons-of-mass-destruction production facilities, and other targets. Long-range, eight-engined B-52 bombers flew alongside shorter-range, single-engine fighter-bombers to strike targets throughout Iraq. The com-

Precision-guided munitions give aerospace power the ability to strike globally and quickly, much like this cruise missile launched from a B-52.

bined effort was designed to isolate Saddam Hussein from his military forces, severely disrupt the air defense systems, and attempt to create a psychological effect on the Iraqi people. Despite the presence of a large enemy air force and air defense system, coalition aircraft got through and destroyed many key targets. A visible example to the Iraqi populace of the coalition's bombing campaign was the disruption of a key aspect of modern life: electricity. Coalition air planners took great pains not to permanently destroy electrical-production facilities—only disable them. Nevertheless, the campaign shut down most electrical power throughout Iraq and created a hardship for its people.

The strategic air campaign ended on 25 January. During the first two days of the campaign, 169 out of 298 strategic targets were struck. The coalition aircraft shut down the Iraqi

AIR AND SPACE SUPERIORITY/STRATEGIC ATTACK

The versatile F-111 strike aircraft

air force, disrupted air defenses, and affected the ability of the Iraqi military to communicate with its deployed forces. These actions allowed coalition forces to expand their assault to different areas. Air superiority was achieved after most of the Iraqi air force was trapped in hangars because their runways were cratered. The first two days of bombardment had destroyed Iraqi aircraft, disrupted ground-controlled intercept (GCI) facilities, and stopped Iraqi air operations. American aircraft and their allies continued to pound airfields, supply lines, command authority, Scud missiles, military support, weapons of mass destruction, and the Republican Guard. Over 18,276 sorties were flown in Phase 1. The coalition lost few aircraft to Iraqi forces in the operation.

The strategic campaign accomplished several goals. However, there were limitations to the strategic-bombardment campaign. Fighter-bombers had a difficult time finding, targeting, and destroying Scud missiles, which continued to hit targets in Israel and Saudi Arabia throughout Desert Storm, raising the possibility of the Iraqis using an NBC warhead against neighboring countries and friendly forces. The failure to stop the Scuds forced the USAF to divert valuable air resources to hunt these missiles. These aircraft could have been used to destroy other targets, like Iraqi ground forces. The Defense Intelligence Agency (DIA) estimates that strategic air missions

F-117 aircraft performed strategic attack missions over Iraq during Operation Desert Storm.

against Scud targets were only 25 percent fully successful.[53] Scud mobile launchers were able to hide, quickly set up, launch their missiles, and move. These characteristics contributed to the difficulty experienced by coalition aircraft in destroying the Scuds.

Coalition aircraft also had problems eliminating NBC weapons, as well as production and storage facilities. These weapons posed some of the greatest threats to coalition forces during Desert Storm and were potential threats in future conflicts in the Persian Gulf. Although the DIA estimated that the Phase 1 effort fully destroyed 76 percent of the targets associated with weapons of mass destruction, the failure to identify all targets was evident after the war.[54] Immediately after the war, UN arms inspectors found that production facilities had moved, targets had not been detected, or weapons had been concealed. Iraq had maintained an NBC weapons program despite the best efforts of the coalition air attacks. This failure illustrated the need for accurate intelligence. Without proper targeting, strategic airpower is seriously hampered. Proper targeting requires timely and appropriate intelligence.

Coalition air forces were able to conduct a massive strategic attack on Iraq. These air forces used surprise, mass, and objective to conduct a sustained campaign during early January 1991. The strategic air campaign allowed the coalition to paralyze many Iraqi military functions. Iraqi air defenses, air

AIR AND SPACE SUPERIORITY/STRATEGIC ATTACK

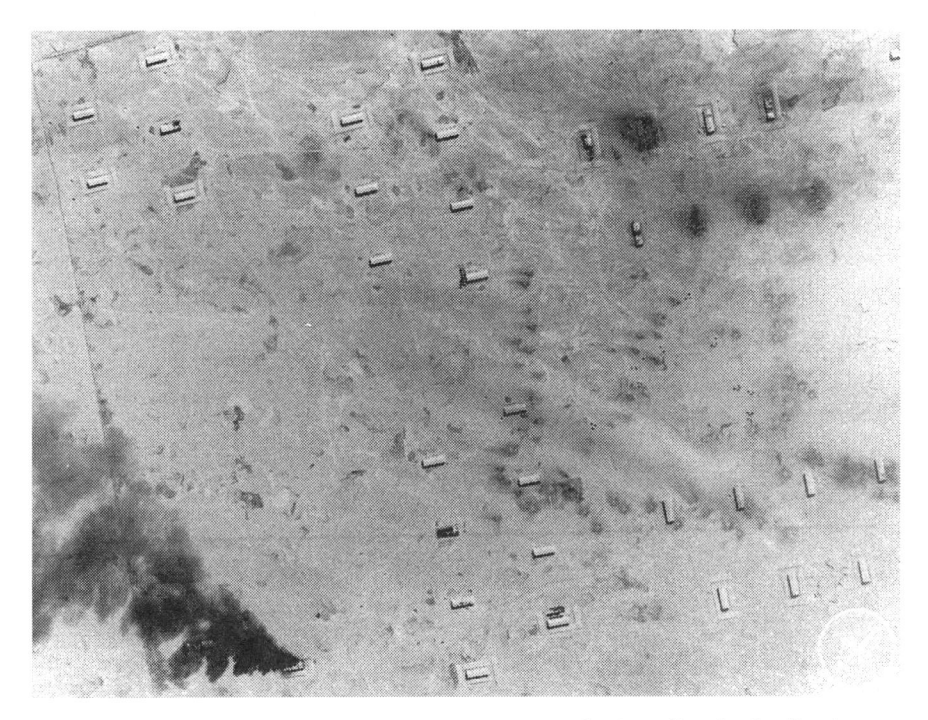

Precision-guided munitions allowed airpower to destroy Scud missile storage facilities with little collateral damage.

forces, and military C^2 capabilities were seriously disrupted throughout the war. This allowed the coalition to conduct the other phases of the war with less resistance from the Iraqis. The effects of the strategic air attack did not totally isolate Iraqi military forces from Saddam Hussein, but the communications links with Kuwait and the outside world were cut. Also, Saddam's air force ultimately fled destruction by seeking asylum in Iran. Additionally, the strategic campaign resulted in a 55 percent shutdown of electricity production by 17 January (88 percent by 9 February). Additionally, 93 percent of Iraq's oil-refining capability was destroyed. Finally, Saddam's elite Republican Guard was immobilized, and many units were reduced to 50 percent combat efficiency.[55] Coalition forces were able to use new advances in precision-guided munitions (PGM), stealth, space, cruise missile, and other technological advancements to achieve these results. Strategic attack created many

Precision attack during Desert Storm. Destruction of these aircraft shelters effectively killed Iraqi aircraft before they could fly.

of the effects desired by Horner. Although it did not end the war, strategic attack was a vital element in preparing to liberate Kuwait.

The Eighth Air Force in the Combined Bomber Offensive, 1943–45

In World War II, the Army Air Corps was confronted with a challenge to find ways to defeat Germany. Many AAF officers in leadership positions who were responsible for planning, building, and employing forces were ACTS graduates and had lived through the public debates during Billy Mitchell's tenure. Several officers and ACTS faculty, such as Laurence S. Kuter, Haywood S. Hansell, Harold L. George, and Kenneth N. Walker, advocated using strategic bombers alone to defeat Germany. Before the entry of the United States into World War II, President Franklin D. Roosevelt had authorized secret high-level military discussions with the British military. From January to March 1941, these discussions resulted in an agreement that Germany had to be defeated first, and a sustained bomber offensive would prepare for an invasion.[56]

On 9 July 1941, Roosevelt asked Secretary of War Henry Stimson and Secretary of the Navy Frank Knox for their estimates of materiel and manpower to defeat Germany, Italy, and Japan.[57] Harold George, who was assigned to the Army's War Plans Division, was authorized to produce the requirements for Army aircraft. He enlisted the aid of Hansell, Kuter, and Walker. Their document, Air War Plans Division-1 (AWPD-1), became a blueprint to defeat Germany by strategic bombardment. The AWPD-1 team assumed that it would take years for the US Army to procure, train, and deploy sufficient aircraft and aircrews to wear down Germany before an invasion could be mounted. To defeat Germany, George estimated the AAF needed 6,860 heavy bombers. The total Air Corps requirement was 63,500 aircraft with 2,160,000 personnel to fight the war. The Air Corps's objectives were to defend the United States, conduct a strategic bombing offensive against Germany to allow an invasion, provide CAS to ground forces after an invasion, conduct a strategic defense against Japan, and—once Germany was defeated—conduct a strategic bomber offensive against Japan.

The AWPD-1 planners believed that a massive strategic attack on Germany would defeat Hitler. In case they were wrong, George and the other planners included other targets to support the invasion of Europe. The plan called for a massive bombing campaign 21 months after America entered the war; this campaign would require at least 4,000 bombers conducting operations for at least six months.[58] The AWPD-1 document was focused on the German economy—no surprise since the ACTS graduates had been educated in the industrial-web theory. This theory was translated into a strategy and force structure. The initial target plans included electrical power, transportation, and petroleum. AWPD-1 contents went well beyond the materiel and manpower estimates requested by Roosevelt. The Air Corps document would become the basis for a strategic air campaign against Germany called the Combined Bomber Offensive (CBO). AWPD-1 contained 154 German targets classified into five major areas: the Luftwaffe and aircraft production (including airfields, aluminum, and magnesium), electrical power, transportation centers, petroleum, and morale.[59] A revision to AWPD-1, AWPD-42, deleted the morale target and substituted submarine bases and synthetic rubber. The German *Kriegsmarine* U-boat submarine fleet was a major threat to Allied convoys that supplied Britain and the Soviet Union with munitions, food, and raw materials.

During World War II, the AAF—the expanded Army Air Corps—was wedded to the idea of employing strategic bombers using high-altitude daylight precision-bombing techniques to destroy specific targets. Using heavily armed and armored bombers, the AAF could deliver bombs at long ranges without fighter escort. Additionally, AAF bombers flying at high altitudes would also help pilots avoid fighter interceptions. These ideas were straight out of both ACTS and the theories of Billy Mitchell. The AAF's Boeing B-17 Flying Fortresses and Consolidated B-24 Liberator bombers were organized into the Eighth Air Force, stationed in England. These bombers were designed and developed to support the idea of high-altitude daylight precision bombing. By early 1942, Eighth Air Force started limited bombing operations against targets in France.

The RAF had serious reservations about the American approach to the CBO. British pilots were unconvinced about the ability to drop bombs with precision from high altitude. The RAF had moved towards area bombing in hopes of crushing the morale and will of the German populace. The British felt

AIR AND SPACE SUPERIORITY/STRATEGIC ATTACK

As part of the Combined Bomber Offensive, a B-17 bomber of the Eighth Air Force attacks the Focke-Wulf plant in 1943.

that industrial targets were not feasible since precision targeting was not a well-developed application. These ideas reflected Trenchard's proposals, discussed earlier. Additionally, flying during daylight, according to the RAF, invited Luftwaffe fighters to harass bombers. British Fighter Command had already demonstrated the folly of sending bombers without escorts against targets, when it defeated the Luftwaffe in the Battle of Britain. Because the RAF did not have adequate fighter escorts that could support the bomber offensive,[60] it switched to night-bombing missions to avoid detection.

The Luftwaffe still possessed a formidable air defense force despite being stretched with commitments from the deserts of North Africa to the steppes of Russia. German air defenses included the Freya early warning radar system, AAA, the new Würzburg fire-control radar, and two fighter aircraft—the

Messerschmitt Bf-109 and the Focke-Wulf Fw-190 (and, later, jet aircraft). The Luftwaffe did not initially use a centralized control system for its air defense system. However, as the CBO continued, the Luftwaffe started to concentrate its forces around seven aerial defensive zones under a single controller.[61] This change increased the efficiency and effectiveness of the Luftwaffe's air defenses.

On 17 August 1942, Eighth Air Force made its debut against German strategic targets when it bombed the Rouen-Sotteville rail marshalling yard in France. Bomber strength started to rise, but so did Luftwaffe opposition. The Eighth conducted missions in France, close to England, to ensure that some fighter escorts were in range of Supermarine Spitfires. Eighth Air Force began to receive longer-range P-47 Thunderbolt and P-38 Lightning fighter escorts. Bomber losses continued as the Luftwaffe Bf-109 and Fw-190 found a vulnerable area against the B-17 and B-24 aircraft—attacking head-on, where the bomber had reduced defensive armament. Luftwaffe air defenses were able to conduct mass attacks against bomber forces and exploit the bombers' lack of defensive armaments after German radar detected the raid. For example, on 17 April 1943, a force of 65 B-17s struck the Focke-Wulf aircraft-production plant in Bremen, Germany. The AAF lost 16 bombers on the raid. The commander of VIII Fighter Command, responsible for fighter escorts, demanded a 20-fighter group reinforcement to avoid the problems faced in Bremen. By May the AAF had received a sufficient number of P-47s and upgraded B-17Fs that had heavier nose armament. On 4 May, a force of 65 B-17Fs and B-24s, Spitfires, and P-47s attacked the former Ford and General Motors plant at Antwerp in the Netherlands. About 70 Luftwaffe fighters attacked, but no bombers were lost. The tactic of sending bombers into combat without escort fighters was ended. Eighth Air Force also had to delay the start of larger missions due to the transfer of bombers and fighters to support combat operations in North Africa and throughout the Mediterranean.

Eighth Air Force got stronger with each passing day through experience and reinforcements, allowing the AAF to strike further into Germany. The long-range escort problem was partially solved by pilots improving their flying experience with the P-47. Emboldened by this new capability, Eighth Air Force planners began to plan a raid on the ball-bearing plants in Schweinfurt and on the Messerschmitt plant at Regensburg. The P-47 escorts would fly near the German border. The fighter pilots would then refuel at their bases and meet the returning bombers. The Schweinfurt and Regensburg raid was scheduled for 17 August 1943. Bad weather and timing problems made it difficult for the fighter escorts to meet the bombers going to and from their targets. Both targets received heavy damage, but 60 of the 315 bombers sent into combat were lost. A follow-up attack on Schweinfurt on 14 October also resulted in heavy losses—60 aircraft from a 230-bomber force. Eighth Air Force could not sustain these numbers of aircraft and aircrew losses. However, replacements were found.

America's relentless economic growth and strength allowed it to manufacture aircraft in large numbers. The AAF started to expand and train more aircrews. Fighter strength started to grow and challenge the Luftwaffe, but the raids into Germany continued. Eighth Air Force planned another major offensive to decimate the Luftwaffe. Operation Argument was designed to disable Luftwaffe fighter-production facilities. These attacks started on 20 February 1944 and would directly curtail the Luftwaffe's fighter operations and force its fighters to meet AAF fighters escorting the bombers. The AAF now flew the P-51 Mustang, a plane superior to either the Bf-109 or Fw-190. These attacks would later be known as Big Week, discussed earlier. The operation was a smashing success. Over 1,000 B-17 and B-24 aircraft participated in the first day of raids. Airfields, aircraft-production facilities, marshalling yards, storage areas, and other targets of opportunity were blasted during Big Week. More importantly, the Luftwaffe's back was broken. It lost airframes and incurred large losses to its ever-decreasing pool of combat-ready pilots. Aircraft production was disrupted, and the Luftwaffe had to build more defensive fighters to defend the Reich instead of building other types of planes. The German military also suffered because the increased emphasis on building fighters reduced the capacity to build ground and naval weapons.

After Big Week, the AAF concentrated on hitting oil and petroleum targets and supporting the Normandy invasion in

France. The AAF also struck rail and road transportation to slow down production efforts. Eighth Air Force continued a war of attrition against the Luftwaffe. Bomber losses were still high. In the first week of March 1944, a single raid against Berlin lost 69 bombers. This was an example of AAF leadership forcing the Eighth to conduct combat operations deep into Germany.[62] Attacks against oil targets would reduce Luftwaffe and German military operations and force the Luftwaffe fighters to engage American bombers and their fighter escorts in combat. Fuel production started to fall. On 5 June 1944, the Luftwaffe Operations Staff was so concerned that it wrote, "The most essential requirements for training and carrying out production plans can scarcely be covered with the quantities of a/c [aircraft] fuel available."[63]

The AAF's participation in the CBO definitely supported the winning of the war against Germany. Eighth Air Force and other AAF units flew 501,536 bomber sorties that dropped 1,005,091 tons of bombs.[64] The campaign did not come without a heavy price—67,646 crewmen were killed, and AAF's bomber losses totaled 8,325 aircraft. The strategic attack disrupted military production, transportation, oil production, and the Luftwaffe; it also prepared the battlefield for an invasion of France. The buildup, training, planning, and employment of B-17 and B-24 bombers reflected ACTS and AAF doctrine and concepts. The AAF was able to force the German military to devote valuable resources towards defending the Reich and allowing American, British, and Soviet ground forces to advance on Germany and ultimately win the war. Instead of contesting these advances, the Luftwaffe was confined to defending Germany against air attacks. The German military, designed for blitzkrieg, was now put on the defensive. This consumed resources, time, opportunities, and training; it also forced a change in strategy. Over 82 percent of the Luftwaffe's strength was assigned to the Reich's defense by 1944.[65]

The strategic air campaign did not win the war singlehandedly, as the ACTS faculty might have thought and hoped. The AAF's CBO efforts focused on defeating the Luftwaffe and the German military's capability by destroying particular industrial targets. Instead, forcing the German fighters to engage Eighth Air Force's superior escort fighters also directly defeated the Luftwaffe. Additionally, having to confront a large German fighter force made the concept of unescorted bomber missions infeasible. The bombing campaign did inflict great damage on fighter production and did succeed in dispersing military production. Professor Wilhelm "Willy" Messerschmitt, designer of the Bf-109 and other aircraft, estimated that this industrial dispersion reduced German aircraft-production ca-

Adolph Hitler inspects bomb damage in a German city in 1944. The Combined Bomber Offensive affected German morale.

pacity by 50 percent.[66] The German economy also suffered through attacks on oil, transportation, and industry.

AAF bombers could have improved their performance in several ways. Besides the inclusion of fighter escorts, better targeting would have increased the effectiveness of the CBO. For example, the United States Strategic Bombing Survey, conducted after the war, believed that the destruction of propeller and aircraft-engine industries would have been more effective than attacking aircraft-assembly plants. Additionally, the attack on ball-bearing plants was found to be not as detrimental to German production as once thought. The Germans could easily import ball bearings, disperse the industry, or create substitutes for this product. Despite the CBO's best efforts, German aircraft engineers and production staffs were able to build a number of jet aircraft and rocket systems that would become operational before the war's end.

The slow buildup of forces also delayed the bombing campaign. Notwithstanding American industrial capacity, bombing the Reich was slowed due to diversions of resources and efforts to other theaters, such as North Africa and the Pacific. Most of the munitions were dropped on Germany in the last months of the war, when Eighth Air Force had a full complement of bombers. Targeting many diverse areas also diluted the bombing effort. German industry was also a resilient target. German production used only a fraction of its full capacity and was able to compensate for AAF bomber damage. Hansell, one of the AWPD-1 authors, admitted that the assumption of Germany's being under full mobilization was an issue.[67] The ACTS assumed that a nation at war would be at full mobilization and that the entire industrial capacity would be targeted. This was critical for the strategic air campaign to work. CBO efforts by themselves did not close down the German economy, but in combination with a Soviet and British-American ground invasion, those efforts caused the German war machine to fold.

Notes

1. Wlliamson Murray, *Strategy for Defeat: The Luftwaffe, 1933–1945* (Maxwell AFB, Ala.: Air University Press, 1983), 45.

2. R. J. Overy, *The Air War, 1939–1945* (Chelsea, Mich.: Scarborough House, 1991), 31.

3. Derek Wood with Derek Dempster, *The Narrow Margin: The Battle of Britain and the Rise of Air Power, 1930–1940* (Washington, D.C.: Smithsonian Institution Press, 1990), 163.

4. Murray, 48.

5. Ibid., 40, table 3.

6. Ibid., 46.

7. Robin Higham, "The Royal Air Force and the Battle of Britain," in *Case Studies in the Achievement of Air Superiority*, ed. Benjamin Franklin Cooling (Washington, D.C.: Center for Air Force History, 1994), 131.

8. Len Deighton, *Battle of Britain* (London: George Rainbird Limited, 1980), 101.

9. Richard Hough and Denis Richards, *The Battle of Britain* (New York: Norton, 1989), 310.

10. Murray, 53, table 9.

11. Chaim Herzog, *The Arab-Israeli Wars: War and Peace in the Middle East* (New York: Random House, 1982), 149.

12. Brereton Greenhaus, "The Israeli Experience," in *Case Studies in the Achievement of Air Superiority*, 576.

13. Ibid., 577.

14. Herzog, 151.

15. Lon O. Nordeen, *Air Warfare in the Missile Age* (Washington, D.C.: Smithsonian Institution Press, 1985), 117.

16. Daniel J. March et al., *The Aerospace Encyclopedia of Air Warfare*, vol. 2, *1945 to the Present* (London: Aerospace Publishing Limited, 1997), 159.

17. Ibid., 162.

18. Edward Jablonski, *America in the Air War* (Alexandria, Va.: Time-Life Books, 1982), 121.

19. David A. Anderton, *The History of the U.S. Air Force* (New York: Crescent Books, 1981), 85.

20. Richard Overy, *Why the Allies Won* (New York: Norton, 1995), 129.

21. Bernard C. Nalty, ed., *Winged Shield, Winged Sword: A History of the United States Air Force*, vol. 1 (Washington, D.C.: Air Force History and Museums Program, 1997), 301.

22. March et al., 160.

23. Richard Hallion, *Strike from the Sky: The History of Battlefield Air Attack, 1911–1945* (Washington, D.C.: Smithsonian Institution Press, 1989), 189.

24. Thomas B. Buell et al., *The Second World War: Europe and the Mediterranean*, West Point Military History Series (Wayne, N.J.: Avery, 1989), 274.

25. Hallion, 196.

26. March et al., 164.

27. Overy, *Why the Allies Won*, 162.

28. March et al., 166.
29. Buell et al., 310.
30. Hallion, 205.
31. Overy, *The Air War*, 77.
32. W. A. Jacobs, "Operation OVERLORD," in *Case Studies in the Achievement of Air Superiority*, 271.
33. Louis Morton, *Strategy and Command: The First Two Years* (Washington, D.C.: Office of the Chief of Military History, 1962), 105.
34. Shigeru Fukudome, "Hawaii Operation," in *The Japanese Navy in World War II: In the Words of Former Japanese Naval Officers*, ed. Raymond O'Connor (Annapolis: Naval Institute Press, 1986), 5.
35. Ibid., 11.
36. Stetson Conn, Rose C. Engelman, and Byron Fairchild, *Guarding the United States and Its Outposts* (Washington, D.C.: Office of the Chief of Military History, 1964), 151.
37. Leatrice R. Arakaki and John R. Kuborn, *7 December 1941: The Air Force Story* (Hickam AFB, Hawaii: Office of History, 1991), 11.
38. James P. Tate, *The Army and Its Air Corps: Army Policy toward Aviation, 1919–1941* (Maxwell AFB, Ala.: Air University Press, 1998), 178.
39. Arakaki and Kuborn, 14.
40. Carl Smith, *Pearl Harbor, 1941* (Botley, Oxford: Osprey, 1999), 37.
41. E. B. Potter, ed., *Sea Power: A Naval History* (Annapolis: Naval Institute Press, 1981), 289.
42. Ibid., 338.
43. Mitsuo Fuchida, "The Attack on Pearl Harbor," in *The Japanese Navy in World War II*, 27.
44. James A. Winnefeld, Preston Niblack, and Dana J. Johnson, *A League of Airmen: U.S. Air Power in the Gulf War* (Santa Monica, Calif.: RAND, 1994), 63.
45. Ibid., 64.
46. Nalty, 456.
47. Ibid.
48. Thomas A. Keaney and Eliot A. Cohen, *Revolution in Warfare? Air Power in the Persian Gulf* (Annapolis: Naval Institute Press, 1995), 55.
49. Richard G. Davis, "Strategic Bombardment in the Gulf War," in *Case Studies in Strategic Bombardment*, ed. R. Cargill Hall (Washington, D.C.: Air Force History and Museums Program, 1998), 558.
50. Ibid.
51. Richard P. Hallion, *Storm over Iraq: Air Power and the Gulf War* (Washington, D.C.: Smithsonian Institution Press, 1992), 158, table 5.3.
52. Stan Morse, *Gulf Air War Debrief* (London: Aerospace Publishing, Limited, 1991), 49.
53. United States General Accounting Office (GAO), *Operation Desert Storm: Evaluation of the Air Campaign*, GAO/NSIAD-97-134 (Washington, D.C.: GAO, 1997), 148.
54. Ibid., 148–49.

55. Keaney and Cohen, 102–3.

56. Michael S. Sherry, *The Rise of American Air Power: The Creation of Armageddon* (New Haven, Conn.: Yale University Press, 1987), 98–99.

57. Geoffrey Perret, *Winged Victory: The Army Air Forces in World War II* (New York: Random House, 1993), 49.

58. Sherry, 99.

59. Stephen L. McFarland and Wesley P. Newton, "The American Strategic Air Offensive against Germany in World War II," in *Case Studies in Strategic Bombardment,* 189.

60. Christopher Shores, *Duel for the Sky* (Garden City, N.Y.: Doubleday, 1985), 173.

61. McFarland and Newton, 197.

62. Richard G. Davis, *Carl A. Spaatz and the Air War in Europe* (Washington, D.C.: Smithsonian Institution Press, 1992), 393.

63. Ibid., 399.

64. McFarland and Newton, 232.

65. Ibid., 237.

66. Ibid., 238.

67. Haywood S. Hansell Jr., *The Air Plan That Defeated Hitler* (Atlanta, Ga.: Higgins-McArthur/Longino & Porter, 1972), 198.

Chapter 4

Functions and Capabilities of Aerospace Power: Interdiction/Close Air Support

Interdiction: Striking the Enemy Before He Can Attack

Surface forces face many challenges, including enemy ground forces threatening their positions. Surface and air commanders face a dilemma. Should air forces directly attack a ground threat, or should they eliminate the threat by reducing its capability to attack? The former case is time sensitive and requires air forces to be ready for action and be responsive to the actions taken by an enemy force. Conversely, the latter case does not result in immediate action. Instead, air forces attack enemy units and supplies before they reach the battlefront. These actions may take time to produce an appropriate effect on the battlefield and are usually conducted in areas away from the immediate front and away from direct support for surface forces.

Air forces are well suited to support interdiction missions, which focus on air operations to destroy, disrupt, or disable enemy military forces before they reach the battlefield. Interdiction missions attempt to reduce the military capability of a ground force to effectively fight a war before friendly forces have to respond by maneuver or fire. For example, if air-interdiction missions are successful, a friendly ground force will not have to engage a fully equipped and manned enemy ground force. These conditions would reduce friendly casualties and increase the probability of success against a foe. Air interdiction can help shape the forces and conditions of a battlefield in favor of friendly ground forces.

There are three methods of conducting air-interdiction missions. First, air operations might try to destroy or reduce the number of enemy soldiers and supplies through attrition. The attack against enemy military forces before they reach a battlefield directly reduces their ability to fight. Second, air forces

US Navy fighter from the USS *Bon Homme Richard* conducting an interdiction mission against a bridge during the Korean War.

can create a blockage that delays or denies the enemy the ability to send personnel and material to the battlefront. This type of action creates a barrier of destruction that prevents the enemy from receiving reinforcements or supplies. The third method is to create systematic inefficiencies to delay logistical support. Air forces might destroy railroads, bridges, or roads to disrupt transportation networks, thus forcing the enemy to take long delivery routes that create distribution problems.[1]

Interdiction targets can take many forms. For example, naval airpower could strike ports and harbors, lines of communications, storage facilities, or submarine bases, albeit with usually lesser payloads than land-based aircraft. Interdiction is not restricted solely to ground operations. Naval forces can also be affected by interdiction missions. Most naval vessels require logistical support or, in the case of battle, reinforcements to continue a conflict. Aviation and ground forces can also conduct interdiction missions by using their helicopters, long-range tactical missiles, and artillery in direct missions against an enemy force. Interdiction missions by air forces provide a flexible capability for a commander to eliminate the requirement to fight a battle or, at the least, reduce the size of the conflict.

Air forces can conduct effective interdiction missions, but they need a concentrated effort in order to work. Ground or naval forces may legitimately require direct aerial support to defeat enemy forces. A commander needs to weigh the issues, costs, and benefits of conducting interdiction or CAS missions. This challenge can pit an air force commander against a surface commander over the use of limited aerospace power resources.

Operation Strangle: Korea, 1951

UN forces in Korea had managed to survive a North Korean invasion of the Republic of Korea (ROK) during 1950. Reversing a humiliating retreat down the Korean peninsula, UN forces conducted an amphibious assault at Inchon and pushed the Soviet Union and North Korean People's Army (NKPA), which was backed by the People's Republic of China (PRC), to the brink of destruction near the North Korean border with the PRC. The PRC responded with an attack across the Yalu River that forced UN and American forces to retreat once more, and the war stalemated in a conflict along a stable line south of Seoul, the ROK capital (fig. 6). The UN faced a PRC ground force of 300,000 men from the People's Liberation Army (PLA) and an NKPA with a combat strength of 553,000 men in November 1950.[2]

A war of attrition ensued throughout the Korean peninsula. The USAF proposed an aerial interdiction campaign to stem the flow of reinforcements and supplies to PRC and NKPA forces. The USAF's Fifth Air Force (5AF), the Navy's Task Force 77 (TF77) carrier force, and the Marine Corps's 1st Marine Air Wing were to conduct the interdiction campaign—Operation Strangle—beginning in the spring of 1951. Gen Matthew Ridgway, commander of UN forces, wanted to recapture Seoul and push the PLA and NKPA north. Operation Strangle would sever

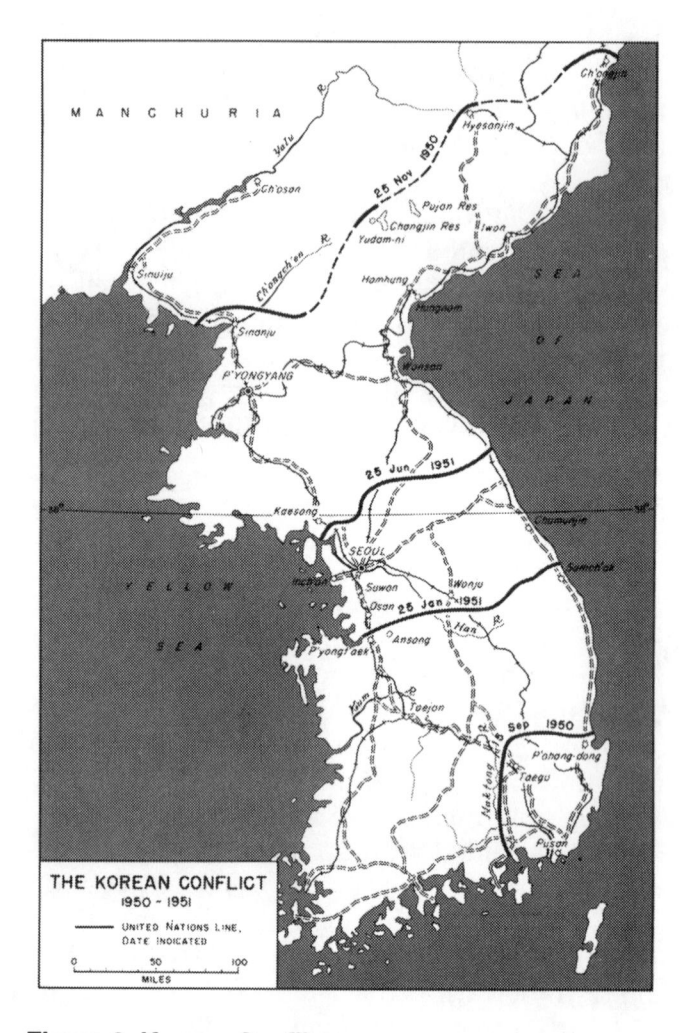

Figure 6. Korean Conflict

the supply lines of these forces, which stretched 150 miles from the Yalu River south.[3]

Fifth Air Force had attempted an earlier interdiction program, Interdiction Plan no. 4 (15 December 1950 to 30 May 1951), to choke off the PRC's use of railroads to resupply its forces. American aircraft, including World War II–era Boeing B-29 Superfortresses and Douglas B-26 Invaders, attacked a myriad of rail lines and connections throughout North Korea.

American intelligence analysts believed that if the rail lines were cut, the PRC would need 10,000 trucks to provide logistical support for its troops. The Chinese and Koreans had only 4,000 trucks between them.[4] The railroad system in North Korea had many parallel and transverse connections that made the network difficult to attack. The air forces could not attack all the connections simultaneously, and repairs were made to cuts in the line with a large labor pool available for construction. So enemy rail traffic continued, albeit using circuitous routes. Limited B-29 bombing sorties and MiG-15 fighters contributed to the reduced Interdiction Plan no. 4's ability to destroy key rail bridges. B-26 bombers tried to intercept motor transports, but the PRC and North Korean drivers switched to night convoys and used camouflage to hide their vehicles from attack during daylight. Fifth Air Force's F-51s, Lockheed P-80 Shooting Stars, and Republic F-84 Thunderjets, acting as armed reconnaissance forces—hunting for trucks and destroying targets of opportunity—soon faced deadly AAA fire. Losses jumped from three in January 1951 to 28 in April 1951. The interdiction program was not working. The PLA still had 18 divisions on the battlefield ready for combat. The railroad system was too tough to destroy.

Operation Strangle was implemented to improve the interdiction effort. North Korea was divided into sections to be attacked by USAF, Navy, or Marine Corps aircraft, which would concentrate on attacking the road network from a rail line to the front.[5] Strangle's targets centered on seven main enemy supply lines running from the PRC to the front. However, as UN air forces destroyed or damaged the roadways, the Chinese and Koreans took measures to counteract the attacks. Instead of using main roads, traffic was diverted to secondary ones. American aircrews did their best to destroy bridges and roads by using time-delay bombs to discourage repairs, but Chinese and Korean labor gangs used rifle fire to explode the bombs or accepted any casualties to repair the damage.[6] UN air forces also dropped tetrahedral tacks to puncture tires, used aerial mines, and cratered roads. North Korean engineer units were stationed at key points along major supply lines to repair any damage. These units rapidly repaired the roads. UN intelligence analysts estimated that road traffic had increased,

B-29 bombers over Korea could not stem the flow of materiel and manpower from North Korean and Communist Chinese forces.

and the PLA and NKPA were able to stockpile 800 tons of supplies a day. They would soon have a large strategic reserve to conduct a major ground offensive.[7]

B-26 bombers continued interdiction operations by flying at night. Attacking convoys required precision; bombing at night compounded the problem since pilots needed to use flares for illumination. Unfortunately, the only combat aircraft using flares, the B-29, had a dismal 50 percent failure rate for its flares.[8] C-47 transports were better, but they were vulnerable to AAA fire; furthermore, defense operations limited their availability for interdiction missions. Weather, terrain, and the difficulty of finding targets at night made these measures questionable. The attack on roads and convoys started to fizzle. Fifth Air Force looked for another alternative to interdict the enemy.

Operation Strangle's focus shifted to attacking the railroad networks. The PRC and North Korea had always used railways to transport the vast majority of their supplies to the front.[9] Intelligence experts from 5AF estimated that only 120 boxcars per day were needed to supply the entire enemy war effort at the front. The rail line interdiction program had three attack options: bomb rail bridges, destroy rolling stock, or sever rail track and roadbeds. Aircraft from TF77 had conducted an extensive bridge-busting program on Korea's eastern coast. Bridges were repeatedly struck, but they were soon repaired or bypassed. Rear Adm R. A. Ofstie, commander of TF77, admitted that the Navy fliers created major gaps in the rail network, but supplies still got through by truck.[10] Additionally, if the communists could repair the bridge, they could anticipate another attack by air forces. They could station AAA units to shoot down the planes. Analysts with 5AF also concluded that since the PLA and North Koreans needed relatively few boxcars to resupply their forces, they could not destroy enough of them to stop their effort.[11] The only remaining option was to bomb railway tracks and roadbeds. Aircraft could attack anyplace along a rail line without fear of AAA. Camouflaging track was difficult, and replacing track would require heavy equipment that the Chinese and Koreans did not possess. Railway track and roadbeds became the main target, along with a few rail bridges.

Aircraft from TF77 and 5AF as well as strategic bombers started to bomb their targets. The majority of air operations in Korea concentrated on this interdiction effort. Gen James A. Van Fleet, commander of Eighth Army, reduced ground requirements for CAS to a total of eight sorties per day per division—a total of a mere 96 sorties.[12] Cutting a rail line in several places also compounded the enemy's repair problems. Fifth Air Force estimated that Operation Strangle, now renamed Saturate, would last 90 days.

Operation Saturate's purpose was to cut the rail lines faster than the enemy could repair them. Rail lines were abandoned or kept open only after a major repair effort was launched. Aircraft from TF77 closed major railway tracks along the eastern coast. However, problems soon started to appear.

Enemy countermeasures were enacted to thwart the interdiction campaign. Use of AAA and automatic weapons directed at aircraft skyrocketed from about 200 weapons in January 1951 to about 1,200 in November 1951.[13] UN losses mounted for all types of aircraft. Because aircrews had to expend more efforts to avoid AAA, bombing accuracy plummeted by half. Additionally, MiG-15s, aided by drop tanks to increase their range south, started to attack aircraft on interdiction missions. This confined the area of operations for most 5AF aircraft. If they were "bounced" by the MiG-15s, then they dropped their bombs before hitting their targets and flew home. MiG-15s also forced B-29 bombers to switch to night attacks to avoid being shot down. Night operations reduced the number of bomber sorties and bombing accuracy, which affected the interdiction effort. North Korean labor units also became more adept at repairing railway track and bridges. South Korean agents of the USAF's Office of Special Investigations observed North Korean labor units fixing railway track within six to eight hours after the attack and replacing large bridges in no more than two to four days.[14] Fifth Air Force would need even more aircraft to keep pace with the North Korean repairs. No additional aircraft were forthcoming to support the effort. US Air Force and Navy resources were also being used in Europe and other contingencies. The technology available to conduct night and precision attacks was not in use. If the interdiction aircraft had obtained such devices, perhaps the assault on roads and railways would have seen better results. Finally, the consumption of supplies by the PLA and NKPA was much smaller than Western intelligence analysts had estimated. American Army divisions required 500 tons per day of supplies. PLA divisions, although 50 percent the size of a comparable American unit, used fewer than 40 tons. Interdiction of such small amounts of supplies would require an extensive effort. By December 1951, 5AF conceded that Operation Saturate had failed.

The interdiction efforts throughout Korea were massive. Aircrews from 5AF flew 87,522 sorties, made over 19,000 railway-track cuts, claimed to have destroyed 34,211 vehicles, wrecked 276 locomotives, and knocked out 3,820 railway cars.[15] Despite these efforts, the PLA and NKPA were still supplied and waged war with the UN. Many ground commanders were convinced that aerial interdiction had achieved little and that the best use of airpower was CAS. The PLA and NKPA were able to stockpile supplies. However, aerial interdiction did disrupt enemy operations, and, more importantly, there was no major offensive conducted by the enemy during or after the interdiction campaign started. Rail lines were cut, and resources were diverted to repair them. Indeed, the aerial interdiction effort did not prove itself to ground-force commanders as airpower advocates had hoped it would. UN forces had to overcome such problems as covering a large area against an enemy who did not rely heavily on logistics and using aircraft not equipped to conduct an interdiction campaign.

The Easter Offensive:
Airpower Halts the North Vietnamese

The American ground involvement in Vietnam had reached a climax in the Tet offensive in 1968. After the combined Vietcong and North Vietnamese offensive had surprised South Vietnamese and US forces, the withdrawal of American ground forces proceeded, greatly aided by intense international and domestic political pressure for a negotiated settlement. The US policy of direct involvement became one of aiding the South Vietnamese government to shoulder more of the defensive requirements while American forces were withdrawn. Under President Richard M. Nixon, the process of Vietnamization proceeded, and only a handful of American ground advisers and few USAF units were stationed in Vietnam. The Paris Peace Accords were dragging on, and the end of hostilities in Vietnam seemed far away, but the American military presence was shrinking fast. The North Vietnamese government gained strength and waited until American forces were at their lowest to begin operations to invade South Vietnam. There were only 95,000 US forces in South Vietnam—down from a high of 500,000 in 1969.[16]

On 30 March 1972, North Vietnamese armor and infantry units rolled across the northern border of South Vietnam through the demilitarized zone (DMZ). Three North Vietnamese Army (NVA) divisions—over 40,000 troops—pushed south, supported by artillery, rockets, and SAMs.[17] The North Vietnamese had been infiltrating regular NVA soldiers into the south in anticipation of the invasion. The NVA also launched an attack from Cambodia in hopes of capturing Saigon, the capital of South Vietnam.

Units of the Army of the Republic of Vietnam (ARVN), defending the northern provinces of South Vietnam, were overrun and forced to retreat. The three-pronged attack on ARVN and the South Vietnamese government threatened to divide the nation quickly. Nixon ordered American airpower to take the field to stem the invasion since he did not want to threaten the withdrawal of further ground troops and thus halt Vietnamization.[18] Nixon ordered the remaining 6,000 American ground forces not to engage the NVA. Airpower could swiftly enter the conflict and leave the area without threatening to create a new, sustained presence in South Vietnam. The USAF's only combat unit stationed in South Vietnam was a McDonnell-Douglas F-4 Phantom wing at Da Nang, but the Air Force also had three wings of F-4s in Thailand. Fortunately, the USAF had several B-52 bomber units stationed at Andersen AFB, Guam. The USAF and Navy were ordered to send more airpower to South Vietnam to stem the rising invasion tide.

Operation Constant Guard was initiated to replenish airpower's strength in South Vietnam and stop the invasion. F-4 strength was boosted from 185 to 374; 124 B-52s were de-

The F-4E fighter, similar to the one shown here, helped stem the tide in the Easter offensive of 1972.

ployed to Guam; and C-130s, F-111As, and KC-135 tankers came from USAF units around the world to South Vietnam. Units were sending aircraft to South Vietnam within 72 hours of the request.[19] The Navy sent two additional aircraft carriers, followed by two more, to the existing two carriers off the coast of South Vietnam. The Marine Corps ordered two squadrons of F-4s, one squadron of A-6 bombers, and two squadrons of McDonnell-Douglas A-4E light-attack aircraft. The US Air Force had removed many of its air resources before the invasion and had to replace much of its capability to fight an air war.

The earlier war in South Vietnam was characterized by a guerilla action. The Vietcong and NVA stayed in the jungle or melted into the local populace to attack and harass the ARVN and American military units. American airpower operated under many restrictions: off-limit targets, artificial zones of responsibility (route packages), piecemeal attacks, centralized command and execution of missions, and other problems. By 1972 the NVA was using T-54, T-55, and amphibious PT-76 tanks. The North Vietnamese had switched to a conventional war to seize territory and defeat the ARVN in the field. The NVA was succeeding. The American military would respond with Operation Freedom Train.

Nixon decided to unleash an extensive bombing and interdiction campaign to stop the North Vietnamese in their tracks—thus, Operation Freedom Train was born. Its objectives were to restrict the flow of supplies to North Vietnam from its allies, destroy enemy military suppliers and stores, and stop the flow of supplies from North to South Vietnam.[20] Eventually, Nixon authorized the mining of North Vietnam's major port, Haiphong. Earlier administrations were afraid to mine or bomb the port due to potential damage to Soviet, Chinese, or other nations' ships, which could have led to extensive political damage to the war effort. Given this self-imposed restriction, the Soviets and Chinese were able to keep the supply lines open to North Vietnam with impunity.

On 3 April, American air forces were authorized to strike SAM, AAA, artillery, and logistical targets as far north as 53 miles above the border of South Vietnam. The Joint Chiefs of Staff (JCS) later authorized the attack of targets throughout North Vietnam's panhandle (the area that connected North and South Vietnam). American air forces were given the green light to inflict maximum damage against the enemy's air defense, artillery, and logistical support. The US Air Force's Seventh Air Force (7AF), the Navy's TF77, and Strategic Air Command's (SAC) B-52s were given certain geographic areas of responsibility. The Seventh had the responsibility of striking targets from the DMZ north to about 100 miles near the 18th parallel, and TF77 would strike north of the Air Force's area for about 25 miles. The task force's interdiction effort would include transshipment points, storage areas, highways, roads, waterways, and any target that supported the NVA's war effort in the south.[21]

Aircraft of 7AF, TF77, SAC, and the South Vietnamese Air Force (VNAF) attacked North Vietnamese supply lines in South Vietnam and throughout the North Vietnamese panhandle. In March 1972, there were 4,237 sorties; the number of missions in April jumped to 17,171 and increased to 18,444 by the end of May.[22] Airpower was heavily involved in the fight. The VNAF contributed about one-third of the total effort. Vietnamization had delivered a trained air force, and it was being used to defend South Vietnam. By 16 April, Nixon expanded the war by allowing B-52s to bomb Haiphong harbor and its surrounding facilities.

Airpower was striking NVA logistics in South Vietnam, the transportation network in the North Vietnamese panhandle, and targets in North Vietnam. Nixon's goal was to halt the North Vietnamese ground offensive and rescue the South Vietnamese—not recapture lost territory.[23] The interdiction effort and an extended bombing campaign in North Vietnam became an effort to coerce the NVA to leave South Vietnam and stop the Easter offensive. Nixon authorized further bombing missions in North Vietnam to begin on 8 May. These raids, Operation Linebacker I, allowed a resumption of bombing. About 1,800 sorties were conducted over North Vietnam in the first three days of Linebacker while other aircraft attacked NVA troops and supply lines in South Vietnam. A total interdiction campaign was initiated to halt all NVA supplies and reinforcements going into South Vietnam.

President Nixon listed three main objectives for the combined air and naval campaign against North Vietnam. During

INTERDICTION/CLOSE AIR SUPPORT

a three-day air campaign, Linebacker would use B-52s and other tactical aircraft to hit targets in the north that would create supply and troop shortages in the south and limit the war-fighting capability of NVA forces in South Vietnam. Linebacker's objectives were to

- reduce the flow of supplies into North Vietnam,
- destroy existing stockpiles of supplies in North Vietnam, and
- reduce the flow south from North Vietnam.[24]

These objectives mirrored the earlier goals to stop supplies and reinforcements into South Vietnam. Now, the entire country of North Vietnam might be affected by restricting the import of resources into Haiphong. The interdiction campaign took on an expanded meaning. B-52 raids threatened to widen the war and escalate the conflict into a new American war unless the NVA withdrew. Linebacker had another goal—to get the stalled peace talks back on track.

North Vietnamese air defenses were not easily defeated, and they were active throughout Linebacker. SAM, AAA, and MiG fighter interceptors were ready to oppose the air assault. The North Vietnamese started to shoot SAMs at record levels during Freedom Train and Linebacker. American air losses for April, May, and June hit 52 aircraft. American air forces continued the attack and racked up 27,745 sorties over the north.[25] Seventh Air Force, TF77, and SAC B-52s started to target rail lines, roads, bridges, and marshalling yards, as well as equipment repair, oil and petroleum storage/refinery, and electrical power facilities as Linebacker geared up. The Navy started to mine Haiphong harbor under Operation Pocket Money. If that operation succeeded, then supplies would have to be rerouted through China—a time-consuming effort—and American air forces could pinch off their transport by attacking the surface-transportation network. The USAF recognized that Hanoi, the capital of North Vietnam, was a key logistics center—key to the country's limited production capability, storage area, and C^2 center. The Hanoi area became a target too. If Hanoi and Haiphong were isolated, the air forces could concentrate on shutting the flow of supplies and reinforcements south.

The Linebacker raids had four phases. The first would strike rail lines in and around Hanoi plus railways leading to China. The second phase concentrated on targeting storage facilities and marshalling yards. Air Force and Navy crews would then hit secondary storage and transshipment points used by the North Vietnamese in response to the first two phases. The fourth phase would strike enemy air defenses: C^2, SAM, AAA, airfields, and other targets. This last phase would start when air commanders believed that air defenses needed to be destroyed to accomplish the first three phases.

Air commanders were faced with a dilemma. Should they concentrate their efforts on striking targets in North Vietnam or stem the immediate flow of supplies in the south? Although the United States had sent many reinforcements to South Vietnam, the air resources to conduct Freedom Train and Linebacker were limited. The targets in North Vietnam were more lucrative, but the number of attack sorties in South Vietnam outnumbered those in Hanoi-Haiphong by a ratio of four to one.[26] However, the raids in the north were aided by the introduction of PGMs. Missions that would have required many aircraft using gravity bombs, unchanged since World War I, were replaced by television- or laser-guided munitions that needed only one aircraft to execute. The number of missions over North Vietnam was also limited due to the lack of night-bombing capability. Air assets in the south did not have to fight radar-guided SAMs, AAA, or MiGs that could attack aircraft under conditions of reduced visibility. This constraint was lessened when 7AF received the all-weather and night-capable F-111A fighter-bomber. The Linebacker raids, although freer from restrictions than previous campaigns, had some limitations. Certain areas in Hanoi were off limits to attack.

Despite these restrictions, Linebacker succeeded in pounding the logistical capabilities of North Vietnam and put pressure on the enemy government to withdraw the NVA from South Vietnam. Once Haiphong harbor was mined and the American air forces could use PGMs to destroy key bridges and rail lines, reinforcements and the resupply effort to support the NVA started to slow down. However, the effort to significantly reduce petroleum supplies to North Vietnam was largely unsuccessful because of North Vietnamese efforts to disperse their oil-distribution system and a well-camouflaged oil pipeline from China that escaped destruction.[27] Interdiction efforts in the south benefited from the lack of an extensive SAM system, the absence of MiGs, better intelligence, and shorter flight times to respond to commanders and increase the sortie rate.

The Easter offensive ultimately faltered by June 1972, when the ARVN, with extensive air support, recaptured much of its lost territory. The North Vietnamese had stockpiled supplies to last through the summer; oil pipelines were not seriously disrupted; and supplies, albeit reduced, were moved from China via truck instead of rail. The interdiction effort did reduce supplies, and the efforts to capture South Vietnam were thwarted. If airpower had not been used, the invasion of South Vietnam would have been unopposed, and the NVA could have controlled the south.

The enemy's use of conventional forces to invade South Vietnam had increased its reliance on logistics, which compromised the NVA's operations because of the vulnerability of its supply lines. Additionally, the heavy demand for supplies made the NVA sensitive to shortages created by the Linebacker bombing campaigns and Freedom Train strikes. The destruction of logistical transportation capability also strained the limited mobility resources available to the NVA. These limited resources could either haul supplies or be used in the south to support combat operations. Lines of communications were disrupted, and the NVA was left with finding ways to overcome these problems. Although the NVA was not ultimately defeated, it was forced to admit defeat at this point, stop its offensive operations, and return to the Paris peace talks. According to Gen William A. Momyer, former 7AF commander, the use of airpower in South Vietnam and Linebacker during the Easter offensive was the most significant factor in turning around the peace negotiations.[28]

Interdiction at Sea: The Battle of the Bismarck Sea

In March 1943, the Allies were slowly pushing the Japanese forces out of New Guinea and the rest of the Southwest Pacific Area (SWPA). Gen Douglas MacArthur, commander of Allied forces in SWPA, was successful in pushing Japanese army units out of Guadalcanal by using his naval, air, and ground forces. The Japanese were being attacked throughout SWPA and required reinforcements throughout the region. American and Australian forces were on the offensive, and the Imperial Japanese army and navy were suddenly on the defensive. The Japanese transferred two divisions from Korea and northern China to shore up their defensive line in New Guinea.[29] Control of New Guinea was still in doubt. If New Guinea remained in Japanese hands, an invasion of Australia was possible. Lt Gen Adachi Hatazo, commander of the newly created Eighteenth Army, decided to relocate his headquarters from Rabaul, New Britain, to Lae, New Guinea, to increase the Japanese army's pressure on the Allied forces. He planned to transit the Bismarck Sea with the 51st Division in a convoy and land in New Guinea (fig. 7).

MacArthur had received intelligence from the US Navy that indicated the Japanese would send the 51st Division via convoy to Lae, with up to 12 transports protected by destroyers.[30] If MacArthur could eliminate the 51st before it reached Lae, then control of the area might fall into Allied hands. Airpower could be used to sink the convoy before the ground forces hit the beaches in New Guinea. The challenge fell on MacArthur's air commander, Maj Gen George Kenney, a recent addition to the Allied SWPA staff. MacArthur had gone through several air commanders because of the lack of progress using airpower. Kenney came armed with some unconventional ideas. High-altitude precision daylight bombing did not work in the Pacific as well as it did in Europe. European targets were industrial ones while Pacific targets frequently were moving ships or ground forces. Pacific bombing operations were hardly a success. B-17 bombers failed to sink any ships in the Battle of Midway in 1942 and were a disappointment throughout the Pacific theater. There was much doubt on MacArthur's staff about the value of airpower.

Kenney believed that the chance of hitting a moving ship would increase if he could change how his Air Force units would operate against the enemy. Kenney did not have any carrier-based aircraft that were designed to sink naval ships. Instead, SWPA air forces needed to modify Kenney's aircraft to

INTERDICTION/CLOSE AIR SUPPORT

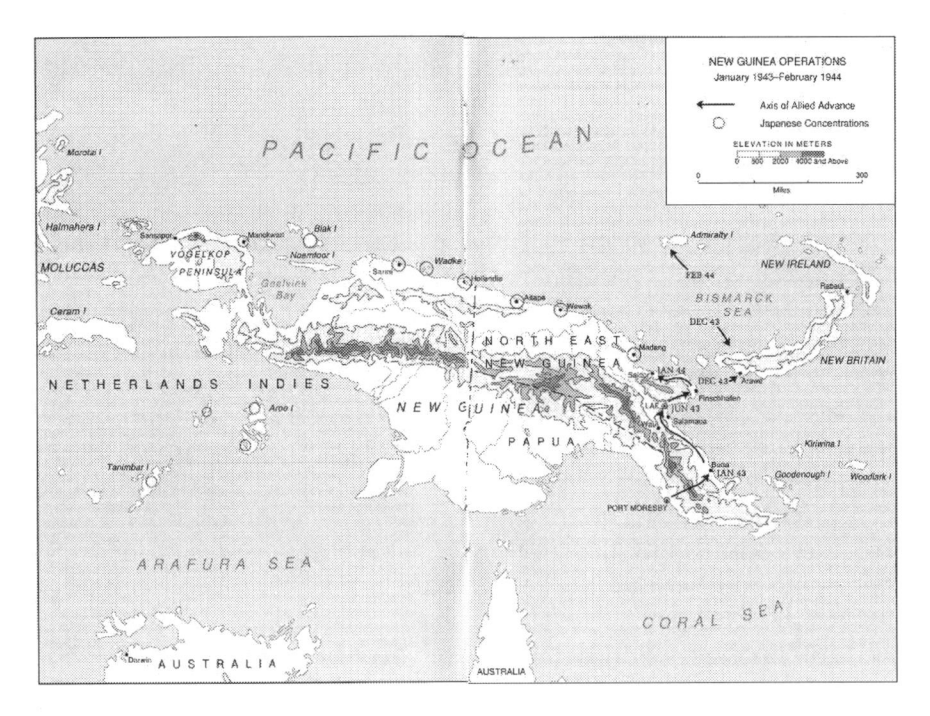

Figure 7. New Guinea

do the job. Kenney had a relatively small force of 207 bombers and 129 fighters. Unfortunately for Kenney and MacArthur, the United States and Britain had agreed that the first goal was for the Allies to defeat Germany first. This meant that the best aircraft were sent to Europe rather than the Pacific. Second-rate aircraft were allocated to Kenney. But this secondary status did not stop him. He ordered his engineers to modify aircraft to meet his needs. For example, SWPA's AAF engineers added forward-firing .50-caliber machine guns to 30 North American B-25C Mitchell medium bombers. The engineers also added four more guns to blisters on the aircraft's side. This modification allowed the B-25 to strafe a ship and knock out any AAA threat on ships' decks. The B-25's bomb payload was also changed to carry 60 small fragmentation bombs and six 100-pound demolition bombs with delayed fuses.[31] Kenney also used parachute-fitted bombs to improve accuracy.

147

SWPA aircrews also practiced bombing targets at an altitude of 150 feet. Kenney soon realized that his aircraft would increase their chances of hitting a ship if they attacked at a lower altitude. B-25 and Douglas A-20 Havoc light bombers experimented with skip bombing or "masthead" attack techniques. This bombing technique was similar in practice to skipping stones; instead of hitting a target from the top, however, a bomb would strike the target—a ship—in its side.

Armed with a warning that the Japanese planned their move towards Lae, Kenney was ready for action with his new air force. B-24 bombers kept Rabaul under observation for any Japanese convoy activity. Hatazo moved out of Rabaul with 6,912 soldiers and crews of the 51st Division and convoy crew members at midnight on 28 February 1943, into the Bismarck Sea towards Lae.[32] The convoy was composed of eight transports and eight destroyers. The Japanese hoped for bad weather to limit visibility and reduce the chances of being attacked by Kenney. They assigned about 80 fighters to provide air coverage over the convoy.[33] Kenney had around 150 aircraft, half of them P-38 fighters. On 1 March, SWPA reconnaissance aircraft spotted the convoy 150 miles west of Rabaul.[34] Land-based aircraft were now poised to defeat a fleet. Mitchell's ideas about airpower sinking ships would be put to the test. If the SWPA aircraft could sink the Japanese, the enemy on New Guinea would be dealt a serious blow.

The Japanese convoy was struck by three waves of long-range B-17 bombers from the 43d Bomb Group, guided by B-24 reconnaissance reports. The B-17s dropped 1,000-pound bombs from an altitude of 6,500 feet. Half of the transports were sunk or sinking. Kenney had intended to sink the enemy ships in deep water to reduce the chance of rescuing enemy survivors.[35] Two destroyers picked up some survivors from the transports and made a dash for Lae to drop rescued soldiers off on New Guinea. The rest of the convoy continued on its fateful way, closer to the bombs of the modified B-25s and fighter aircraft.

SWPA medium bombers and fighters were ready to finish off the convoy. On 2 March, 30 modified B-25Cs, A-20s, and Australian Beaufighter aircraft were ready to strike. Flying in low, the aircraft avoided Japanese Zero fighter coverage that was ready to pounce on any B-17s. The Japanese fighter coverage was flying at 7,000 feet above the convoy and was caught off guard by Kenney's low-level bombing strikes.[36] From 1000 hours to nightfall, Allied airpower repeatedly struck the Japanese convoy. Aircraft attacked at wave height, low, and medium altitudes. Skip bombing and strafing worked magnificently. The US Navy's Seventh Fleet added to the fray by sending patrol torpedo boats to attack the convoy. At the end of the day, all of the remaining transports were sunk, four of the eight destroyers sunk, and many Japanese aircraft shot out of the skies. The Japanese convoy lay broken and burning in the Bismarck Sea.

The next day, 3 March, aircraft continued to strafe the remnants of the convoy. American and Australian aircraft were victorious, sinking 12 ships in three days. Out of 6,912 Japanese troops and crews on the convoy, 3,664 were killed. Fewer than 700 soldiers reached Lae. The Allies lost only four planes shot down, with 13 killed and 12 wounded.[37] This interdiction mission also influenced the Japanese strategy of directly sending reinforcements to their forces in New Guinea. The Japanese would not send supplies or troop replacements directly to Lae. Instead, they would send them up to 200 miles away from Lae and either transport them on smaller high-speed boats and submarines or overland through the jungle. The introduction of small barges and high-speed ships made their supply and reinforcements vulnerable to US Navy patrol torpedo boats and SWPA aircraft.[38] The Japanese lost an estimated 20,000 personnel transiting the sea from Rabaul to New Guinea after the Battle of the Bismarck Sea.[39] In both cases, the transfer of reinforcements and supplies was slower and consumed more resources by forcing Japanese engineers to build a road across northern New Guinea and use smaller vessels.

Land-based airpower was able to defeat a naval force almost single-handedly. Despite the lack of dive-bombers and torpedo attack planes designed to sink ships, Kenney's skip bombing and modified aircraft completed the job. The typical interdiction mission of attacking and disrupting men and materiel on the land took on another face: destruction of enemy resources at sea. Airpower could deliver a valuable tool of maneuver to force the Japanese to take excessive actions to avoid destruction by the SWPA forces. The Japanese were vulnerable, especially to interdiction of their naval assets that provided reinforcements and logistics support to island outposts. The US Navy also aided these efforts by using its submarine forces to sink any ships that escaped detection by air. The aerial interdiction efforts also grew as the Japanese started to lose their ability to contest the skies over the Pacific. The American aircraft industry also got into high gear and produced modern fighters and bombers in quantity; these were shared in the European and Pacific theaters. This had the effect of tightening the noose around Japan's neck. Japanese living conditions on New Guinea were getting abysmal. Approximately 40 percent of the Japanese force fighting in the steaming jungles of New Guinea were suffering from disease or starvation.[40]

MacArthur could now start a campaign of island hopping. These actions centered on avoiding pitched battles on enemy-held islands and letting the Japanese "starve on the vine" by cutting off their supplies. Since airpower was a deadly threat to the Japanese navy, this strategy was an effective method of defeating the enemy and avoiding American and Australian casualties. The Battle of the Bismarck Sea forced the Japanese largely to abandon any major efforts to take the offensive against the Americans and Australians on New Guinea. After isolating the Japanese, Kenney believed his air forces could then concentrate on supporting ground operations.[41] The Japanese dug into their island empire to await the oncoming Allied offensives—this spelled doom for the Japanese.

SWPA forces were also fortunate that they had intelligence indicating the Japanese were going to move their forces from Rabaul to Lae. The interception of Japanese naval codes gave Kenney advanced notification of the size of the convoy, departure and destination locations, and an approximate timing of the move. SWPA air forces were able to marshal sufficient reconnaissance aircraft to seek out the Japanese convoy.

Allied success at the Battle of the Bismarck Sea illustrated the importance of airpower to many skeptical ground commanders in the SWPA. MacArthur finally recognized the value of airpower. His opinion on airpower left no doubt when he advised a subordinate of Sir Louis Mountbatten, commander of the Southeast Asian theater, in fall 1943 to "tell him he will need more air and when you have told him, tell him again from me that he will need more air! And when you have told him that for a second time, tell him from me for the third time that he will still need more air!"[42] This transformation was due, in no small part, to the efforts of Kenney and the Battle of the Bismarck Sea.

Supporting the Troops with Close Air Support

One of a ground commander's worst nightmares is to be attacked and surrounded by an overwhelming number of enemy troops. Ground commanders normally have at their disposal artillery, surface-to-surface missiles, armor, and other weapons to help repel such attacks. Starting in World War I and reaching maturity in World War II, airpower provided a much-needed function of close air support. CAS provides direct assistance, through bombing or strafing, to troops directly engaged with enemy forces or in proximity to friendly forces. This is especially true for light infantry, airborne forces, or ground units getting ashore from a seaborne invasion. For example, if friendly forces are surrounded and being attacked, aircraft could bomb enemy forces that have encircled the friendly forces.

CAS has been the subject of many debates since its introduction on the battlefield. Airmen argued that interdiction was a more valuable use of limited aerial weapons. Conversely, ground commanders saw the immediate need of CAS to protect and support their soldiers in battle. Airmen could control and plan interdiction missions, but they would be "on-call" to respond to a CAS request. Interdiction allowed commanders to be more proactive and seek out the enemy, whereas CAS was a reactive function that tied up resources waiting for a mission. However, CAS was and still is a very valuable tool for all commanders.

No military function or capability is infallible. Strategic attack and interdiction missions may not completely stop an enemy force from conducting operations against friendly ground forces. An example is a surprise combined air and ground

A-10s providing CAS in Kosovo in 1999

attack, such as the 1973 Yom Kippur War, in which Egyptian forces stymied and pushed Israeli armored and infantry units out of their defensive positions. This forced the IDF/AF to concentrate on CAS to stop the advance. Throughout modern war, cooperative efforts in the air and on the ground have proven to be an effective team for defeating enemy ground forces. The US Marine Corps almost exclusively devotes its own "organic" fixed-wing air forces to the support of ground operations.

Air and space forces need to balance the requirements and priorities for all of their functions: air and space superiority, strategic attack, interdiction, and CAS. If interdiction works, friendly ground forces will not even see a significant portion of an enemy's force. If not, airmen may need to apportion many of their resources to CAS. In either case, an aerospace leader needs to decide upon the appropriate number of interdiction and CAS missions, given the current situation. Conducting an exclusive interdiction campaign without regard to CAS may lead to a defeated friendly ground force and make the successful interdiction campaign a moot point. Conversely, using all air and space resources for CAS might not be an effective application of limited aerial weaponry. Aircraft might stay idle, and enemy forces might entrench their rear-area logistical support structure and defenses. Such a situation might lead to having to use even greater numbers of ground and air forces to defeat the enemy later on.

The debate over whether to use interdiction or CAS is a continuing one. Understanding the issues and the functions of CAS and interdiction will help one become aware of these concerns. Future military commanders need to use all their forces as effectively and efficiently as possible to maximize their firepower, maneuver, and exploitation of the battlefield. In certain situations, priorities may change, and either interdiction or CAS may become the more critical mission for the day. The availability of resources or political objectives may dictate switching from one type of mission to the other. This is one of the most valuable aspects of air and space power—the ability to conduct many types of missions, with limited resources, and in a short time frame.

Airpower Fails at Kasserine Pass

By early 1943, the US Army had landed and begun operations against German and Italian forces in North Africa. The Allies were slowly pushing the German Afrika Korps (DAK) out of Africa and forcing its retreat to Sicily and the Italian mainland. Although relatively new to the war, American ground commanders were itching to get into combat and prove their worth. The DAK's leaders, including *Generalfeldmarschall* Erwin Rommel, realized they were being put into a vise between the growing American strength in the west and the oncoming British Eighth Army in the east. Rommel planned to scrape together enough German and Italian forces to launch an offensive against the green American Army and then concentrate on the British. American and German forces would eventually meet at Kasserine Pass in Tunisia. In this battle, American ground forces would be defeated. Airpower—specifically, the lack of both CAS and air superiority—would be partly blamed. Based on this experience, the Allies would adopt a new doctrine that changed the face of airpower.

In the early days of World War II, Army Air Corps assets did not operate as an independent force. Instead, aircraft squadrons were divided among ground units. The ground commander was responsible for assigning missions to his aircraft. The only exception to control of air resources by ground officers was long-range strategic-bombardment units. They were controlled by a centralized source to conduct independent actions in direct support of a war effort. Small aviation forces were assigned to ground commanders to ensure rapid and exclusive CAS in operations.[43] There were still questions about who would control airpower and what was the most effective use of these resources.

Adding more confusion to this situation was a new Army doctrine incorporated into Field Manual (FM) 31-35, *Aviation in Support of Ground Forces*. CAS and other support missions were put under the control of the highest ground commander in-theater, but subordinate ground commanders could not direct the use of air units to conduct missions. They had to request missions through an air-support commander via a

Erwin Rommel, the Desert Fox, was a cunning foe to Allied forces in North Africa.

INTERDICTION/CLOSE AIR SUPPORT

theater commander. Ground commanders objected since their ability to use all available forces and ensure their unity of command was now disrupted. The control of airpower, especially CAS, was in doubt in 1942 and would seriously affect operations in North Africa, as well as later actions.

The Germans launched their strategy of conducting an offensive against the Americans and holding off British attacks in the west. German and Italian units conducted a massive offensive, and Allied forces were overrun. Tanks, half-tracks, artillery, munitions, supplies, and airfields were abandoned to the onrushing Germans. The Battle of Kasserine Pass in Tunisia, initiated on 18 February, began when Rommel ordered two DAK armor divisions to strike and push American forces out of the area (fig. 8). The Americans had built up a defensive line to contain further German advances in the area. German forces smashed American units and forced several units to retreat by the next day.

Allied air and ground units were thrown into the battle to stem the DAK's offensive. Airpower was rushed into the battle. Air Vice Marshal Sir Arthur Coningham, from the Western Desert Air Force, which supported the British Eighth Army, was put in command of the Allied Air Support Command. This command had responsibility for all tactical air-support missions, including CAS.[44] Coningham quickly saw many problems. Almost all of the Allied air missions were defensive in nature. Although the air forces conducted CAS missions, air units were hesitant to go on the offensive. Additionally, targets were numerous, but bombers and fighters tended to protect their assigned ground units. Coningham insisted that the existing tactic of creating "air umbrellas" to provide a protective bubble for ground units had to stop. Coningham demanded that air missions attack troop concentrations and vulnerable trucks. By going on the offensive, Allied aircraft should cause enemy attacks on ground forces to subside.

This change of policy would turn the fortune of war around for the Allies. One aspect that Coningham could not control, however, was the weather. Torrential rains turned airfields into seas of mud. Sortie rates dropped. Additionally, the loss of airfields close to the battlefront caused aircraft to fly at their maximum range to fight a battle. Payloads were reduced for

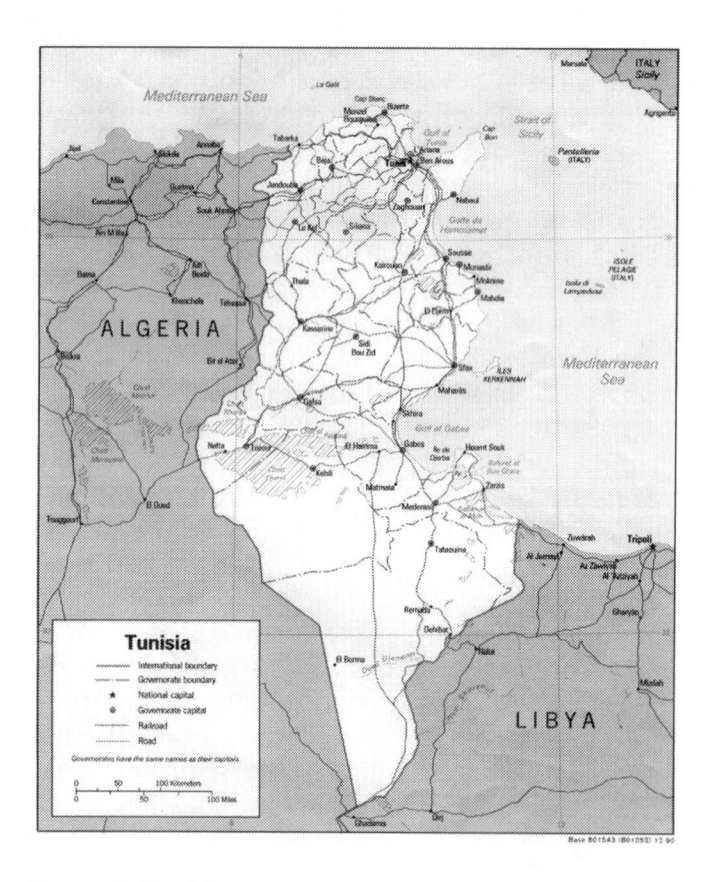

Figure 8. Tunisia

bombers, and fighters had less time contesting the skies against the Luftwaffe or strafing targets.

Allied ground forces eventually pushed the DAK out of the area, and Kasserine Pass was cleared on 21 February. By 22 February, the Germans were in retreat. Weather conditions continued to hamper air operations. As the weather improved, Coningham was able to enact a priority system of air missions throughout the area. Air units were no longer under the direct control of ground commanders. Coningham convinced Gen Dwight D. Eisenhower, commander of Allied forces for all of North Africa and the Mediterranean, that CAS needed to be allocated by priority due to the scarcity of aircraft.[45] Ground commanders would expect less CAS. However, ground commanders whose limited air resources did not give them enough CAS support in previous situations now received, in an emergency, more resources from a pool of centrally controlled aircraft.

Recriminations about the failure of airpower to support ground commanders started in earnest after the DAK was pushed back. Air-ground cooperation was lacking. There were insufficient aircraft to conduct important missions; aerial reconnaissance proved to be of little value to commanders; and bombing missions were too slow in execution to be effective. Experienced ground forces were afraid of firing on aircraft, unless they were fired upon, for fear of being attacked.[46] In other cases, ground forces shot at any aircraft—including friendly ones. Changes to air doctrine and policy were badly needed.

Coningham identified several areas to improve the support of ground forces. First, instead of creating a defensive umbrella that concentrated on air defense over a limited area, airpower should strive to gain air superiority over the entire region. Air units, theoretically, could have local air superiority over their area but could lose it if the Luftwaffe attacked each air umbrella one at a time. The Luftwaffe could use mass and the offensive to separately defeat the Allied air forces. Overall air superiority was a primary objective above all other requirements. Second, Coningham ordered a halt to the application of airpower on an on-call basis controlled by separate ground commanders. Another commander might view one ground commander's priority as a mere nuisance. Due to scarce air assets, requirements and requests for airpower could best serve the overall theater commander by centralizing the assignment of air missions. Third, Coningham pressed for control of air resources by an airman, not a ground commander. An airman better understood and had a broader theater perspective for the application of air superiority, strategic attack, interdiction, and CAS than did a ground commander. Ground commanders, in Coningham's eyes, fought the land campaign; air commanders fought two: the battle for air superiority and the battle in support of the ground commander to win the land campaign.[47] These observations would become codified into a new Army doctrine that would eventually affect the future of CAS.

The experience at Kasserine Pass and the overall performance of airpower in North Africa indicated a need to revise Army doctrine. Army Chief of Staff Marshall authorized Eisenhower to form a team of air and ground officers to revise the existing doctrine. The new doctrine, FM 100-20, *Command and Employment of Air Power*, reflected many of Coningham's ideas. FM 100-20, which differed greatly from FM 1-5, took effect on 21 July 1943—a swift change for a policy that included such radical changes. FM 100-20 codified the concept that air and land are "co-equal and interdependent; neither is an auxiliary of the other."[48] Although this segment of the doctrine did not give the AAF total independence, it was a great step towards equity between air and ground commanders. Air commanders still worked through a theater commander, but lower-level ground commanders could not treat air units as if they were subordinates.

The manual went further by defining the priority of employing airpower. Air superiority was first as a prerequisite for "any major land operation," followed by interdiction and CAS. The lesson of first achieving air superiority provided an opening for the growing AAF to push for a wider theater perspective for airpower. Interdiction also reflected the thought of using offensive actions to create situations in which ground forces did not have to fight larger surface conflicts. CAS received the third priority.

FM 100-20 also identified the idea that one of airpower's greatest strengths was its inherent flexibility. Airpower could provide an air or ground commander many capabilities. Aircraft could attack other aircraft, bomb strategic targets, strafe railways, or support operations near ground forces. The authors of FM 100-20 stressed that centralized control of these resources would enhance this flexibility to react in dynamic situations. Aircraft could mass and focus on different targets and defeat the enemy better than if they were acting in a piecemeal fashion. Additionally, an airman would control these air resources better than would a ground commander. An airman—knowledgeable about air missions, aircraft, and employment tactics, and aware of the air environment—could better serve the requirements of the ground commander.

INTERDICTION/CLOSE AIR SUPPORT

Out of the ashes of Kasserine Pass arose the foundations of new doctrine and policy that affected not only CAS, but also airpower's future in the AAF and the forthcoming US Air Force. The failure of CAS became a rallying point for discussing broad ideas of airpower. Not every reader agreed with FM 100-20. Some thought that it was an "AAF Declaration of Independence."[49] Others believed that the document was too "British" because of Coningham's influence in North Africa. Regardless of opinion, the doctrine of tactical air support was forged in North Africa and became a defining moment for CAS.

Gunships for Close Air Support in Vietnam

In 1965 a new weapon that carried miniguns in a transport airframe—the gunship—supported American Army units in South Vietnam. This marriage of modern gunnery weapons and relatively slow, propeller-driven transport airplanes flew in face of the USAF's push to employ jet aircraft. After this development, Army units were able to get large volumes of accurate CAS. Although the gunships were slow, they provided a stable platform to deliver their deadly firepower, and they could loiter over an area for long periods of time. They were designed to support the soldier on the ground for CAS missions. The use of the first gunships in Vietnam is a good illustration of how airpower's flexibility greatly supported a ground commander's requirements.

Top American military leaders were concerned about several aspects of the United States's increasing involvement in South Vietnam. Rising Vietcong insurgency efforts threatened much of South Vietnam's army. The Vietcong and NVA were increasingly targeting South Vietnamese villages and citizens. Guerilla raiders harassed American airfields with rocket attacks. American military ground operations began to move from air base defense to active operations against the Vietcong as ground strength grew. The Vietcong usually launched attacks at night to take advantage of the dark and increase their chance of success in a surprise attack. At the same time, the USAF was testing a specially fitted Douglas C-47 with three 6,000-round 7.62 mm SUU-11A miniguns and flare dispensers fitted on the left side of the plane. These aircraft were designed for nighttime CAS missions. On 2 November 1964, Gen Curtis E. LeMay, Air Force chief of staff, ordered that a prototype gunship test the concept in Vietnam.[50]

The gunship tests started in December and showed great promise under combat conditions. Gunship attacks against boats, trails, and buildings demonstrated accurate fire. On the first nighttime mission during 23–24 December, the gunship attacked a Vietcong force that had surrounded an outpost. The test gunship dropped 17 flares and fired 4,500 rounds. The attack was broken off, and the outpost saved. The gunship was then sent to another surrounded outpost that was also saved by gunship fire.[51] A more dramatic example of the gunship's prowess was a combat mission flown on the night of 25 February 1965. The prototype gunship fired upon a Vietcong force that was on the offensive in the Vietnamese highlands. The gunship poured 20,500 rounds into the enemy assault and killed about 300 Vietcong guerillas.[52]

The gunship tests were a resounding success. On 13 July 1965, the Air Staff authorized the formation of a squadron of AC-47 gunships and their deployment to Southeast Asia by 9 November.[53] But there were critics of the AC-47 program who feared that the slow-moving, low-altitude AC-47s were vulnerable to ground fire. Furthermore, the 7.62 mm miniguns were ineffective at ranges up to 1,500 feet. If the AC-47s operated at a lower altitude, they were within the range of enemy 23 mm and 37 mm AAA.[54] However, the AC-47 became a versatile weapon, demonstrating its ability to conduct CAS by operating at night and producing a high volume of fire that could also destroy vehicles. These characteristics would make the AC-47 quite valuable to an interdiction effort. The AC-47 would provide interdiction capabilities against enemy troop and truck movements in Laos.

The AC-47 "Spooky" gunships were organized under the 4th Air Commando Squadron (4ACS). Seventh Air Force's Operations Order 411-65 identified the 4ACS's missions as defending hamlets against night attack with flares and firepower, supplementing strike aircraft in the defense of friendly forces, and providing long-endurance escorts for convoys.[55] The 4ACS also provided interdiction by hitting targets in Laos and along the infamous Ho Chi Minh Trail, a main north-south route

The AC-47 gunship provided invaluable CAS in the Vietnam War.

network of roads, where supplies and manpower supplied the Vietcong and NVA in South Vietnam (fig. 9).

The AC-47 provided a significant boost for CAS. From July to September 1965, it was responsible for defending over 500 villages and hamlets and breaking up 166 enemy attacks.[56] The US Army and other forces were given an aerial tool for quickly delivering a huge amount of firepower that could break the attack of an enemy force. For example, in February 1967, AC-47 gunships were providing CAS to Marine Corps, ROK, and South Vietnamese military forces in the northern part of South Vietnam in Operation Lien Ket I, 16 miles southwest of Chu Lai. NVA forces were threatening the area in early 1967 and had to be stopped.[57] Six AC-47 aircraft were assigned to support marines and other forces. The Spooky aircraft provided 12 hours of support, firing over 123,000 rounds. This effort accounted for over 200 confirmed enemy dead and another 520 probably killed in the area.[58] This example illustrates the value that AC-47s had for ground forces. These aircraft acted as airborne artillery to provide direct, accurate, timely, and sustained CAS for troops engaged in battle.

The AC-47 was still hampered by some operational limitations. It had a speed of only 200 knots, was vulnerable to

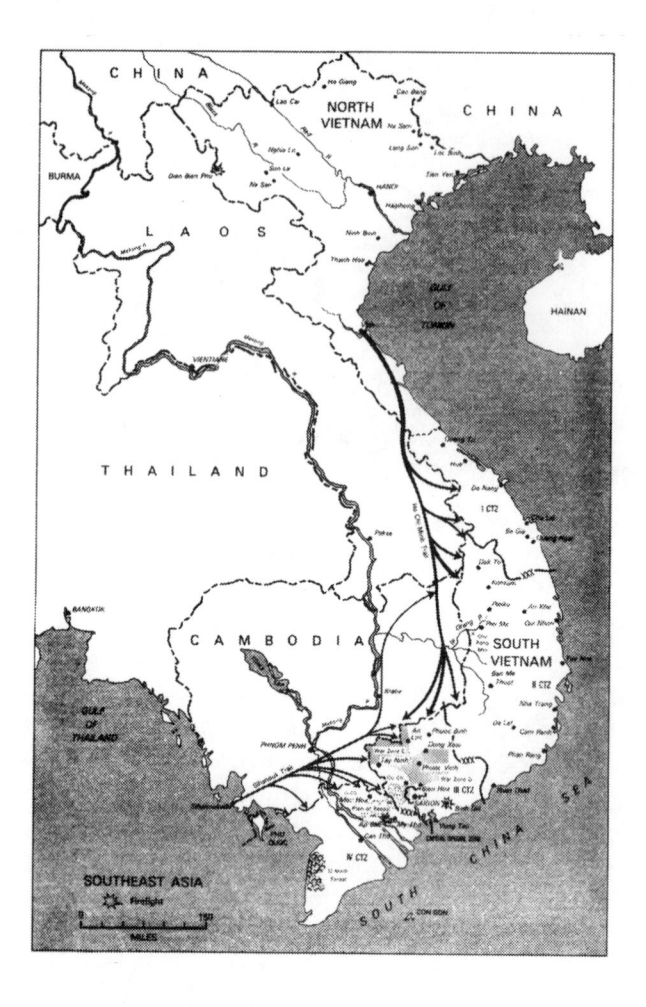

Figure 9. Southeast Asia

ground fire, and was not as maneuverable as other aircraft. Also, the AC-47 had limited cargo space that put constraints on the types and placement of its weapons and restricted the amount of ammunition and flares it could carry. Also, the AC-47's low wings restricted the vision of gunners and blocked certain firing angles. Still, the AC-47 was cited as "the best deterrent we have to attack by mortar, recoilless rifle, or rocket" on airfields and bases.[59] Field commanders in Vietnam wanted more AC-47s. By 1967 two more squadrons were formed and

INTERDICTION/CLOSE AIR SUPPORT

began actively supporting ground forces. The USAF's AC-47 aircraft operated until 1969.

A new replacement aircraft, the AC-119G Shadow, was added in 1968. The AC-119 was designed to carry armament similar to the AC-47's. The aircraft carried 7.62 mm miniguns, a new illumination system, fire-control equipment, and other detection systems. The interim AC-119G was introduced, but a more advanced gunship was on the horizon—the Lockheed AC-130A Spectre.

The AC-47 met with so much success that engineers from Air Force Systems Command had already started plans to develop a more capable gunship by February 1965. The four-engined, propeller-driven C-130A Hercules transport plane was chosen as a test prototype. This gunship would carry night-detection sensors in addition to flares to improve its ability to strike at night. Engineers also wanted to experiment with radar and infrared systems that improved its ability to find enemy targets at night, under jungle foliage, and in difficult terrain. The forward-looking infrared system would help detect heat from vehicle engines and lights, even after they were turned off. The aircraft also had a night-illumination system with 1.5-million-candlepower capability and 24 flares. Additionally, the proposed AC-130A tested a combination of 7.62 mm miniguns and 20 mm M-61 Vulcan cannons. The longer-range 20 mm guns put the aircraft out of reach of the Vietcong's AAA. The AC-130A was also much faster than the AC-47. Its enhanced-detection system was linked to a fire-control system that could provide better aiming and preparation for firing. The AC-130A would provide a significant increase in weaponry over the AC-47's.

The AC-130A prototype, like the test AC-47, conducted combat trials over Southeast Asia from February to November 1968. The gunship proved its worth by conducting CAS missions, but it was called upon for more interdiction missions. During the combat-trial period, it spotted 1,000 trucks, attacked 481, and destroyed or damaged 361 vehicles.[60] The gunships also sank boats, struck roads and waterways, and directly supported troops. After the test period, Secretary of the Air Force Harold Brown approved a mixed gunship force of AC-47, AC-119, and AC-130A aircraft. Brown was concerned that a huge force of AC-130s might cut into the tactical-airlift transport capability in the area. He proposed that AC-119 aircraft replace the AC-47s for CAS and base defense and release the AC-130As to concentrate on night interdiction first and CAS in a secondary role.[61] The AC-47s would phase out with AC-119s, which themselves would be phased out in favor of AC-130As.

The success of the AC-130A against trucks in its combat tests led to a major change in the aircraft's priorities. AC-130s were tasked to conduct night interdiction and armed reconnaissance missions to destroy wheeled and tracked vehicles.[62] CAS became a tertiary priority of the aircraft after it conducted night-interdiction missions involving bombing and then hitting the target with fire suppression. The technology of the gunship's weapons and detection systems, as well as the aircraft's capabilities, allowed the commander to expand its mission beyond CAS.

Although the gunship was originally designed to support ground forces with CAS, new technology and innovation allowed engineers and combat personnel to devise new methods to support ground forces. These actions increased the options that a commander could take to blunt Vietcong and NVA efforts in South Vietnam. The gunships were capable of CAS, interdiction, and armed reconnaissance missions. These aircraft reflected the flexibility that airpower provides to a commander under many diverse conditions. The gunship's designers and users were able to use existing transport aircraft and weapons to develop a unique weapon system in record time: months compared to the years normally required for an aircraft-acquisition effort. Engineers and combat personnel worked together to refine requirements and build and test the aircraft under actual fighting conditions. Users of the aircraft also had the foresight to test and expand the weapon's use from CAS to interdiction. Designers of the gunship also improved the aircraft in response to enemy defenses.

CAS missions were aided by the introduction of the AC-47, AC-119, and AC-130 aircraft. Instead of fast-flying jets, ground units had aircraft that could loiter slowly over a target and deliver a withering amount of fire. Additionally, these gunships could provide several levels of support, including CAS, interdiction, and armed reconnaissance. These capabilities allowed a commander to provide many different types of support. The US Air Force has used gunships, which were proven in Vietnam, for CAS and special-operations missions since their inception.

Close Air Support in the Korean War: A Navy and Marine Corps View

CAS missions were highly valued by ground commanders as much in the Korean War as they are today. The issue of getting enough CAS missions has always been a sore point among the services. During the opening months of the Korean War, UN forces were pushed from the border between North and South Korea to a perimeter around the port city of Pusan. Retreating UN ground forces were forced into this corner and were desperate to hang on and not be swept into the Sea of Japan. Ground units made CAS requests for immediate support. Artillery and ammunition were in short supply to support these ground units. The Air Force was asked to shoulder more responsibility for CAS but was also shorthanded in available aircraft.[63] B-29 bombers were pressed into CAS service. General MacArthur, commander of UN forces in Korea, wanted the UN's Eighth Army to route all CAS requirements through the Air Force's 5AF. This centralized control of CAS missions reflected the doctrine established by FM 100-20. However, the Pusan defense was critical, and many demands for CAS were sent directly to the US Navy's TF77, some with the concurrence of 5AF.

Fifth Air Force was responsible not only for CAS, but also for air superiority throughout the theater and for interdiction missions. Air superiority was needed to allow it to unleash the tactical airpower to conduct CAS and interdiction. USAF, Navy, and Marine Corps aircraft were fighting the air war independently and threatening the coordination of action. Lt Gen George E. Stratemeyer, commander of 5AF, wanted all operational control of air resources under his purview. He requested that MacArthur agree to this proposal. Stratemeyer's request was approved with modifications—he could control only land-based aircraft (which included Marine Corps assets) and had operational coordination (veto power over proposed missions) with naval airpower. The Navy could still control airpower to support several missions, including amphibious assaults. This arrangement would create problems for the use of airpower in the future.

The use of CAS was one of the problems that would remain unanswered in this debate. The Air Force and Army had one system established by FM 100-20 and the World War II experience. The Navy and Marine Corps had another method shaped by the Latin American and World War II (Pacific theater) experiences. Both systems were designed under specific assumptions, needs, and forces. Each service believed that its CAS approach was appropriate for its operations in Korea. Both systems would create problems for Stratemeyer.

After World War II, the US Army revised its doctrine concerning air-ground operations, conceding that tactical airpower was under the control of a theater air commander who could assign air missions. The theater air commander was still under the command of a theater commander, but airpower was centrally controlled. These missions were controlled out of an Army and Air Force joint operations center (JOC) located at Army headquarters. The JOC allowed Army and USAF officers to coordinate actions, but the decisions to conduct a mission remained firmly in the hands of a USAF commander.[64] On 3 July 1950, the first JOC was established in Itazuke Air Base in Japan and later moved to Korea as UN forces pushed north from Pusan.[65] Radar, air traffic control, communications, and other systems were shipped and installed to support JOC operations in Korea. After the first month of the war, over 4,300 CAS sorties were flown in support of the ground forces, stopping enemy tank, truck, and vehicle movement during daylight.[66]

Under the JOC system, the USAF established subordinate organizations to improve air-ground operations that affected CAS. Air Force personnel manned a tactical air control center (TACC) that was colocated with the JOC. The TACC received air mission requests, coordinated the action with the JOC, and ordered execution of the mission. The TACC allowed USAF forces to get prioritized missions from the JOC and control the number of missions conducted in-theater. The Air

Force also formed air liaison officers (ALO) who coordinated missions under the tactical air control party (TACP) system. The ALO served on the ground with Army units, under the TACPs, and was equipped with appropriate communications equipment to stay in contact with CAS aircraft and a forward air controller (FAC)—an airborne USAF pilot directing air operations from a plane. If the TACP identified a likely CAS target (from ground-unit requests), the pilot would contact the Army division it worked for and request a mission. The division would then pass the request up through the division, corps, and then to the JOC for action. As soon as the JOC approved the mission, the TACC would direct an aircraft for action. This aircraft would then contact the FAC for directions and guidance to the target. The process could take 40 minutes.

Air Force and Army officers in the JOC also decided whether Army artillery could provide support rather than CAS; USAF officers were reluctant to approve CAS missions within 1,000 yards in front of troops.[67] Army commanders preferred to rely on their own artillery within this range, but if the situation were critical or demanded additional firepower, they would call on airpower to conduct the mission.[68] Army ground commanders started to request more CAS as the war lengthened and enemy activity increased. In August 1952, Gen Mark W. Clark, the US Army Far East commander, observed that ground commanders frequently asked for CAS missions that their organic artillery could provide faster and more efficiently than could limited air forces.[69] Clark believed that the Army could not replicate the same system as a rival, dedicated air-ground Marine Corps system because organization, training, and artillery allocations differed greatly. The Air Force/Army system was highly structured and tightly controlled by the Air Force. Initially, the JOC system did not include Navy or Marine Corps requirements or links to their airpower resources. Later, Navy and Marine Corps officers were included in JOC operations, which improved coordination among TF77, Marine Corps, and 5AF operations. Incredibly, before the consolidation of JOC operations, the services used different map systems, which led to great confusion over target locations.[70]

Navy and Marine Corps airpower focused on CAS in a different light. The Navy/Marine concept of air-ground operations was tested in the 1920s and throughout the Pacific campaign in World War II. During Marine amphibious assaults around the Pacific, air liaison teams operated with ground forces, much like the ALO system. Navy and Marine Corps air forces in Korea were focused on the CAS mission. Although their air resources conducted interdiction missions later in the war, the early phases of the conflict were dedicated towards support of ground forces. Conversely, the US Air Force was conducting strategic attack, interdiction, and CAS during the same phase. Coordinating CAS missions became a problem of priorities.

Navy and Marine Corps support of onshore operations was based on the assumption that lightly armed Marine Corps forces did not have sufficient artillery support.[71] While the Army had its own heavy-artillery units, similarly sized Marine Corps units relied on naval fire support from ships offshore and on air support. The lack of artillery forced the Marine Corps to devote its limited aircraft resources to focus on CAS. It could commit few resources to other missions. Navy and Marine Corps air resources were trained specifically for the CAS mission and were considered an aerial-artillery asset to be used in lieu of ground fire support. Attacks on enemy positions close to Marine ground forces were the rule rather than the exception.

Navy pilots did share a common objective with their Air Force contemporaries: the value of air superiority. The USAF valued air superiority because of the freedom to attack and the freedom from being attacked. The Navy believed in the same principles but had an added concern—defending the carrier fleet and protecting an amphibious landing force from attack. The Navy also had to contend with antiship aerial attack, reconnaissance, antisubmarine actions, and other missions. Interdiction and CAS were viewed as equal priorities.[72] Conversely, the Air Force and Army had agreed that interdiction preceded CAS in priority as early as FM 100-20. The Marines had an added incentive to keep CAS a high priority. If they could not keep their independent CAS capability, the Navy might subsume their air resources, and they would lose their air capability.

INTERDICTION/CLOSE AIR SUPPORT

CAS from Navy Corsairs in the Korean War

Navy and Marine Corps CAS requests were normally started by a Marine Corps TACP assigned to a ground unit. These TACPs were similar to the Air Force/Army TACP units. Requests were sent to a Marine brigade's tactical air direction center (TADC), which was at a lower level than the TACC that provided more decentralized decision making and potentially faster response time. Separate TADCs traded timeliness for coordination of theater operations. Marine Corps TADCs worked well to support Marine units only, but the USAF TACC had to coordinate support for Army and other ground units. Later, radio links and improved coordination among TADCs, Air Force TACCs, and Navy/Marine TACCs helped alleviate this problem. The onshore Marine Corps TACC or Navy TACC at sea did prioritize air missions but assumed that a TACP request was valid and immediately ordered CAS strikes against the target.[73] Still, the TACC was able to get CAS to troops faster. The Marines also used a ground FAC to control strikes, unlike the airborne Air Force FAC. The Air Force and Army tried ground-based FACs but found radio communications difficult in the mountainous Korean terrain.[74] Radio interference created communications breakdowns, so the USAF turned to light observation aircraft for the task. The degree of control of the air strikes reflected the focus of air support.

Both the Navy/Marine Corps and Air Force/Army had differences, but once they recognized these differences, they could meet requests for CAS more efficiently. Air Force officers needed to realize the importance of Navy and Marine CAS efforts to secure and defend an amphibious landing and to provide fire support to Marine units without major artillery support. The proximity of carriers to amphibious and Marine operations made it possible for aircraft to stay airborne and ready to provide on-call CAS missions. Marine Corps air units could ensure a CAS strike mission within five to 10 minutes.[75] Most USAF units were well behind the battlefront and were better prepared to launch their missions from a ground on-call status rather than an aerial one. The Air Force also recognized that, like the Army, Marine ground commanders did not command air resources but had to coordinate their requests among other commanders through a TACC priority system. While Navy/Marine Corps CAS advocates railed against the confining, centralized control advocated by the Air Force, the Air Force rejected the "go it alone" attitude of the Navy/Marines. Centralized control resulted in slower response time for a Marine ground commander. Conversely, the USAF was concerned about Navy/Marine Corps CAS missions being conducted to the exclusion of other theater priorities. Although the two systems differed, there was room for cooperation. The Air Force believed that the Navy/Marine Corps system was better suited for the early stages of an amphibious assault—not a battlefront where airpower would become a substitute for artillery.[76]

CAS was a vital element to the success of ground operations in Korea. After improving communications and coordination among the services, the JOC concept did work. Understanding each service's views on CAS helped improve the relationships among them. Additionally, better aircraft, equipment, maps, targeting, and battle-damage assessment significantly improved operations. However, differences in perspectives among services plagued the use of CAS. The Air Force still considered CAS secondary to air superiority, strategic attack, and interdiction. Increasing its commitment to CAS would have reduced its capability to conduct these other missions.

After the Korean War, an Air-Ground Operations Conference was held to evaluate CAS. The findings concluded that the JOC system was effective and improved throughout the war. Army, Navy, and Marine Corps representatives wanted a commitment to an allocation of air missions devoted to CAS and wanted it assigned to a ground commander after all other missions were assigned. The Army considered Air Force CAS restrictive, compared to that of the Marines. For example, response and support time were slower; USAF aircraft loitered over a target area for 30 minutes, whereas Marine aircraft stayed for 73 minutes; and, more importantly, each Marine Corps division received 37 CAS sorties a day, while Army units got only 13.[77] These missions would be preplanned but could be allocated to other missions in an emergency. This would avoid questions of a ground commander's misusing assigned missions for less important missions. The three services also wanted more ground TACP units and the airborne FAC as a spotter—not the director of CAS missions. Predictably, the USAF representative disagreed since the set allocation might endanger airpower's flexibility to support the theater campaign. This issue was not resolved and remains a point of contention to this day.

Issues among the services surrounding CAS are as contentious today as they were in the Korean War. Control of air missions, requests for support, and the priority of CAS, compared to other missions, are still a topic of hot debate. Ground commanders still want dedicated CAS. Aerospace leaders will continue to wrestle with the challenge of choosing the priority of air missions among competing demands. Services will continue to debate who is in charge—the supported or supporting command for CAS. This challenge will become greater as emerging threats create situations that conventional artillery and a reduced military cannot handle. Greater cooperation, communication, understanding, and joint doctrine may solve some of these problems. However, the competing demand for limited resources may drive ground forces to elect the development and employment of substitute capabilities for CAS.

Notes

1. Eduard Mark, *Aerial Interdiction: Air Power and the Land Battle in Three American Wars* (Washington, D.C.: Center for Air Force History, 1994), 1.
2. Billy C. Mossman, *Ebb and Flow: November 1950–July 1951* (Washington, D.C.: Center of Military History, 1990), 23 and 55.
3. Bernard C. Nalty, ed., *Winged Shield, Winged Sword: A History of the United States Air Force*, vol. 2 (Washington, D.C.: Air Force History and Museums Program, 1997), 40.
4. Mark, 294.
5. Conrad C. Crane, *American Airpower Strategy in Korea, 1950–1953* (Lawrence, Kans.: University Press of Kansas, 2000), 82.
6. Ibid., 83.
7. Mark, 307.
8. Ibid., 305.
9. Robert F. Futrell, *The United States Air Force in Korea, 1950–1953*, rev. ed. (Washington, D.C.: Office of Air Force History, 1983), 437.
10. Wilbur H. Morrison, *Pilots, Man Your Planes! The History of Naval Aviation* (Central Point, Oreg.: Hellgate Press, 1999), 282.
11. Futrell, 439.
12. Walter G. Hermes, *Truce Tent and Fighting Front* (Washington, D.C.: Center of Military History, 1992), 106.
13. Mark, 302.
14. Ibid., 315.
15. Futrell, 471.
16. A. J. C. Lavalle, ed., *Airpower and the 1972 Spring Invasion* (Washington, D.C.: Office of Air Force History, 1985), 1.
17. Victor Flintham, *Air Wars and Aircraft: A Detailed Record of Air Combat, 1945 to the Present* (New York: Facts on File, 1990), 273.
18. Mark Clodfelter, *The Limits of Air Power: The American Bombing of North Vietnam* (New York: Free Press, 1989), 153.
19. Ibid.
20. Mark, 375.
21. Ibid., 376.
22. Lavalle, 106, table 6.
23. Robert A. Pape, *Bombing to Win: Air Power and Coercion in War* (Ithaca, N.Y.: Cornell University Press, 1996), 197.
24. Lavalle, 106.
25. Mark, 378.
26. Ibid., 383.
27. Ibid., 391.

28. William W. Momyer, *Air Power in Three Wars* (New York: Arno Press, 1980), 333.

29. Ronald H. Spector, *Eagle against the Sun: The American War with Japan* (New York: Free Press, 1985), 226.

30. Geoffrey Perret, *Old Soldiers Never Die: The Life of Douglas MacArthur* (New York: Random House, 1996), 333.

31. Wesley Frank Craven and James Lea Cate, eds., *The Army Air Forces in World War II,* vol. 4, *The Pacific: Guadalcanal to Saipan, August 1942 to July 1944* (1950; new imprint, Washington, D.C.: Office of Air Force History, 1983), 141.

32. John Miller, *Cartwheel: The Reduction of Rabaul* (Washington, D.C.: Office of the Chief of Military History, 1959), 40.

33. Eric M. Bergerud, *Fire in the Sky: The Air War in the South Pacific* (Boulder, Colo.: Westview Press, 2000), 590.

34. George C. Kenney, *General Kenney Reports: A Personal History of the Pacific War* (Washington, D.C.: Office of Air Force History, 1987), 202.

35. Perret, 333.

36. Edward J. Drea, "Into the Jungle: New Guinea," in *Pearl Harbor and the War in the Pacific,* ed. Bernard C. Nalty (New York: Smithmark Publishers, 1991), 103.

37. Miller, 41.

38. E. B. Potter, ed., *Sea Power: A Naval History* (Annapolis: Naval Institute Press, 1981), 315.

39. Bergerud, 592.

40. Spector, 228.

41. Joe Gray Taylor, "American Experience in the Southwest Pacific," in *Case Studies in the Development of Close Air Support,* ed. Benjamin Franklin Cooling (Washington, D.C.: Office of Air Force History, 1990), 311.

42. Perret, 342.

43. Daniel R. Mortensen, *A Pattern for Joint Operations: World War II Close Air Support, North Africa* (Washington, D.C.: Office of Air Force History and US Army Center of Military History, 1987), 12.

44. Wesley Frank Craven and James Lea Cate, eds., *The Army Air Forces in World War II,* vol. 2, *Europe: Torch to Pointblank, August 1942 to December 1943* (1949; new imprint, Washington, D.C.: Office of Air Force History, 1983), 157.

45. Mortensen, 72.

46. George F. Howe, *Northwest Africa: Seizing the Initiative in the West* (Washington, D.C.: Center of Military History, 1991), 480.

47. Mortensen, 76.

48. War Department, Field Manual (FM) 100-20, *Command and Employment of Air Power,* 21 July 1943, 1.

49. David Syrett, "The Tunisian Campaign, 1942–1943," in *Case Studies in the Development of Close Air Support,* 185.

50. Jack S. Ballard, *The Development and Employment of Fixed-Wing Gunships, 1962–1972* (Washington, D.C.: Office of Air Force History, 1982), 11.
51. Ibid., 20.
52. Ibid., 21.
53. Ibid., 26.
54. Earl H. Tilford, *Setup: What the Air Force Did in Vietnam and Why* (Maxwell AFB, Ala.: Air University Press, 1991), 176.
55. Ballard, 35.
56. John J. Sbrega, "Southeast Asia," in *Case Studies in the Development of Close Air Support*, 444.
57. George L. MacGarrigle, *Combat Operations: Taking the Offensive, October 1966 to October 1967* (Washington, D.C.: Center of Military History, 1998), 203.
58. Ballard, 52.
59. Ibid., 53.
60. Ibid., 90.
61. John Schlight, *The War in South Vietnam: The Years of the Offensive, 1965–1968* (Washington, D.C.: Office of Air Force History, 1988), 241.
62. Ballard, 107.
63. James F. Schnabel, *Policy and Direction: The First Year* (Washington, D.C.: Center of Military History, 1992), 109.
64. Allan R. Millett, "Korea, 1950–1953," in *Case Studies in the Development of Close Air Support*, 348.
65. Roy E. Appleman, *South to the Naktong, North to the Yalu: (June–November 1950)* (Washington, D.C.: Center of Military History, 1992), 95.
66. Ibid., 256–57.
67. Richard P. Hallion, *The Naval Air War in Korea* (Baltimore: Nautical & Aviation Publishing Co. of America, 1986), 43.
68. Futrell, 705.
69. Hermes, 326.
70. Morrison, 274.
71. Hallion, 43.
72. Millett, 351.
73. Ibid.
74. Hallion, 44.
75. Futrell, 120.
76. Millett, 352.
77. Crane, 62.

Chapter 5

Functions and Capabilities of Aerospace Power: Rapid Mobility/Space and Information

Mobility Operations: Moving Manpower, Munitions, and Machines

Aerial combat operations do not always involve fighter planes shooting enemy planes or bombers attacking targets deep within an adversary's homeland. Airpower can conduct operations that significantly aid land forces. CAS directly aids the effort of a ground-force commander. An operation that greatly aids land forces is airpower's ability to move those forces quickly around the globe. Mobility operations can also transport cargo, from a single soldier to heavy tanks, thousands of miles in a day. Additionally, transport aircraft can provide supplies to a land force in terrain difficult to reach by land or sea routes. This capability also lends itself to not having to station ground forces around the world. Instead, if an emergency arises, airpower can transport forces to the theater and replacements to fight any battle. The ability to move these forces quickly and in significant numbers can also provide a deterrent effect on an adversary who may not be willing to face a swift, decisive action by a mobile ground force. These same capabilities are also applicable to humanitarian missions. Medical aid and food can be sent to many inhospitable regions by air transport. Conditions that require the timely delivery of medicine, food, clothing, shelter, and technical assistance can be met by global air mobility. Airlift can also deliver supplies and personnel to combat zones using tactical air mobility.

The movement of personnel and equipment is a key capability of airpower. The versatility of large transports allows a commander to conduct many different types of operations. Transports can deliver soldiers from their home country to a destination, move them within a region, or fly them from one region to another. This reduces the number of soldiers or forces that may be required for worldwide commitments due to the ability to move and better share resources at an appropriate location. Merchant or cargo shipping can transport more people and material than can air mobility. However, if timing is critical, air transportation can provide a more effective and efficient solution to the problem. Additionally, air transportation is better able to deliver these resources if the location is landlocked, does not have infrastructure capable of handling merchant shipping, or does not have the road or rail system to carry cargo to its destination inland. Air mobility is not a substitute for oceanic shipping. It is just another tool available for a commander to consider. Moving equipment is another capability of air mobility. A transport can literally carry a heavily armored tank thousands of miles. Additionally, an air transport can move aircraft by putting them on board a plane, as with tanks, or through another method.

Air mobility in World War II

RAPID MOBILITY/SPACE AND INFORMATION

Most modern military aircraft also have the capability of aerial refueling. This allows an air force to rapidly move combat-capable aircraft from one theater to the next without stopping to prepare them for shipping, putting them in transit, and making them operational for combat after they make the trip. This capability reduces the need for a series of bases for aircraft to land, refuel, take off, and go to another airfield before arriving at their final destination. Rapid reinforcement of air resources might mean the difference between winning or losing a war. More importantly, it could prevent a conflict by deterring or frightening a potential adversary from attacking, much like transporting a large land force into an area in conflict. Aerial refueling allows air forces to mass their aircraft at crucial points and times. Aircraft can also stay on station longer to fight or extend their range of operations to meet unknown or difficult situations. Aerial refueling provides more options to the commander—it becomes a force multiplier.

Air transport has always been an important part of airpower. The dream of rapid transport of men, material, and machines has become a reality. Jet aircraft with large carrying capacities have greatly supported many operations in the past. Global coverage to move material from one continent to another gives a national decision maker many options for fighting, deterring, or meeting requirements for providing relief during natural disasters. Like their weapons-capable brethren, air-transport aircraft must be responsive and capable of operations at a moment's notice.

Failure at Stalingrad: Air Supply Falls Flat

In late 1942, the German and Soviet armies were locked in mortal combat over control of the city of Stalingrad, located in the southern USSR on the Volga River. The Volga was a "vital artery" to keep supply lines open from the Black Sea.[1] Stalingrad was the site of several munitions, tank, tractor, chemical, oil-processing, and other production facilities. Named after Soviet leader Joseph Stalin, it was a symbol of the War in the East. The German Sixth Army attempted to push Soviet ground forces out of the city. The Soviets planned on a house-to-house fight that would ensnare the German forces. Sixth Army was eventually encircled and defeated at Stalingrad; this became one of the major turning points of the war because the Germans had to shift from an offensive to a defensive focus in the USSR. The Battle of Stalingrad saw some of the bitterest fighting in World War II, with the Germans suffering over 800,000 and the Soviets 1.1 million casualties in the campaign.[2] In the immediate area of Stalingrad, the Germans suffered 147,200 casualties and over 91,000 captured.[3] Only 5,000 German prisoners returned home in 1955.

The house-to-house fighting allowed the Soviets to grind the Germans in a slow attrition. The German Sixth Army's major advantage—armored forces and mobility—was useless in the rubble of this type of street fighting. The Soviets were able to defend buildings and trade space for time. Initially, the Germans prevailed by pushing most of the Soviets from the city by October 1942. Soviet forces had another idea. Two Soviet armies began to encircle the German forces around Stalingrad. The commander of the German forces asked that he be allowed to retreat to avoid encirclement and save his forces. Hitler refused since the taking of Stalingrad had become a symbol of the fortunes of the Soviet campaign. The Soviets had never succeeded in defeating a German army, and it was inconceivable they would do so now. Hitler ordered his troops in Stalingrad to consolidate their positions and hold on until reinforcements could break through. Temperatures started to fall as Soviet pressure on the besieged Germans increased. Hitler and Göring promised that the Luftwaffe would provide German forces with as much as 600 tons of supplies a day.[4] Sixth Army staff officers originally calculated that their men needed 750 tons but later reduced this to 500 tons.[5] Göring would later agree to airlift this amount. The Luftwaffe would have a big chore since it had only 30 Junkers Ju-52s in the area for the operation. Several Luftwaffe commanders in the area were concerned. *Generalleutnant* Martin Fiebig, responsible for the airlift, wrote that "supplying Sixth Army by air was not feasible." Even Göring doubted the Luftwaffe's ability to conduct the airlift. He could "do nothing but agree" with Hitler, or else he would be "left with the blame."[6] Further, the weather and enemy situation were unpredictable factors.[7] Winter flying

In 1941, German forces in the Soviet Union faced severe supply shortages at Stalingrad.

conditions were miserable, and the Soviets started to threaten Luftwaffe airfields.

The Ju-52 was the Luftwaffe's main transport aircraft. It had served well in the early phases of World War II but was beginning to suffer losses greater than its production. Still, the Ju-52 had proven itself by supplying six German divisions encircled at Demyansk in the winter of 1941–42. Ju-52s were scheduled to transport 300 tons of supplies per day to the Germans in Demyansk.[8] This was the world's first major airlift operation to supply a ground force entirely by air. The Luftwaffe collected Ju-52 aircraft, pilots, and training units from throughout the eastern front to conduct the operation. Soviet bombers had damaged airfields, which limited the airlift efforts. By the end of February 1942, the Luftwaffe was capable of providing only half of the ground forces' requirements. Luftwaffe Ju-52s were keeping 100,000 troops supplied, if barely, and in three months delivered 24,300 tons of cargo, airlifted 15,446 men into Demyansk, and removed 20,093 casualties.[9] Luftwaffe transport capabilities were severely weakened with this effort. Losses included 385 flying personnel and 262 aircraft. The Luftwaffe demonstrated its ability to airlift supplies and reinforcements. The Demyansk experience was costly and illusionary insofar as the Luftwaffe believed it exemplified what its airlift fleet could accomplish. A similar situation at Stalingrad provided an opportunity for the Luftwaffe to demonstrate its ability to perform another mobility operation (fig. 10).

But Stalingrad was not Demyansk. The requirements to keep Stalingrad were greater. The number of soldiers in Stalingrad

Figure 10. The Eastern Front (Adapted from *Case Studies in the Development of Close Air Support,* ed. Benjamin Franklin Cooling [Washington, D.C.: Office of Air Force History, 1990], 116)

was three times the number in Demyansk. Also, the Soviets had a strong air force near Stalingrad, where the Luftwaffe contested air superiority. Additionally, the Luftwaffe did not have the number of transport aircraft to support the airlift. The idea that this would be another Demyansk would prove faulty. Additionally, planning and decision making for the airlift took place in Berlin. Air commanders from the area around Stalingrad were not consulted.

If the Germans in Stalingrad could survive in the pocket, a planned breakthrough by German armored forces might save the city. Hitler assumed that the Luftwaffe would be capable of completely resupplying Sixth Army by air and that the Sixth could defend itself in the face of massive Soviet forces. The entire German military was under a strain since it was fighting on simultaneous fronts in the USSR, North Africa, and the Balkans. Luftwaffe assets were drained away from the USSR to support North Africa. The Luftwaffe was forced to press Heinkel He-111 bombers into service as transports. The decision to use these aircraft came at the cost of reducing the attack capability of the German air force. The Luftwaffe also had to contend with the weather, limited ground support, and enemy air opposition while operating a small transport fleet. At least the Demyansk operation had had sufficient transports. On 29 November, the first day of the resupply effort, the Luftwaffe put 38 Ju-52s and 21 He-111s into the air. Only 12 Ju-52s and 13 He-111s delivered their cargoes to Stalingrad. Each Ju-52 could carry about a ton of cargo while an He-111 could fly in about 1,000 pounds. The Luftwaffe needed 800 Ju-52s to supply the 500 tons per day to the Sixth Army. The Luftwaffe had only 750 aircraft in the entire fleet.[10] Some estimates were as high as 1,052 Ju-52s, assuming an abysmal 30 to 35 percent for operational readiness of the aircraft.[11]

This first-day effort was far less than the 500 tons per day promised by Göring. *Generaloberst* Wolfram von Richtofen, commander of the Luftwaffe's Fourth Air Force, which had responsibility for the airlift, estimated that he would be able to field 298 Ju-52s on 25 November.[12] This was far short of the required 800 Ju-52s to supply the effort. The Luftwaffe's ability to keep Göring's promise seemed slim. The lack of Ju-52s would have to be made up with the less-capable He-111s and other aircraft. Richtofen had recommended that the Sixth Army break out of Stalingrad, but Hitler rejected the proposal. The Luftwaffe was caught in a no-win situation.

The Stalingrad defensive continued in the cold, wintry weather. From 1 to 23 December, the Luftwaffe airlifted supplies averaging 90 tons per day.[13] This allowed the German forces to survive but do nothing else. They could not counterattack or force a breakthrough from their encircled positions. The major airlift of the period came on 7 December, when 300 tons were delivered to Stalingrad. Airlift capabilities rose marginally in January, when Sixth Army received an average of 120 tons per day. This was still only 20 percent of the required and promised amounts. If the supplies were not met, surrender and defeat would soon come to the Germans.

The Luftwaffe stripped units of any aircraft that could fly. Ju-52s, obsolete Junkers Ju-86 trainers, Focke-Wulf Fw-200 Condor naval bombers, Messerschmitt Me-323 transports, Gotha 242 transports, and He-111s supported the effort. Training crews and aircraft were also sent east, which further reduced the ability of the Luftwaffe to increase its airlift capability. The Soviet air force was not oblivious to this effort, concentrating its fighter strength to intercept the transports and stop the flow of supplies. The Luftwaffe's failure to master offensive counterair superiority was in doubt because of losses, bad weather, and the need to escort the transports safely into Stalingrad. Soviet air defenses concentrated their efforts near the front. Moreover, cold weather limited maintenance, group support, and cold-start procedures—temperatures of -30° C were not uncommon. By mid-January 1943, only 15 of 140 Ju-52s, 41 of 140 He-111s, and one of 20 Fw-200s were capable of flying the airlift.[14]

Luftwaffe efforts could hardly deliver any tonnage at all, let alone the estimated required amounts to Sixth Army. The 600-ton requirement seemed like an underestimate. Ammunition requirements for a corps, about one-third smaller than Sixth Army, were 400 tons per day. In heavy fighting, this could increase to 598 tons (or 295 Ju-52 sorties) per day or 990 tons for heavy fighting.[15] Sixth Army would need much more than the 600 tons to survive. Luftwaffe officers had tried to persuade the German *Wehrmacht* headquarters that the Luftwaffe could not support the effort. Instead, it might be able to supply a portion of the requirement, but either a breakout by Sixth Army or a breakthrough by a relief column would save the ground forces. Actual supplies airlifted into Stalingrad were estimated to be 50 to 80 tons per day.[16] The airlift effort might only allow the besieged defenders to hold their positions.

There are several reasons for the failure to provide adequate mobility and support at Stalingrad. First, the Germans failed to adequately plan and analyze the situation. The reliance only on airlift operations was questionable. Only an immediate breakout or breakthrough could have ensured proper reinforcements and supplies to the defenders. The inflexibility of Hitler's decision to defend the salient at all costs ensured Sixth Army's destruction. Second, the inadequate transport force significantly lessened the Germans' ability to muster enough mobility forces to deliver supplies into Stalingrad. Hitler's decision to send airlift forces into North Africa also hurt his efforts in the USSR. Between November 1942 and January 1943, the Luftwaffe lost 250 Ju-52s in Tunisia—aircraft it could hardly afford do without.[17] Third, the Luftwaffe had only one adequate airfield to supply Stalingrad. Soviet ground forces eventually closed it and forced Luftwaffe transports to fly longer distances, which reduced daily sorties and made them more vulnerable to interception by Soviet aircraft. Soviet artillery and ground operations threatened airfield operations throughout the area. Fourth, unpredictable weather caused flight and ground-support problems. Weather delays and cancellations were common. Maintenance operations and the process of getting aircraft to work in freezing conditions exhausted the ground crews. Fifth, the Luftwaffe did not have air superiority. Transports were easy targets, even with fighter escorts. The Soviets claimed to have shot down 676 Ju-52s, but the Luftwaffe admitted only 266 planes lost.[18] Soviet aircraft also continued to attack Luftwaffe airfields, and the Luftwaffe could do little to stop it. For example, on 2 January 1943, Soviet ground-attack aircraft claimed to have destroyed 72 German aircraft on the ground.[19] Overly optimistic predictions and inadequate airlift resources ultimately led to the failure of the resupply effort. Soviet army forces eventually forced the surrender of the German Sixth Army on 30 January 1943.

Transporting an Army: Operation Desert Shield

The airlift of men, material, and machines from the United States to Saudi Arabia and the subsequent effort to supply forces and maintain those forces comprised the largest airlift in history. The US Air Force and its Civil Reserve Air Fleet (CRAF) provided rapid-response capability to all services that supported the coalition efforts of Operations Desert Shield and Desert Storm. Although sea lift carried more material and munitions than did airlift, the latter was able to deploy combat-ready soldiers within hours of a presidential decision to deploy ground and air forces to the Persian Gulf. Similarly, critical units or spare parts were delivered in-theater and distributed through an intratheater air-express service to move vital cargoes to their destination.

Civilian airliners supported the massive deployment of troops during Operation Desert Shield.

The American effort to defend Saudi Arabia and deter further Iraqi aggression in August 1990 relied upon swift movement of military forces from the continental United States to locations thousands of miles away in the Persian Gulf. Fortunately, the USAF had two dedicated major commands that could support this Herculean effort: Military Airlift Command (MAC) and Strategic Air Command. MAC had the responsibility to transport personnel and cargo worldwide with its fleet of Lockheed C-5 Galaxy and C-141 Starlifter jet aircraft. Additionally, MAC was responsible for intratheater airlift with Lockheed C-130 Hercules propeller-driven aircraft, which supported tactical missions. SAC was the Air Force's and nation's primary nuclear-deterrent force, but it also maintained and operated aerial-refueling Boeing KC-135 Stratotankers and McDonnell-Douglas KC-10 Extender aircraft.

The USAF's mobility forces had to move cargoes up to 7,000 miles one way. These distances and the amount of support required would take upwards of 80 percent of the C-141 fleet and 90 percent of all C-5 aircraft.[20] The 110 C-5 and 234 C-141 aircraft carried personnel, tanks, palletized cargo, helicopters, and other equipment to fight the war. These two aircraft types served as the bulwarks of the strategic, long-range airlift effort, moving close to 64 percent of the cargo and about 27 percent of the personnel transported by strategic airlift.[21] The USAF also operated 32 percent of its C-130 fleet in Desert Shield/Desert Storm. This fleet delivered up to 300,000 tons of cargo, using over 47,000 sorties throughout Saudi Arabia and the Persian Gulf area. These efforts were significant, but airlift resources were not sufficient. On 17 August 1990, President Bush authorized MAC to order CRAF to support the airlift. This fleet included commercial airliners that had accepted subsidies and preferential contracts in return for making themselves available for emergency activation to support airlift operations. This marked the first time CRAF had been activated in its 38-year history. Four days later, the president issued Executive Order 12727 to mobilize 200,000 reservists, many of them involved in mobility operations, for a period not to exceed 180 days.[22]

The airlift effort lasted about 206 days, moving approximately 17 million tons per mile per day (the product of aircraft cargo weight in tons and the distance flown).[23] C-5 and C-141 aircraft carried the cargo, while CRAF carried mostly passengers since its aircraft were configured for passenger service but not readily capable of transporting outsized cargo (e.g., tanks). The strategic airlift of dry cargo material accounted for only 15 percent of the total war effort, but it carried about 99 percent of all passengers deployed to and from the Persian Gulf.[24] At the peak of operations, from December 1990 to January 1991, strategic-airlift aircraft were landing every 11 minutes, 24 hours a day. This equated to 127 aircraft that conducted a sortie per day. Airlift operations rose to support the initial deployment of forces into Saudi Arabia and to support combat operations after the start of Desert Storm in January 1991.

On 7 August 1990, President Bush authorized the deployment of military forces into Saudi Arabia to defend the kingdom. MAC had to start moving forces almost immediately, initiating thousands of sorties. MAC quickly deployed an airlift-support team to the Persian Gulf to set up a coordination and control office. On 8 August, the first elements of the Army's 2d Brigade of the 82d Airborne Division from Fort Bragg, North Carolina, were sent to Saudi Arabia to send a clear signal of America's commitment and to deter further Iraqi aggression.[25] The JCS also sent two squadrons of F-15C fighters, Maritime Prepositioned Squadrons 2 and 3 (which contained heavy equipment and supplies) from Diego Garcia and Guam, two aircraft-carrier battle groups, and an airborne warning and control system (AWACS) unit to the Persian Gulf, along with the ready brigade from the 82d Airborne. MAC supported the move of the F-15s, AWACS aircraft, and Army brigade.

Requests to move major units and cargo started to overwhelm MAC. Its airlift fleet was limited, and it relied on Air Force Reserve personnel to man half of its crews.[26] The airlift effort needed aircrews and aircraft. On 17 August, Gen Hansford T. Johnson, commander in chief of MAC, ordered a limited activation of CRAF, which added 17 passenger and 21 cargo planes to MAC's fleet. The president would later issue a call-up of reserves. Within a month of MAC's beginning the airlift, it had moved 50,000 tons of cargo and 70,000 passengers.

There were 100 combat aircraft on the ground in Saudi Arabia, as well as a brigade from the 82d Airborne, personnel from a Marine air-ground task force, and elements from an air-assault division. These forces allowed the UN to provide an immediate but limited defensive force against the Iraqis. The next deployments would concentrate on building up a force to expel the Iraqis from Kuwait.

On 9 November, President Bush ordered more military forces into the theater. Passenger movement expanded. Heavily armored Marine Corps and other combat divisions were rushed into the theater. This movement also created a demand for additional cargo to support more personnel. MAC used all available CRAF aircraft and started to reduce its cargo missions by modifying C-141 aircraft to carry passengers. Logistics distribution and transportation systems were inundated in the United States and in Saudi Arabia with the deluge of requests and deliveries. This emphasis on airlift did not change until the start of Desert Storm—the attack on Iraqi forces.

The start of offensive operations against Iraq, beginning on 17 January, brought several challenges to MAC. The Iraqis began to launch Scud surface-to-surface ballistic missiles, which threatened airfields in Saudi Arabia. Several CRAF aircrews refused to enter a war zone, and there was great fear that the Scuds might carry chemical or biological weapons. Most CRAF airlines indicated that they would fly into the area only during daylight hours since Scud attacks occurred at night.[27] This affected the timing and scheduling of flights, which could lead to the possible cancellation of 24-hour operations. MAC officials moved airfields out of the range of Scuds, provided CRAF aircrews with chemical defense gear and better intelligence, and made a concerted effort to convince airline executives to accept their request to return to the previous working relationship. CRAF operations resumed their 24-hour-per-day schedule. On 17 January, another 76 CRAF aircraft were activated; only nine cargo planes were used since MAC had contracted the others to fly earlier.[28] Another challenge was the Scud attacks on Israel. President Bush ordered the deployment of US Army Patriot SAM units to defend Israel. The Patriot was originally developed as an antiaircraft missile, but modifications to its software allowed it to intercept tactical ballistic missiles like Scuds.

MAC needed to use almost all of its C-5 fleet to move the Patriot missile batteries because of their size and extensive support equipment. Within 24 hours of notification, two Patriot batteries were landing in Tel Aviv's Ben-Gurion Airport on 19 January.[29] The batteries were made minimally operational that day. Coincidentally, the Iraqis started a Scud attack on Israel that same day. Within three days of being airlifted, the Patriots began operations to intercept Scud missiles. The airlift forces were able to respond rapidly to an emerging threat and move priority cargo and personnel to different regions to support a national directive.

MAC still needed to support air and ground operations. The United States had deployed almost 500,000 personnel to the theater. They needed food, water, medicine, munitions, and all types of equipment. MAC also had to prepare for personnel movements back to the United States and other locations worldwide after the war.

Intratheater airlift was also a significant effort. C-130 sorties actually outnumbered those of all other aircraft types in Desert Shield/Desert Storm.[30] The C-130s acted as "feeder" airlines to the strategic-airlift C-5, C-141, and CRAF aircraft that made the intercontinental flights. These routes were scheduled to provide routine distribution of cargo and personnel. Helicopters could extend the feeder airlines to locations inaccessible to C-130s. The aircraft supported operations throughout the Persian Gulf and delivered reinforcements and supplies to frontline troops. F-16 units were moved overnight by C-130s to get closer to the battlefield.[31] The C-130 fleet was critical to intratheater logistics and included the first units to be deployed to serve in that capacity. These aircraft delivered air tasking orders (ATO) (daily aircraft-operations orders) that shaped the conduct of the war, delivered reconnaissance film, and provided advanced logistics support to units on the move, among other missions.

C-130s transported the entire XVIII Airborne Corps during the ground-combat phase of Desert Storm. The corps moved from its base in Saudi Arabia to a position 400 miles west. Airlift aircrews beat the estimated requirement of averaging a landing every 10 minutes during a 24-hour period for 14 days by averaging a landing every seven minutes![32] This airlift operation moved 9,000 tons of equipment and over 14,000 airborne troops.

Aerial refueling allowed the UN's coalition air forces to conduct training, patrol capabilities, and a major air campaign. Aerial refueling also allowed the strategic airlift and transit of combat aircraft. US Air Force, Navy, Marine Corps, and foreign air forces provided several different types of tankers that kept fighters and AWACS aircraft on station to defend Saudi Arabia. These aircraft also allowed attack aircraft to strike deep into Iraq or loiter over the battlefield to conduct CAS and interdiction missions. SAC tankers flew over 360 sorties a day and averaged 1,433 refuelings a day.[33] Refueling capability supported 60 percent of all attack sorties.

Aerial refueling allowed the initial F-15 force to arrive in Saudi Arabia within one day; with their armaments, the F-15s were able to fly operational missions a day after their arrival. Over 1,000 aircraft were able to carry their armaments and arrive on station, ready for combat. A tanker bridge that involved more than 100 tankers was constructed between the United States and Saudi Arabia. Aircraft such as the F-15 used five refuelings to make the trip nonstop.[34] Refueling operations were the largest and most extensive in history.

MAC and SAC were able to successfully conduct a massive airlift operation that directly aided the victory in Desert Storm. They moved personnel and critical cargo quickly. However, ground commanders wanted three times the airlift capability that MAC and SAC possessed. Additionally, increased usage of C-5 and C-141 aircraft caused operational readiness rates to fall because of maintenance requirements. The rush to airlift materials also caused priority difficulties, payload inefficiencies, and planning problems. These problems highlighted concerns about realistic training, planning factors, retention of sufficient numbers of aircrews, and integration of CRAF aircraft into MAC operations.

The airlift operation did, however, work well. Using C-141 aircraft near the end of their operational lives and undergoing a massive downsizing of forces after the Cold War, MAC provided the largest airlift operation in history. The value of mobility resources was underscored when air forces were rapidly moved to fight in Desert Storm, Army units were sent directly into the theater within hours, and combat-ready equipment was deployed in a minimum of time.

Airlift Saves Berlin: Operation Vittles

Airpower has increasingly been called upon as a tool of choice to provide humanitarian aid worldwide. Air transports can deliver food, medicine, equipment, supplies, and personnel within hours of an emergency. This capability has been available for several years. One of the first instances of airpower's being called upon to support people in need occurred in 1948, when the Soviet Union blockaded Berlin and tried to sever it from the Western powers. By agreement, Britain, France, the United States, and the Soviet Union administered a divided Berlin. The city itself was located within the Soviet-controlled zone of occupation that would later become the People's Democratic Republic of Germany or East Germany. The Soviets attempted to squeeze the allies out of Berlin and reduce their influence in Eastern Europe.

Stalin, leader of the Soviet Union, wanted to further consolidate the Soviet sphere of influence in Eastern Europe. The American, British, and French presence in Berlin was a reminder of Western influence. West Germany was being rebuilt under the Marshall Plan and might become a self-sustaining country, which would make the East German regime's economic efforts pale in comparison. The allies also introduced a new currency in Berlin over which the Soviets had no control. Stalin wanted the allies out of the city.[35]

On 15 June 1948, the Soviets placed restrictions on traffic between Berlin and the western zones of occupation held by the American, British, and French powers. The Soviets wanted Western currency usage ended in Berlin since the Soviet zone of occupation surrounded it and they believed Berlin was part of the Soviet-controlled economy. The Soviets issued a new currency, the ostmark, for use throughout Berlin. Gen Lucius D. Clay, American military governor of the military zone in Berlin, refused to compromise. The Soviets could withdraw their demand, go to war, or intensify their blockade. At 0600 on 24 June, the Soviets cut off all road, rail, and water traffic from Berlin to West Germany. Electricity from the Soviet zone of occupation to Berlin was shut off due to "coal shortages."[36] The Western powers could either agree with the Soviets or get out of Berlin.

President Harry Truman ordered US forces to stay in Berlin, which became a symbol of America's fight against spreading communism. Secretary of Defense James Forrestal recalled Truman's bluntly stating, "We [are] going to stay, period."[37] Without food, supplies, and power, the Western powers had only an estimated 36 days of food and 45 days of coal in stock to supply 2.3 million civilians and military personnel.[38] The city needed 3,800 tons of supplies daily in summer and 4,500 tons in winter; the winter requirement was later raised to 5,600 tons.[39] Without surface transportation, the only possible solution was an immediate airlift. Clay was unconvinced that the USAF could conduct such an operation. He wanted to send a relief column supported with armored vehicles through the Soviet zone of occupation to resupply Berlin. Truman disagreed with Clay and ordered an airlift. The USAF and RAF began an effort to airlift food, supplies, and coal into Berlin. These actions became known as Operation Vittles or the Berlin airlift.

United States Air Forces in Europe (USAFE) would bear the brunt of the airlift missions. USAFE had two troop-carrying groups of Douglas C-47 Dakota transports. Lt Gen Curtis E. LeMay, commander of USAFE, estimated that his force could airlift about 225 tons per day—less than half of the 500-ton-per-day requirement for the military-occupation force alone.[40] LeMay requested that Headquarters US Air Force send additional heavier-lift Douglas C-54 Skymaster aircraft, which were sent to LeMay along with an order to provide airlift for the civilian population as well. LeMay and Clay agreed on a 24-hour-a-day airlift with 54 C-54 and 195 C-47 aircraft that could lift 1,500 tons per day.[41] LeMay was forced to rely on the less-capable C-47s until sufficient numbers of C-54s were assigned to Europe. The British could provide about 750 tons per day. When Clay asked LeMay if he could lift coal and other supplies, LeMay responded, "The Air Force can deliver anything."[42] However, LeMay needed even more capability to meet

C-47s, like the one shown here, provided invaluable service during the Berlin airlift.

these demands. The Air Force stripped units in the United States, Guam, Hawaii, and other locations to muster enough C-54s to support the airlift. The US Navy sent 24 C-54s. USAFE had 225 C-54s ready to support the airlift. Earlier, USAFE estimated it needed 162 C-54s, without C-47 support, to meet Berlin's requirements. USAFE now had sufficient air resources to begin the operation.

The USAFE and RAF efforts were merged into the Combined Airlift Task Force (CALTF). The Soviets allowed CALTF to operate three air corridors, each 20 miles wide, under previous agreements (fig. 11). The Soviets patrolled the corridors with fighters and monitored activity with radar and communications equipment. The first airlift missions started on 26 June with an 80-ton delivery. LeMay had started to airlift some supplies to Berlin earlier in anticipation of the blockade. These initial trials started on 21 June with a six-ton load that grew to 156 tons the next day.[43] By 28 June, the RAF started airlift missions. As transports became available to CALTF, the tonnage increased. The Soviets started to harass the transports.

RAPID MOBILITY/SPACE AND INFORMATION

The US Air Force reacted by sending two squadrons of B-29 bombers and Lockheed F-80 Shooting Star fighters to Europe in case hostilities ensued. The B-29s were not capable of carrying nuclear weapons, but they were highly publicized as "atomic bombers."[44] The atomic-bomb-capable B-29s remained in the United States.

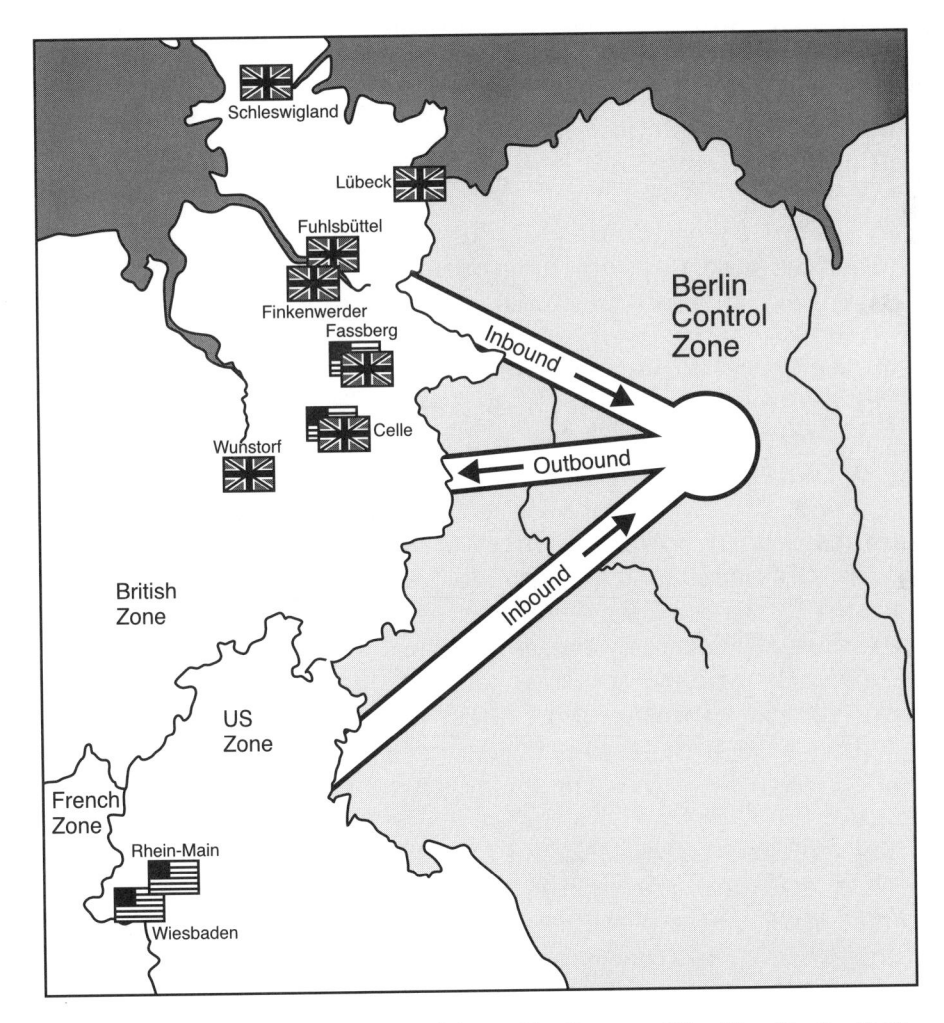

Figure 11. Berlin Airlift (Adapted from *To Save a City: The Berlin Airlift, 1948–1949* by Robert G. Miller [Washington, D.C.: Air Force History and Museums Program, 1998], iv)

Maj Gen William H. Tunner, commander of CALTF, created a production-line effort to get aircraft on schedule for departure, spaced within the corridor, landed, cargo extracted, and returned to West Germany for another sortie. Tunner built his airlift upon the heavier-airlift C-54 aircraft, which had triple the carrying capacity of the C-47.[45] The larger-capacity aircraft would reduce the number of sorties and ease coordination. USAFE and RAF aircraft were guided by radar and were spaced three minutes apart. Radar- and ground-controlled approach (GCA) systems kept strict discipline for the aircraft. Winter storms, night operations, and the GCA handled other problems. Each plane had only one opportunity to approach and land; if it could not, the plane was ordered back to West Germany.

C-54s on the ground were quickly unloaded and refueled. Tunner reduced time on the ground to 30 minutes.[46] Aircrews would call 10 minutes ahead of landing to coordinate with ground operations to ensure that a specialized crew was available to off-load a particular cargo, such as coal, and arrange for a parking spot for each aircraft. Aircrews stayed on the plane while it was unloaded and refueled. Similarly, the loading of coal and food became a science. A loading team could put a bagged, 10-ton cargo of coal into an aircraft in about 15 minutes, and a portable conveyor belt could load 20 tons of coal in 35 minutes, compared to a ground crew's 45 to 60 minutes.[47] Tunner believed that his aircrews could achieve maximum efficiency by using standardized procedures. Crews were given standard training courses, flight information, procedures, and controls. C-54 airlift operations operated like a machine with little variance. Tunner's efforts paid off, as C-54s carried more than their civilian versions by about 8,500 pounds.[48]

The nonstop operations did take a toll on aircraft. Engines needed overhaul and spare-parts replacements. Landing on rough, steel-planked runways required above-normal tire repairs. USAFE and augmented maintenance crews could not perform all of the maintenance. These crews had to replace over 90 engines per month and repair 23 tires a day, along with repairs and routine checks on hydraulics, electrical systems, airframes, and other problems. C-54s also required 200-

and 1,000-hour routine maintenance checks. After 200 flight hours, a C-54 was sent to a depot in England for a series of inspections. After passing the inspections, the plane was loaded with engines ready for overhaul and sent back to the United States for the 1,000-hour maintenance work. This removed the aircraft from operations for up to 44 days. After the airplane underwent the maintenance work, it was loaded with cargo and repaired engines to return to Germany. Tunner used a complex scheduling system to ensure that he had a minimum of 319 C-54s available from a peak force of 400 aircraft to conduct operations.[49] About 75 were in maintenance at any one time. Still, scheduling was not enough.

Tunner started to employ German nationals to conduct limited, routine maintenance work in Berlin. These replacements would allow American maintenance crews to concentrate on other vital repair work. USAFE hired former World War II Luftwaffe personnel. Maintenance manuals were translated into German to aid the effort. The program worked so well that ex-Luftwaffe personnel outnumbered American maintenance crews at the end of the Berlin airlift.

Operation Vittles was meeting all expectations and requirements. Berlin's citizens were fed, clothed, and heated through airpower. The 24-hour-a-day operation lasted for 462 days, with the exception of a 15-hour period in November 1948 that closed airlift operations due to poor weather. On 15 April 1949, CALTF established a delivery record of 12,940 tons in 1,398 sorties.[50] Airlift capability grew from 2,000 tons per day on 31 July to an average of 5,583 tons by 18 September 1948. It continued even higher despite the winter weather. The Soviets' blockade had failed. The West had won. On 9 May 1949, the Soviets announced that the blockade would be lifted on 12 May. Operation Vittles continued to deliver supplies through the air in case the Soviets reinitiated the blockade.

Airlift operations performed magnificently. Through 30 September 1949—the end of the Berlin airlift—CALTF delivered 2,325,000 tons of cargo. Berlin did not fall. The city continued to conduct business and factory production under "normal" conditions. The US Air Force carried about 1,783,000 tons of cargo. During the period, approximately two-thirds of this cargo was coal.[51] American and British aircrews flew 567,537 flying hours with a takeoff or landing occurring every minute. Unfortunately, CALTF lost 12 aircraft in crashes that killed 30 American military members and one civilian.

The Berlin airlift demonstrated the feasibility and effectiveness of mobility operations. Combined and joint operations were showcased in this effort. American and British airlift joined forces to supply Berlin with almost every requirement imaginable. The C-54s demonstrated the advantages that large cargo planes had over the smaller C-47s. These aircraft showed that large aircraft were more efficient than the nimbler cargo aircraft. Additionally, Operation Vittles was a visible showcase for global-mobility operations in peace and, potentially, in war. The Berlin airlift was the largest one of its kind up to this point in history. It was conducted solely for humanitarian reasons, yet it had serious political implications for the future of Western Europe. Planning and coordination allowed a massive airlift operation to be sprung in weeks, altering Stalin's position on Berlin. He could continue the fruitless effort; attack the combined American, British, and French forces; or end the blockade. He chose a humiliating defeat and pulled back the blockade. The newly created US Air Force had survived its first challenge and won.

Space and Information: The Enabler of Operations

Aerospace power is a combination of air and space functions and capabilities that have enhanced combat operations on the battlefield and have aided national-security decisions. Space operations have significantly increased the quality and amount of information that has directly affected the ability of commanders to observe enemy operations, communicate with forces, plan actions, prepare forces for combat, and support war-fighting capabilities. Additionally, space systems provide deterrent value for the nation's security. Satellites provide a constant stream of information about possible ICBM launches. Space-based imagery also allows the nation to identify potential threats from new weapons. These opportunities provide more alternatives to decision makers. Some of the uncertainty that military commanders face is reduced, and the chance of success on the battlefield is increased with this information.

Computer and information technology has significantly increased since the days of the first computer—ENIAC—in 1946. The acquisition, manipulation, transmission, and storage of vast amounts of information have revolutionized warfare. Intelligence information about enemy capabilities that formerly took days or weeks to gather, format, and distribute now takes minutes. The transmission of battle plans might involve a single distribution through a network of computers instead of printing and physically delivering the orders to their recipients. While the United States utilizes this information for many defense issues, it must also defend against powers that may try to disable or destroy the ability to use such information. The nation also conducts information warfare, which seeks to defend the country's use of information and to deny the same capability to a foe. This capability is similar to air superiority in that it allows the nation to act without fear of attack on its information.

Space and information operations are tightly connected. Information in warfare and information warfare rely on the gathering and rapid transmission of large quantities of data. Satellites can provide a means to observe an area of the globe unhindered by the limitations of manned aircraft and national borders. These systems can operate on a 24-hour schedule that may provide near-constant coverage over a specific region. Global communications with satellites also provide near-simultaneous connections without regard to terrain. This capability has also aided aircrews in the receiving of navigation information. These opportunities have not only helped military but also commercial organizations. The rapid and accurate use of information has transformed the world economy. This has been a boon to industry, but it has also become a potential target for an adversary.

There have been several space and information operations that have had national impact. Space operations are still relatively new compared to air operations, but space systems have gained much influence relative to aerial systems over recent years. Information technology is growing at an exponential rate and provides many new avenues to exploit and defend against exploitation. These opportunities will provide the future aerospace leader with an additional arsenal to meet tomorrow's challenges.

Finding a Needle in a Haystack: The Great Scud Hunt

During Desert Storm, a major problem that plagued coalition forces was the inability to destroy Iraqi surface-to-surface ballistic missiles launched against targets in Israel and Saudi Arabia. The Iraqis were able to launch a number of Scud missiles that killed several people and could have created more damage had they been armed with NBC warheads. Part of the problem of finding these missiles involved determining the location of launchers, mobile or fixed. The US Air Force's Defense Support Program (DSP) was a key component of the Scud hunt.

The Scud was not a precision weapon. The Iraqi government used it as a terror weapon rather than a military one. Saddam ordered that Scuds be used in his war with Iran from March to June 1985, when the Iraqis attacked factories, a nuclear plant, and civilian targets. Saddam attempted to use Scud strikes against Israel to fracture a tenuous alliance between Western and Arab nations during the Gulf War.[52] The Iraqis hoped that their Scud attacks might provoke an Israeli military response that would put the coalition Arab nations in a tough position of siding with Israel against another Arab country. The Iraqis launched the first Scud attack on 17 January 1991 and followed with seven missiles that struck near Tel Aviv and one missile against Dhahran, Saudi Arabia. The coalition had to stop Scud launchings in order to keep Israel from taking unilateral action that might affect the operation of the war. After hearing about the Scud launches, Secretary of Defense Dick Cheney stated that "the number one priority is to keep Israel out of the war."[53]

The Scud was a relatively primitive ballistic missile based on the World War II–era German V-2. The Iraqis purchased several missiles from the Soviet Union and developed several indigenous missiles. Saddam's missile force was composed of the Scud 1-C, Scud-B, and the Iraqi-made Al-Hussein and

A Scud missile that failed to reach its target

Al-Abbas/Al-Hijarah Scud derivatives. The Soviet-built Scuds had a limited range of 175–85 miles, with a circular error probable of 2,900 feet; they could carry a payload of 2,200 pounds.[54] The Al-Hussein had a longer range but a reduced payload of 1,000 pounds; though less accurate, it could reach a speed of Mach 5. Iraq's Al-Abbas and Al-Hijarah had the longest range—465 miles—with only a 650-pound payload; they were less accurate than the Al-Hussein.

Iraqi missile crews could launch the Scuds in two ways: from fixed sites and through mobile transporter erector launchers (TEL). Scuds deployed from fixed sites offered more accuracy since their guidance systems were better aligned against target coordinates. However, these sites were also vulnerable to air attack. TELs offered a more difficult target since a launch crew could fire its missile from many locations against an enemy. Such launches were less accurate than launching from a fixed site, but mobile sites could remain hidden from detection until firing. After a launch, the TEL was driven away and hidden.

The United States had two options to reduce the chance of Scuds hitting Israel. American forces could deploy a missile-defense system or conduct an air campaign against the missiles and their launchers. The US Army deployed and operated the Patriot missile in an anti-ballistic-missile role to shoot down Scuds. Additionally, the coalition air forces used ground-attack aircraft to locate and destroy Scud launching sites. Both systems required detailed information about the timing and location of the missile launch. The usual flight time from launch to impact was only seven minutes.[55] Patriot missile units required warnings, and strike aircraft used location data to find the launch site. Scud missiles were not militarily important. They had a small warhead and were inaccurate. Their true value was their political impact.

The United States had three DSP satellites in the Persian Gulf theater. DSP satellites were originally developed to detect Soviet ICBM launches and submarine-launched ballistic missiles through infrared signatures, thus providing strategic warning to national leaders. In 1990 the JCS realized that DSP could also identify launches of less-capable tactical ballistic missiles, including Scuds, and authorized United States Space Command to release this data for regional combat commanders.[56] This entailed a move from a strategic, national role to one that provided detailed launch time, location, missile class, direction, and an assessment of the launch to a war-fighting commander for immediate, day-to-day operations to defeat tactical ballistic missiles. This change would require alterations in operating conditions to provide tactical missile warning along with the satellites' primary mission of providing early warning against an ICBM attack on the United States.[57]

DSP satellites, along with ground-based radar systems in Turkey, could detect ballistic missile launches from Iraq. Only these systems could provide warning and targeting information concerning the Scud attacks. The United States operated three DSP satellites in the area for such purposes. The DSP used an infrared telescope to monitor Earth every 10 seconds. A sensor within the telescope would detect the infrared energy from a Scud and send an electronic signal to a ground station for processing. Cloud cover could mask detection of the mis-

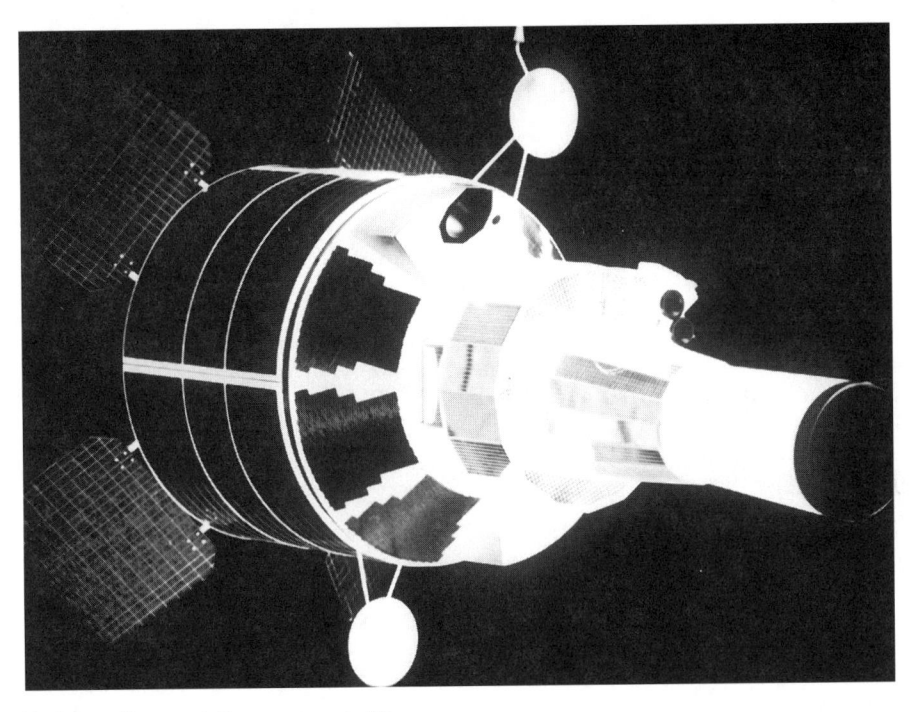

Defense Support Program satellite

sile's "launch plume." The Scud could be detected only after it broke through the clouds.

Once the missile was detected, satellite data was sent to ground stations for relay to a processing center in the United States. Initial data was sent to an Air Force Space Command station in Woomera, Australia, and then sent via a Defense Satellite Communications System (DSCS) link to another ground station at Buckley AFB, Colorado. The data was then transmitted to US Space Command's Missile Warning Center at the North American Air Defense Command in Cheyenne Mountain near Colorado Springs, Colorado. The data was then analyzed, and launch information transmitted back to the Persian Gulf through DSCS to US Central Command in Saudi Arabia. The data was transmitted by a telephone call or through the automated Tactical Event Reporting System. Central Command would send the warning to a Patriot missile battery commander or air commander via the Air Force Satellite Communications System. These commanders relayed the information via radio link to their subordinates to take air defense actions or to hunt for the Scud TEL or fixed site. This process took about five minutes.[58] Given the fact that the missile's flight usually lasted seven minutes and that Patriot missile crews needed time to align their missiles and detect the incoming missile with their own radar systems, there was little margin for error.

The Air Force Space Command, US Central Command, US Space Command, and others tried to reduce the warning time. From 17 to 20 January, the warning time averaged 5.4 minutes but was significantly reduced to 3.3 minutes after Air Force Space Command analysts became experienced with the detection of Scud launches. This added crucial time to allow Patriot and aircraft crews to prepare for operations. Air Force Space Command officials suggested that a direct connection between DSP and Central Command be established that would reduce warning time to 90 seconds.[59] Unfortunately, this proposal required training, secure communications, procedures, and equipment that would take too long to make the system operational.

At first, the Patriot missile defense system was touted as a great success. Scuds were fired upon and allegedly brought down. Unfortunately, the Patriot's performance was challenged when an analysis by the General Accounting Office of Patriot warhead kills indicated a 9 percent success rate against Scuds.[60] Patriot missile batteries in Israel were also criticized in a 1991 Israeli Defense Ministry report that claimed there was no evidence that the Patriots hit Scuds. However, DSP information identified each Scud launch and was relayed to the appropriate individuals. One can only speculate as to whether the delay in receiving information or the performance of the Patriot missile caused the drop in interception rate. However, DSP information did provide at least a limited warning time and guidance information for the Patriots.

The Great Scud Hunt over Iraq by coalition aircraft was also a disappointment. McDonnell-Douglas F-15E Strike Eagles attacked fixed sites on the first day of Desert Storm in order to eliminate the threat to Israel. Initial battle-damage assessment indicated that the effort destroyed 36 fixed and 10 mo-

A Patriot missile battery, ready for action

bile TELs,[61] the latter representing the real problem. The Iraqis used preselected launch sites to improve accuracy and hide their TELs. Bombing missions were conducted against Scud production facilities, fixed sites, potential hiding places, and mobile launchers.

The hunt for the mobile TELs was limited because of the time required to calculate the location of the launch and send aircraft to attack. Only 215 sorties were made against TELs—approximately 15 percent of all air attacks against Scuds.[62] This slim number indicated the difficulty of coordinating near-real-time detection, targeting, and attacks on these types of systems. Although the coalition air forces had information, this limited effort underscored the difficulty of striking TELs. F-15Es and other aircraft, such as F-16s, were equipped with targeting and infrared detection systems to attack TELs at night and with limited visibility. Even if the Scud was sighted,

The F-15E provides long-range strategic strike and interdiction.

targeting and delivering weapons against the TEL proved difficult. On 42 occasions in which pilots identified TELs, only eight were attacked due to sensor limitations.[63]

The Great Scud Hunt had limited success insofar as increased patrolling by F-15E, F-16, and other aircraft may have reduced the number of launches. The first week of the campaign saw 34 missiles fired against targets. During the last week, the rate dropped to 17.[64] But the Great Scud Hunt used 2,493 sorties that involved F-15E, F-16, A-6E, A-10, B-52G, F-117A, and RAF Tornadoes.[65] This effort took away valuable aircraft missions that Central Command could have diverted to other areas, such as CAS or interdiction.

DSP's ability to find, track, and warn coalition forces worked very well. Air Force Space Command personnel were able to adjust DSP from a strategic missile warning system to one that detected tactical ballistic missiles. Warning times were reduced. Accurate information was given to commanders. Unfortunately, even this advanced warning time was not enough to halt the deaths of 42 individuals in the war. The relatively rapid warning time required better coordination and information distribution. A five-minute warning time may have been adequate for a response, given a 30-minute missile flight. Tactical commanders had, at best, only a 3.3-minute warning time for a Scud flight time of seven minutes. The warning times were even shorter when Scuds were launched under heavy cloud cover. Additionally, tactical commanders had to launch air strikes or conduct antiballistic-missile operations that took more time and exact coordination. The Scud experience caused the United States to initiate a series of Patriot system improvements and speed up efforts to develop a tactical ballistic missile defense system. In the future, aerospace leaders need to concentrate not on detection capabilities, but on command, control, and battle management of information and its rapid distribution to users.

Corona: The First Space-Reconnaissance System

After the end of World War II, the United States and the Soviet Union entered another war—the Cold War. Each nation developed nuclear weapons and the means to deliver them. A devastating strategic attack against cities and military forces could occur within hours from a bomber or minutes from a land-based or submarine-launched ballistic missile. The United States needed accurate information to assess the Soviet Union's capability to launch a nuclear attack. If the Soviets were building a new weapon, then the United States might need to develop a counterweight to this threat or increase its deterrence against such a weapon. This would affect the nation's chances for survival.

The United States developed and deployed a series of programs designed to gather information about the USSR's military capabilities. Several aircraft systems were used to gather electronic, communications, and photographic information. These schemes ranged from the use of high-altitude balloons carrying cameras to aircraft that would enter the Soviet Union's airspace to gather strategic information. Soviet air defenses started to improve their capabilities to shoot down these balloons and aircraft with advanced SAMs guided by radar systems and interceptors. Additionally, the Soviets increased the number of jet interceptors capable of reaching reconnaissance aircraft. The Central Intelligence Agency (CIA) and US Air Force combined to develop a high-altitude photographic aircraft—the Lockheed U-2. CIA officials believed its high-altitude operation could escape SAMs and jet interceptors.

U-2 operations overflew the USSR, gathering photographic information about Soviet strategic bomber and missile developments. These missions ended when the Soviets shot down a U-2 on 1 May 1960, captured its pilot, and exposed America's aerial spy missions to the world. This shootdown denied the US government its premier strategic-reconnaissance system.

The CIA and the Air Force had commissioned several studies to explore the use of Earth-orbiting satellites to take photographs over the Soviet Union. Satellites seemed to be a reasonable, albeit untried, substitute for aircraft. The Soviets had already sent a satellite into orbit when they launched *Sputnik I* on 4 October 1957. Satellites were seen as a less vulnerable alternative than another aerial system. There were no known Soviet antisatellite weapons, and an unmanned reconnaissance satellite did not have a pilot to support or lose if the satellite were shot down. Additionally, the satellite could take photographs over several regions in the Soviet Union faster than an airplane could. While the U-2 was readied for its missions to get information about Soviet systems, the Air Force was charged in 1955 with developing a highly classified space system—Weapon System (WS)-117L—that would provide continuous surveillance of preselected areas of the world related to an adversary's war-making capability.[66]

The Lockheed Corporation received a contract on 29 October 1956 to build WS-117L. The project would provide the CIA with an operational system in 1960. President Eisenhower wanted a satellite system in place earlier. CIA and USAF officials decided to initiate an interim reconnaissance satellite that might be deployed faster. This system—Corona—was designed to use a camera that photographed its targets while the satellite made several orbits over a designated area. The film would be returned to Earth via a recoverable reentry capsule that an Air Force plane would capture in midair over the Pacific.

The Corona program helped answer many questions about the Soviet Union's military programs. Airfields, factories, missile silos, research and development centers, military bases, and other targets were photographed. However, Eisenhower wanted the existence of Corona kept secret. A cover story was concocted, and the project was called Discoverer in public—an attempt to mask the reconnaissance program's purpose as a scientific satellite program.

The Corona program was originally designed for a mission of limited duration. A Thor launch vehicle would put Corona into a polar orbit from Vandenberg AFB, California. Each Corona vehicle had a 70-degree panoramic Itek camera with a resolution of 35 to 40 feet.[67] Later missions included two cameras and improved resolution to six feet. The first Corona vehicles carried enough film for a 24-hour mission that allowed the satellite to make 17 orbits.[68] The vehicle would start photographing a wide area of the Soviet Union because it could not distinguish particular targets, unlike the U-2, whose pilot controlled the camera. A radio signal from the ground would initiate the reentry phase of the flight. The film was recovered in a parachute-equipped reentry vehicle caught in midair by a C-119 recovery aircraft stationed at Hickam AFB, Hawaii. Later, modified JC-130s improved the recovery process.

Discoverer I was launched on 28 February 1959. This test case was designed to evaluate the Thor booster rocket's ability to put a dummy payload into orbit. Air Force engineers tracking *Discoverer I*'s progress lost contact with the vehicle 950 miles from Vandenberg. Failures plagued the early Discoverer program. Problems involving the Thor booster rocket, camera, reentry system, and other shortfalls caused much concern about Corona's future. Finally, on 10 August 1960, *Discoverer XIII* put an instrument payload into orbit that was recovered by ship after it reentered the atmosphere, despite the fact that a C-119 recovery aircraft had failed to catch it. President Eisenhower displayed an American flag that had gone into orbit in the reentry vehicle. This public act helped cement Discoverer's cover story but, more importantly, proved that Corona could work.

The prime targets for photographic missions were the Soviet Union's ICBMs. The United States did not know how many missiles the Soviets possessed or their capabilities. During the presidential campaign debates, President Eisenhower's administration was blamed for creating a "missile gap" between the United States and the USSR. The Soviets were credited with a growing ballistic missile advantage, and the United States needed to build up its strategic force. Although the U-2 had provided valuable photographs over several targeted areas, much of the Soviet Union was uncharted by the CIA. Approximately 65 percent of the Soviet Union's landmass could hold ICBMs.[69] The CIA estimated that the Soviet Union could have 150 to 400 ICBMs by mid-1961. Corona could help confirm or deny this estimate.

Discoverer XIV was launched on 18 August 1960. The camera used 20 pounds of film to photograph 1,650,000 square miles of the Soviet Union, more than the total U-2 program of 24 flights.[70] The film allowed photointerpreters to identify 64 new airfields and 26 SAM bases. However, clouds obscured the film, and the camera's resolution did not allow the photointerpreters to count aircraft. Later advancements in camera technology would improve this capability. The vehicles started to carry more film, stereo cameras, two film-recovery capsules, more fuel to keep Corona in orbit longer, and other additions.

Corona proved to be a great success for the nation. The program was able to photograph 23 of 25 Soviet ICBM complexes by March 1964. Three months later, all ICBM complexes were photographed.[71] The missile gap was debunked when the Soviets were shown to have about 10–25 ICBMs in 1961.[72] Believing the missile gap, some people in the administration of President John F. Kennedy wanted to build 10,000 Minuteman ICBMs; instead, Kennedy reduced the number of missiles to 1,000, which saved valuable resources and reduced the chance of a massive arms race. The Kennedy administration observed no appreciable buildup of Soviet or Warsaw Pact military activities (including ballistic missiles) during the Cuban missile crisis. This allowed President Kennedy to strengthen his fortitude to maintain a naval blockade around Cuba. Another example of Corona's value was its ability to determine the amount of destruction that Israel inflicted on Arab forces in the Six-Day War in 1967. The United States knew the extent of the Israeli victory and the amount of damage suffered by the Arabs. During the Vietnam War, Corona photographed SAM sites and gave commanders the status of individual missile complexes. More importantly, the United States gained invaluable information about Soviet and Communist Chinese strategic weapons, nuclear energy, and space programs. The Corona program gave the United

The Minuteman ICBM force was built to counter a perceived Soviet missile threat.

States a reliable, continuing system that provided a glimpse into the Soviet and Chinese national defense programs.

The Corona program became the backbone of US intelligence capability during its long lifetime.[73] Corona missions flew from 1961 through 25 May 1972. This period covered 145 missions and 165 film-capsule recoveries. Corona cameras took 866,000 images covering 99,722,000 square miles.[74] This accomplishment created a wealth of timely information for national decision makers. Corona allowed American leaders to gather information about Soviet successes and failures in weapons and space developments, force-structure sizes, and deployments. This gave presidents a significant advantage in dealing with arms negotiations, weapons development, and diplomatic actions.

The information from Corona was a valuable light in a sea of intelligence darkness in the early 1960s. The program provided certainty to intelligence and gave national leaders confidence to make critical decisions. The United States and the Soviet Union were on the brink of building massive numbers of nuclear-armed weapons. The Soviets were threatening American interests in Western Europe over Berlin and off the coast of Florida in Cuba. Instead of overreacting and creating an artificial confrontation, national leaders were able to use up-to-date information to dispel false estimates or misinformation. Not only did Corona identify all major ballistic-missile launch complexes, but also it identified space centers, construction facilities for ballistic-missile submarines, weapons plants, SAMs, antiballistic-missile sites, and other high-value targets.[75] This information allowed America's national leaders and military forces to target these locations and create detailed maps. Additionally, the Corona information allowed President Nixon to begin serious arms-limitation negotiations with the Soviet Union.

The United States continues to use imagery satellite systems for military and arms control purposes. These systems provide critical, time-sensitive information that gives a commander near-instantaneous information about an enemy's force dispositions, battle damage, movements, and terrain conditions. Instead of film, these systems use electronic storage and transmission of photographs to ground stations that can send them in digital form around the world. These advances have given today's imagery satellites a significant advantage over the Corona system.

Information Averts a Nuclear Showdown: Cuba, 1962

In October 1962, the United States and the Soviet Union were at the brink of nuclear war over the Soviet Union's placement of intermediate-range and medium-range ballistic missiles (IRBM and MRBM) in Cuba, just 90 miles away from Florida (fig. 12). The Soviets' placement of both these missiles and Ilyushin Il-28 Beagle light jet bombers gave the Soviet Union a potent nuclear-strike capability. The Soviet Union was hoping to deploy these missiles without the United States's knowledge. President Kennedy was already aware of the missiles' presence and was prepared to demand their removal. On 22 October 1962, Kennedy called this action "deliberately provocative and unjustified . . . that cannot be accepted by this country."[76] The American discovery of Soviet chairman Nikita Khrushchev's placement of the missiles was greatly aided by aerial-reconnaissance aircraft that provided up-to-date photographic evidence of SAM, aircraft, IRBM, and MRBM deployments around Cuba. Photographic analysts from all services and the CIA gave the White House evidence of these actions with which to confront Khrushchev and eventually force him to dismantle the missiles and pledge never to put them in Cuba again.

Cuba had recently been through a turbulent period of revolution. Fidel Castro had risen to power and aligned himself as a Cuban nationalist revolutionary with Marxist leanings. Castro overthrew the Cuban government on 1 January 1959. He did not want to align himself with American businesses or government due to their support of the Cuban government that he had just overthrown. The Soviet Union moved swiftly to fill this void and provided military and economic aid to Castro's new communist government. Cuban-American relations were strained when anti-Castro forces, supported by the CIA, attempted an invasion of Cuba at the Bay of Pigs in April 1962. The Kennedy administration was highly embarrassed by this failure.

Khrushchev was encouraged by these events. He thought that he could influence and pressure Kennedy into making several concessions, more so than his predecessor, Dwight Eisenhower.[77] Kennedy and Khrushchev met in Vienna, Austria, to discuss several important mutual issues: arms control, relations between the two nations, and other points of contention. Kennedy supported the status quo while Khrushchev wanted more—the communist revolution was in full swing,

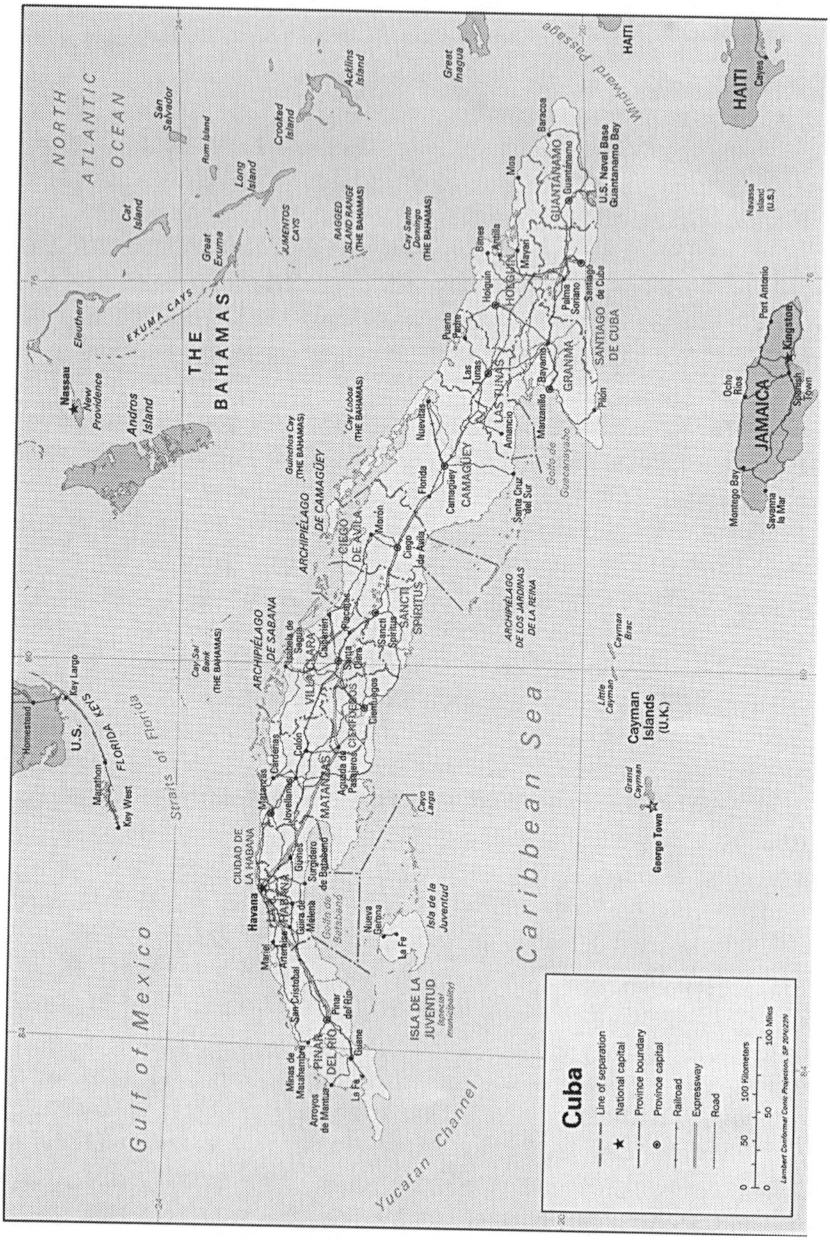

Figure 12. Cuba

and the Soviets wanted recognition as a superpower on par with the United States. The Soviets also were interested in gaining control of Berlin.

Khrushchev became bolder. He decided to pressure the United States into removing IRBMs and MRBMs based in Turkey, Italy, and Britain. Khrushchev considered the placement of nuclear-armed missiles a personal affront and demanded their withdrawal.[78] Although the Soviet Union had a few ballistic missiles and strategic bombers capable of reaching North America, the Soviets did not have as many capable nuclear forces as did the United States. If the Soviets could deploy operational IRBMs and MRBMs, the two countries might become more strategically balanced. Additionally, the attempted Bay of Pigs invasion was thought to be a signal of American intention to eventually wrest control of communist Cuba. Khrushchev could protect Cuba by providing a nuclear retaliatory force. In May 1962, the Soviet premier decided to build several missile bases in Cuba, thinking, "Why not throw a hedgehog at Uncle Sam's pants?"[79]

The Soviet Union would move MiG-21 interceptors, Il-28s, MRBMs, IRBMs, SAMs, AAA, construction equipment, and 42,000 construction and military personnel to Cuba. The Soviets secretly launched Operation Anadyr to ensure a missile deployment in Cuba by October 1962.[80] Soviet dockworkers unloaded the missiles, and Russian construction crews built missile complexes to avoid Cuban involvement and potential leaks. Castro was concerned about the secrecy and believed that public disclosure would be a better course for Cuba and the Soviet Union. Khrushchev disagreed. The deployment's secrecy would surprise Kennedy, especially with a November congressional election approaching, and force him to accede to several Soviet demands. Also, if the Americans found out about the deployment, they could attack Cuba or blockade the island. The deployment proceeded without notice until a CIA U-2 flight over Cuba provided photographic evidence of newly constructed SAM sites.

The CIA had reason to believe that the Soviets were sending massive numbers of military weapons to Cuba. On 22 August, Kennedy was advised of the large arms shipments, and he ordered increased aerial surveillance of the island. The vulnerability of the CIA's U-2 program became evident when one of its planes was shot down over the Soviet Union in May. The Cubans did not, as the CIA first believed, possess the same air defense systems or capabilities as the Soviets. US Air Force and Navy reconnaissance, patrol, and surveillance missions were stepped up.

On 29 August, a CIA U-2 mission took off from McCoy AFB, Florida. It photographed two SAM sites and six more under construction.[81] By themselves, the sites were of little threat to the United States. However, the patterning of the sites suggested that their mission was to defend a ballistic missile complex. The SAMs were operational, and ballistic missile deployment might occur soon. On 4 September, Kennedy warned Khrushchev not to introduce offensive missiles into Cuba. Khrushchev denied any knowledge of ballistic-missile development in Cuba. The CIA ordered more U-2 flights for 5, 17, 26, and 29 September and for 5 and 7 October.[82] The United States sped up the race for more information. Three more SAM sites were identified, but no IRBM or MRBM weapons were found. On 8 September, a US Navy Lockheed P-2 Neptune antisubmarine aircraft photographed the Soviet freighter *Omsk* carrying several suspicious oblong containers that might contain ballistic missiles. IRBM and MRBM cargoes were being shipped to Cuba.

Further construction work on Cuba was noted by reconnaissance flights. Secretary of Defense Robert S. McNamara ordered the US Air Force's SAC to take control of all U-2 flights. The Soviets had operational SA-2 SAMs. If a U-2 were shot down, the aircraft would be by piloted an Air Force military officer—not a CIA civilian employee. On 14 October, a U-2 from SAC's 4080th Strategic Reconnaissance Wing flying out of Patrick AFB, Florida, took 928 photographs during a six-minute flight over Cuba. The photographs showed MRBMs ready for deployment at two sites—San Cristóbal and Sagua la Grande. The MRBMs were on transporters outside of shelters. Propellant-loading equipment was present. President Kennedy was shown the photographs on 16 October.

The aerial reconnaissance effort shifted from high-altitude, wide-area views to more detailed, low-level missions. The Air Force's McDonnell RF-101C Voodoo aircraft from the 29th

Nuclear warhead bunker at San Cristóbal, Cuba

Tactical Reconnaissance Squadron out of Shaw AFB, South Carolina, were ordered into action. The U-2 photographs had already identified several areas for tactical-level reconnaissance to gather more information. On 17 October, the RF-101Cs photographed what appeared to be two IRBM sites at Guanajay and Remedios.

The United States added other information-gathering resources. The National Security Agency used Boeing RB-47E USAF electronic-intelligence aircraft, flying three missions per day, to gather data on Cuban surveillance radar and SAM radar systems. Navy RC-121C Super Constellation aircraft were used to listen to radio and other communications throughout Cuba. Naval ships were also used to eavesdrop on Cuban and Soviet communications.[83] The United States used all possible means to gather information about suspected ballistic missile activity.

The combination of U-2 and RF-101C flights provided all the evidence that Kennedy needed. Nine missile sites were identified at four locations. There were six MRBM sites—four at San Cristóbal and two at Sagua la Grande. Each site had four missile launchers with the capability of two launches. The Soviets could deploy up to 48 SS-4 Sandel missiles with a range of 2,000 kilometers.[84] The Sandel could strike targets as far north as Washington, D.C., and cover 40 percent of America's SAC bases.[85] The other three sites were IRBM complexes at Guanajay and Remedios. Like the MRBM sites, these also had four launch sites with a two-missile system. This indicated that the Soviets could launch 24 SS-5 Skean IRBMs, each with a maximum reach of 4,100 kilometers.[86] All major American cities except Seattle were in range of the SS-5. These MRBMs and IRBMs could carry about a one-megaton nuclear yield.

In private discussions and in the UN, President Kennedy was able to confront the Soviets with photographic evidence that they had placed offensive missiles in Cuba. Kennedy put American military forces on alert. US Air Force aircraft were sent to the southeast. Kennedy ordered a quarantine—in reality, a naval blockade—around Cuba to stop all shipping. SAC's 156 operational ICBMs were ready to launch, and its nuclear-armed bomber fleet dispersed. Reconnaissance flights continued over the island with a flight every hour. RF-101Cs and US Navy LTV RF-8 Crusaders crisscrossed the island to update information about missile-deployment status. AAA fire was noticed, but no SAMs were fired. Unfortunately, on 27 October a SAM shot down a U-2 over Cuba, killing Maj Rudolph Anderson. Kennedy sent a letter to Khrushchev via the Soviet Embassy in Washington, telling him that if he did not withdraw the missiles, further action would take place.

American air, naval, and land forces were readied for a possible invasion and strike against the missiles. American reservists and guardsmen were activated for service. The United States was ready to repeat another Bay of Pigs invasion; this time, however, American servicemen would assault Cuba with the full backing of the nation. On 28 October, Radio Moscow reported that the missiles would be withdrawn—the United States had successfully forced Khrushchev to back down without firing a shot. The Soviet Union was humiliated. The United States accomplished this with the use of photographic evidence and the deterrent power of its military. America also started to dismantle its tactical ballistic missiles in Britain, Italy, and Turkey. The US government also promised not to invade Cuba. To ensure Soviet compliance with the agreement, reconnaissance planes continued to fly over Cuba, this time to inspect departing freighters with their missile cargoes. Aircraft also observed the removal of missiles and missile-support equipment. Rapid, accurate information had affected the fortunes of the two superpowers. A nuclear confrontation was averted, and the lives of millions of people had been saved.

Notes

1. Earl F. Ziemke and Magna E. Bauer, *Moscow to Stalingrad: Decision in the East* (Washington, D.C.: Center of Military History, 1987), 365.
2. Charles Winchester, *Ostfront: Hitler's War on Russia, 1941–1945* (Botley, Oxford: Osprey Publishing, Limited, 2000), 62.
3. Earl F. Ziemke, *Stalingrad to Berlin: The German Defeat in the East* (Washington, D.C.: Office of the Chief of Military History, 1968), 79.
4. Ibid., 59.
5. Joel S. A. Hayward, *Stopped at Stalingrad: The Luftwaffe and Hitler's Defeat in the East, 1942–1943* (Lawrence, Kans.: University Press of Kansas, 1998), 236.
6. Ibid., 246.
7. Ibid., 236.
8. Ziemke and Bauer, 188.
9. David Donald, ed., *Warplanes of the Luftwaffe* (London: Aerospace Publishing, 1994), 152.
10. Hayward, 248.
11. Von Hardesty, *Red Phoenix: The Rise of Soviet Air Power, 1941–1945* (Washington, D.C.: Smithsonian Institution Press, 1991), 107.
12. Ziemke, 61.
13. Ibid., 75.
14. Winchester, 7.
15. Ibid., 73.
16. Hardesty, 110.
17. Hayward, 245.
18. Hardesty, 110.
19. Hayward, 284.

20. Richard P. Hallion, *Storm over Iraq: Air Power and the Gulf War* (Washington, D.C.: Smithsonian Institution Press, 1992), 137.

21. James K. Matthews and Cora J. Holt, *So Many, So Much, So Far, So Fast: United States Transportation Command and Strategic Deployment for Operation Desert Shield/Desert Storm* (Washington, D.C.: Research Center, United States Transportation Command, and Joint History Office, Office of the Chairman of the Joint Chiefs of Staff, 1996), 37.

22. Thomas A. Keaney and Eliot A. Cohen, *Revolution in Warfare? Air Power in the Persian Gulf* (Annapolis: Naval Institute Press, 1995), 4.

23. Ibid., 154.

24. Bernard C. Nalty, ed., *Winged Shield, Winged Sword: A History of the United States Air Force*, vol. 2 (Washington, D.C.: Air Force History and Museums Program, 1997), 448.

25. Frank N. Schubert and Theresa L. Kraus, *The Whirlwind War: The United States Army in Operations Desert Shield and Desert Storm* (Washington, D.C.: Center of Military History, 1995), 51.

26. James A. Winnefeld, Preston Niblack, and Dana J. Johnson, *A League of Airmen: U.S. Air Power in the Gulf War* (Santa Monica, Calif.: RAND, 1994), 29.

27. Ronald N. Priddy, *A History of the Civil Reserve Air Fleet in Operations Desert Shield, Desert Storm, and Desert Sortie* (Cambridge, Mass.: Volpe National Transportation Center, 1994), 148.

28. Keaney and Cohen, 158.

29. Schubert and Kraus, 248.

30. Keaney and Cohen, 156–57, table 5.

31. Winnefeld, Niblack, and Johnson, 230.

32. Nalty, 452.

33. Keaney and Cohen, 160.

34. Ibid.

35. John Lewis Gaddis, *We Now Know: Rethinking Cold War History* (New York: Oxford University Press, 1997), 47.

36. Jeremy Isaacs and Taylor Downing, *Cold War: An Illustrated History, 1945–1991* (Boston: Little, Brown, and Co., 1998), 69.

37. Daniel L. Haulman, *Wings of Hope: The U.S. Air Force and Humanitarian Airlift Operations* (Washington, D.C.: Air Force History and Museums Program, 1997), 3.

38. Isaacs and Downing, 70.

39. David A. Anderton, *The History of the U.S. Air Force* (New York: Crescent Books, 1981), 137.

40. Charles E. Miller, *Airlift Doctrine* (Maxwell AFB, Ala.: Air University Press, 1988), 177.

41. Ibid.

42. Anderton, 137.

43. Roger G. Miller, *To Save a City: The Berlin Airlift, 1948–1949* (Washington, D.C.: Air Force History and Museums Program, 1998), 22.

44. Isaacs and Downing, 75.

45. Bernard C. Nalty, ed., *Winged Shield, Winged Sword: A History of the United States Air Force*, vol. 1 (Washington, D.C.: Air Force History and Museums Program, 1997), 428.

46. Walter J. Boyne, *Beyond the Wild Blue: A History of the United States Air Force, 1947–1997* (New York: Saint Martin's Press, 1997), 42.

47. Miller, *Airlift Doctrine*, 180.

48. Anderton, 140.

49. Miller, *Airlift Doctrine*, 181.

50. Boyne, 42.

51. Miller, *Airlift Doctrine*, 181.

52. Hallion, 180.

53. Michael R. Gordon and Bernard E. Trainor, *The Generals' War: The Inside Story of the Conflict in the Gulf* (Boston: Little, Brown, and Co., 1995), 234.

54. Jeffrey T. Richelson, *America's Space Sentinels: DSP Satellites and National Security* (Lawrence, Kans.: University Press of Kansas, 1999), 158. Circular error probable measures the radius of a circle where 50 percent of a warhead or weapon falls near a target.

55. David N. Spires, *Beyond Horizons: A Half Century of Air Force Space Leadership* (Peterson AFB, Colo.: Air Force Space Command, 1997), 255.

56. Richelson, 161.

57. Winnefeld, Niblack, and Johnson, 193.

58. Spires, 254.

59. Ibid., 255.

60. Richelson, 168.

61. Ibid., 171.

62. Keaney and Cohen, 73.

63. Ibid., 76.

64. Gordon and Trainor, 240.

65. Richelson, 171.

66. Kenneth E. Greer, "Corona" (document is now declassified), in *CORONA: America's First Satellite Program*, ed. Kevin C. Ruffner (Washington, D.C.: CIA History Staff Center for the Study of Intelligence, 1995), 4.

67. Cris Kruschke, "CORONA: A Program Profile," *Quest* 7, no. 1 (Spring 1999): 25.

68. Curtis Peebles, *The Corona Project: America's First Spy Satellites* (Annapolis: Naval Institute Press, 1997), 55.

69. Ibid., 88.

70. Dwayne A. Day, "The Development and Improvement of the CORONA Satellite," in *Eye in the Sky: The Story of the Corona Spy Satellites*, ed. Dwayne A. Day, John M. Logsdon, and Brian Latell (Washington, D.C.: Smithsonian Institution Press, 1998), 61.

71. Greer, 37. Document is now declassified.

72. Central Intelligence Agency, National Intelligence Estimate, 11-8/1-61, "Strength and Deployment of Soviet Long Range Ballistic Missile

Forces," 21 September 1961 (document is now declassified), in *CORONA: America's First Satellite Program,* 141.

73. Albert D. Wheelon, "CORONA: A Triumph of American Technology," in *Eye in the Sky,* 47.

74. Peebles, 259.

75. *CORONA: America's First Satellite Program,* xiv.

76. Donald Kagan, *On the Origins of War and the Preservation of Peace* (New York: Doubleday, 1995), 437.

77. Ibid., 467.

78. Gaddis, 264.

79. Isaacs and Downing, 190.

80. Norman Friedman, *The Fifty-Year War: Conflict and Strategy in the Cold War* (Annapolis: Naval Institute Press, 2000), 275.

81. Victor Flintham, *Air Wars and Aircraft: A Detailed Record of Air Combat, 1945 to the Present* (New York: Facts on File, 1990), 349.

82. Anderton, 152.

83. Jeffrey T. Richelson, *A Century of Spies: Intelligence in the Twentieth Century* (New York: Oxford University Press, 1995), 315–16.

84. David Miller, *The Cold War: A Military History* (New York: Saint Martin's Press, 1999), appendix 8, 407.

85. Isaacs and Downing, 191.

86. Miller, *The Cold War,* appendix 8, 407.

Chapter 6

Functions and Capabilities of Aerospace Power: Airpower Unleashed

Aerospace power advocates can point to several cases in which airpower and space power were used in many unique ways. Innovative, flexible applications provided a variety of options for a commander. Creative applications of airpower and space power confounded a foe and allowed a military force to adapt to environments that a country never before faced. Doctrine, weapons, and experience were used to overcome the shortcomings of airpower in order to sweep aside opposition. Flexibility was the key to unlocking many problems facing a commander. Long-distance combat, numeric superiority, and other limitations were overcome through bold, ingenious planning.

A future aerospace leader needs to extend his or her thinking to solve complex military problems. The British recapture of the Falkland Islands demonstrates multiple uses of limited airpower and the innovative approach to reducing Argentina's military advantages. The Israeli military also used advanced technology and superior military forces to overcome numeric advantages. The Bekaa Valley campaign was a demonstration of joint air and ground operations that pushed Syrian forces out of a highly threatening position against Israel. Finally, the Soviet Union's campaign to defeat the Luftwaffe in World War II was an example of skillful planning and attacking German weaknesses with Soviet strengths. The Soviet air force was on the brink of collapse but resisted the might of a German onslaught and won. American aerospace leaders might face a similar challenge in the future.

These case studies do not involve American military forces. Foreign air forces do not handle military situations in the same way that the United States does. Readers can better prepare for operating with allies or fighting future air forces if they understand the motivations and gain an appreciation of how foreign forces fight. Although American air forces have great capability, there is always the potential for a foe to identify and exploit any weakness in our forces. Studying the results of how different actors might react to situations will only strengthen the reader's ability to make strategic decisions.

At the End of Empire: The 1982 Falklands War in the Air

In future military operations, the United States may have to fight and win further from home with far fewer forces than in the past. One factor will remain constant in the future—America's reliance upon airpower for victory. How might airpower contribute to a successful, extended "bare base" operation far from home? A student of airpower should examine how the British overcame both numerically superior Argentinean military forces and difficult geographic challenges during the Falklands War of 1982. Airpower significantly contributed to success in the British campaign. Conversely, the Argentinean air force's and navy's misuse of airpower played a significant role in their defeat. This case discusses the background of the war, ways in which the British and Argentinean forces used airpower, and the significant airpower lessons to be learned from the war.

The conflict between the United Kingdom and Argentina was not new. The British had gained the Falkland Islands as a possession in 1833 through eviction of Argentinean colonists (fig. 13). Since that time, Argentinean governments have repeatedly tried to reestablish their claims to the Falklands (known to the Argentineans as Islas Malvinas). The Argentineans repeatedly attempted to regain possession of the islands and worked through the UN to settle their claims. These legal efforts did not succeed. In the past, the Falklands served the British as a naval base near strategic Cape Horn, as a whaling station, and as a justification for a presence in Antarctica. Possession of the islands has also served as a visible outpost to an ever-shrinking British Empire. The Falklands are literally at the end of the Empire—7,100 miles southwest of the British Isles.

Figure 13. Argentina and the Falkland Islands (Islas Malvinas)

The territory is composed of a series of islands approximately 400 miles east of the southern coast of Argentina. Most activities on the Falklands took place on two main islands—West Falkland and East Falkland (fig. 14). The capital and main city was Port Stanley, with a population of 1,000 people (total population of the Falklands was about 2,000). In 1982 Port

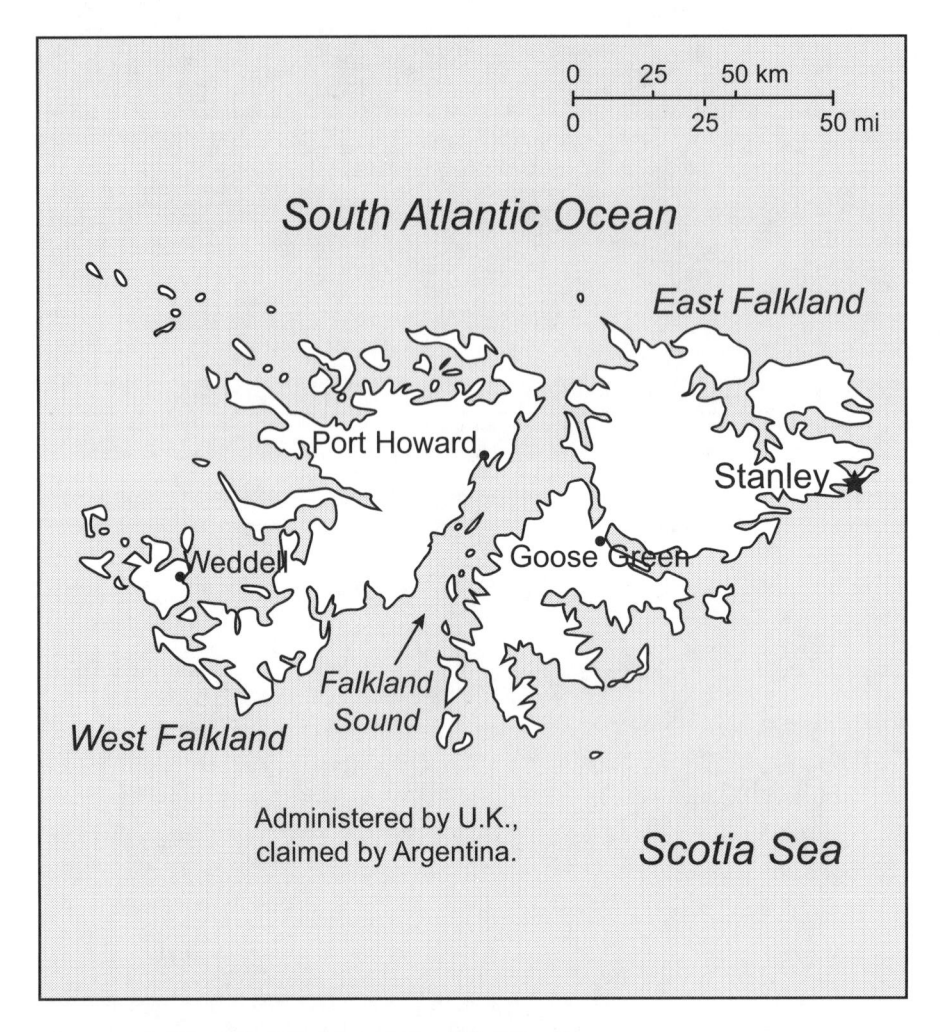

Figure 14. West Falkland and East Falkland

Stanley also contained the island's major airport, which contained a 4,100-foot airstrip that could not support large jet-aircraft operations.

Argentinean attempts to unseat British rule of the Islas Malvinas were precipitated by several events. Under their military junta, Argentinean civil and military forces attempted to take possession of South Georgia, a British island east of the Falklands, on 19 March 1982. About 60 Argentinean civilian scrap workers were sent to the island to dismantle an abandoned whaling station. These workers raised their nation's flag on South Georgia and claimed it for Argentina. With little overt British reaction to this "invasion," the Argentinean military government decided to take the Falklands. However, the British had sent military observation teams from the Falklands-based HMS *Endurance* and Royal Marines on 25 and 31 March. British Royal Navy (RN) nuclear submarines were also dispatched to the area on 25 March. Apparently, the Argentineans were unaware of this response. Ironically, a British firm had hired the Argentinean scrap workers to dismantle and salvage the abandoned whaling station.

Another key event that influenced the Argentinean invasion decision was British domestic politics. John Nott, British minister of defense, had proposed several defense cuts, which included the retirement—without replacement—of the HMS *Endurance*, the only permanently stationed British naval presence on the Falklands. Nott also recommended that the RN's only two aircraft carriers—HMS *Hermes* and *Invincible*—be removed from the active inventory and sold to Australia due to budget reductions. He made plans to reduce air and ground forces as well. In light of the scant reaction concerning the invasion of South Georgia, a shrinking British military force, and the long distances from British military bases, and seeking a way to bolster the unpopular military government, on 23 March the Argentinean junta decided to recapture national prestige by invading the Falklands. The Argentinean invasion force left port on 25 March and successfully landed on the Falklands on 2 April. After token resistance, the British governor of the Falklands surrendered to the Argentineans. The latter's military forces quickly installed an AN/TPS-43F radar, air traffic control center, and air defense systems at the Port Stanley airport. Argentinean ground forces deployed more than 10,000 troops around the Falklands.

Both nations had aviation forces equipped to fight a major conflict; however, conditions dictated by the Falklands severely affected aircraft operations. Argentinean forces had one of the largest airpower forces in Latin America. Conversely, the British forces had a wide range of aircraft types capable of conducting missions, from long-range operations to tactical support. The United Kingdom did, however, lack the numbers of aircraft available for long-range and extended deployments. The British military needed to develop other counters to the numerically superior Argentinean air forces.

The Argentinean air force, *Fuerza Aerea Argentina* (FAA), and naval aviation force, *Commando Aviacion Naval Argentina* (CANA), had a mix of single-purpose aircraft. FAA forces had 225 combat aircraft, several of them capable of striking the Falklands from Argentina.[1] These aircraft included approximately 21 Dassault Mirage IIIEA fighter-bombers, 26 Israel Aircraft Industry Dagger fighter-bombers (based on the Mirage design), nine English Electric Canberra B.Mk.2 bombers, 60 IA-58 Pucara twin turboprop ground-attack planes, and about 68 McDonnell-Douglas A-4B/C/P Skyhawk light-attack aircraft. The FAA also possessed seven Lockheed C-130 transports, Boeing 707 jets, helicopters, and other aircraft. Many of these aircraft would have to operate at their maximum ranges since Argentina did not possess many air-to-air-refueling tanker aircraft, nor could many of its combat-loaded jets operate from the Port Stanley airport. The FAA did operate two KC-130 tankers. The Mirages and Daggers did not, however, have air-to-air-refueling capability. The major CANA forces during the conflict included 10 A-4Q Skyhawks, 10 Aeromacchi MB-339 light strike forces, and five Dassault Super Etendard attack aircraft. The Super Etendards were especially dangerous to British naval forces since they were equipped with French-built AM-39 Exocet antiship missiles, but CANA had an inventory of only five missiles. Additionally, CANA could use A-4Qs deployed on the Argentinean carrier *Vienticinco de Mayo* to attack the British fleet. FAA and CANA deployed 24 Pucaras, six MB.339A jets, four Beech T-34C Mentor trainers, and several helicopters to Port Stanley and a smaller airfield at Goose Green. A combination of 20 mm and 35 mm AAA and Roland and Tigercat SAMs defended these two airfields. The FAA also used two companies of officer cadets to operate the air defenses at the airfields.[2]

With the above forces, the FAA and CANA pursued several combat objectives: to attack any possible British invasion force, to oppose any invasion, to provide CAS to Argentinean ground forces, and to defend Argentinean soil from any British attack. Although Argentinean air forces could operate their high-performance jets, they had to fly from locations over 400 miles away. This range limitation reduced aircraft payloads and loiter time to target and attack British forces, as well as response time and sortie generation since the Argentineans could not station the majority of their aircraft at Port Stanley. Conspicuously absent was any airborne early warning (AEW) or major use of air-to-air-refueling capability for FAA or CANA.

The RAF and RN had better aircraft than the FAA or CANA, but the limited number of aircraft and the long distances affected their ability to deploy forces and conduct operations. Past budget cuts had forced the RAF to transition to a smaller force. For several decades, the RAF had maintained a force of "V" long-range strategic bombers. Its lone five Avro Vulcan aircraft force—No. 44 Squadron—was saved from deactivation and placed on alert after the Argentineans invaded the Falklands. The Vulcan had the range to strike targets at 4,600 miles. The RAF was in the process of replacing the Vulcan with shorter-range Panavia Tornado strike aircraft. The RAF also maintained several Handley Page Victor K.2 air-to-air-refueling tankers (modified bombers), McDonnell-Douglas F-4 Phantoms, British Aerospace Buccaneer strike jets, C-130 and VC-10 transports, Sepecat Jaguars, Hawker-Siddley Nimrod maritime reconnaissance and strike aircraft, and an assortment of helicopters. The F-4s, like the Vulcans, were slated for replacement by Tornados. The RAF and RN had a force of multipurpose British Aerospace Harrier and Sea Harrier close-support vertical/short takeoff and landing jets.

The RAF and RN air forces' immediate objectives were to establish an air bridge between the United Kingdom and Ascension Island, to protect a British invasion task force, and to support and defend British ground-invasion forces. The British did not have long-range aircraft capable of striking the Falklands or Argentina from bases in Great Britain. The RAF needed an assembly point for long-range strike, reconnaissance, mobility, and tanker operations. The nearest British-controlled airfield, Ascension Island, was about 3,900 miles away from the Falklands. The RAF could not operate anything other than its Vulcans, Victors, Nimrods, C-130s, and VC-10s from Ascension Island's Wideawake airport. Ascension Island would serve as a base for airborne strike and reconnaissance missions and logistics support, as well as a natural springboard to coordinate and consolidate forces for an attempt to retake the Falklands. The RAF expanded operations at Wideawake from a three-flight-per-week runway to one handling over 400 flights per day.

Another objective of British airpower was to provide protection for moving an invasion fleet from the United Kingdom or for moving one assembled at Ascension Island. Fortunately, the RN did not immediately scrap the carriers HMS *Hermes* and *Invincible* after Nott released his policy. Those carriers would serve as the basis for the initial task force. They were normally operated with five Sea Harriers and about 10 Sea King helicopters each. The Sea Harrier was the aircraft of choice by default since it could take off and land from ships that could move close to the Falklands. The carrier task force could increase the Sea Harrier payload by reducing the effective operating range and make these aircraft a more viable military force. The RN's Sea Harrier aircraft were armed with US-supplied AIM-9L Sidewinder all-aspect air-to-air missiles (AAM) for combat air patrol missions over the fleet. Additionally, aircraft were also required for ground-attack sorties to support and defend any British ground operations once an invasion force landed on the Falklands. British task forces subsequently carried RAF Harrier GR.Mk.3s to replace Sea Harriers lost to attrition and to supplement ground-attack missions.

An initial British task force left Great Britain on 5 April for Ascension Island en route to the Falklands. The task force consisted of the HMS *Hermes* and *Invincible*, support ships, 20 Sea Harriers, and dozens of helicopters. Additional ships, including troop transports, would follow.

Although the Argentinean air forces' jet aircraft were not able to use the Port Stanley airport, the FAA had significant airpower resources based on the Falklands. If the British could neutralize FAA operations on the Falklands, then a serious threat to the British invasion and ground operations would be removed. The Argentineans would then have to rely on major air support from the mainland. Without major air-to-air-refueling capability, Argentinean aircraft could strike British forces only at extreme ranges. This allowed any British task force to more effectively employ Sea Harrier CAP and air defense weapons to increase the chance of fending off Argentinean air attacks and successfully projecting combat power. The British could also strike the FAA and CANA bases on the mainland using their Vulcan fleet. However, British attacks on the mainland might result in a widening of the war. As a result, the British limited Argentinean airpower in two ways—by stationing a force in Chile and by attacking the Falklands from Ascension Island.

The British government deployed several aircraft to Chile. Argentina and Chile had a long history of territorial disputes over several southern islands. A successful occupation of South Georgia and the Falklands by Argentina could pave the way for future Argentinean military "island taking" adventures. The Chilean government, therefore, had a stake in the British military attempt to retake the Falklands and head off Argentinean expansion. Allegedly, the RAF stationed several aircraft in Punta Arenas in Chile, close to the Argentinean border. Sometime after 10 April, the RAF was allowed to station RAF Canberra PR.Mk.9 and RN Nimrod R.Mk.1 aircraft, ready to perform reconnaissance and electronic intelligence missions.[3] Additionally, the British press reported that a squadron of RAF F-4 Phantoms was deployed to Chile.[4] The F-4s were in range to attack several FAA and CANA airfields. This threat drew off Argentinean FAA fighter forces to ensure they could mount DCA missions against the F-4s. This action reduced potential FAA airpower against a British invasion force.

Additionally, the RAF used its Vulcan and Victor forces to attack the Port Stanley airport. The RAF conducted seven Vulcan missions (code-named "Black Buck") during the campaign in an attempt to render the airfield inoperable to the FAA. On 1 May, a Vulcan B.2 from Wideawake conducted Black Buck 1. This Vulcan mission required 18 air-refueling operations and 15 Victor K.2 tanker sorties, with the bomber in flight for 14 hours and 50 minutes.[5] The Vulcan dropped 21 1,000-pound bombs, but only one bomb struck the airfield. The single bomb did crater the center of the airfield, but the damage was quickly repaired. A later Black Buck mission included a successful antiradar mission using AGM-45 Shrike missiles against the AN TPS-43F radar at the Port Stanley airport. Although the damage caused by the Black Buck missions was minor, the psychological impact on the Argentinean government was great. The British proved their ability to strike long distance from Wideawake. This action takes on more significance when one realizes that Buenos Aires is much closer to Wideawake than the Falklands. After Black Buck 1, the FAA pulled out fighters from support of the Islas Malvinas to bases further north to protect Argentinean cities.[6] Black Buck 1 was only the warm-up act. The British task force, equipped with Sea Harriers, was now in range for ground-attack operations.

The initial British task force had finally arrived within 90 nautical miles of East Falkland. Immediately following the Black Buck 1 mission, 12 Sea Harriers from HMS *Hermes* headed towards Argentinean positions to complement the Vulcan raid. Nine Sea Harriers attacked Port Stanley using 1,000-pound general-purpose bombs and BL.755 cluster-bomb units. This attack temporarily made the airfield unusable. The attack on Goose Green was more successful since it resulted in the destruction of three FAA Pucara aircraft. The Sea Harriers returned to the task force without loss. The RN's HMS *Glamorgan, Alacrity*, and *Arrow* followed up the air attacks by conducting shore-bombardment operations within 12 miles of Port Stanley.[7] Three FAA Daggers attacked and caused minor damage to all three ships. The task force's Sea Harriers that were used in the airfield attack were rearmed with AIM-9L Sidewinders in anticipation of further Argentinean attacks on the fleet.

The sudden attacks by Vulcans and Sea Harriers on Argentinean military forces on the Falklands were a shock to the Argentineans. They knew of the existence of the British task forces and had spotted them on 21 April with an FAA Boeing 707; the thought of an imminent invasion caused immediate reaction by the FAA and CANA. The FAA launched sorties from mainland airfields in San Julian and Rio Gallegos against the British task force. The Argentineans launched A-4 and Canberra aircraft supported by Mirage III and Dagger fighters against the RN's ships. The A-4s were unsuccessful in finding any targets. The Canberras did spot the task force and attempted to attack. Sea Harriers intercepted them, and one Canberra was shot down by an AIM-9L. Additionally, the only air-to-air engagement of the war took place as a result of the FAA's first attack on the RN fleet. Mirage IIIs from the FAA's only dedicated interceptor unit clashed with Sea Harriers conducting CAP missions over the task force and lost two aircraft to AIM-9 missiles. The FAA also lost a Dagger. British airpower ruled the skies after the first day of conflict. However, Argentinean airpower was poised to strike a more deadly blow to the British forces in the coming weeks.

On 2 May, the British nuclear attack submarine HMS *Conqueror* found and sank Argentina's second-largest naval vessel, the cruiser *General Belgrano*. The sinking of the *Belgrano* resulted in the Argentinean navy's retreat to coastal waters for the remainder of the war and caused the *Vienticinco de Mayo* to withdraw to port. British naval forces were not under threat from Argentinean surface naval forces for the remainder of the war. More importantly, the CANA A-4 forces on the *Vienticinco de Mayo* were denied the opportunity to operate closer to British invasion forces and complicate British defensive efforts by immobilizing the carrier. British forces could now concentrate on air defense efforts to protect their fleet. The Argentinean government's hope of defeating the British invasion forces rested on its FAA and CANA land-based aircraft and ground forces deployed on the Falklands.

Two CANA Super Etendards based at the Rio Grande airfield found the British task force, which had earlier been shadowed by a CANA surveillance SP-2H Tracker aircraft. CANA was aware of the fleet's composition and general location. The Etendards were armed with one AM-39 Exocet antiship missile. The aircraft were operating at close to their maximum operating range, in poor weather, and with no air cover. Both aircraft launched their missiles. One missile failed to find its target. However, the second one struck the HMS *Sheffield*, a type 42 destroyer performing radar picket duty for the task force. The Exocet's warhead failed to detonate, but the fire caused by unused missile fuel and the ship's aluminum construction resulted in massive destruction.[8] There were 26 RN fatalities, and the ship sank under tow six days later. The loss of the *Sheffield* was a shock to the British government. The FAA and

HMS *Broadsword*, a veteran of the Falklands War of 1982, was attacked by Argentinean sea- and land-based air forces.

CANA displayed their ability to deliver a tremendous new threat to British naval forces. Additionally, the attack demonstrated the poor judgment of the British in not using an AEW system to detect an enemy air attack. The British eventually deployed Sea King helicopters in an AEW role, but these aircraft were neither designed nor properly equipped for the mission.

British fortunes also turned sour in another manner. Sea Harriers struck the Goose Green airfield on the same day as the attack on the *Sheffield*. One aircraft was lost to AAA fire. The next day, two Sea Harriers from the *Invincible* collided in poor weather when they were conducting search and rescue operations for the *Sheffield*. These actions seriously reduced the number of operating Sea Harriers, amounting to 15 percent of the original Sea Harrier force. The task force needed aircraft-attrition replacements since these losses occurred before the main effort of the force—the amphibious invasion. RAF Harrier GR.Mk.3s were modified for air-to-air refueling, flown from Great Britain to Ascension Island, and then transferred to the commercial-container cargo ship MV *Atlantic Conveyor* for transport to the Falkland Islands area. The *Atlantic Conveyor* ultimately reequipped the *Hermes* and *Invincible* with six Harrier GR.Mk.3s, eight Sea Harriers, and 10 helicopters.

The British military also stepped up attacks on Argentinean forces on the Falklands, relying on other unique forces to leverage its limited airpower. Units from the British Special Air

Services commando forces operated as forward air observers and helped neutralize FAA bases on the Falklands. On 14 May, Special Air Services forces attacked an FAA airfield at Pebble Island near West Falkland. The raid destroyed six Pucaras, four T-34Cs, and a transport aircraft, not only reducing Argentinean ground-support aircraft available to thwart the invasion, but also demoralizing the Argentinean ground forces. They realized that British forces, with more to come, were slowly isolating them.

Argentinean aviation forces, however, continued to attack British naval forces throughout May. Typically, FAA A-4 Skyhawks, escorted by Mirage IIIs, would deliver 1,000-pound bombs against naval targets of opportunity. For example, on 12 May, 12 Skyhawks attacked the HMS *Glasgow* and HMS *Brilliant*. A 1,000-pound bomb was dropped on the *Glasgow* but passed through the hull without exploding. The FAA had serious problems involving faulty bomb fuses throughout the war. The attacks on *Glasgow* and *Brilliant* cost the FAA three A-4s (two to Sea Wolf SAMs and one to pilot error). The Argentineans failed to stem the rising tide of British forces building up around the Falklands. Additionally, British naval forces carrying more aircraft, helicopters, supplies, and ground forces streamed south from Ascension Island. The war entered its final phase—a British amphibious invasion to wrest control of the Falklands from the Argentineans.

The British were not deterred by the Argentinean air attacks. British airpower transitioned from a force primarily devoted to fleet defense and attacks upon Falklands airfields to one ready for invasion of the Falklands. RAF and RN resources focused their efforts on protecting the ground forces that had landed and on supporting the ground offensive. However, the FAA and CANA still possessed the ability to strike and destroy portions of the task force. By 21 May, the British forces had landed at San Carlos Bay with a main objective of retaking Port Stanley. Approximately 2,000 British troops composed of commando units and paratroops hit the beach.

In the next few days, the FAA and CANA put up a vigorous effort to disrupt the invasion force by attacking naval vessels and the beachhead. The Argentineans launched several strikes composed of A-4, Mirage III, and Dagger aircraft against the

British task force and sank the frigates HMS *Ardent*, *Antelope*, and the destroyer *Conventry*. Another three RN frigates suffered heavy damage. While the loss of these naval vessels was serious, the British were to suffer a heavier blow.

On 25 May, two CANA Super Etendards, armed with one AM-39 Exocet each and displaying exceptional flying skill, found the MV *Atlantic Conveyor* after flying over 800 miles from their mainland bases. The pilots fired their missiles. One Exocet hit the *Atlantic Conveyor* and started an onboard fire that eventually caused the ship to sink; the other missile failed to find its mark. The Super Etendards were refueled by KC-130s.[9] Fortunately for the British task force, all Harrier aircraft had earlier been transferred, but the task force lost six Wessex helicopters, one Lynx helicopter, three heavy-lift CH-47D Chinook helicopters, 12 seamen, and several tons of critical supplies. British ground forces lost invaluable helicopter lift to support their operations against Port Stanley. Instead of the rapid mobility offered by helicopters, the British ground forces had to move on foot up mountainous terrain under winter conditions.

Argentinean air strikes were not exclusive to the task force. On 27 May, a force of A-4 and Mirage III aircraft struck British ground forces near the British beachhead. These aircraft attacked the British main logistics center on the Falklands and destroyed significant numbers of guns, mortars, ammunition, and antitank missiles and launchers. Additionally, a major medical dressing station was rendered unserviceable for the rest of the war.[10]

The Argentinean attacks were also very costly to the FAA and CANA. Argentinean pilots flew not only long distances from their bases, but also faced a gauntlet of Sea Harriers, sea-based SAMs, AAA, land-based air defense systems, and electronic countermeasures (ECM) as well. The Argentineans lost over 40 aircraft, mostly to Sea Harriers, during this period. Argentinean air strikes would never again approach the intensity or scope of previous efforts.

RAF Harriers and RN Sea Harriers continued to support the advance of British ground forces towards Port Stanley. By 5 June, Harrier operations were enlarged by the addition of an 850-foot steel-mat airfield on the San Carlos beachhead. This provided British aircraft with a refueling point and reduced the vulnerability of aircraft from attacks by the FAA and CANA on the HMS *Hermes* and *Invincible*. These land-based aircraft were able to generate additional sorties and reduce response time to support the ground commander's requirements.

The Argentineans put up some last-ditch efforts to support their besieged ground forces on East Falkland. British ground forces attempted an amphibious assault seven miles south of Port Stanley in Buff Cove on 8 June. The FAA attacked the logistics landing ships HMS *Sir Tristram* and *Sir Galahad* with five A-4 and six Dagger jets. Mirage IIIs conducted a diversionary raid on San Carlos to draw away the Sea Harrier CAP. *Sir Tristram* and *Sir Galahad* suffered major damage, the latter losing 50 men. On the return flight home, the Daggers attacked the HMS *Plymouth*, a frigate, and disabled her when four 1,000-pound bombs struck the ship (none exploded). A second wave of Argentinean aircraft also sank the assault ship HMS *Fearless*.

These attacks failed to halt the British encirclement of Port Stanley. The FAA and CANA supported Argentinean forces around Port Stanley, but they were ineffective due to the inability of their air forces to stop British resupply efforts. The Argentinean ground forces were unable to halt the British advance through the island. Conversely, Sea Harrier and Harrier GR.Mk.3 aircraft continued to attack Argentinean ground positions. By 14 June, Argentinean forces around Port Stanley surrendered, and the war was over.

The Argentinean and British air forces conducted two different air campaigns. The Argentineans were reduced to a defensive mission close to home, while the British mounted an expeditionary force to retake the Falkland Islands without nearby land bases. Both forces recognized the value of airpower. The Argentineans relied on land-based airpower, and the British concentrated on sea-based airpower. The British also used several innovative applications of airpower throughout the campaign.

One can trace the failure of FAA and CANA forces to several factors. These include less-capable aircraft, failure to achieve air superiority, lack of modern force multipliers, failure to mass during attack, and limited air refueling.

Although the Argentineans were numerically superior, many of the aircraft and equipment used were not top of the line. The FAA's main strike aircraft, the A-4 Skyhawk and Canberra bombers, were 1950s design and production. Argentinean aircraft also carried few electronic aids and defensive armaments; most did not have air-refueling capability, which severely limited their range. The equipment used by the Argentineans was also faulty. Bomb fuses failed to operate, due in part to Argentinean aircraft dropping their ordnance at low altitudes to avoid the RN CAP and air defenses. This left insufficient time for bombs to fuse. CANA Super Etendards did score impressive strikes against ships with their Exocet missiles. However, the Argentinean government failed to stock enough of these weapons or break an embargo by the French government on the missiles. The FAA and CANA also did not use laser-guided munitions, unlike the RAF in its ground attacks against Argentinean ground positions.[11]

The FAA and CANA did not achieve air superiority over the Falklands. Argentinean military forces did not attempt to expand the runways at Port Stanley's airport to operate their Mirage III or Dagger aircraft. If the FAA had deployed their interceptors on the island, British military operations would have been more hotly contested. The Sea Harriers might not have had the ability to control the skies, and A-4 and Super Etendard aircraft operating from a closer land base could have generated more sorties to attack the British task force, invasion, and ground operations.

Argentinean air forces did not employ many of the modern force multipliers that we see today. The FAA and CANA generated up to 300 strike sorties from 1 May to the surrender at Port Stanley on 14 June, but many sorties operated without sufficient reconnaissance or intelligence. The Argentineans carried out several reconnaissance sorties, but the aircraft used for these missions (e.g., Boeing 707, C-130, P-2 Neptunes, and others) were neither designed nor equipped for this task. Additionally, many attacks against the task force were made against naval targets of opportunity. As a result, the FAA and CANA hit picket ships (e.g., frigates and destroyers). The FAA and CANA did not know where the British carriers or major troop transports (e.g., the requisitioned luxury liners SS

Canberra and *Queen Elizabeth II)* were located. Sinking these ships would have dealt a major blow to the invasion because of the loss of military ground forces and the political effect of high casualties.

Another Argentinean failure involved the use of the principle of mass. Although the FAA and CANA had numerical superiority, they never generated a full-scale attack against the British task force or invasion force. Argentinean air strikes were limited to fewer than a dozen aircraft at a single time. Imagine what might have happened if the Argentineans had used a 75-aircraft attack wave against the British task force. The Sea Harrier CAP and ship air defenses caused major losses among Argentinean aircraft, but some did get through to their targets; a large-scale attack could have overwhelmed the defenses and proved disastrous for the invasion force. Poor planning resulted in a failure to mount large-scale attacks.

Another shortfall in FAA and CANA operations was low sortie generation. Argentinean sortie generation was considerably less than that of RN or RAF forces. Although the British had few aircraft, they were able to project more combat power than the numerically superior Argentineans. The FAA planned over 505 combat sorties—445 were launched, but only 280 reached their targets.[12] The CANA launched only six Super Etendard and 34 A-4Q sorties. In contrast, for example, the British launched the following numbers of sorties from 1 May through 14 June: 1,335 Sea Harrier (1,135 CAP missions), 600 Victor K.2, 111 Nimrod, 126 Harrier GR.Mk.3, and 2,253 Sea King helicopter.[13]

Lastly, the Argentineans' lack of major air-refueling capability significantly affected their operations. This limitation diminished aircraft range, loiter time, and the ability to search for targets. FAA and CANA aircraft could attack only ships or surface targets within their range, thus limiting their available targets. Mirage III and Dagger aircraft had to operate at the extreme boundaries of their ranges. This significantly contributed to their inability to contest the skies for air superiority with the Sea Harriers, much like the failure of the Luftwaffe's Me-109Es to control the air against RAF Spitfires and Hurricanes 40 years earlier in the Battle of Britain. They could not loiter and protect A-4 or other aircraft. Also, FAA and CANA aircraft had to attack at the first target of opportunity and could not search for more lucrative targets due to fuel constraints.

Although FAA and CANA failed to stop the British recapture of the Falklands, their pilots served with distinction. Under extremely difficult conditions (e.g., better armed Sea Harriers, long distances, extensive air defenses, and other factors), these pilots were able to sink several major RN surface combatants and support ships. The prospect of facing AIM-9L armed Sea Harriers providing CAP would alarm the bravest of pilots. The effectiveness of CAP is illustrated by the RN pilots' results. They launched 27 AIM-9Ls and scored 24 hits, which destroyed 19 aircraft (11 Mirage III and eight Dagger interceptors). Despite these dangers, FAA and CANA pilots and crews rose to the challenge to defend the Islas Malvinas.

British airpower took a distinctly different approach by planning the campaign in distinct phases and coordinating joint forces successfully to invade and eject Argentinean forces. The British were able to effectively use their smaller forces and maximize their performance. The Argentinean strategy boiled down to a phased defensive operation that seemed more reactive than British actions. In a nutshell, the British relied on an overall offensive campaign against a defensive one waged by FAA and CANA airpower. British airpower objectives, after creating the air bridge to Ascension Island, were to protect the task force and ensure that air support was available for the ground invasion.

The first task for the RAF and RN was to neutralize the Argentineans' airpower and deny them control of the air. The RN initially deployed only 20 Sea Harriers. The British needed to draw on these limited resources and other forces to reduce Argentinean airpower. These operations included conducting CAP over the task force with Sea Harriers armed with AIM-9Ls, launching the Black Buck missions, keeping CANA's only carrier in port, attacking airfields with Special Air Services forces and Harriers, and deploying seaborne and land-based air defense systems. Although the British forces were not able to achieve air supremacy throughout the theater, their limited forces did thwart many FAA and CANA attempts to bomb the task and invasion forces. More importantly, the combination of local air superiority using CAP, superior training and armament, and favorable attrition rates significantly reduced the Argentinean numerical advantage. The high Argentinean attrition rate affected FAA and CANA efforts to stop the British invasion efforts.

The reduction in the number of threats from Argentinean air forces also led to the RAF's and RN's ability to support ground operations for the British invasion. Argentinean ground forces had air defense weapons, but efforts by RAF and RN fixed- and rotary-wing aircraft still managed to ensure that ground units could retake many major military objectives around the Falklands. The use of multipurpose aircraft like the Sea Harrier enabled the British to switch roles from CAP to ground attack. Additionally, the coordination between ground elements and CAS immeasurably aided the effort to evict Argentinean ground forces from defensive positions.

Whereas the FAA and CANA did not use force multipliers, the British relied on several to compensate for the operational difficulties they faced. Air refueling significantly improved the RAF's ability to strike long distance from Wideawake. The RN was able to use aerial refueling to extend Nimrod reconnaissance and intelligence-gathering missions. The British also employed strategic airlift. The use of Ascension Island as a long-distance logistics base forced the RAF to rely on strategic airlift from its C-130 and VC-10 forces to ensure that the task force received vital personnel, spare parts, and supplies.

Unlike the Argentineans, the British were able to restore the Port Stanley airport quickly after the war. RAF F-4s conducted full operations from the airport on 17 October by using AM-2 matting. The RAF also extended the airfield by 2,000 feet. Argentinean forces had AM-2 matting before the conflict and could have started extension of the airfield before it was attacked. If the conflict had continued, the airfield's ability to support RAF operations would have provided new opportunities to strike Argentina directly.

Although the British maintained a multilayer defense for the task force, Argentinean forces still scored some impressive hits. Sea Harriers and SAMs shot down many Argentinean aircraft, but the RN was hampered by inadequate AEW coverage and defenses against such weapons as the Exocet missile. Additionally, bomb damage from Skyhawk, Mirage III, and Dagger aircraft sank four ships and could have done serious damage to six more if the bombs had exploded. This illustrated the vulnerability of naval forces to aircraft despite all of the RN's defensive precautions. More importantly, antimissile defenses against the Exocet were lacking. Air-to-surface missiles showed their deadly effect in the absence of adequate defenses.

Despite this problem, the RAF and RN defeated a force much larger than their own. Argentina lost an estimated 103 aircraft and helicopters to all causes in the conflict.[14] The British government made claims of another 14 aircraft probably destroyed and 15 destroyed on the ground. The RAF and RN lost 34 airframes in the war due to AAA, SAMs, accidents, or losses from ship attacks by the FAA and CANA. British airpower played a significant role in defeating a foe by participating in a joint undertaking that occurred far from home under difficult circumstances. Proper planning, employment, and use of force multipliers all played major roles in the retaking of the Falklands. However, the innovative use of force by British airpower may offer more fertile ground to explore for future force employment. The Falklands War demonstrated the ability to project military forces in innovative ways. The British task force operated far from logistics sources and won a major victory in the process. Because the United States may face similar situations in the future, the Air Force must learn from the experience of British forces in the Falklands.

Eighty-Five to Zero: Israel's Bekaa Valley Campaign

Aerial warfare has progressed from "knights of the sky" meeting in aerial duels over the western front in World War I to a sophisticated electronic battle waged above the battlefield. A key element of modern airpower involves the defeat of ground-based air defense systems in order to wage aerial combat. During World War I, biplanes on both sides of the conflict avoided or countered other biplanes, small-arms fire, barrage balloons, and first-generation antiaircraft weapons. By the 1980s, many nations' militaries had sophisticated air defense systems with radar, airborne warning, radar-guided AAA, defensive ECM, and SAMs. The Israeli Defense Forces/Air Force encountered these types of systems during the 1973 Yom Kippur War. Unfortunately for the IDF/AF, the early stages of the engagement over the Suez Canal almost proved catastrophic for an air force unprepared to meet those defenses. The IDF/AF quickly adapted to the situation, with the aid of the United States, to defeat Egyptian and Syrian air and ground forces. In June 1982, Israel was to face another conflict—this time in Lebanon. It had learned its lessons about defeating integrated air defense systems (IADS) and would apply those lessons in the Bekaa Valley.

In 1974 a civil war between Christian and Islamic militia groups erupted in Lebanon. Islamic groups such as the Palestine Liberation Organization (PLO) sought and received aid from some Arab countries. Syria was one of those supporters and a willing participant in the conflict. On 31 May 1976, it intervened in the civil war to halt the conflict.[15] The Syrian government made no effort to disguise its support for the Islamic groups, especially the PLO. Syrian forces included the 3d Armored Division and a variety of aircraft such as the MiG-21, Su-7, and helicopters. These forces and others transited from Damascus to Beirut through the Bekaa Valley, which ran north to south (fig. 15).

Syrian and PLO involvement in the Lebanese civil war created several problems for Israel. An Islamic-controlled Lebanon would allow terrorist groups like the PLO easy access to conduct guerilla or artillery raids on northern Israeli settlements. Although Israel had signed the Camp David peace accords with Egypt, Syria still posed a threat to Israel. Syrian forces in Lebanon added another question mark to Israel's strategic position in case of war. Israel also felt a moral responsibility not to see a "holocaust" among the Christian factions perpetrated by Islamic groups if Syria succeeded in tipping the military balance in favor of such groups as the PLO.[16] Thus, Israel was slowly dragged into Lebanon.

As the Lebanese civil war continued, the PLO began a campaign to strike Israeli settlements from encampments in southern

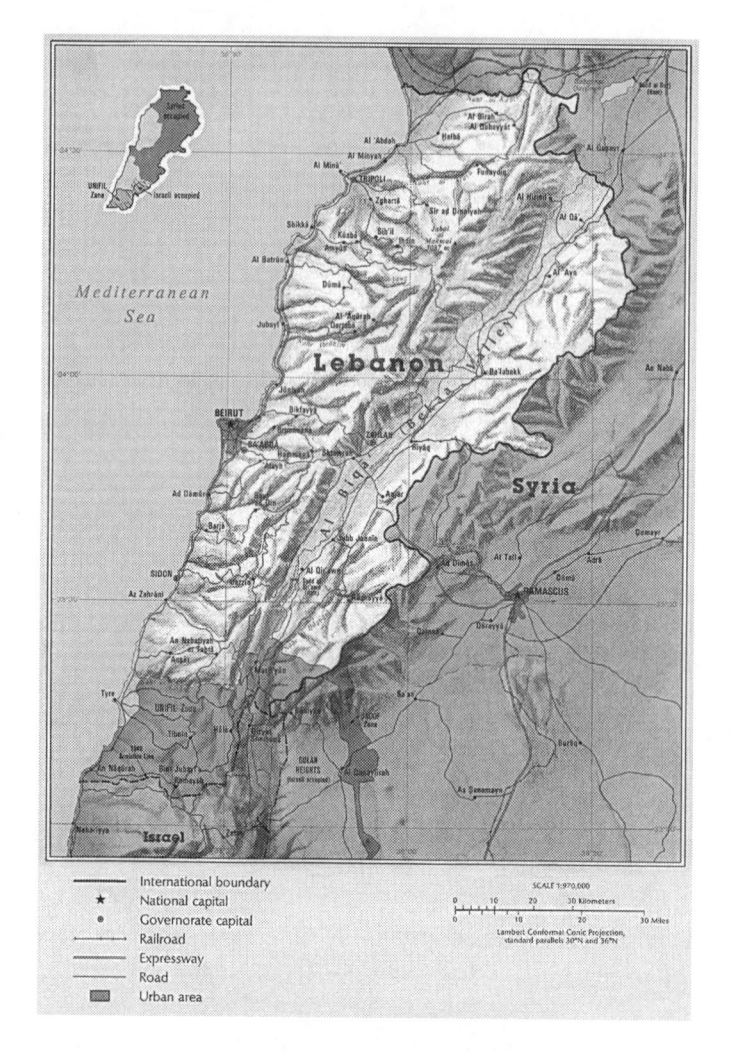

Figure 15. Lebanon and the Bekaa Valley

Lebanon. The frequency of guerilla raids escalated through the early 1980s. By spring of 1982, Israeli defense minister Ariel Sharon had publicly warned the PLO and Syria that it was his government's intention to cross the Lebanese border in force and destroy the PLO infrastructure unless the attacks stopped.[17] With the Israelis pulling out of the Sinai peninsula in observance of the Camp David accords and achieving peace with

Egypt, Syria became Israel's main enemy. The Israeli government could release military forces from the Egyptian frontier for future operations in Lebanon against the PLO and Syria. A justification for launching the Lebanese invasion came after another PLO attack. This time a terrorist group linked to the PLO attempted to assassinate Shlomo Argov, the Israeli ambassador to the United Kingdom, on 3 June 1982 in London. On the next day, the IDF/AF conducted 60 air strikes on PLO outposts in southern Lebanon; the PLO responded with stepped-up artillery and Katyusha rocket attacks on Israeli settlements.[18] The Israeli Cabinet met and authorized an invasion of Lebanon.

An Israeli armored force composed of 500 tanks spearheaded a force of 60,000 troops over the Lebanese border at 1100 on 6 June 1982. Israel launched Operation Peace for Galilee, ostensibly to eliminate the threat from the PLO and other terrorist groups located in southern Lebanon, to demilitarize the Lebanese border, and to remove Syrian forces from the country. Israeli military forces would need to establish a demilitarized zone from the border up to a distance of 40 kilometers (about 25 miles) to remove the threat of future artillery or rocket attacks. The PLO and Syrian military controlled a series of mountainous areas surrounding the Bekaa Valley. The Syrians had deployed several radar, AAA, and SAM systems to protect their forces from the Israelis. In order to eject PLO and Syrian forces from the Bekaa Valley, the IDF/AF needed to contend with these defenses. The IDF/AF faced a situation similar to that encountered with Egypt in 1973—a heavily defended air defense umbrella but with a more deadly combination of modern air defense weapons and emplacements hidden among rugged mountains instead of exposed on the flat desert terrain of the Sinai. The Syrians also possessed many advanced MiG-23 and MiG-25 fighters that compounded the IDF/AF's problems.

The IDF/AF and the Syrian Arab air force had clashed intermittently over the skies of Lebanon from 1978 through 1982. The Israeli government authorized air strikes into Lebanon starting in 1979. On 27 June 1979, the IDF/AF struck PLO targets in Tyre and Sidon with a force of A-4 Skyhawks and F-4E Phantoms supported by CAP from F-15A and Kfir fighters (an Israeli-modified Dassault Mirage jet). American-supplied AEW E-2C aircraft supported these attacks by detecting enemy aircraft and directing their interception by fighter aircraft. Twelve SAAF MiG-21s responded to the Israeli assaults—only seven returned. This was the first of many encounters between the IDF/AF and SAAF. From 1978 through 1982, SAAF lost over two dozen aircraft to the IDF/AF.[19]

IDF/AF aircraft conducted reconnaissance missions over southern Lebanon, including the Bekaa Valley, with RF-4E aircraft and remotely piloted vehicles (RPV), which included the Ryan Teledyne 1241 (AQM-34L) Firebee and the Israel Aircraft Industry Scout. The Firebees were fitted with electronic and optical sensors to track the locations of Soviet-built mobile SA-6 SAM units and gather information about radar frequencies.[20] The Scout RPVs were equipped with television and wide-angle film cameras for postattack analysis.

The Israelis' ground forces advanced on two fronts, up the Lebanese coast and through the Bekaa Valley. These initial drives into southern Lebanon, supported by attack helicopters and air strikes, pushed back some 15,000 PLO guerillas and 100 tanks.[21] PLO encampments were destroyed or captured. The Israelis attempted an amphibious invasion of Sidon but were repulsed. The IDF then tried a ground attack a second time to invade Sidon but was met with SAAF attacks. IDF/AF fighters easily dominated the SAAF intruders and shot down at least two MiG-21s and six ground-attack aircraft.[22] The Israelis were pushing the PLO and Syrians out of Lebanon. The PLO forces were in danger of being crushed. The Syrian government had no alternative other than moving against the IDF task force to save the PLO and stop any further Israeli advance into Lebanon.

The Israeli advance up the Bekaa Valley started to slow as the PLO and Syrian ground forces put up continued opposition from their deployments in the surrounding mountains. The Bekaa Valley was an important route for Syrian forces and military supplies, but it also housed several PLO encampments. Israeli forces would need to push both the PLO and Syrian army out of this area. However, the IDF ground forces could not do the job alone and relied on the IDF/AF for CAS and protection from SAAF attack. Israeli air support for Bekaa

AIRPOWER UNLEASHED

Valley operations faced a challenge similar to that of the 1973 Yom Kippur War. Unlike its actions in earlier encounters, the Syrian military had heavily defended its positions with 15 SA-6, two SA-3, and two SA-2 SAM batteries.[23] Once employed, however, the Syrian military did not reposition any SAM batteries, build dummy sites, entrench, or properly site the missile batteries during its stay in the Bekaa Valley. These actions would haunt the Syrians later in the campaign. The defenses also included radar and AAA emplacements. This air defense system stretched the length of the Bekaa Valley to the Syrian border.

In light of its experience in the Yom Kippur War, the IDF/AF had modified its tactics and strategies to handle attacks on IADS. If the IDF/AF could not neutralize these systems, it could not achieve air superiority over the SAAF. Failure to gain and maintain air superiority would lead to a disaster akin to what occurred in the early stages of the 1973 war. This time, the IDF/AF was well prepared. RF-4E and RPV reconnaissance missions had located many of the Syrian SAM, AAA, and radar sites. Prior to any air strikes, a coordinated attack by IDF special forces, artillery, and rockets would soften the Syrian air defenses. IDF ground forces used American-made Lance surface-to-surface missiles in these attacks. Additionally, they used a newly deployed surface-to-surface antiradiation missile of Israeli design, the Ze'ev (Wolf), to strike radar systems.[24] Additionally, the IDF/AF employed a specially modified Boeing 707 to jam Syrian radar signals, fighter-control networks, and navigation aids. The Boeing 707 also had side-looking radar that allowed pilots to detect locations of SAM batteries and other systems, as well as enemy radar frequencies used to tune IDF/AF aircraft ECM pods. The RPVs gathered the appropriate frequencies for this jamming, and the IDF/AF also used them in the initial attack to get up-to-date information.[25] The Israelis also used CH-53 helicopters for stand-off jamming missions. The Israelis armed their strike aircraft with a variety of PGMs to attack radar and SAM sites. The IDF/AF had acquired US-made long-range AGM-78 Standard and AGM-45 Shrike antiradiation missiles to destroy radar sites. Fortunately for the IDF/AF, the Syrians did not use dummy radar sites emitting signals to confuse antiradiation missiles fired against operating radar systems. Finally, the IDF/AF operated an AEW system composed of two orbiting E-2C Hawkeye aircraft. These aircraft allowed Israeli commanders to gather real-time information about SAAF movements for IDF/AF fighter pilots and provided an invaluable tool for maintaining C^2 over the battlefield. The Israelis also used a system of Westinghouse low-altitude AN/TPS-63 radar units deployed under tethered balloons to maintain continual surveillance over the SAAF.[26]

The first attack against the Bekaa Valley air defenses was launched on 9 June at 1414. An attack force composed of 40 F-4E Phantoms, A-4 Skyhawks, and Kfirs, supported by F-15 and F-16 fighters, struck Syrian air defenses. The IDF/AF launched several RPVs to confuse Syrian radar operations and to gather current frequency data when these radar operators detected and locked SAMs on the RPVs. The attack-force aircraft were well equipped with ECM pods and chaff to counter radar detection (the Firebees may have used chaff as well).[27] The main targets were Syrian ground-controlled intercept facilities, SAM radar sites, and SAM batteries. The destruction of GCI facilities would leave the SAAF incapable of directing any DCA missions against the IDF/AF or attacks on the IDF ground forces. The elimination of SAM radar sites would render any SAM battery sightless. Lastly, air strikes against the SAM batteries would eliminate SAAF's ability to threaten any Israeli airborne systems conducting either OCA or CAS operations.

The IDF/AF sent 26 F-4Es armed with AGM-65 television-guided Mavericks and the Standard and Shrike antiradiation missiles to make the initial strikes. The F-4Es launched their antiradiation missiles from a range of about 22 miles to avoid any SAMs after the Syrians turned on their radar systems when they detected the RPVs.[28] The A-4s and Kfirs followed up the F-4E strikes with GBU-15 cluster-bomb attacks on the SAM sites. These aircraft destroyed several GCI facilities, radar installations, and 10 of the 19 SAM batteries within 10 minutes. Eventually, the IDF/AF would destroy 23 SAM batteries in the Bekaa Valley over the entire campaign. These batteries included replacements for ones previously attacked and destroyed by the IDF/AF. A second wave of IDF/AF aircraft struck additional radar and SAM locations. A third IDF/AF series of attacks mopped up any remaining targets. Syria responded by sending aircraft to stop the IDF/AF. The SAAF, without a clear picture of the air situation due to its loss of radar and GCI capability, sent out a large force of approximately 60 to 100 aircraft. Their mission was to push the IDF/AF out of the Bekaa Valley and to protect any retreating Syrian ground units.[29]

The SAAF sent a force of MiG-21, -23, -25, and Su-22 aircraft out to attack an IDF/AF force of unknown strength and location. The second wave of IDF/AF aircraft was in the midst of mopping-up operations against the Syrian air defenses. Israeli F-15 and F-16 escort aircraft engaged the Syrian interceptors in one of the largest dogfights since World War II. Israeli aircraft had AIM-7F Sparrow, AIM-9L Sidewinder, and Israeli-made Shafrir 2 and Python 3 AAMs, along with internal guns. The Sparrow allowed IDF/AF pilots to strike SAAF aircraft at beyond visual ranges and beyond the range of any of the Soviet-made AAMs used by the Syrians. Additionally, the AIM-9L all-aspect mission allowed Israeli fighter pilots to attack SAAF jets head-on. Israeli AAMs eventually accounted for 93 percent of all IDF/AF kills. The Soviet infrared-guided AA-2 Atoll and AA-8 Aphid AAMs were usable only if the SAAF pilot managed to maneuver and attack an IDF/AF plane from the rear. This put the Syrian pilots at a severe disadvantage in a dogfight.

Syrian air losses over the Bekaa Valley were heavy. After dogfights, the SAAF claimed to have shot down 26 IDF/AF jets while losing 16 aircraft. The Syrians later readjusted this total to 19 enemy aircraft destroyed at a loss of 16 MiGs. The IDF/AF boasted that it had shot down 29 SAAF planes without loss. The Israelis reduced their claim to 22 Syrian jets, again without any losses. Most of the SAAF losses were due to "modified" AIM-9L AAMs. These missiles were specifically modified from IDF/AF experience in Lebanon since 1976.[30]

In a single day, the Syrians' air defenses in the Bekaa Valley were virtually destroyed, and a significant number of their aircraft shot down. The Soviet Union was so concerned about the IDF/AF's ability to defeat its designed and manufactured SAM and radar systems that it sent Col Gen Yevseny S. Yuvasov, deputy commander of the Soviet Air Defense Force, to investigate the actions in the Bekaa Valley.[31] If the Israelis, armed with American equipment, could easily sweep away the Soviets' air defense systems, then what could they expect from the United States Air Force? The poor performance of the Syrian air defense system underscored the lessons learned from the earlier air campaigns in 1973 and World War II. Although ground forces may have a superior air defense umbrella, airpower can often defeat the most heavily armed air defense systems.

Air combat continued between the IDF/AF and SAAF for two days. On 10 June, the IDF/AF destroyed the last two original SAM batteries in the Bekaa Valley. Israeli ground forces, supported by Bell AH-1S Cobra and Hughes 500MD Defender helicopters (the 500MD was armed with TOW antitank missiles), started a drive into the Bekaa Valley to dislodge PLO and Syrian forces. The IDF/AF provided top cover against any SAAF attack to the ground forces. The SAAF attempted to stop the IDF ground forces and suffered the loss of 26 MiGs and three helicopters. The Syrians admitted to the loss of only five MiG-21s, three MiG-23s, and six helicopters.[32]

SAAF could not sustain this loss rate. The IDF/AF and SAAF continued their air operations on 11 June over the Bekaa Valley. An Israeli armored column attempted to cut a road from the Bekaa Valley to Beirut. SAAF was not successful in stopping the Israeli ground forces; nor did it halt the hemorrhage of aircraft losses. The attack cost the Syrians 18 more planes. At 1200 on 11 June, Israel and Syria reached a tentative cease-fire. Because the PLO was not included, the IDF/AF continued to support air operations in southern Lebanon against the PLO.

The IDF/AF claimed an exceptional victory in the air and against the Syrian IADS. Israel claimed it shot down 85 SAAF aircraft in air-to-air combat with no losses in the Bekaa Valley campaign. The IDF/AF's force of 37 F-15A aircraft accounted for 40 SAAF jets (equally divided between MiG-21 and MiG-23 aircraft), while the 72 F-16As killed 44 more Syrian jets. One Syrian plane was shot down by an F4-E. The Syrians claimed they lost 60 aircraft while shooting down 19 IDF/AF aircraft. Even if Israeli claims are discounted, this campaign still achieved outstanding results in air-to-air combat against the SAAF. US estimates of IDF/AF losses include two A-4s, one F-4E, one F-16A, and seven aircraft damaged.[33]

The IDF/AF's successful air campaign in the Bekaa Valley is a textbook example of how to achieve air superiority. The campaign was conducted in two phases. First, the IDF/AF attacked and defeated SAM, AAA, radar, and GCI systems. This action significantly reduced the ground threat to IDF/AF aircraft and blinded the SAAF. SAAF aircraft were handicapped by their inability to receive up-to-date information about their IDF/AF foe. Second, Israeli fighter aircraft defeated the SAAF in the skies over the Bekaa in major dogfights during the three-day air campaign. Not only did the IDF/AF plan and execute its mission well, but also the SAAF and Syrian military contributed to their own demise by their poor operational performance. Syrian fighter pilots could not achieve air superiority or deny it to the IDF/AF. The SAAF could not stop any IDF/AF effort to destroy air defenses in the Bekaa Valley.

The IDF/AF planned the defeat of the Syrian air defense system, based on its experience in the 1973 Yom Kippur War. The IDF/AF maintained reconnaissance and intelligence gathering by RF-4E and RPVs prior to and after the commencement of hostilities. Israeli attack plans reflected information gathered by electronic and optical means on the location of air defense weapon systems and radar frequencies before the 9 June air strikes. This information allowed the Israelis to concentrate on destroying Syrian air defense and C^2 systems without making extensive and time-sensitive search efforts. The Israelis made extensive use of RPVs as decoys and as a means of gathering intelligence throughout the campaign. Although these IDF/AF systems were not armed in the Bekaa Valley, future US Air Force unmanned aerial vehicles could carry weapons (e.g., antiradiation missiles or other PGMs) capable of carrying out missions akin to the Israeli F-4Es' defeat of SAMs or radar systems. The Israelis also deployed airborne jamming assets on specially equipped aircraft and aircraft-carried pods. In contrast to its initial efforts to dislodge Egyptian air defenses in 1973, the IDF/AF used many electronic aids to defeat Syrian forces and deny them many of their defensive capabilities.

The IDF/AF's aircraft, weapons, and other force multipliers also contributed to its success. The Israelis obtained advanced weaponry, superior C^2, and better coordination between ground and air forces. F-15 and F-16 aircraft demonstrated their superiority over Soviet-supplied MiG planes. American AIM-7s and AIM-9s (and Israeli derivatives) provided an additional edge for the better trained and motivated Israeli pilots over their Soviet-armed and -trained foes. Advanced technology gave the IDF/AF the ability to locate and kill SAAF aircraft before those planes could get off a single missile shot. Attacks on radar and SAM systems by antiradiation missiles also allowed the Israelis to defeat those systems beyond the effective range of SAAF weapons. Once blinded, the Syrian air defenses could not stop the IDF/AF from attacks on SAM and AAA sites with their less sophisticated weapons. Finally, the use of AEW assets allowed the Israelis to detect SAAF aircraft taking off from their bases, hence eliminating any chance of surprise attacks. This information also allowed the IDF/AF to provide better C^2 of its limited assets to meet an airborne threat or divert aircraft to hit ground targets. This real-time information greatly contributed to the IDF/AF's intercepting and defeating SAAF forces over the campaign.

The IDF/AF and ground forces also integrated their operations within the Bekaa Valley. The IDF/AF first defeated the air defense systems, achieved air superiority, and supported ground forces in their occupation of southern Lebanon. The key to success in the Bekaa Valley was knocking out the air defense systems and then turning airpower loose to support the IDF ground forces. The Syrian military's reliance on an air defense umbrella to protect itself from an air attack proved deficient, much like early American doctrine during the North African campaign in World War II.

Syrian forces, in contrast, were poorly deployed and did not perform well in the field. SAM and radar systems were placed in locations that were not optimal for defeating the IDF/AF. For example, SAM sites were not dug in or placed in proper fields of fire. Several SAM sites were located on the tops of mountain peaks, which precluded them from depressing their launchers to attack low-flying Israeli jets. The Syrians did not operate CAP over the SAM, GCI, AAA, and radar systems before the IDF/AF conducted its attacks; they suffered massive losses attempting to do so later. Radar and other air defense systems did not attempt to relocate throughout the campaign, making them sitting ducks for the Israeli warplanes. The SAAF was merely reactive to the IDF/AF strike and went on the defensive. Conversely, Israel maintained the offensive throughout the campaign and accomplished its goal of pushing the PLO and Syrians out of the Bekaa Valley.

Stopping the Luftwaffe Cold: The Soviet Tactical Air Effort in World War II

On 22 June 1941, the largest military campaign in World War II started on the German-Soviet border. This was Fall Barbarossa, the German invasion of the Soviet Union. The campaign would engulf the major portion of the German military effort in World War II until the final defeat and destruction of Berlin in 1945. The struggle would result in more than 30 million deaths and many more wounded—casualties on a scale never before seen in human history. This military front was the scene of large ground armies slugging it out over vast plains, mountains, frozen steppes, and countless scenes of urban street fighting. Thousands of tanks shot it out at the Battle of Kursk, and hundreds of thousands of soldiers fought untold personal engagements in the rubble of Stalingrad. The battle was fought not only on the ground, but also in the skies. What role did airpower play in this gigantic struggle?

The German Luftwaffe was still smarting from its humiliating defeat at the hands of the RAF during the Battle of Britain. Part of its problem was its doctrine, force structure, and strategy. The Luftwaffe continued to cling to a doctrine that supported Germany's earlier blitzkrieg strategy of rapidly knocking out enemy ground forces and supporting continued land operations. This meant that Luftwaffe doctrine did not have to address the need for a significant strategic-bombing force; instead, it chose to concentrate on a CAS force. As a result, the Luftwaffe was primed for a quick campaign without any aerial counterattacks. The Luftwaffe's force structure worked well against countries in the relatively close quarters of western and central Europe, like France or Poland. However, fighting against the Soviets on a much larger continental front, the Luftwaffe failed to achieve the same blitzkrieg success it enjoyed in 1939 and 1940.

Curiously, the Soviet air force (*Voyenno-vozdushnyye sily* or VVS) was designed and built to support the operation of the Soviet army, just as the Luftwaffe was designed to support the German army. Although not built to support a blitzkrieg strategy, the VVS was designed and organized as an auxiliary of the Soviet army. The Luftwaffe's rise to power before World War II occurred because of rapid, sustained buildup, but the VVS's prewar development was severely hampered by Stalin's purges of top VVS and aircraft-industry leadership. From 1936 to 1939, approximately 75 percent of the VVS's top leaders were removed from office. Since the VVS lacked the aircraft, leaders, doctrine, or infrastructure to fight the Luftwaffe on an equal footing, it found itself unprepared for war in 1941.

How did the VVS ultimately force the Luftwaffe to a standstill and help lead the Soviet Union to victory over Germany? These actions are particularly interesting, given the fact that the VVS was virtually destroyed in the air and on the ground during the first day of Fall Barbarossa. What did it do to win the war against the superior Luftwaffe and gain mastery of the skies on the eastern front? The VVS's approach towards fighting Germany is a lesson in how a defeated air force can use its strengths and ability to change its operations to achieve victory under very trying conditions.

The VVS lost over 1,200 aircraft in combat to the Luftwaffe on the first day of Fall Barbarossa. The Germans attacked simultaneously along the Soviet border from the Baltics to the Black Sea on 22 June. Although the Soviets had dispersed their airfields, most of their aircraft losses were due to Luftwaffe strafing and bombing attacks—not air-to-air combat.[34] The VVS had over 10,000 aircraft assigned to Europe at the time, but most of the planes were obsolete and deployed far forward, towards the enemy. The Russians' forward aircraft deployments were a result of the recent acquisition of Polish territories under their nonaggression pact with Germany. This land grab allowed the VVS to station aircraft in the new territory but placed them within easy reach of the Luftwaffe. On the first day of Fall Barbarossa, VVS aircraft were parked wingtip to wingtip on rough airfields. Within a week, the Luftwaffe had crushed the VVS in Europe. About 2,000 VVS aircraft were destroyed within 72 hours, and the German High Command claimed VVS losses at 4,017 planes within the first seven days of the campaign.[35] Only 150 German aircraft were claimed to be lost in the operation after the first week.

The Luftwaffe reigned supreme over the VVS as a result of these early operations. But the VVS soon fought back with a vengeance. The Soviet armies withdrew and started to fight a defensive war. The VVS began a war of attrition and started to chip away at the Luftwaffe. By 27 September 1941, the Luftwaffe had lost 1,603 aircraft, almost as many as the 1,733 planes it lost in the Battle of Britain.[36] By the end of 1941, however, the VVS's losses approached over 8,500 aircraft, which forced it to change its focus. The Soviets put more emphasis on gaining air superiority and defeating Luftwaffe fighter forces. The VVS also concentrated on its role as flying artillery for the Soviet army to counteract German panzer forces. Although the VVS had many obsolete aircraft, it tried to sweep the skies of Luftwaffe planes at all costs.

How then did the VVS accomplish this mission? A key strategy was to use mass to crush German military forces. Fearing for their aircraft industry, the Soviets moved entire production lines across the Ural Mountains, away from possible capture or destruction. This Herculean effort required the Soviets to move 10,000,000 workers; 1,360 production plants; and 1,500,000 tons of equipment to start production.[37] Before the war, in 1939 and 1940, Soviet industry had produced about 10,000 aircraft per year.[38] By June 1944, the Soviet aircraft industry was able to boost production from 2,000 aircraft per month in 1942 to well over 3,355 planes per month. These aircraft included improved versions of existing aircraft and several new types that proved rugged, simple to maintain, and effective in combat. By contrast, the Luftwaffe's reliance on a blitzkrieg force structure resulted in the production of the wrong types of aircraft and very few new aircraft types until late in the war.

The VVS's ability to produce aircraft rivaling and eventually surpassing the Luftwaffe's was as much an illustration of Soviet determination and dedication to win the war as the failure of the Luftwaffe's strategic attack. The Luftwaffe did not learn its lesson from the Battle of Britain of developing a viable, long-range strategic-attack capability. The German air force was still oriented towards the support of the ground war. As a consequence, it could not stop the flow of VVS aircraft or other war materiel to the Soviet front. The Luftwaffe also did not have the doctrine or experience to conduct an extensive interdiction campaign. Although Luftwaffe pilots had tried interdiction efforts in Poland and France, they were not equipped to conduct operations over the broad expanse of the USSR. The Luftwaffe failed to destroy rail lines, materiel in transport, and transportation centers.

The Luftwaffe's reliance on blitzkrieg strategy did not prepare it for the long, continuous combat operations on the Russian steppes. German force structure and tactics relied on a lightning war fought with fencing-foil precision. What the Germans faced, however, was a meat-cleaver war that continued unabated until Berlin's final surrender. Fighting near major salients, such as Stalingrad, and maintaining a presence along the entire front highlighted the war. The Luftwaffe could not support the front everywhere with the same effort. The Germans frequently stripped areas not under immediate attack to concentrate their forces to gain air superiority. This strategy succeeded at the cost of other fronts and further attacks.

Continued attrition of German aircraft was a significant factor in the destruction of the Luftwaffe in the Soviet Union. Unlike the Soviets, the Germans delayed introduction of new aircraft types and did not mobilize their economy to a full war footing until well into the war. Germany produced 27,185 aircraft from 1941 to 1942 for all fronts, compared to Soviet production of 41,171 for the same period.[39] The 1942 production rate would not allow the Luftwaffe to sustain simultaneous offensive operations in the Soviet Union and on all other fronts. The Germans had to send aircraft to support their operations in the Balkans and the Mediterranean, as well as to defend the Reich. By 1943 the Soviet front became a secondary priority for the Luftwaffe as the defense of the Reich against American and British long-range strategic bombers consumed valuable fighter resources. This action further reduced the possibility of knocking out the VVS. In fact, in 1943 the Luftwaffe fielded only 375 single-engine fighters devoted to air-superiority missions on the Soviet front against thousands of VVS aircraft.[40]

Russian devotion to duty and fierce courage were also key ingredients in the victory over the Luftwaffe. The Luftwaffe maintained control of the air from 1941 to 1942 due to its superior planes, pilots, and experience. During the early stages of Fall Barbarossa, the VVS, desperate to stem the onslaught of the Luftwaffe, began ramming Luftwaffe aircraft using a tactic called *taran*, an extreme measure taken by Soviet fighter pilots after they had run out of ammunition.[41] Pilots would ram their aircraft against Luftwaffe bombers and attempt to disable the aircraft. VVS pilots aimed their fighters at the German aircraft's control surfaces or attempted to cut the German bomber in half. The pilots would then either land their fighters or attempt to parachute away from the damaged plane. This tactic remained part of VVS pilots' options against the Germans until they achieved air superiority on all fronts in 1943.

Conversely, the Luftwaffe was shortsighted in its application of seasoned pilots and limited aircraft. Starting in the 1939 buildup, the Luftwaffe stripped training units of their best pilots and assigned them as frontline combat crews. This policy hastened the demise of the Luftwaffe by reducing the quantity and valuable quality of replacement pilots. This self-defeating process forced less-qualified instructor pilots to provide an ever-decreasing capability to produce combat crews. As the Luftwaffe raided its own meager training bases for more combat crews, training quality diminished even further. For example, during the Soviet encirclement of 100,000 German ground troops in February 1942 at Demyansk, the Luftwaffe attempted to resupply those forces via airlift. Luftwaffe transport resources were ordered to send 300 tons per day to the encircled forces. German transport instructor pilots and training aircraft were sent to the Soviet Union to allow the Luftwaffe to conduct the airlift. Although the airlift was successful, it came at a steep price: 265 aircraft lost. The Luftwaffe

High Command came away from the experience believing it could break a Soviet ground encirclement through aerial resupply alone. This illusion proved disastrous at Stalingrad. Additionally, the poor performance of VVS fighter operations at Demyansk forced the Soviets to build better fighters and improve their tactics. These actions would ultimately lead to the VVS's achievement of air superiority.

The experience at Demyansk spurred the VVS to make needed reforms. Better air and ground coordination would ensure that encircled German forces would not escape again. The Soviet *Stavka*, or high military command, replaced the VVS commander with Alexander Novikov, who provided the drive, energy, and ability to modernize the VVS. Just as the RAF changed its fighter tactics in the Battle of Britain, so did Novikov modify VVS operations to counter the Luftwaffe's tactics and began building more capable aircraft. He also formed air armies. Instead of keeping the current, segmented VVS operations (e.g., separate bomber, fighter, and other commands), the air army put elements of each type of command under a single organization, controlled by a Soviet ground commander. The separate VVS commands had previously worked independently—most of the time in an uncoordinated manner.[42] The new air armies were able to provide improved support and quickly strike at German positions throughout the front. This gave the VVS and the Soviet army the needed flexibility of a fluid, continental front against the Germans. Novikov also formed huge air armies as reserves to plug gaps along the front. The increased production of aircraft allowed the VVS to keep 43 percent of its strength in these reserve air armies by the end of the war. The air armies also grew in number from 1,000 in 1942 to well over 2,500 by 1945. These forces were able to batter not only German ground forces, but also the Luftwaffe.

The Luftwaffe's reliance on a blitzkrieg force structure and doctrine contributed to its inability to meet the VVS challenge of a long-term attrition campaign. One of the key elements of the Luftwaffe's blitzkrieg doctrine was the use of surprise to win air superiority.[43] Germany's early World War II campaigns were aimed at rapid capture of enemy airfields and destruction of opposing air forces through a combination of armored advances and CAS. German fighters would pick off the remaining air opposition in air-to-air combat. The Russian campaign significantly altered the Luftwaffe's plans. The VVS was not totally destroyed in the early days of Fall Barbarossa, and German air forces could not remain supreme throughout the campaign over the Russian skies, as they did in France or Poland. During the campaign, Germany did not significantly alter its doctrine or strategy to compensate for the changing tides of war. Instead, the Luftwaffe was locked into a slugging match with the VVS that it could not win. Ultimately, the numbers of VVS aircraft that faced Germany overwhelmed the Luftwaffe's limited resources.

The best known example of the Luftwaffe's failure in the Soviet Union is the encirclement of Stalingrad from 19 November 1942 to 3 February 1943 (see chap. 5). The Soviet army had surrounded 230,000 Axis troops of the German Sixth Army in the city of Stalingrad. The Luftwaffe attempted to provide aerial resupply to the trapped forces, as it had done in Demyansk. Unfortunately, the loss of irreplaceable pilots and transports at Demyansk played a major role in the Luftwaffe's failure at Stalingrad. The Luftwaffe had been in continuous combat from 1939 and was at the end of a long logistical tail in the Soviet Union. It was also fighting against an improved VVS. German air force officials were forced to use their meager resources in unconventional ways to halt the Soviets at Stalingrad. Transport units used bombers to carry supplies to make up a fleet of 800 aircraft, but improved Soviet fighter operations and dwindling Luftwaffe fighter capability resulted in major German losses. German transport losses skyrocketed to 481 aircraft and, on average, achieved a resupply rate of less than 31 percent of the daily objective.[44] The Soviets were successful in capturing Stalingrad, and the German Sixth Army was lost. This ensured the collapse of the main German offensive on the central Soviet front.

The Luftwaffe never recovered after Stalingrad. Conversely, the VVS gained in strength and momentum after this major victory. VVS aircraft were able to stem all further German ground opportunities from then on. The last major German offensive on the front, Operation *Zitadel*, on 5 July 1943, was Hitler's last attempt to drive a wedge between the Soviet armies in the center and southern fronts at Kursk. The Germans attempted to stop a potential Soviet drive into the middle of the German line by encircling two Soviet armies, much like Stalingrad, but this time with the Soviets entrapped. Kursk was the key. If it fell, the Germans would have a new life in the Soviet Union. Kursk would eventually become the largest tank battle in history. The Luftwaffe committed 70 percent of its forces on the Soviet front to the battle—over 2,050 aircraft against 2,900 VVS planes.[45] The Soviets lost hundreds of tanks in the initial attacks. However, VVS fighter and ground-attack aircraft counterattacked against the Germans. VVS quantity and quality stopped the German advance and allowed the Soviet tank forces to regroup and attack. The VVS lost well over 1,000 aircraft, but so did the Luftwaffe. This titanic armored and air battle caused massive losses to the Germans. German failure at Kursk, Italy's fall, plus stepped-up American and British strategic bombing over Germany forced the Luftwaffe to withdraw fighter units to strengthen defenses closer to home. This allowed the VVS to take the offensive against the Germans and dominate the skies until the end of the war.

The battle at Kursk brought to an end Germany's final attempt to conquer the Soviet Union. The Luftwaffe did not stop the VVS, even after stripping aircraft throughout the front to gain air superiority over Kursk. The VVS was still able to pound German ground forces. Ironically, the VVS was able to use a Luftwaffe air doctrine based on support of ground forces to push out the German invaders. However, the VVS approached the doctrine differently and modified its strategies in light of conditions on the front. The Luftwaffe's weaknesses were exposed in the frozen wastes—not only its inability to conduct winter fighting, but also its failed logistics and ill-planned force structure.

Once the Luftwaffe was deposed, the VVS maintained the offensive from Kursk to Berlin. It was able to retain the initiative because of its ability to produce massive numbers of aircraft. The failure of the Luftwaffe to destroy Soviet production facilities allowed the Soviets to build thousands of modern aircraft and continue a long war of attrition. Additionally, the Allies were able to supply the Soviets with thousands of other aircraft and supporting war materials throughout the war until the Soviets could increase their own aircraft production. This uninterrupted supply of domestic and imported aircraft allowed the Soviets to achieve a minimum 10-to-one superiority in terms of operational aircraft towards the end of the war.

Massive production, attrition, Luftwaffe mistakes, and sound doctrine allowed the Soviets slowly to gain air superiority. The lessons learned in blood from early failures in 1941 and 1942 eventually forced the VVS to concentrate on gaining air superiority. This allowed the Soviets to defend against Luftwaffe attacks and gave the VVS the freedom to strike against German ground units with relative impunity. The VVS then concentrated its forces against vulnerable German sectors during the offensives of 1944 and 1945.

Even without a strategic bombardment force like America's or Britain's, the VVS was still able to beat the vaunted German military machine with only a tactical air force. The Soviets used tactical aircraft because of limited resources, experience, wartime emergencies, and doctrine. Soviet aircraft were further refined to operate under rugged conditions (such as unimproved airfields, winter conditions, long logistical lines, and limited maintenance). The Soviets were able to adapt to conditions that the Luftwaffe faced in 1941 and 1942 and to prevail, while the Germans became bogged down. This example illustrates the possibility of winning a major war without strategic airpower. Some may argue that the Combined Bomber Offensive supported the Soviets by reducing German military production and drawing away the opposition's fighter strength. Conversely, the Luftwaffe's failure to destroy VVS airfields and aircraft-production facilities was due to a lack of strategic airpower. However, the VVS's emphasis on tactical support kept the Soviet army in the field and allowed it to grind down the German war machine. The VVS eventually was able to meet German quality with Soviet quantity and attrit the once mighty Luftwaffe to a shell of its former self.

The VVS's force structure clearly reflected its doctrine. About 35 percent of Soviet airpower was devoted to air superiority and 46.5 percent to CAS. The remainder was predominantly reconnaissance—not strategic bombardment.[46] The Soviets had no intention of using a blitzkrieg-style offensive, given the size and breadth of the front they faced. Throughout the campaign, the main focus for the VVS was ground support. In the early part of the war, the Soviet air force was able to trade space for time. This exchange allowed the Soviet Union to regroup and rebuild. The Luftwaffe did not expect a counterattack but believed it would have a quick victory in 1941. The Soviet Union planned an attrition strategy that eventually put even more pressure on the overwhelmed Luftwaffe. The Soviets' ability to remain flexible and to adapt doctrine, strategy, and force structure became an important element of their victory. Airpower strategists in the future need to be aware of changing conditions and realize that some situations may not require such time-honored or dogma-inspired uses of airpower as strategic bombardment.

Summary

Aerospace functions and capabilities are not meaningless definitions and terms. Wars and conflicts have been won or lost because a side could not accomplish a certain mission or failed to include the function or capability in its plans. Air and space superiority, strategic attack, interdiction, CAS, mobility, space and information, and flexibility in operations were key components in many conflicts. No one method exists for successfully using these functions. Creative and innovative uses of these air and space activities can provide a commander many alternatives and options to settle a conflict.

Future technology, threats, and limited resources will greet aerospace leaders. They will need to apply many of the lessons learned from previous conflicts and many concepts about aerospace power to successfully harness air and space resources. Future weapons will become more precise and deadly. Engagements with adversaries are becoming more complex. Aerospace power will also become more involved in these challenges as the nation seeks new methods to reduce casualties and quickly settle conflicts. Applying a single aerospace function or a combination of functions to support this goal has become an art that tests our best minds. It will remain a continuing issue in the twenty-first century. Flexibility in planning and execution is the key to aerospace power.

Notes

1. Earl H. Tilford, "Air Power Lessons," in *Military Lessons of the Falkland Islands War: Views from the United States*, ed. Bruce W. Watson and Peter M. Dunn (Boulder, Colo.: Westview Press, 1984), 37.

2. Victor Flintham, *Air Wars and Aircraft: A Detailed Record of Air Combat, 1945 to the Present* (New York: Facts on File, 1990), 372.

3. Ibid., 370.

4. Bryan Perrett, *Weapons of the Falklands Conflict* (New York: Blandford Press, 1982), 90.

5. Flintham, 372.

6. David C. Isby, Jane's Air War 1, *Fighter Combat in the Jet Age* (London: HarperCollins, 1997), 148.

7. R. G. Funnell, "'It Was a Bit of a Close Call': Some Thoughts on the South Atlantic War," in *The War in the Air, 1914–1994: The Proceedings of a Conference Held by the Royal Australian Air Force in Canberra, March 1994*, ed. Alan Stephens (Fairbairn Base, Australia: RAAF Air Power Studies Centre, 1994), 214.

8. Perrett, 47.

9. Lon O. Nordeen, *Air Warfare in the Missile Age* (Washington, D.C.: Smithsonian Institution Press, 1985), 199.

10. Funnell, 219.

11. Nordeen, 205.

12. Flintham, 379.

13. Ibid., 378.

14. Jeffrey Ethell and Alfred Price, *Air War South Atlantic* (New York: Macmillan Publishing Co., 1983), 247.

15. Chaim Herzog, *The Arab-Israeli Wars: War and Peace in the Middle East* (New York: Random House, 1982), 68.

16. Ibid., 339.

17. Ibid., 341.

18. Nordeen, 182.

19. Charles Stafrace, *Arab Air Forces* (Carrollton, Tex.: Squadron/Signal Publications, 1994), 59.

20. Flintham, 69.

21. Nordeen, 182.

22. Flintham, 69.

23. Nordeen, 182.

24. Kenneth P. Werrell, *Archie, Flak, AAA, and SAM: A Short Operational History of Ground-Based Air Defense* (Maxwell AFB, Ala.: Air University Press, 1988), 147.

25. Flintham, 69.

26. *The Aerospace Encyclopedia of Air Warfare*, vol. 2, *1945 to the Present*, ed. Chris Bishop and Sophearith Moeng (Westport, Conn.: AIRtime Publishing, 1997), 180.

27. Werrell, 147.

28. Bishop and Moeng, 180.

29. Isby, 111.

30. Brereton Greenhous, "The Israeli Experience," in *Case Studies in the Achievement of Air Superiority*, ed. Benjamin Franklin Cooling (Washington, D.C.: Office of Air Force History, 1994), 600.

31. Nordeen, 182.

32. Flintham, 70.

33. Nordeen, 184.

34. The Aerospace Encyclopedia of Air Warfare, vol. 1, *1911–1945*, ed. Daniel J. March and John Heathcott (Westport, Conn.: AIRtime Publishing, 1997), 90.

35. Samuel W. Micham Jr., *Eagles of the Third Reich* (Novato, Calif.: Presidio Press, 1997), 138.

36. David C. Isby, "The Air and Sea War in the East," in *War in the East: The Russo-German Conflict, 1941–45* (New York: Simulations Publications, 1977), 174.

37. Kenneth R. Whiting, "The Soviet Air Force against Germany and Japan," in *Case Studies in the Achievement of Air Superiority*, 190.

38. R. J. Overy, *The Air War, 1939–1945* (Chelsea, Mich.: Scarborough House, 1991), 49.

39. Whiting, 203.

40. Isby, "The Air and Sea War in the East," 175.

41. Von Hardesty, *Red Phoenix: The Rise of Soviet Air Power, 1941–1945* (Washington, D.C.: Smithsonian Institution Press, 1991), 27.

42. Ibid., 86.

43. J. E. Kaufmann and H. W. Kaufmann, *Hitler's Blitzkrieg Campaigns: The Invasion and Defense of Western Europe, 1939–1940* (Conshohocken, Pa.: Combined Books, 1993), 26.

44. Isby, "The Air and Sea War in the East," 175.

45. Chistopher Shores, *Duel for the Sky* (Garden City, N.Y.: Doubleday, 1985), 141.

46. Overy, 54.

Chapter 7

Planning for Aerospace Operations

Aerospace forces provide many capabilities and alternatives that a commander can use independently or in unison with land and maritime forces. The proper balance between airpower and land power was clearly an issue during World War II at Kasserine Pass in Tunisia. This debate caused the Army to create FM 100-20, *Command and Employment of Air Power*, which served as a concept for airpower in World War II and future conflicts. It stressed that the Army Air Forces should attain air superiority and then conduct interdiction and close air support, in that order. This doctrine provided guidance for simple to complex tactical operations. At the same time, the AAF was conducting strategic bombardment operations against Germany and, later, Japan. Billy Mitchell and the philosophies of the Air Corps Tactical School encouraged the AAF leadership to focus on strategic bombardment. Many AAF leaders wanted to concentrate on independent operations that could win the war through the Combined Bomber Offensive alone. Ground commanders wanted more airpower devoted to ground operations to support an eventual invasion of Europe. However, the Combined Bomber Offensive did not win the war single-handedly although it significantly helped reduce Germany's industrial and military strength, enabling the Allies to land in France. Although these issues were debated over a half century ago, they still have validity within the aerospace power community and other military communities. Planning for aerospace-power applications involves many such concerns that must be settled before an air campaign is conducted. Air Force officers need to be knowledgeable of the possibilities and limitations of aerospace assets and should advocate conditions that optimize the effectiveness of aerospace power.

During Operations Desert Shield and Desert Storm, the proper application and operation of aerospace power was debated. These issues were very similar to the ones raised in World War II. A group within the Air Force advocated that the best method to defeat the Iraqis was a massive strategic bombardment campaign that, in their opinion, would provide a knockout punch to Iraqi leadership and the Iraqis' war-making capability. This would pave the way for an easy coalition victory. Other Air Force leaders believed that the Iraqi forces on the Saudi Arabian border dictated a more tactical approach to airpower to support defensive operations. Fortunately, Saddam Hussein did not attack across the Saudi border. However, the coalition used a four-phased air campaign approach that combined the strategic bombardment campaign with a tactical ground-support operation. The planning for this campaign involved national priorities, military objectives, service doctrines, force capabilities, political environments, the threat, and other factors. Planning for an air campaign is one of the most crucial aspects of conducting a war and will continue to increase in complexity.

This chapter introduces some of the most basic concepts and rudimentary aspects of conducting air campaign planning (including planning for space forces) to conduct operations. These tools and concepts are not meant to be a simple list of procedures that one blindly follows. Flexibility is the key to aerospace power. Innovation and a changing threat will force aerospace planners to adapt to change and exploit situations to gain an advantage over a foe. Rigid planning and the conduct of operations might give a foe the opportunity to anticipate a friendly force's plan and prepare a countermove or avoid an attack. Conversely, failure to provide a flexible plan may lock aerospace forces into a course of action that neither supports friendly forces nor effectively hampers the enemy. Air campaign planning is an art that all aerospace leaders must understand and practice.

Air Campaign Planning Concepts

An aerospace leader needs to understand how to organize, plan, and operate forces to meet a set of goals or objectives under difficult environmental conditions. Aerospace operations are the result of many decisions and linkages. Military actions must support national political objectives. If military action is appropriate, military objectives are developed that are subsets of national political objectives. Aerospace operations are a part of these military objectives. Without this direction, aerospace operations would be ambiguous at best and damaging to national objectives at worst. Depending on the level of operations, the planning to support these actions may be very extensive. These plans can range from a theater-level air campaign that deals with a massive strategic attack to a series of air-ground operations. Theater-level campaign plans are designed to include all aspects of a military operation or campaign over a geographic area. These plans include air, land, space, and maritime operations. They also affect national and allied forces. A theater commander may have four different campaign-planning activities conducted simultaneously. The theater commander might have air and space, land, maritime, and special operations plans being developed and integrated into an overall theater campaign plan. Air campaign plans must support higher-level theater campaign plans, and lower-level aerospace tasks must support the air campaign plan. These plans must provide a framework to satisfy objectives, force availability, logistics, timing, contingencies, alternative actions after the conflict, and measures of effectiveness to compare progress towards meeting the objective. Aerospace power involves such diverse elements as air and space superiority, mobility, strategic attack, interdiction, CAS, and other support. How should a staff of professionals organize and plan for these types of operations?

Air campaign planning should help a commander satisfy several requirements. Although an overall air campaign plan provides the basis for further air and space planning, this process serves as a vehicle to force commanders and staffs to think about a situation or problem facing the nation. There is no set methodology for solving aerospace problems. Doctrine provides guidance but may not illustrate enough detail to make specific aircraft assignments. Conversely, regulations or other similar documents might force strict compliance as a primary goal, but these actions are normally on a smaller scale than an air campaign plan. However, air campaign planning and other levels of similar details should at least provide a common focus that satisfies a commander's goals and objectives and makes clear to subordinates the purpose of the operation.

Air campaign planning provides a vehicle for organizing several military operations to attain a particular set of objectives with certain forces, at specified times, and with a desired number of effects. The process of selecting a single plan or series of plans can involve the evaluation of several alternatives and options that may vary the force level and direction of operations and possibly influence the level of casualties for an action. Alternatives may also be dictated by different environments, adversarial characteristics, friendly strengths and weaknesses, and timing of missions. A commander may also need to evaluate these alternatives by comparing the potential risk of failure to the probability of a positive outcome. Additionally, not only does the commander need to consider air and space forces, but also the interaction between these forces and the effect that land and maritime forces will have on the operation. Acting independently, these forces may require more forces than would a joint effort.

Completing an aerospace planning effort may require a complex schedule of operations. In Operation Desert Storm, the coalition air forces' overall air campaign plan involved four phases that required extensive coordination among all military forces. These actions provided commanders a time-sequenced chain of events that subordinates would need to prepare for future detailed actions. Additionally, the phasing of operations allowed commanders to prioritize actions, objectives, and targets. Commanders must decide how to determine the phases from objectives, such as Desert Storm's achievement of air superiority in phase one; the geographic goals of destroying all Luftwaffe airfields in France; or meeting a condition (e.g., conducting a CAS campaign if ground opposition increases or conducting interdiction if no such increase occurs). Once a phasing schedule is developed, a further evaluation of targets, priorities, and a lower level of objectives can be defined.

Phasing the air campaign plan allows the commander to determine the priority of operations. If phasing is completed sequentially, there is a distinct order for the completion of target attack against the enemy. Perhaps the reason for a sequential attack is due to requirements to complete destruction or disruption of targets in a particular order. For example, before an air force can destroy a factory, it needs to disable an

PLANNING FOR AEROSPACE OPERATIONS

F-16s providing air superiority

air defense system to increase the probability of the factory's destruction with reduced risk of aircrew casualties. Conversely, an air force could also attack targets in parallel, which would confuse an enemy and complicate his air defense efforts. Phases might overlap or be accomplished at the same time. This capability allows the air force to strike many different types of targets at the same time and increase a commander's options. Aircraft could strike mechanized infantry units and supply dumps, and engage in an aerial battle with the enemy—all at once. This might greatly confuse a foe or help complete a phase in the air campaign plan.

The specific targets for the air campaign usually concentrate on centers of gravity—key components that affect the running of the military or the nation. Successfully attacking these COGs can help disable the enemy's war-making capability, morale, political decision making, and so forth, thus interfering with the running of the government, economy, military, and society. For example, COGs discussed by John Warden include leadership, organic essentials, infrastructure, population, and fielded forces—critical in achieving both the theater's and commander's overall objectives and goals. COGs may shift as the theater campaign proceeds and the enemy reacts to the air campaign's operations. For example, the destruction of fuel sources may shift the COG from destruction of the enemy's armored forces to chemical weapons. Depending upon political constraints or an aerospace force's ability to destroy a target without causing collateral damage (i.e., unintended civilian damage), the force might not be able to attack some COGs.

Air campaign planning must also organize the appropriate forces to conduct the operation. Air and space forces involved in the operation must be notified and ready to perform a series of potentially complex actions. Commanders must coordinate actions for logistics, timing, aerial refueling, reconnais-

Strategic attack. B-29 bombers destroy the Chosen oil refinery at Wonsan, North Korea.

sance, and many other tasks. The sequence of attacks from divergent forces must ensure the proper number and types of munitions, fighter escort, and other support. Available forces might not have particular capabilities to strike the enemy, which may affect the use of weapon systems or the sequence and choice of attacking certain targets. Organizing available forces to achieve a desired effect is the most important aspect of assigning these forces.

One of the most important considerations involved in air campaign planning is the enemy's strength and condition. Air campaign planners might consider the enemy's strategies, forces, objectives, weaknesses, and strengths. The enemy might have certain objectives that one should deny before a friendly commander can start an air campaign. The enemy might be willing to sacrifice a certain number of forces to accomplish this objective or deny it to a friendly force. Understanding these constraints will improve the chances of achieving friendly air campaign goals and objectives. This understanding of how an enemy operates can help a commander predict or estimate how he might react to selected actions. These projections might allow a commander to anticipate countermoves and challenge the enemy in a more informed manner. These projections might also open up some vulnerability to attack. Additionally, if one allows the enemy to take the initiative and go on the offensive, one loses the ability to control events. Staying on the offensive might be easier if one can anticipate and counter the adversary's moves.

These considerations provide some of the information necessary to put together an air campaign plan. Situations will differ over time and may force an aerospace commander to review and modify his or her plan between campaigns or day-to-day actions. Concentration on one area during a successful air campaign might not work with other campaigns. The campaign in Desert Storm might not have worked in Vietnam. However, some common areas provide a framework for organizing activities to conduct an air campaign. These events provide a way to think about and debate the merits of alternatives for committing forces and fighting the enemy.

A Framework for Air Campaign Planning

The information necessary to conduct air campaign planning is extensive and varies with time. Organizing the information into a coherent plan requires a logical method to ensure consistent, thorough consideration. One may use a five-step approach towards planning: researching the combat environment, determining the air and space objectives, analyzing COGs, determining the air and space strategy, and putting the campaign together.[1] These steps provide a way to think about an air campaign. This process also gives the planner a road map to gather information about the campaign.

This five-step method directly links the objectives and effects desired by an aerospace commander. The process allows the planner to build a campaign from a theater commander's general directions to specific guidance on targets. Normally, the five-step method is not sequential. Some planning steps continue throughout the process and are revised with time. Gathering information about the enemy's military capabilities should happen continuously to give planners and aircrews up-to-date information about such activities as the opposition's fighter capabilities or ground movements, which can affect the timing of missions or specific targets. The process involves specialists from many different areas of expertise. For example, intelligence officers can provide valuable information and insights into the enemy's capabilities. Additionally, they can give advice about specific targets in the COGs. Other individuals with expertise in logistics, munitions, weather, space, aircraft operations, and information systems come together to create the plan. This process then serves as a communications device to ensure that relevant units required to conduct the air campaign are aware of the plan's details and can provide maximum support for operations. The five-step method allows aerospace teams to best satisfy a commander's objectives and goals for a theater campaign.

Researching the Combat Environment

This stage involves "doing your homework." Before planning an air campaign, the planner needs to understand the environment in which forces will be engaged. Such information includes political, military, economic, leadership, geographic, and other significant data. This stage involves not only enemy capabilities, but also friendly forces and the physical environment. Planners need to understand the strengths and weaknesses of the enemy. This knowledge may provide insights for designing a plan to exploit a defect in an adversary's suit of armor. Such information can significantly change the alternative courses of action presented to a commander. Additionally, an enemy force's dispositions, capabilities, and locations can influence the types of friendly forces needed, target identification, and deployment locations for friendly forces. Information about an enemy's political, social, and economic structure might give planners insight into the foe's motivations, objectives, and strategies.

Air campaign planners should also evaluate friendly forces' capabilities. Information might include available forces, treaties, rules of engagement, command relationships, and other relevant considerations. This evaluation not only includes forces under the direct control of a national air force commander, but also any alliance or coalition member's forces as well. Do forces have the proper munitions, training, and personnel to conduct proposed operations? Planners may need to request additional reinforcements or release forces to other theaters with this information. Suppose the planners are given the task of evaluating how to attack an enemy based on an island. Friendly forces in the theater may include several fighter and bomber squadrons. Perhaps the planners might need more aerial-refueling aircraft and transports to ensure that adequate support is present to conduct strike operations. Planners might also ask for additional aircraft carriers. If the enemy's air strength is modest, then planners might not need as many fighters. These forces might be released to fight in another theater that has a greater need for them. Current forces may also dictate alternatives and options available to planners to present as courses of action to a commander. Possession of only a few forces might indicate a defensive strategy until more forces are available to attack an enemy. This situation would resemble the one in the early days of World War II in the Pacific theater. Forces were first sent to Europe to defeat

Germany. After sufficient forces were assigned to the European theater, American commanders in the Pacific started to receive more and better equipment and manpower. Before receiving Pacific-bound reinforcements, American forces were on the defensive and had to react to Japanese advances throughout the area in the early years of World War II.

Finally, researching the combat environment also includes evaluating its physical condition. The area's geography may dictate certain requirements and considerations for friendly forces. Operations Desert Shield and Desert Storm forced planners to maximize the use of global transportation to ship everything from personnel to heavy vehicles. This large-scale movement of manpower and materiel required a combined aerial-, maritime-, and surface-transportation effort. The shipment of large items, such as armored fighting vehicles, forced coalition air planners to consider actions that relied on jet transports to move other cargo. Additionally, these requirements also forced other planners to use slower maritime resources. Logistics is one of the most critical support issues affecting present and future military capabilities. Current supply stocks, host-nation support agreements, airfield capabilities, and existing and future supply infrastructure all require immediate attention. These factors significantly controlled the timing of operations in Desert Storm. The desert environment also influenced planning. Great distances between airfields and targets made aerial-refueling capabilities critical to conducting an air attack. Often, planners for friendly forces tend to cast the enemy in their own image. They tend to believe the enemy would fight in the same way and have the same objectives as friendly forces. This is usually not the case. Planners need to put themselves in the enemy's shoes to understand what his motivations are and how he might fight.

Determining Air and Space Objectives

This step is the most important aspect of air campaign planning—defining what air forces are to achieve in a campaign. Objectives help focus thoughts and actions. They should be developed from higher-level national objectives and the theater commander's objectives. Without direction, air and space forces might aimlessly conduct disorganized and contradictory actions, some of which might prove harmful to friendly forces. Well-defined objectives should help planners avoid these problems and better coordinate proposed actions. A force can "demonstrate resolve" to show that a nation is ready to act, but it must have a clear objective. For example, a nation might protest another country's action and show resolve by deploying forces near the offending country. However, unless the nation clearly illustrates its purpose, it could be a meaningless gesture. If the nation provides a condition, such as threatening air strikes unless forces are withdrawn from a disputed territory within 24 hours, this sends a clear picture to the offending country.

Objectives should have four characteristics: clarity, conciseness, attainability, and support for higher-level objectives.[2] A planner might not provide the most effective or efficient plan to higher-echelon commands without these characteristics. Either the planners can ask for more guidance from higher commands, or they can continue planning, assuming a commander's intent. Air campaign planners might need to estimate what a commander intends to accomplish.

Objectives must be clear. They should provide distinct guidance for all parties involved in the planning process. Objectives must convey a common understanding of what is to be accomplished in the plan. This condition should greatly improve the planners' ability to translate the national and theater commander's objectives into detailed airpower and spacepower objectives. For example, a theater commander's objectives might include destruction of all weapons of mass destruction held by the enemy. An air campaign plan may focus on an objective to destroy nuclear-material processing plants. Planners might assign strategic bombers to attack these targets. However, before they can successfully meet this objective, friendly forces might first need to achieve air superiority as a theater air objective. These air and space objectives must support higher-level command objectives, or else one needs to question the relevance and wisdom of those airpower and space-power theater objectives.

These objectives should not be designed as "open ended." Commanders and planners require some measure to help determine when they have accomplished the objectives. This process may include defined factors about which intelligence specialists might gather information to ensure the objectives are met. This quantitative measure may help in many respects. If one of the theater air objectives was to achieve air superiority, then one way to measure attainment of the objective might be the destruction of 90 percent of the enemy's fighter forces. Intelligence sources might have an accurate estimate of the number of enemy fighters before the start of the conflict. Assuming that friendly forces have a reliable method of determining enemy air losses, this measure of effectiveness might work. Conversely, an "end state" that requires a break in the will or morale of the civilian populace is more difficult to measure. Intelligence officers might see mass civilian migrations from enemy cities to rural relocation centers. This might be indicative of the civilian populace's fear of attack. However, in the Battle of Britain in 1940, many civilian families left cities bombed by the Luftwaffe, but British morale never broke during the war.

Objectives must also be tempered by political, legal, moral, and social constraints. Bombing cities, even with PGMs, might involve civilian deaths due to human error. The taking of innocent lives is unacceptable to most nations. Restrictions involving attacks near shrines, religious structures, borders, embassies, hospitals, and other targets might limit the ability of planners to consider several objectives. Perhaps an objective is to disable a nation's industrial capacity to support its war-making capability. The industry might be located near the heart of the nation's medical and cultural centers. Although the air force has the ability to bomb targets with great accuracy, mistakes do happen. The accidental bombing of a children's hospital would have major international and domestic political ramifications that could alter the course of the war. This is especially true with worldwide television and media coverage that can heighten awareness of a single bombing mistake. International and domestic political opposition to the conflict could sprout and end further aerial bombardment.

These constraints might limit the courses of action available to the commander.

Determining Centers of Gravity

Once air objectives are agreed upon, planners need to determine the critical characteristics, capabilities, and strengths that allow the nation to survive and conduct military operations. The planners need to look at COGs that affect how the enemy functions. Additionally, planners also may want to evaluate the friendly forces' COGs. This analysis will provide information that may help friendly forces take steps to prevent destruction by enemy forces. Once these COGs are identified, planners should determine the strategic effect of their destruction or disruption on an enemy's capabilities.

The evaluation of COGs is affected not only by the air objectives, but also by the capabilities and doctrines of the attacking air forces. An air force with only a few fighters would have a difficult time conducting a heavy-bombardment campaign against a widespread industrial complex. Additionally, an air force with a doctrine that focuses on high-altitude, precision daylight bombing—like the AAF in World War II—might concentrate on an enemy's COGs supporting the industrial-web theory—factories, for example. Again, one is cautioned about casting an adversary in one's own image. The industrial-web theory may work for highly centralized industrial nations that do not import military equipment. Small, agrarian nations or guerilla movements might not have the same COGs. Similarly, John Warden's five-ring model took a different spin regarding an enemy's COGs, the most important of which was leadership. Ideas from Warden and other theorists can alter planners' ways of determining these important COGs.

There is no magic formula or set method for determining COGs. After identifying the "true" COGs, planners may even determine that their air force cannot significantly destroy, disable, or disrupt the enemy's operations within a particular COG. This realization may force planners to consider concentrating on other COGs or asking for reinforcements to disable a particular target. These COGs will later become the basis for developing a set of targets for air forces to attack. Planners must also assign priorities to the COGs, which can help them determine when to attack them and the number of sorties necessary to ensure they are destroyed or disabled. If the planners can calculate the number of forces for each COG, the aerospace commander can build a force sufficient to support and conduct the campaign.

COGs may also change during the campaign. Political forces within the enemy nation could alter leadership. Destruction of the enemy's natural resources might force him to shift from a resource-based economy to an industrial one, assuming he has the capacity and time to do so. Purely conventional military forces could switch to a guerilla or terrorist orientation. Planners and analysts will need to determine how these COGs change as time and actions alter the enemy's behavior and interests.

An analysis of friendly COGs is also important. If a foe counterattacks or conducts a surprise attack, friendly forces could be dealt a devastating blow. One cannot assume that the enemy will remain on the defensive. He might launch an offensive against weaknesses in the friendly forces. This analysis helps planners calculate the necessary defensive effort to assure that offensive operations can run smoothly throughout the campaign.

Determining Air and Space Strategy

Strategy is the art of defining how to meet an objective. Once air objectives are determined, an aerospace commander must develop a strategy to meet his or her theater air objectives. Strategy is a balancing act that pits forces, the risk of failure or success, and a commander's imagination to meet an objective. The commander needs to weigh courses of actions to best satisfy his or her specific requirements to accomplish a mission. This stage should clearly define how an aerospace leader would use all airpower and space-power forces to accomplish theater-level objectives and all air and space objectives.

Planners must consider many aspects of creating an overall air campaign plan. Air and space strategy should also fit into other campaign strategies that involve land or maritime forces and their joint usage. Conversely, the air and space strategy for a particular campaign may be just a small part of a series of air and space actions that support a major conflict. In the air and space strategy, planners might discuss the use of parallel or serial attacks. They should also consider the phasing of operations. Air and space forces could first achieve air and space superiority and then conduct different types of attack. Likewise, these forces could attempt to gain control of the air and at the same time begin all manner of military operations, including strategic attack, interdiction, reconnaissance, mobility, and CAS. The phasing of operations is normally identified by a major event or attainment of a specific objective. The plan might also devise a strategy that centers on independent action, such as a strategic bombardment campaign designed to halt the enemy. Conversely, the air and space campaign plan may focus on supporting land or maritime campaign plans only.

A strategist might not have the luxury of maintaining a static strategy. As events occur in the campaign, the enemy's and friendly force's objectives and situations could change, dictating the use of different strategies. If the purpose of strategy is to describe how to achieve an objective, then changing a friendly or an enemy objective can force planners to modify strategies. This means that planners must continually monitor current situations and adjust their plans accordingly throughout the air campaign.

Unfortunately, air and space resources are limited. National leaders need to prioritize their resource allocations for defense expenditures or force-structure decisions. If we had unlimited resources, air forces might have equal capabilities for air superiority, strategic attack, and other actions. Depending on the air force's situation, leaders could develop force structure to emphasize certain abilities to satisfy particular requirements. The proposed strategy should concentrate on using the strengths of friendly forces against the weaknesses of the enemy. This focus on an asymmetric approach to warfare allows the commander to pit his or her best force capabilities against the least-capable forces of the enemy. Indeed, if one conducts this type of strategy, he or she must be wary of a foe who conducts a similar strategy. Understanding a friendly force's weaknesses and COGs will help alleviate some of these limitations by planning for their adequate defense.

Putting the Campaign Together

The first four stages of air campaign planning help the aerospace commander and planners gather information and concepts and then coordinate actions. The next step is to put the information together into a coherent, clear plan of action so that air and space forces located throughout the theater can conduct operations. The commander must consider all alternatives and courses of action to select the best possible plan to achieve the theater commander's objectives. The plan must strike a balance between being too optimistic and overly pessimistic. Some planners could assume that a smaller enemy military capability poses little danger to friendly forces and that these forces will soundly defeat the enemy. Although a foe might have a smaller air force, he could attack a much larger military force, much like the Israelis did against Egypt and Syria in the Six-Day War. The plan should also avoid overly pessimistic options. Defending against every possible enemy attack against a friendly COG is futile and wasteful. Air campaign plans should have a reserve capability to handle unexpected situations, but the reserve amount must be tempered by resource availability and the amount of risk a commander is willing to assume.

The air campaign plan must provide information about objectives, specific targets, timing, force assignments, level of damage desired, and roles and responsibilities among forces. The specific form of the air campaign plan may change over time, but the basic ideas and concepts concerning planning for combat are not likely to change soon. Identifying enemy and friendly capabilities, forming objectives, noting key aspects of different sides, developing strategy, and organizing a plan are concepts that should endure into the future.

Air Campaign Planning Concerns

Developing an air campaign plan involves several people and organizations. The process allows many different organizations with divergent ideas to work together to develop a coordinated plan. Each air campaign plan may vary, depending upon the air and space objective, threat, and available forces. These dynamic concerns may affect the proposed organizations, schedules, information, decision points, and dissemination of the air campaign plan. Such concerns motivate planners to add more effort and coordination as the challenges of creating an air campaign plan increase with the complexity of the circumstances.

The overall theater campaign plan can help determine the organizational level and objectives in the air campaign planning phase. If the theater campaign plan specifies that only a particular type of operation is desired, then a limited number of organizations may be involved with the planning effort. A limited campaign will obviously reduce the number and scope of organizations for the operation. A campaign involving only airpower and space power—such as Allied Force, the 1999 air campaign in Kosovo—may not require a large organization, like the one that supported Desert Storm, which coordinated air, ground, and maritime operations. Conversely, a true coalition air campaign plan that includes land and maritime forces can involve several organizations and foreign nations. Desert Storm's air campaign planning effort involved many nations, services, and national organizations (e.g., intelligence agencies), which forced planners to consider complex issues and increase the time required to coordinate actions and conduct operations.

Air campaign planning may not always be completed in one location. Small, forward-based planning organizations might deploy to a location near the battlefield. If this forward echelon can create sufficient planning activities to support the war, then it could use resources available through support services back home or away from the immediate front. Modern technology allows for instantaneous global communications that may enable this option. Home-based intelligence, weather forecasting, and other support might not have to deploy to the field. Required information could be transmitted to the forward echelon for inclusion in the air campaign plan. The availability of timely and accurate information reduces the planning cell's requirements to support a large staff and diminishes its vulnerability to attack. Conversely, the lack of support personnel may increase the coordination time or requirement definition because their absence might create a misunderstanding or lack of perspective necessary for a true aerospace operation (as would be the case in the absence of space-operations personnel). If all planning is conducted away from the battlefield, planners might not understand the concerns, interests, and requirements of the air campaign in the same way a set of deployed, dedicated planners would.

Due to the nature of modern warfare and aerial combat, the coordination among air, space, land, and maritime forces is key for mission success. Liaison efforts among ground forces for CAS, air defense efforts, special forces, land forces for mobility, and naval fleet activities can affect operations. For example, even though the air forces might want to conduct a series of strategic attacks on the enemy's homeland, they should coordinate with land-component commanders and forces. Soldiers might be deployed in the area or ready to attack the same target. Additionally, if the air campaign planners need to use transport aircraft, the land-component commander should be told that tactical airlift for resupply, transport, or parachute deployments might be curtailed.

After an air campaign plan is completed, units do not use the plan as the sole basis for initiating aircraft sorties; they will receive more detailed plans for executing operations. Conducting air and space operations requires much preparation. Targets need to be identified, munitions prepared, aircraft repaired, pilots briefed on the operation, and other operational considerations satisfied. The timing of operations can also change hourly. Although operational units should have a basic concept of the campaign, they might need only a few days of detailed plans because of the focus and potential for change. The air campaign plan might represent the overall campaign, with general guidance for aerospace leaders. Operational units require more directed plans to prepare missions within the next few days and then conduct an attack.

In Desert Storm, commanders received a master attack plan (MAP) that provided more detail than did the air campaign plan (e.g., times on target for missions, target names, aircraft types, and number of aircraft to conduct the operation for the next 72 hours).[3] This information provided a more comprehensive view of air and space operations in-theater, thus preparing operational units for combat. Although the MAP did not specify individual aircraft, it gave affected units an overview of operations. Current information and intelligence data help develop the MAP. If an attack does not produce the desired outcome, the commander might want the target struck again. Additionally, the MAP identified the availability of munitions and aircraft so that operational units could prepare for their missions. The plan also listed a prioritized set of targets.[4] Planners and operational units would use the MAP to make decisions about specific targets. The plan also helped planners identify specific weapons to be used against targets.

Although the MAP identified targets and weapons, more detailed information was required to conduct operations. Planners issued units an air tasking order (ATO) that provided a detailed operational plan for the next 24 hours. ATOs were normally in production up to 48 hours before they were implemented. This forced air campaign planners to work on one ATO 24 hours in advance of the operation, while operational units were executing the missions. Often, ATOs were delayed, and changes were frequent. The ATO provided detailed information about communications, radio call signs, airspace control, aerial refueling, munitions loads, aircraft performance data, and specific unit actions that affected theater operations (e.g., AWACS aircraft, reconnaissance systems, etc.). If this information is not available, then aircraft from different units might try to attack the same target at the same time.

During Desert Storm, 116,818 sorties covered by ATOs were planned in 43 days.[5] Published the day before their execution, ATOs were immediately flown to the operational units to ensure they had sufficient time to prepare for operations. Changes were common—about 500 a day for a total of 22,942. Operational units needed to monitor and adjust to changes to ensure that they hit the right target, at the correct time, with the proper weapons. Aerial-refueling locations and timing were

Command and control—key to success. This AWACS aircraft can direct airpower in combat.

other key aspects of the ATOs. If units attempted to refuel at the wrong times, they would have to wait because other units were scheduled ahead of them or because refueling support was insufficient.

Critics of the ATO process complained about the unresponsiveness and slow processing time for the plans. Although it took 48 hours to prepare the ATO, air units had to satisfy immediate requirements to follow it. This pushed operational units to create a surge of action in a short period of time and repeat the process the next day, placing a great deal of strain on aircrews and support personnel. Producing the ATO faster would allow operational units to better prepare for operations. Additionally, operational units wanted fewer changes. Unfortunately, campaign planners had no control over dynamic situations, aircrews being ordered to reattack targets, and bad weather. Operational units also wanted to do away with the process and "do their own coordination,"[6] which likely would have led to much confusion and disorganization among military forces.

This series of plans provides different levels of information for specific purposes. An overall air campaign plan gives general guidance to meet theater campaign objectives. This infor-

After an air interdiction mission, vehicles are unable to transport troops or supplies.

mation identifies air and space objectives that support an overall theater campaign. The MAP provides further delineation of specific targeting and detailed information for planning sorties. Finally, the ATO assigns individual pilots and aircraft to attack or conduct other operations. These planning documents allow a commander to coordinate actions and assure that sufficient resources are assigned to the appropriate target.

Air Campaign Planning: National Implications

Air campaign planning is not limited to theater considerations—it also has national implications. Today, a single aerial attack can alter the shape of an entire war. Planning for warfighting contingencies provides security options for the national leadership. Conducting general air campaign planning for different scenarios gives political and military leadership a basis for conducting more detailed efforts. Air campaign planning also allows military commanders to acquire, prepare, and test plans before they are executed in combat. If targets are not carefully identified or if heavy collateral damage is inflicted on civilians, national policy or objectives might change. The quintessential set of national security and military plans involves nuclear operations, since approval of the release of nuclear weapons would affect the country's survival.

Planning for an air campaign takes much concentrated effort. ATO development depends upon very specific situational planning. Although one might not be able to conduct detailed preconflict planning, aerospace leaders could prepare regional or likely conflict scenarios for planning contingencies. Before Desert Storm, several possible air campaign plans were modified for particular conditions in-theater. Such preconflict planning efforts create opportunities to evaluate potential requirements, approaches, targets, and training exercises that later become the basis for detailed, specific campaign plans. Questions about the free world's access to Persian Gulf oil forced military planners to consider many scenarios involving different countries, all designed to thwart an invasion by an adversary. These contingency plans are the basis for further planning, including one for an air campaign. The latter should not begin with the outbreak of hostilities. An understanding of potential conflicts and ways to use air and space resources can help define the forces required to fight a future conflict. The AAF used a request from President Franklin Roosevelt to develop aircraft requirements before America entered World War II as a blueprint for an air campaign plan against Germany. The Allied effort to conduct strategic air operations against Germany would have been considerably slowed without the early planning and mobilization to build an aircraft force structure. Such contingency plans might also become the foundation for planning exercise deployments to allow operational forces to train in the same way they will fight.

Air campaign planning also provides tangible evidence that the nation is committed to defend or support allies in a conflict. If the nation provides adequate forces and trains them appropriately to execute the plan, then this effort might have value as both a show of strength to allies and a deterrent to potential enemies. Preparing for future conflict by using potential air campaign plans also allows planners to determine whether the proposed concepts are feasible. Testing a concept or an idea for the first time in combat is probably not the best way to evaluate the capabilities of an aerospace power force. The only exception might occur as the result of a new discovery or the desire of military leaders to achieve strategic surprise by introducing a new method of conflict. Air campaign plans, if not immediately implemented, might be modified via a war game that is used as an exercise or a test of combat capability.

The specific conditions and objectives found in the air campaign plans for Desert Storm and subsequent deployments such as Deliberate Force (Bosnia) and Allied Force (Kosovo) reflected national and international political objectives. The linkage between national political objectives and ATOs is important. Theater campaign plans need to reflect national political objectives. Additionally, air campaign plans must support the theater campaign plans. ATOs, at the lowest level of air campaign planning, represent a detailed, one-day view of operations in the air campaign plan and must support the efforts of the national leadership. This is especially true today because of the lethality, precision, and global reach of air and space forces. A single aircraft can certainly affect the outcome of a war. Conventional cruise missiles, laser-guided weapons, weapons using satellite navigation, and other munitions can accidentally inflict massive casualties upon military forces or civilians, which may affect operations in the conflict. For example, on 13 February 1991, USAF aircraft bombed the Ameriyya air-raid shelter in Baghdad, thought to be a command post, resulting in several hundred civilian deaths. The attack raised international protests and forced a review of individual target lists on the daily ATO by the US secretary of defense and Joint Chiefs of Staff.[7] Similarly, during Allied Force, a B-2 bomber accidentally destroyed part of the Chinese Embassy in Belgrade, Yugoslavia. This unfortunate accident forced changes in strategic bombing by reducing the number of eligible targets in subsequent attacks on Belgrade. In both cases, instant media attention highlighted the damage and increased the pressure on national leaders to alter actions that might affect political objectives.

The clearest connection between national political objectives and air campaign planning is the possible employment of nuclear weapons. Stringent control by national leadership is para-

Aerial refueling allowed B-2s based in the United States to strike targets in Kosovo.

mount. In the United States, the Single Integrated Operation Plan (SIOP) outlines attack options involving the aerial delivery of nuclear weapons. Depending on dynamic conditions, the conflict, forces, timing, targets, and desired effects will change daily. The president of the United States can select the options and, effectively, the ATO to accomplish the operation. Nuclear forces in the Cold War were on instant alert with aircraft ready to take off and conduct nuclear operations. ICBM launch crews were ready to send missiles to their targets within minutes. The SIOP was continually tested, evaluated, reviewed, and exercised as a deterrent and visible sign of America's aerospace power. The US Navy also had a significant role in the SIOP with its submarine-launched ballistic missile forces. The control of nuclear weapons is vested in national leadership, and that leadership has significantly tied aerospace power planning to the country's survival.

The flexibility, global ranges, lethality, and rapid speed of aerospace weapons significantly affect air campaign planning efforts for air forces. These characteristics can also have a say in the outcome of a conflict in terms of developing a force, training for contingencies, or influencing national policies. Air campaign planning is not static. An aerospace leader faces continual, dynamic changes in threats, capabilities of friendly forces, objectives, and availability of resources. Proper preparation for contingencies and actual conditions can help that leader win a battle and, eventually, a major conflict. Air campaign planning is a first step towards applying the aerospace functions of air and space superiority, strategic attack, interdiction, CAS, mobility, and space and information operations in a larger role involving other nations and services.

Notes

1. Lt Col Maris McCrabb, "Air Campaign Planning," *Airpower Journal* 8, no. 2 (Summer 1993): 11.

2. *Air Campaign Planning Handbook* (Maxwell AFB, Ala.: Joint Doctrine Air Campaign Course, College of Aerospace Doctrine, Research and Education, 1998), 14.

3. Thomas A. Keaney and Eliot A. Cohen, *Revolution in Warfare? Air Power in the Persian Gulf* (Annapolis: Naval Institute Press, 1995), 128.

4. Daniel R. Gonzales, *Evolution of the Air Campaign and the Contingency Theater Automated Planning System (CTAPS)*, MR-618-AF (Santa Monica, Calif.: RAND, 1996), 12.

5. Ibid., 21, table 3.1.

6. Ibid., 25.

7. Jeffrey Record, *Hollow Victory: A Contrary View of the Gulf War* (McLean, Va.: Brassey's, 1993), 124.

Chapter 8

Taking Off into the Wild Blue Yonder

Air and space forces are relative newcomers to warfare. The desire to fight an enemy by taking the high ground has been an objective of surface commanders. The first military application of aerial devices involved balloons, used in 1794 during the French Revolution. Other inventors and military thinkers sought different devices for flying through the air. One of the earliest inventors was Leonardo da Vinci, who proposed the use of gliders, helicopters, and other fantastic flying machines in the fifteenth century. Inventors and visionaries created new weapons and concepts for commanders to gain the high ground through the use of the air. Rockets, used by the Chinese, were introduced to European armies. The first flying machine other than a lighter-than-air balloon—the Wright Flyer—graced the skies in 1903. By 1907 the US Army was using this aircraft as a reconnaissance vehicle. Italy started to use the airplane as a weapon as early as 1911, and other nations incorporated it into their war plans in World War I. After World War II, space systems added another step to conquering the high ground. The first man-made object orbited Earth in 1957. Since that time, man has set foot on the Moon, and space vehicles have explored the solar system and beyond. Military space systems have developed along with these civilian efforts and have significantly increased the global reach of aerospace power.

Aerospace power depends, in large part, on technology and the ability of a trained labor force to sustain and supply it. The use of airplanes was made possible only by technology and innovation. The development of machines capable of escaping gravity has enabled nations to use the air and space environments to conduct many existing and new military missions. These capabilities have opened a number of new options for a nation to exploit the aerospace realm by increasing the reach, lethality, and speed of air and space vehicles. However, proposed alternatives to fighting created by aerospace vehicles through existing conventions have raised many issues. Some of these concern new technologies and their effects on warfare, while others are "classical" debates within the military services.

Although aerospace forces face numerous current issues, some debates will affect aerospace power into the twenty-first century and beyond. Air forces will continue to debate whether their primary focus should concern the conduct of strategic operations, ground support, or a combination of both. The advancement of microelectronics, computer systems, and miniaturization has allowed scientists and engineers to develop unmanned aerial vehicles (UAV), which may eliminate the need for manned aircraft in some areas. The advancement of space systems has increased the potential for hypersonic travel, which may allow true aerospace vehicles to deliver munitions or supplies worldwide very quickly. This capability may lead to questions about the integration of these innovations into current force structures. Political, military, social, and economic changes in the world have altered the threats and conflicts involving many nations. With the end of the Cold War, several nations have reduced their military forces, yet diverse and deadly threats still confront the world. Air and space forces may need greater mobility and the capability of fighting a number of different conflicts while committing fewer forces. Information warfare will also become an issue for future conflicts, possibly expanding the scope of conflict and operations that affect aerospace forces. The advancement of technology and innovation has also challenged national, military, and aerospace leaders. How aerospace commanders handle these new capabilities will be a contentious issue in the future. National leadership is increasingly called upon to use military forces in many unique situations. Peacekeeping and humanitarian missions are becoming the norm—more so than in the past. Military leaders have focused on incorporating many different types of forces into a joint capability to support these missions. Doctrine, organizations, training, strategy, and operations have been significantly affected by this new emphasis. These challenges can affect the employment of forces and alter the face of war.

These are only a few of the concerns that present and future aerospace leaders will face in a turbulent world. However, aerospace power challenges today will certainly change and influence events with which tomorrow's leaders must contend.

Thinking about and solving future problems will require keen decision making and planning. Understanding such broad issues will help individuals evaluate solutions to many future problems.

Strategic or Ground-Operations Support?

Some advocates of an independent air force argued that the primary mission of the service was to conduct independent, strategic bombardment. Veterans from the Combined Bomber Offensive, former ACTS faculty and students, and believers in strategic bombardment were in AAF leadership positions after World War II. The invention and use of the atomic bomb also provided a glimpse into the future face of war worldwide. Hopes that the terror of nuclear weapons would deter an opponent were tantalizing for many AAF officers. Nuclear weapons could stop aggressive moves around the globe. Additionally, reliance on these devices and the need for fewer bomber aircraft would allow a nation to reduce the size and importance of other services. As an independent service, the Air Force could win a war or at least severely damage an enemy so that the other services would have a better chance of prevailing on the battlefield. This issue created a national debate concerning the use of airpower.

Critics both inside and outside the Air Force questioned many aspects of this view. If nuclear weapons were used, could war be waged in such an environment?[1] Nuclear deterrence might work against other nuclear powers, but would the United States use these weapons against a nonnuclear power? If not, what value would nuclear-capable bombers have against a guerilla movement or small-scale conventional conflict? To get resources, the Air Force might have to reduce its conventional forces. The sacrifice of fighters, tactical fighter-bombers, and other aerial weapons designed to provide CAS and interdiction would reduce war-fighting capability against conventional forces. Unfortunately, this concern became a deadly problem for Air Force units flying many World War II–era aircraft in the Korean War.

Concepts involving strategic air attack changed dramatically after the end of the Cold War. The Air Force started to emphasize conventional PGMs instead of nuclear weapons. The service had conducted strategic attacks using conventional weapons earlier, but new threats, weapons, and national objectives forced a modification of ideas about strategic air warfare. The Air Force also used aerial platforms that differed greatly from nuclear-armed bombers. During the Vietnam War, the Air Force and Navy used fighter and attack aircraft to bomb key targets throughout North Vietnam. In 1986 those two services combined forces to jointly attack Libya with "tactical" aircraft—not the traditional large, multiengined bombers. The goal was to create a strategic effect by striking particular targets. By the early 1990s, national and military leaders had de-emphasized nuclear weapons. Conventional weapons, because of lethality and precision guidance, could hit an adversary more potently than could older, nonnuclear weapons. Technology gave aerospace leaders alternatives to nuclear weapons for conducting strategic attacks.

The idea of emphasizing independent strategic warfare versus a ground-support strategy is still an open issue. During Operation Desert Shield, a plan to use airpower alone to force the Iraqi government to withdraw its forces from Kuwait was proposed for adoption. This plan, known as Instant Thunder, was designed by Col John Warden as "a focused, intense air campaign designed to incapacitate Iraqi leadership and destroy key Iraqi military capability in a short period of time."[2] The Instant Thunder campaign sought to isolate Saddam Hussein from control of the nation, destroy Iraqi offensive and defensive capability, disable national leadership, eliminate Iraq as a threat to other foreign nations, and minimize infrastructure damage so as to reduce reconstruction efforts at the conclusion of the war. Air forces would concentrate on COGs that included leadership, C^2, key production and distribution centers, weapons of mass destruction, and threats from offensive ballistic missiles and aircraft. The air forces conducting this campaign would use PGMs, two squadrons of B-52s, one squadron of F-111s, one squadron of F-15Es, 32 squadrons of fighter/attack aircraft, and one squadron of F-117s. Additionally, the attack would use conventional Tomahawk land-attack missiles from naval forces.

Warden believed that his plan would cripple the enemy within six days if attacks were conducted around-the-clock. On the first day, the USAF and other forces would conduct 1,200 sorties against a strategic target list that included telecommunications, electricity, oil, nuclear weapons, and other targets. Up to 900 sorties per day by coalition aircraft would follow to reattack strategic targets; they would then turn their attention to the Iraqi chemical and military-support infrastructure. Warden's goal was to destroy the national leadership's ability to command and control activities; eliminate Iraq's ability to conduct strategic offensive and defensive operations; disrupt the economy; reduce oil exports; and prepare the battlefield for combat operations. Warden's emphasis on a strategic air campaign was absolute. He dismissed any suggestions by Gen Colin Powell, chairman of the Joint Chiefs of Staff, regarding the diversion of air resources to support ground operations until Instant Thunder had attained its objectives.[3]

Others within the USAF disagreed. Ground-support operations in the form of CAS seemed more of a priority to ground commanders. The potential threat of Iraqi ground forces invading Saudi Arabian territory seemed a more imminent and diverse threat. If the strategic air campaign did not stop the Iraqi military capability, what would air forces do to halt a possible invasion? There were many questions about the target selection and short time frame, as well as concerns about the complexity of the plan and a focus on tactical versus strategic effects. The presence of Iraqi armored forces only a few hundred miles away from Riyadh also caused concern.[4] The closest American armored units were in Germany. At the time, airpower was the only tool that could halt these forces.

The question of employing strategic versus ground-support operations should not be considered an "either or" proposition. Numerous factors can affect the decision to emphasize either strategic or tactical warfare. If a country does not have many strategic targets that can affect the conduct of a war, emphasizing an extensive strategic air campaign might be inappropriate. For example, if the purpose of the strategic air campaign was to defeat the means of military production, then a country that imports military equipment may not offer sufficient targets for such a campaign. Instead, an interdiction program might be more appropriate. In the Korean War, in which the People's Republic of China and the Soviet Union supplied the North Korean military forces, the allied strategic air campaign was limited due to the paucity of North Korean factories or oil refineries.[5]

Ground forces also require air support. However, on-call CAS could leave aerial assets idle; they might also be used against less important targets than strategic ones if control is left to ground commanders. Using air resources for ground support is a contentious issue among aerospace and ground commanders. Strategic attack affects the adversary's entire war effort, but the CAS campaign takes time for successful implementation. Conversely, ground commanders could require immediate CAS to ensure they are not encircled and defeated by a superior enemy ground force. However, assigning all aerial forces to conduct CAS operations might bleed away forces that could affect the naval, air, and ground war by attacking targets that would eventually halt enemy actions at either the theater or national level.

During Operation Desert Storm, coalition air forces conducted a strategic air campaign and then implemented a ground campaign. After commanders were satisfied that the Iraqi military was sufficiently battered, they launched a combined air and ground campaign. However, this classic campaign was conducted against a conventional army. What would happen if the coalition fought a guerilla force in the jungle, on mountains, or in a heavily urban area with many civilians? Conditions can dictate that airpower and space power might not be able to use strategic or CAS missions as they were conducted against Iraq. Future aerospace commanders must consider a number of factors to advise, consult, coordinate, and decide on the appropriate application of aerospace power in various scenarios. Mixing a strategic air campaign with ground operations will continue to be a highly debated issue. The value of aerospace power is its flexibility to conduct a variety of operations. Aerospace leaders will need to organize and apply these flexible forces to satisfy many commanders' needs and requirements, especially as the United States faces many unknown threats in widely divergent environments.

Unmanned Aerial Vehicles and the Future of Aerial Warfare

Future aerial vehicles will face a number of advancements in air defenses that can limit their capabilities. SAMs and AAA could be supplemented by directed-energy weapons and a number of other systems. Aircrews facing these dangers may encounter a deadly reception that could result in high casualties. Avoidance of aircrew casualties or capture is an important factor in planning air attacks. Some methods for avoiding such situations include using longer-range, precision offensive weapons and increasing aircraft survivability by improving avionics or other defensive countermeasures. Another method involves using pilotless aircraft.

UAVs will not replace piloted aircraft entirely. However, the use of these types of vehicles may alter the structure and application of aerospace forces in the future. UAVs can be used for reconnaissance, SEAD, and bombing missions. Advancements in electronics, information networks, sensors, processors, and miniaturization of aircraft components increase the effectiveness and efficiency of aerial operations. Transferring information at high speed through satellite connections and processing through advanced computer systems might allow a "pilot" to operate the vehicle safely from locations thousands of miles away. This reduces the potential for casualties, reduces the cost of the vehicle (no life-support systems for aircrews), increases options for a commander to attack heavily defended targets with a centralized command center, and increases the number of vehicles available for a commander because of their smaller size, mobility requirements, and support needs. Crews, maintenance personnel, and other equipment may not need to deploy to a theater, freeing mobility assets to send other critical materiel or personnel to fight a conflict. Commanders might be willing to "sacrifice" these vehicles to attack targets in exchange for a certain result. A pilotless aerial vehicle also might perform better since accel-

The shape of future airpower? A Predator UAV on a reconnaissance mission

eration and G-force limits are extended without a pilot, thus increasing the UAV's ability to avoid missiles and other defenses.[6] Aircraft designers might have more options for building a low-observable version of the UAV if it is smaller than a typical piloted aircraft.

UAVs have certain limitations. They depend heavily on sensors and data links to operate. If those devices are disabled or destroyed, the UAV either will not operate or will operate with limited capabilities. Heavily jammed areas could significantly affect UAV operations. Human pilots can generally operate the aircraft without these types of sensors and data links. UAVs that do not rely on periodic updates but use preprogrammed instructions are feasible. However, a preprogrammed UAV may lose its ability to react to changing environments and situations. A centralized control center for UAVs may also become a potential target for terrorists or become a vulnerability if a natural disaster or other event affects its operation.

Air forces have used UAVs in the past, mostly for bombing missions that used a preprogrammed, one-way mission profile. Today, the fact that UAVs can take off and land makes them reusable in a variety of missions. Most current-day proposals focus on a man-machine interface that allows a vehicle to maneuver to avoid defenses, attack targets of opportunity, and initiate other actions that require immediate changes to a flight profile. Technology has greatly advanced capabilities, enabling true UAVs to conduct many of the same missions that piloted vehicles can accomplish today.

The US Army and Navy were interested in an unmanned guided flying vehicle as early as 1916.[7] This proposed World War I–era "Bug" was a pilotless aircraft that could carry a payload to attack enemy positions. Actually a flying bomb or torpedo, it performed well in a series of tests. Col Henry "Hap" Arnold (future AAF commander) wanted to order 100 of them for use in proposed tactical missile units on the western front in World War I. Unfortunately, Arnold never received permission to implement his plan. The Germans experimented with the V-1 winged cruise missile, launching over 1,200 of these aerial bombs against London in World War II.[8] The United States and other nations have used cruise missiles for several years now. Similar in principle to the Bug and V-1, these weapons boast improved inertial guidance and performance. During the Vietnam War, the USAF successfully used remotely piloted vehicles for reconnaissance missions.

In the future, aerospace leaders may decide to use a predominant force of UAVs in particular situations or phases of an air campaign. UAVs will alter the face of combat. Perhaps due to the absence of a pilot and any potential casualties to aircrews, national leaders will be more willing to use this form of airpower rather than surface forces. Additionally, the availability of UAVs might prompt more aggressive action rather than diplomacy.

The Advancement of Space Forces: An Independent Force?

In the 1960s, the Air Force attempted to create a true aerospace force. The future of space forces looked bright. Space satellite systems, boosters, and other developments were forecasted for acquisition, development, and use. One program—the Dyna-Soar, a forerunner of the space shuttle—was a proposed manned reconnaissance and bomber vehicle. Unfortunately, the Vietnam War and a national focus on civilian space activities forced a reduction in many of the Air Force's space programs. Satellite reconnaissance, communications, navigation, early warning, weather, and other support programs have illustrated the value and necessity of incorporating space-based capabilities for aerial operations as well as ground and maritime actions.

Technological advances in propulsion, materials, electronics, computers, communications, and other discoveries have helped ignite interest in space systems. Reliance upon the Global Positioning System (GPS) satellite constellation for navigation and weapons delivery by all services has increased the need to continually operate and improve the system. One limitation of space power, however, is the time-sensitive and costly process of sending a space system into orbit. Many of today's satellites are very fragile, slow to build, and expensive. If a problem occurs in the orbiting system, either a ground crew can try to send instructions to the vehicle in an attempt to fix it or use an expensive space shuttle mission to retrieve it. Deploying a satellite into orbit usually requires the use of an expendable rocket or the space shuttle; both options require much effort and many resources. These impediments have curtailed attempts to make space systems more responsive to the requirements of war fighters.

The Air Force and the National Aeronautics and Space Administration are experimenting with a series of hypersonic and transatmospheric vehicles, which promise routine, inexpensive access to space. These vehicles may become the bridge between true aerial vehicles and orbiting space systems. They can lift off from Earth's surface, operate at high altitudes or in space, and then return. Depending on their payload, these vehicles can perform a number of missions that space and aerial platforms can conduct today—and they can fly faster, further, and higher than contemporary vehicles. The USAF and other air forces might face issues related to the integration of these new vehicles in their organizations and ways to operate them in the future.

Some individuals might advocate making space forces independent from the Air Force. Their arguments could highlight differences in the environments in which air and space forces operate. Aerial vehicles rely on lift. Space vehicles, because they operate in a vacuum, rely on thrust. This simple difference illustrates the gulf between the two environments and puts a different focus on their forces. Although they are still Earth-based, like aircraft, space systems are usually unmanned and operate from the farthest reaches of human interaction. Advocates of an independent space force insist that such a force can better serve the nation by concentrating on space issues. Their argument resembles that of the early proponents of an independent air force, who supported the idea of a separate service capable of increasing the capabilities of airpower rather than being shackled by an organization focused on land operations.

Space power is evolving and can provide even greater flexibility and strategic reach than airpower. However, questions still arise concerning the use of weapons in space; cost; technical, legal, and doctrinal matters; and theoretical aspects of the use of space power. Technology and specific equipment provide opportunities, but space-power advocates have to define the use of space not only in terms of operations there, but also in terms of terrestrial actions. Today, space power appears limited to a supporting role for aerial and surface operations.[9] Until economic, political, and military issues are resolved, allowing space power to conduct a broader range of military operations (e.g., bombardment and other force applications), the question of an independent space force will continue to be debated.

Technological advancements in the 1920s and 1930s that involved guidance, propulsion, and payload improvements pointed many visionaries towards an independent air force. Similar advances in hypersonic and transatmospheric vehicles may do the same for space forces. Instead of an independent space force, the operation of a combined aerospace force might allow for a better joint use of forces. Adm William A. Moffett gained lasting naval fame when he combined the divergent maritime surface operation with naval aviation. Aircraft were able to support naval surface operations and amphibious landings. Space forces that operate at high altitudes and low earth orbit can support aerial forces. As technology advances, hypersonic and transatmospheric vehicles will gradually conduct more missions that were once the sole responsibility of aerial operations. Moffett's model will be more applicable in this case. Aerospace power may evolve into a broader, space-heavy

Communications satellites, a vital part of space power, multiply a military force's combat power.

force. Naval aviation is now a premier force at sea with aircraft-carrier battle groups. Battleships have gone by the boards, and the once proud "gun club" is no more. Can the same situation apply to the Air Force of the future? Space forces might become the primary source of operations, supported by aerial forces. These actions will occur only if the technology, commitment, and vision to match these new and expanding capabilities can be translated into a military force that promotes national objectives.

Exploiting space itself, compared to affecting terrestrial events, may become more of a key COG in the future. Today, access to space holds political, economic, and military applications that significantly affect operations on Earth's surface. Space offers much opportunity for political cooperation—witness the International Space Station, which has led to many nations working together for a single purpose. Also, the growing commercial value of communications satellites and the use of information networks in opening international trade have increased the value of space access immensely over the last few years. Finally, military power can greatly expand into truly global access, even if weaponry is not introduced into space. Hypersonic and transatmospheric vehicles can expand rapid mobility, reconnaissance, situational awareness, satellite deployment, and other activities. Space has become an increasingly significant portion of the nation's military capability. Questions about an independent force versus an integrated force will be debated for years. Future aerospace leaders must be aware of the issues involving space as the field becomes a dominant factor in future force employment.

Building a Mobile Force

A nation can deter and fight aggression in many ways. During the Cold War, the United States and its allies maintained a large military on many bases throughout the world, ready to contain and possibly fight the Soviet Union. These forces were geared towards conducting either a conventional or nuclear war. After the Cold War, the United States made drastic cuts in personnel, weapons, and bases. The demise of the Soviet Union forced national leadership to rethink many of its military concepts that had guided the country for decades. Ethnic, religious, territorial, and other conflicts started to become issues after the controlling influence of the Soviet Union ended. Also, traditional regional disputes have become more common and deadly for a variety of reasons, such as the proliferation of different weapon systems. Overseeing national, alliance, and UN commitments to enforce security arrangements and sanctions has also forced the extended deployment of air forces. These concerns, which have challenged the American military to identify future threats and prepare its forces to fight in many different situations, are magnified in light of the decrease in military force structure and the reduction in resources available to modernize military forces.

Instead of manning the same number of Cold War installations with fewer personnel, one method entails making forces more mobile and capable of deploying and fighting in different environments and situations. This philosophy is not new. The

United States Marine Corps has embraced this concept throughout its history. The Marines developed expeditionary forces to support deployments from the most northern regions to jungle warfare throughout the world. Naval vessels were able to move the Marines and their equipment to sites worldwide. Air forces can also conduct these types of operations. Although the Air Force did not create an explicit expeditionary force until today, throughout its history it has been able to craft and deploy aircraft and personnel to fight a war in many emergency situations. For example, the Air Force was able to fight major conflicts in Korea, Vietnam, and Iraq by planning and shaping an appropriate force and quickly moving it into the theater. Today, this emphasis on expeditionary forces has taken over much of the service's planning.

Temporary, extended, and unforeseen deployments of air forces worldwide have created several constraints on force deployments. Many of them are conducted from foreign bases and have relied upon ad hoc organizations to fill requirements. This has created concerns about personnel deployments, training, and readiness. Since these types of deployments are the norm today and for the foreseeable future, an organizational and doctrinal change has become necessary. The emphasis on a more mobile, contingent force is quite different than the Cold War–era stationing of forces ready to fight a set-piece war. The change to an expeditionary force will alter the types of personnel and forces, as well as the way the nation will fight in the future.

Mobile forces will require different types of capabilities to enable an expeditionary nature. Although the Air Force can move many forces and personnel quickly, it is limited in the size and amount of cargo it can move at any one time. This constraint will force leaders to prioritize the cargo it will choose to move. Additionally, large numbers of aircraft, equipment, and personnel may also create a more lucrative target to an adversary. Further, these forces will require additional support. Indeed, a smaller force can be deployed faster and is less vulnerable as a target; it is also more likely to receive basing approval from the host nation.

These smaller forces will need to operate on their own without as much support as required by previous ones. Thus,

C-17s can transport combat equipment and personnel worldwide.

equipment and munitions must be more reliable. This means that aircraft and equipment must be easily maintained and operated with fewer personnel and less material support. Munitions and equipment must be more capable of accomplishing their missions the first time, without having to repeatedly reattack the target. Improving a weapon's lethality can increase the probability of a successful attack on first try. Conversely, if current target information or deployment of the weapon is incorrect, potential collateral damage or civilian casualties might be great, thus creating new political concerns that can affect the conduct of the operation.

Information becomes very important to this new capability. Pilots must have accurate targeting data and mission-planning data delivered to them quickly. Missions may change, or targets may be modified. American forces need to maximize their combat effectiveness and efficiency by solving problems with fewer forces. Shared knowledge will help accomplish these objectives. Similarly, other personnel and support functions can support operations better with accurate and near-real-time information. Maintenance, civil engineer, medical, and security personnel, as well as others, can accommodate changes and emergencies faster by relying on distributed information.

Fast, accurate information requires vast computing and communications networks. Much of this equipment is not easily transportable. However, one may not need to send most of the personnel and equipment to the theater. Much of the information-management support can stay in the continental United States or a regional center. Advanced technology has allowed the United States to transfer information through communications satellites and other devices. Additionally, information might be directly available from information sources in directly usable form. For example, GPS satellites can give military forces in the field accurate navigation locations with a satellite receiver. Likewise, small satellite receivers may provide a commander with data on imagery, weather, and so forth. Other systems, such as airborne C^2, could provide mobile support that would have otherwise been restricted to a large, permanent command center. Technology has allowed machines to replace many traditional functions, reducing the need for additional personnel.

The new emphasis on expeditionary capability also requires increased mobility resources. Larger-capacity transports that can deliver cargo and personnel are required for the initial movement and subsequent operations. Other expeditionary forces will also require rapid support. These requirements will demand a capability to move many forces to different locations under varying conditions.

Personnel will also have to perform under more demanding conditions. Instead of focusing on one foe or region, future aerospace leaders must be able not only to become deployable worldwide, but also work with more allies under extremely sensitive political conditions. Military officers must be able to solve difficult problems at several levels. Junior officers will interact with foreign allies, train to operate under arctic to desert conditions, maximize the use of existing equipment, operate with fewer resources, and be ready to deploy at a moment's notice. These future leaders must be decision makers who can operate under tactical conditions but with a strategic view towards winning a conflict. The ability to solve serious problems with an appreciation for applying aerospace forces at critical times is paramount for future aerospace leaders.

Expeditionary aerospace forces will require a new discipline and way of thinking among personnel. Rotational duties will become more the norm than the exception. These forces will become more attuned to schedules and training requirements to solve problems. Additionally, if whole units deploy to support operations, everyone in an organization will become combat-focused for the deployment. No longer will selected personnel move to a forward location. Personnel—from combat crews to financial managers to services specialists—will travel together and train, live, work, and operate as one team. This situation is similar to the Navy's ship deployments. Aircraft carriers are moving cities that have every capability, from police to cooks to firemen, and everyone operates as a team. Land-based airpower will perform in a similar manner by taking all of its technical capability to the field.

Information: The Key to Victory

Aerospace power relies not only on technology, but also on information. The control and exploitation of information can channel an adversary into certain behaviors and actions. Conversely, if friendly forces do not have the correct information about a target, they can misidentify it, use an inappropriate weapon against it, or be unable to tell whether or not an attack against it was successful. Reliance on commercial computer and information networks has forced military organizations to think about conducting attacks against an enemy's information resources and defending against similar information attacks by an adversary. Increased emphasis on information will have profound implications for future aerospace forces. Personnel, equipment, decision-making processes, and other influences will alter the ways air and space forces operate.

Why is information so important in today's military? It has always been critical to success in warfare. Finding an enemy or determining industrial targets is crucial for planners trying to disable an adversary's economy by scheduling sorties or attacks. Additionally, coordinating activities with other services depends on timely information. Conversely, enemy intelligence services would like to know the location, intent, and plans of friendly forces to avoid an attack or launch a countermove against those forces. In the past, military forces have used a variety of sources to gain information from spies, library research, aerial photography, satellites, and so forth. Although today's forces use many of these same sources, the information is more rapidly disseminated and more easily obtained.

Smaller forces must rely on striking targets the first time with great confidence of destroying or disabling them. Aerospace power is much affected by these changes. Air and space forces must be able to deploy forces for combat, treaty enforcement, deterrence, and support of operations. A commander's decision to conduct particular operations must rely on data for deploying rapidly and defending forces; providing necessary targeting information to conduct selective attacks might allow expeditionary forces to react to short-notice emergencies faster than previous force structures.[10] Information will help aerospace forces to deploy rapidly and employ forces; improve military capabilities to combat weapons of mass destruction; increase options available for a commander to operate; provide better situational awareness of enemy actions in the battlefield; and provide sufficient firepower to appropriate target sets. These abilities may allow present and future aerospace forces to combat a variety of operations with fewer forces and, hopefully, improve the planning and evaluation of enemy capabilities. The availability of appropriate information during timely situations can provide leverage to forces and improve their efficiency and effectiveness against much larger forces. This may require aerospace forces to invest in a variety of information-gathering, processing, and analysis systems. Aerospace leaders must contend with a variety of issues to understand expanded information threats. Information imbues all aspects of modern life: political, social, economic, and military. Access to and exploitation of information can significantly affect doctrine, policy, strategy, and alternatives for confronting and handling these situations.

Several aspects of modern-day life have heightened the value of information to military operations: low costs, the blurring of traditional boundaries, perceptions, warnings, coalitions, and the increased vulnerability of the United States.[11] Modern technological innovations in the civilian-information sector have far outstripped the military's development of similar systems. Military information-processing applications were once the driving force to develop computers, networks, and communications devices. Today, the military must rely on many civilian inventions and commercial products to stay current. Once-classified military systems now have less capability and growth potential than commercial ones. The low cost of procurement has allowed less-developed countries to access much information to exploit or attack other systems. Individuals or terrorist groups can gain the same information available to many nations. For example, the United States developed a number of imagery satellite systems worth billions of dollars. Today, better imaging systems can provide the same or superior products almost instantaneously to individuals for a lower cost. Persons familiar with a computer, modem, and the Internet can gain substantial information to conduct operations.

Space power in the field. Ground forces can now benefit from satellite communications.

Information does not have borders and may not be limited solely to governments. Military-related information was once limited to certain government organizations. Today, weather, imagery, navigation, and other information is accessible to the private sector, other governments, and the general public. Many of these systems have also been transferred to civilian government and private organizations. Computer networks and their control are in the hands of numerous commercial organizations worldwide. If one were to inquire about the source of information required by the military, he or she would find a patchwork of public and private organizations and individuals. For example, a French satellite taking imagery of American ports may use a commercial data-processing center in Germany that uses a multinational data-communications system for a terrorist user. If the United States government wanted to deny access to certain types of information, it would have to work with numerous organizations to cut off an adversary.

Low-cost access to information also creates several opportunities to allow many state and nonstate actors to voice their opinions worldwide and affect the perception of participants in a conflict. Different points of view expressed around the world can be used for legitimately voicing concerns, or they can be used to confuse or misinform parties. Confusion about the "facts" of the case can affect national relationships, domestic debates, and one's understanding of the nature of the conflict. A small group of dedicated information specialists can create an effective propaganda machine to combat much larger opponents.

Information is available at the speed of an electron. It can be reproduced instantaneously and sent around the world with a simple keystroke. The complexity of information systems also makes detection of and reaction to information-based attacks or concerns difficult to assess. Damage to databases, communications systems, and processing systems may take time to detect and to make relevant parties aware of problems in their information systems. Hidden computer viruses or other damaging programs might lay dormant until a foe needs to initiate an attack. Information attacks might be subtle, incremental actions, or they could be a series of massive attacks. A defender against such attacks may not have adequate time to prepare or fix complex problems. Additionally, using the Internet may allow a foe to conduct information warfare anonymously. A nation or an individual could strike a country undetected. This aspect of information operations inhibits long-range forecasts about threats; it also increases the difficulty of planning for and defending against activities or of ensuring that national leadership is aware of potential threats. Since many industries and services use information, the enemy has numerous potential targets to consider. Utilities, financial institutions, health-care organizations, postal services, and other modern-day conveniences use information systems. How can the nation plan for such attacks and successfully defend diverse institutions under both private and public control?

Parties using an information attack might choose a selective strike against particular nations. Some countries might be more vulnerable to interruptions of work in financial institutions; others might be affected greatly by the disruption of mass transportation, such as railways or roadways. If several nations try to band together to fight this threat, they may not be able to coordinate activities because of confusion about the nature of the threat. The unknown nature of the information attack might not allow nations to understand either the scope of the attack or the participants involved. Additionally, coalitions or alliances that share information might be vulnerable through their "weakest" member. Hacking into a sovereign nation's information systems might allow an adversary to gain access to an ATO or other information, with or without the knowledge of the intended victim.

The unprecedented access to and availability of information systems have increased the vulnerability of many nations. National security threats to a country's existence were once thought to be limited to nuclear weapons or conventionally armed bombers. Today, the reliance on information-intensive activities has improved the standard of living for the populace. However, this improvement in lifestyles has also increased the potential to affect more people's lives by eliminating selected information. For example, most American citizens and businesses use checking accounts to pay for domestic and international transactions. Suppose an unfriendly nation decides to disrupt the Federal Reserve System's ability to clear bank checks in the United States. Everyday commerce would be gravely affected.

Individuals and companies making or receiving payments and planning expenditures may have to think about methods to circumvent this problem, if possible. American and international economies would be slowed without this key component of commerce.

Aerospace forces also rely heavily on information. Awareness of the potential use and vulnerabilities of information is an important first step towards understanding how to operate in this new environment. Aerospace forces can elect to follow several routes. Control of information is important. Access to selected information might be designed to secure the availability of data to selected users. Information and security experts could increase efforts to protect information. Conversely, airpower and space-power forces, such as satellites and aircraft devoted to gaining data about a foe or denying access to an adversary, already conduct many of these types of operations. Integration of these efforts into current air and space operations will take time. Denying information to a foe may be more of a challenge than conducting weapons-dropping missions on an enemy. Problems associated with creating special organizations, training personnel, and equipping units to handle the explosion of potential information-related problems will increase exponentially in the future. This will compound the problems that aerospace leaders will face, along with the "conventional" aspects of air superiority, CAS, interdiction, and other functions.

Technological Solutions for an Unknown World

Aerospace forces are based on devices that rely on applying scientific and engineering principles and an educated workforce to support practical applications. Advancing technology has enabled aerospace leaders to substitute machinery for manpower. Giulio Douhet was convinced that battleplanes might revolutionize warfare and make the outcome more humane. Other airpower theorists tried to apply technology to reduce friendly casualties or end conflicts faster than contemporary methods would. Advancements in air and space weaponry have increased commanders' alternatives. For example, space exploration allowed the fledgling USAF to experiment with a number of capabilities that allowed it to replace or supplement manned aerial vehicles with unmanned machines. Tomorrow, advancements in information, materials, and the miniaturization of components might provide newer methods to fight a war.

The ways in which aerospace leaders plan and exploit new technology will be an important factor in shaping future capabilities. There are several ways to think about using technology. Individuals or organizations can create new technologies based on a desire or requirement. Aerospace forces might evaluate what they need for future capabilities and spend resources to get special applications of technology for specific missions. This emphasis on technology is a more directed approach towards advancing weapon-systems development. Conversely, military forces might adapt available technology or recently discovered applications for military use. Aerospace leaders might need to become more innovative in using the technology. The challenge to aerospace leaders is to adapt to change. Unfortunately, organizational resistance to change might affect how leaders use new inventions, or the discovery might lay idle until the service faces an emergency—or, in many cases, until an adversary adopts the technology. In case an enemy makes strides in technology, the emphasis will quickly shift to finding a countermeasure or defense. Unfortunately, the aerospace force may have lost a prime opportunity to exploit the new technology—hence, air and space forces become reactive, not proactive, to the technology. A principle of war calls for staying on the offensive, but reactive behavior gives an adversary the advantage of taking the initiative and potentially taking offensive action against friendly forces. Indirectly, the avoidance of initiative may give an adversary valuable time to exploit the technology.

Aerospace forces in the United States had relied primarily on directed research and development to produce weapon systems, many of which were started as solutions to problems facing the nation. Doctrines and strategies were initially created, and then an aerospace force was created to support them. This approach provided a "top-down" view of high-level objectives. This philosophy provides a logical, planned direction for technology. After the Vietnam War, the USAF evaluated combat losses due to SAMs, AAA, and interceptor aircraft. The Yom Kippur War of 1973 between Israel and Egypt highlighted the value of air-defense weapons against aircraft. Development of advanced air-defense systems would make future aircraft losses even greater.

One approach to reducing potential losses and increasing combat effectiveness involved developing a radar-evading aircraft that would reduce aircraft vulnerability. The USAF started an advanced-technology program that would reduce the radar cross section (RCS) that enemy air defenses could detect to guide missiles, guns, or aircraft. By 1974 the Defense Advanced Research Projects Agency (DARPA) approved contracts to develop RCS reduction technology—known as Project Harvey.[12] Eventually, the USAF would use this technology to produce and deploy the F-117A stealth combat aircraft. The new technology, which allowed the United States to strike enemy targets in heavily defended areas using a single radar-evading airplane, was a breakthrough in aerospace engineering and has been applied to other aircraft, missiles, and aerial vehicles.

The focused approach to top-down innovation works under many conditions involving whether or not sufficient resources are available, whether or not objectives have been identified, and whether or not activities happen during war or peace. These factors can affect time, motivation, experience, and development of the proposed applications of new technology. The application of advanced technology can help a nation prepare to shape future conflicts and world events. Stealth aircraft allowed the United States to conduct an extensive strategic-bombardment campaign in Operation Desert Storm, without loss, against one of the most heavily defended areas in the history of aerial combat. This capability shaped the conduct of the conflict and allowed coalition air-campaign planners to attack different targets with many combinations of aircraft.

New aircraft, space, and basic research efforts are expensive. For example, the USAF research, development, test, and evaluation budget request for fiscal year 2001 is $9.7 billion, and the procurement of aircraft, missiles, and other systems includes an additional $14.1 billion.[13] These amounts represent a total of 33.4 percent of the USAF budget. The Air Force has assigned approximately 97,000 people to conduct research, development, test, acquisition, and support for aerospace weapons and support systems.[14] These resources represent a commitment to advance, apply, and maintain advanced technology in many systems. Aeronautical, space and missile, electronic, and munitions systems are supported by a variety of test centers, laboratories, and other scientific and engineering centers. These efforts frequently take much time to design, build, test, and deploy weapon systems. The F-117A used many existing systems, such as the engine and landing gear, to reduce development time. The initial operational capability of the first F-117A unit was granted in 1983, nine years after DARPA initiated Project Harvey.[15] Conversely, the Rockwell B-1B concept-to-deployment of an operational aircraft took decades of focusing on new technology.

Justification for long development and production times for weapon systems assumes that threats and foes do not change readily during this period. In the Cold War, many weapons could afford a slow, deliberate development phase. Technology was created and tested extensively to ensure that weapons worked with great reliability. Unfortunately, threats have changed dramatically since the end of the Cold War. Some weapons, such as the Northrop-Grumman B-2 stealth bomber, were designed to find, attack, and destroy nuclear-armed systems within the Soviet Union. After the Cold War, national leaders decided that they did not need the number of B-2 bombers initially estimated to defend the nation. However, modifications to America's long-range bombers allowed aircraft designed in the Cold War era to maintain their combat edge by equipping them with conventional cruise missiles and PGMs. Engineers and scientists were able to update munitions, enabling these aircraft to fight another way. Unfortunately, not all weapon systems could claim this distinction. Reduced budgets and mission requirements forced the retirement of a series of Cold War–era aircraft and other systems.

During peacetime, engineers and scientists have the luxury of time to correct mistakes or test alternatives. But technology and innovation during an active conflict is a different situation altogether. Aerospace leaders faced with an emergency condition might need to modify existing weapon systems or rush

B-2 Spirit bomber

the development of the weapon without adequate experimentation or extensive development. Motivation among design engineers and scientists may be higher for this type of effort since the nation may be faced with destruction unless a solution is found. Additionally, the military may not face the same level of scrutiny or questioning about the development of weapons as it would during peacetime.[16] The approval of wartime efforts may require a compressed schedule to implement a proposed program. This shortened timing may result in higher costs and potentially more mistakes or errors in the development program than would be the case for peacetime projects. But wartime designs and technology applications allow aerospace forces to immediately test, under combat conditions, whether the effort is worthy of increased production. Immediate feedback to weapons designers can speed the modification of systems to satisfy a commander's requirements.

Aerospace systems are very susceptible to problems in technological advancement. Innovation allows for experimenting with new and untested ideas or concepts for a force structure. In the rush towards developing a new weapon, many resources and valuable time can be squandered without clear direction. During World War II, the Luftwaffe designed and produced several jet aircraft. Top Luftwaffe leadership concentrated its efforts on building a jet fighter to defend Germany against American and British bombing efforts and regain air superiority along all fronts. The Messerschmitt Me-262 Schwalbe, designed as an interceptor, was ready for service by May 1944. Hitler's desire for revenge against the Allied bombing of Germany motivated him to order the program reoriented to a fast bomber.[17] Many of the aircraft were diverted from their main purpose of attacking bombers and their escorts. If devoted to an air defense role, the aircraft could have changed the character and success of the Combined Bomber Offensive and, ultimately, the conduct of the war. Questionable national direction and goals blocked the revolutionary path to the introduction of jet aircraft.

Conversely, wartime necessity under clear direction can also produce many successful results. Several nuclear scientists and physicists, including Albert Einstein, heavily influenced the United States government to conduct atomic-energy research for the purpose of developing an atomic bomb.[18] By 1941 the Army was the lead development agency for such a project. The rush to develop this weapon required much duplication and parallel effort to ensure creation of a workable device. After tremendous amounts of money, manpower, and materials were expended, the AAF exploded nuclear weapons over Hiroshima and Nagasaki in August 1945. In four years, a weapon of great power was created. During Desert Storm, coalition forces were not able to attack targets that were heavily entrenched or buried deep in the earth. Air Force engineers were able to develop the GBU-28 penetrating bomb in less than 17 days. The 25-foot-long and 4,700-pound weapon was designed, built, and tested before its transport to the Persian Gulf. Within five hours of its delivery to coalition forces, two GBU-28s were loaded onto F-111 aircraft for an operational mission.[19]

Today, military forces must rely increasingly on civilian innovation. Information and computer systems are only two examples of this change. Reduced defense budgets, a rapidly changing strategic and international environment, and demand for a more responsive process to acquire weapons have forced engineers and scientists to use many commercial sources for innovation. Aerospace forces must alter their expectations to incorporate commercial technology and adapt existing inventions for weapon systems. The reliance on civilian technology and standards has become the focus for development efforts.

Such reliance has many advantages. Competitive free markets can separate and identify the best and most cost-effective technology for an application. Military forces can literally reap the benefits of obtaining tested, superior, and cost-effective solutions to difficult problems. Using a military-controlled development program might result in a narrow development of technology for specific uses. But civilian technology can be used in a number of applications instead of staying locked behind a classified wall of military silence. Rather than limiting the number of persons working for a technical solution, innovation—assuming the commercial world is looking at the problem—can be expanded to an entire world of engineers and scientists who are working on the project. This may lead to different approaches for handling or solving the problem that were never imagined by military or government decision makers. These are but a few of the advantages of applying civilian technology and adapting this approach to weapons development. However, aerospace leaders must balance several shortcomings to this approach with military technological-development efforts.

First, the ability to design custom weapons or systems is limited to available civilian innovation. Unless, by coincidence, civilian technology is applicable to military needs, development of aerospace weaponry will be delayed or may not have the same desired characteristics or capabilities that aerospace leaders require for the future. Another limitation of civilian innovation is control over dual-use technology for military applications. If the military uses the same civilian technology as is used for commercial products, adversaries may be able to develop countermeasures to the system after examining its operating capabilities and faults in the technology. An adversary can also exploit commercial technology. Countries without large budgets for research and development may be able to build their own weapons with this inexpensive technology. Civilian dual technology may even lead to the proliferation of weapons and create an arms race. The United States has relied on its ability to use advanced technology to overcome a number of operational limitations, such as geographic distances, disparities in force sizes, and so forth. If nations have access to the same technology, many of them will benefit from this situation, while others, like the United States, may see a once-held advantage disappear.

New technology and developments have allowed countries to avoid always "fighting the last war."[20] Innovations such as nuclear weapons, tanks, aircraft, and so forth have changed the face of warfare. Future aerospace leaders must adapt to advances in military innovation. Information warfare, space systems, stealth aircraft, and other advances have challenged air and space forces in the recent past. These systems have altered doctrines, strategies, and force structures. Technology advancement is not limited to aerospace forces. Other military systems will also add new and better capabilities. Aerospace leaders should be aware of how ground and maritime forces have applied technology. This awareness helps friendly forces plan and fight together by integrating the strengths and addressing the weaknesses of all forces. Similarly, understanding technology will also help future planners think about a perceived adversary's capabilities and threats.

Fighting Jointly

Today's American military forces are trained, organized, and structured to fight with their sister services as a joint team. Improved operations, decreased resources, and rising complexity in warfare have forced increased joint operations among services. This emphasis is apparent in joint doctrine, organizations, purchases of weapons, and training of forces. Each component has unique capabilities that can add to the successful execution of an air campaign. For example, Army forces can provide massive fire support against air-defense systems by using tactical missiles and artillery. Army and Marine Corps forces can also use helicopter and aviation forces to disable and destroy many different targets along a front. Naval forces contribute aviation forces and cruise missiles to strike deep into enemy territory. If the Air Force does not take advantage of these capabilities, it will have to divert its limited resources to accomplish these missions, perhaps delaying the attainment of other objectives. Additionally, having several divergent forces take action against an enemy can cause confusion and complicate his defensive effort.

If a nation fights with only a single force, an enemy can more easily plan for the assault. If an enemy knows he will be threatened by a land-based air force, he can prepare SAMs, AAA, radar, and interceptor forces to defend the homeland. However, if the force is joint, the planning for attacks from the sea or from tactical missiles may require additional defensive forces, which may weaken the overall capability of the adversary to defeat other friendly forces. Also, by massing a larger force, the joint effort might stun the enemy with the speed and size of the attack, a situation that other friendly or allied forces could exploit.

Joint operations have been significantly affected by the rapid impact of world events. Disruption of access to a raw material in a small country might have a detrimental effect on the world economy or political relationships. This reaction can, in turn, compel a nation to send military forces to stabilize an area or take other active measures to restore a situation. Countries might need to send selected units to support these actions in an expeditious manner. Different services have unique capabilities and forces that can create and shape situations to a nation's advantage. Selecting the right combination depends upon forces able to successfully integrate force capabilities in a joint manner.

Dealing with unknown or ill-defined requirements, using smaller forces, and making rapid decisions will shape future military organizations. Operations ranging from nuclear to humanitarian missions cannot rely on a single military service or capability. Concentrating on a single capability will provide narrow operational options and alternatives to national leaders. Force capabilities should not be so thinly stressed that they can do all missions but cannot reduce a persistent threat to a nation. National leaders need to make careful choices about force capabilities. One method for overcoming this issue entails creating forces that can substitute capabilities for particular forces. For example, Jack Slessor suggested that airpower could patrol and restore order in the British colonies just as well as Royal ground forces in the 1930s. Space systems have substituted for ground-based communications systems in many areas, reducing costs and increasing capabilities.

Future military commanders must be experts in conducting their own specialties and in knowing how other military forces operate. Knowledge of ground and maritime operations is a prime ingredient in the development of aerospace leaders. The ability to work in a joint or multinational force structure has become a prerequisite for operating large theater-level forces. Although the United States has fought in World War I, World War II, the Korean War, the Vietnam War, the Gulf War, and other conflicts involving joint and multinational operations, the increased political and military influence of foreign countries has grown exponentially. Understanding how ground and maritime forces fight may also increase the ability of a student of aerospace power to compare and contrast its strengths and weaknesses. Such a study can only improve the student's knowledge of aerospace power and its future applications.

Summary

Aerospace commanders must not only consider how to apply aerospace forces, but also know how to approach many future issues and concerns. Changing world events, technology, national goals, and other events are factors that change the way nations can use air and space forces. However, advocates of airpower and space power may have to deal with several enduring issues. What is the best role for airpower and space power? Can air and space forces win a war independently of other forces? How can the nation incorporate new technologies, weapons, and missions?

A strong foundation in knowing the capabilities of aerospace forces can only strengthen an individual's ability to use them in war or humanitarian missions. This knowledge helps in developing new weapons, deploying forces, and working with different military services and nations. The dynamic nature of aerospace operations will force future leaders to evaluate their actions and other services in a more critical manner to enable them to solve increasingly complex problems. Undertaking a career-long study of aerospace power is one way of assuring that this foundation remains strong, relevant, and viable. The long-term appreciation of these subjects not only will improve our ability to control aerospace power, but also will solve unknown issues that await us in the future.

Notes

1. Trevor N. Dupuy, *The Evolution of Weapons and Warfare* (Indianapolis: Bobbs-Merrill, 1980), 269.
2. Briefing, "Iraqi Air Campaign Instant Thunder," Persian Gulf War Records, n.d., US Air Force Historical Research Agency, Maxwell AFB, Ala.
3. Col Richard T. Reynolds, *Heart of the Storm: The Genesis of the Air Campaign against Iraq* (Maxwell AFB, Ala.: Air University Press, 1995), 72.
4. Ibid., 127.
5. John R. Bruning, *Crimson Sky: The Air Battle for Korea* (Dulles, Va.: Brassey's, 1999), 209.
6. Air Vice Marshal Tony Mason, *The Aerospace Revolution: Role Revision and Technology: An Overview* (Washington, D.C.: Brassey's, 1998), 145.
7. Stephen Peter Rosen, *Winning the Next War: Innovation and the Modern Military* (Ithaca, N.Y.: Cornell University Press, 1991), 237.
8. Kenneth P. Werrell, *The Evolution of the Cruise Missile* (Maxwell AFB, Ala.: Air University Press, 1985), 58.
9. Gregory Billman, "The Inherent Limitations of Space Power: Fact or Fiction?" in *Beyond the Paths of Heaven: The Emergence of Space Power Thought: A Comprehensive Anthology of Space-Related Master's Research*, ed. Bruce M. DeBlois (Maxwell AFB, Ala.: Air University Press, 1999), 548.
10. David A. Ochmanek et al., *To Find, and Not To Yield: How Advances in Information and Firepower Can Transform Theater Warfare*, MR-958-AF (Santa Monica, Calif.: RAND, 1998), 67–68.
11. Roger C. Molander, Andrew S. Riddile, and Peter A. Wilson, *Strategic Information Warfare: A New Face of War*, MR-661-OSD (Santa Monica, Calif.: RAND, 1996), 16.
12. Curtis Peebles, *Dark Eagles: A History of Top Secret U.S. Aircraft Programs* (Novato, Calif.: Presidio Press, 1995), 141.
13. United States Air Force, *Air Force FY00/01 President's Budget Highlights* (Washington, D.C.: Department of the Air Force, 1999), 2.

14. "Organization," *Airman: Magazine of America's Air Force*, January 2000, 16.

15. Peebles, 170.

16. Rosen, 23.

17. James L. Stokesbury, *A Short History of Air Power* (New York: William Morrow and Co., 1986), 236.

18. Martin van Creveld, *Technology and War: From 2000 B.C. to the Present* (New York: Free Press, 1991), 252.

19. Richard P. Hallion, *Storm over Iraq: Air Power and the Gulf War* (Washington, D.C.: Smithsonian Institution Press, 1992), 243.

20. Rosen, 1.

Glossary

AAA	antiaircraft artillery
AAF	Army Air Forces
AAM	air-to-air missile
ACTS	Air Corps Tactical School
AEW	airborne early warning
AFB	Air Force base
AFDD	Air Force Doctrine Document
ALO	air liaison officer
ARVN	Army of the Republic of Vietnam
ATO	air tasking order
AWACS	airborne warning and control system
AWPD-1	Air War Plans Division-1
C^2	command and control
CALTF	Combined Airlift Task Force
CANA	Commando Aviacion Naval Argentina (Argentinean naval aviation force)
CAP	combat air patrol
CAS	close air support
CBO	Combined Bomber Offensive
CIA	Central Intelligence Agency
COG	center of gravity
CRAF	Civil Reserve Air Fleet
DAK	German Afrika Korps
DARPA	Defense Advanced Research Projects Agency
DCA	defensive counterair
DCS	defensive counterspace
DIA	Defense Intelligence Agency
DMZ	demilitarized zone
DSCS	Defense Satellite Communications System

DSP	Defense Support Program
EAF	Egyptian Air Force
ECM	electronic countermeasures
FAA	*Fuerza Aerea Argentina* (Argentinean air force)
FAC	forward air controller
FM	Field Manual
GCA	ground-controlled approach
GCI	ground-controlled intercept
IADS	integrated air defense system
ICBM	intercontinental ballistic missile
IDF/AF	Israeli Defense Forces/Air Force
IJN	Imperial Japanese Navy
IRBM	intermediate-range ballistic missile
JCS	Joint Chiefs of Staff
JOC	joint operations center
MAC	Military Airlift Command
MAP	master attack plan
MRBM	medium-range ballistic missile
NATO	North Atlantic Treaty Organization
NBC	nuclear, biological, and chemical
NKPA	North Korean People's Army
NVA	North Vietnamese Army
OCA	offensive counterair
OCS	offensive counterspace
PGM	precision-guided munitions
PLA	People's Liberation Army
PLO	Palestine Liberation Organization
PRC	People's Republic of China
RAF	Royal Air Force
RCS	radar cross section
RJAF	Royal Jordanian Air Force
RN	Royal Navy
ROK	Republic of Korea

RPV	remotely piloted vehicle
SAAF	Syrian Arab Air Force
SAC	Strategic Air Command
SAM	surface-to-air missile
SEAD	suppression of enemy air defenses
SIOP	Single Integrated Operation Plan
SWPA	Southwest Pacific Area
TACC	tactical air control center
TACP	tactical air control party
TADC	tactical air direction center
TEL	transporter erector launcher
UAV	unmanned aerial vehicle
UN	United Nations
USAF	United States Air Force
USAFE	United States Air Forces in Europe
VNAF	South Vietnamese Air Force
VVS	*Voyenno-vozdushnyye sily* (Soviet air force)

Index

Adlerangriff (Eagle Day), 83
aerial
    artillery, 168
    bombardment, 104
    interdiction, 133, 138–39, 150
    reconnaissance, 157
    refueling, 12, 90, 177, 185, 189, 226–29, 232, 235–37, 239, 268, 271–72, 281
aerospace industry, 29–30, 32
aerospace vehicles, 29, 289–90
airborne artillery, 161
airborne early warning (AEW), 227, 232, 239, 244, 246, 250
air campaign, 110–11, 200, 264–65, 267–70, 277, 280, 284, 292, 297, 317
air campaign plan/planners, 67, 264–73, 276, 278–85, 287
air control, 52–53
Air Corps, 39, 56–57, 59, 62–63, 103–4, 119–20
Air Corps Tactical School (ACTS), 39, 56, 58–59, 72, 99, 119–20, 124, 126, 263, 291
aircraft
    A-6 Intruder, 113, 141
    A-6E, 204
    A-10, 204
    AC-47 "Spooky" gunship, 160–64
    AC-119, 163–64
    AC-119G Shadow, 163
    Aeromacchi MB-339, 226
    AH-64 Apache helicopter, 112
    Aichi D3A1 Val, 103, 107
    airborne warning and control system (AWACS), 186, 189, 281
    Avro Vulcan, 227, 229–30
    battleplane, 42–43, 45, 48, 58, 310
    Beaufighter, 148
    Beech T-34C Mentor, 226, 233
    Bell AH-1S Cobra helicopter, 248
    Boeing 707, 226, 230, 236, 245
    Boeing B-17 Flying Fortress, 79, 93, 104, 120, 122–24, 146, 148–49
    Boeing B-29 Superfortress, 134–36, 138, 165, 193
    Boeing B-52, 112–13, 140, 142–43, 204, 292
    Boeing KC-135 Stratotanker, 141, 185
    Boeing RB-47E, 215
    bomber, 49–50, 56–59, 62–63, 65, 72, 80–85, 88, 93–95, 108, 112, 120, 122–24, 126, 135–37, 147, 150, 155–56, 175, 205, 211, 229, 255, 257, 271, 291–92, 297, 309, 315
    British Aerospace Buccaneer, 227
    British Aerospace Harrier, 227–32, 234–39
    Bug (pilotless aircraft), 297
    C-119, 207
    Canberra PR.Mk.9, 229–31, 236
    carrier, 60–61, 101, 103–4, 106, 113, 146
    CH-47D Chinook helicopter, 234
    CH-53 helicopter, 245
    close-support vertical/short takeoff and landing, 227
    Consolidated B-24 Liberator, 79, 93, 120, 122–24, 148
    Curtiss P-36A, 104
    Curtiss P-40 B/C Tomahawk, 104
    Dassault Mirage, 90–91, 226, 244
    Dassault Mirage III, 230–31, 233–38, 240
    Dassault Mirage IIICJ, 88
    Dassault Mirage IIIEA, 226
    Dassault Super Etendard, 226, 231, 234, 236–37
    dive-bomber, 103, 149
    Dornier Do-17, 81
    Douglas A-20 Havoc, 148
    Douglas B-26 Invader, 134–36
    Douglas C-47 Dakota, 136, 159, 191–92, 194, 196
    Douglas C-54 Skymaster, 191–92, 194–96
    E-2C Hawkeye, 244, 246
    EA-6B, 112
    EF-111A, 112
    Electric Canberra B.Mk.2 bomber, 226
    electronic warfare, 112
    escort fighter, 81, 93, 124
    F-16 Fighting Falcon, 22, 188, 203–4, 246–50
    F-51, 135
    F-100 Super Saber, 4

F-105 Thunderchief, 18
fighter, 57–59, 80–81, 85, 94–95, 97–98, 103, 112, 121–22, 124, 135, 148, 150, 155–56, 175, 182, 189, 192, 249, 255–59, 269–71, 274–75, 291–92
fighter-bomber, 88–90, 113, 115, 144
fighter-interceptor, 111
Focke-Wulf Fw-190, 99, 122–23
Focke-Wulf Fw-200 Condor, 182
General Dynamics F-111 Aardvark, 113, 141, 144, 292, 315
Gotha 242, 182
gunship, 159–61, 163–65
Handley Page Victor K.2, 227, 229, 237
Hawker Hurricane Mark I, 82–85, 237
Hawker-Siddley Nimrod, 227, 229, 237, 239
Heinkel He-111, 81, 181–82
helicopter, 100, 112, 132, 185, 188, 226–28, 232–34, 240–41, 244, 248, 289, 318
Hughes 500MD Defender helicopter, 248
IA-58 Pucara, 226, 230, 233
Ilyushin Il-28 Beagle, 88, 211, 213
interceptor, 57–59, 82, 205, 236, 247, 312
Iraqi, 91, 115
Israel Aircraft Industry Dagger fighter-bomber, 226, 230–31, 233, 235–38, 240
Israel Aircraft Industry Scout, 244
JC-130, 207
Junkers Ju-52, 178–79, 181–83
Junkers Ju-86, 182
Junkers Ju-87, 81
Junkers Ju-88, 81
KC-130, 226, 234
Kfir, 243, 246
Lockheed AC-130A Spectre, 163–64
Lockheed C-5 Galaxy, 185–86, 188–89
Lockheed C-130 Hercules, 141, 163, 185, 188, 226–27, 236, 239
Lockheed C-141 Starlifter, 185–89
Lockheed F-80 Shooting Star, 193
Lockheed F-117, 113, 204, 292, 312–13
Lockheed P-2 Neptune, 214, 236
Lockheed P-38 Lightning, 94, 99, 122, 148
Lockheed P-80 Shooting Star, 135
Lockheed U-2, 205–8, 213–16
long-range bomber, 48–49, 64, 99, 103, 227, 255, 313
LTV RF-8 Crusader, 216
Lynx helicopter, 234
Marine Corps, 112, 135, 152, 165, 168
MB.339A, 226
McDonnell RF-101C Voodoo, 214–16
McDonnell-Douglas A-4 Skyhawk, 4, 141, 226, 230–31, 233–38, 240, 243, 246, 249
McDonnell-Douglas F-4 Phantom, 18–19, 112, 140–41, 227, 229, 239, 243, 246, 248–49
McDonnell-Douglas F-15 Eagle, 22, 109, 113, 186, 189, 202–4, 243, 246–48, 250, 292
McDonnell-Douglas KC-10 Extender, 185
Messerschmitt Bf-109, 81–85, 99, 122–23, 125
Messerschmitt Bf-110, 81–83
Messerschmitt Me-109E, 237
Messerschmitt Me-262 Schwalbe, 315
Messerschmitt Me-323, 182
MH-53J Pave Low helicopter, 112
MiG, 143–45, 247–48, 250
MiG-15, 135, 137–38
MiG-21 Fishbed, 88, 91, 213, 241, 244, 247–48
MiG-23, 243, 247–48
MiG-25, 243, 247
MiG-29, 111
Mitsubishi A6M2 Zero, 103, 107, 148
Mystere IV-A, 88
Nakajima B5N2 Kate, 103, 107
Navy, 135, 165
North American B-25C Mitchell, 147–48
North American P-51 Mustang, 93–94, 98–99, 123
Northrop-Grumman B-2 stealth bomber, 285, 313
nuclear bomber, 216, 291–92
Panavia Tornado, 113, 204, 227
pursuit, 48, 56–59, 65, 82, 103
RC-121C Super Constellation, 215
reconnaissance, 104, 112, 148, 150, 205, 211, 217, 227
Republic F-84 Thunderjet, 135
Republic P-47 Thunderbolt, 93–94, 99, 122–23

RF-4E, 244–45, 249
Rockwell B-1B, 313
Ryan Teledyne 1241 (AQM-34L) Firebee, 244, 246
Sea King helicopter, 228, 232, 237
Sepecat Jaguar, 227
SP-2H Tracker, 231
special operations, 112
stealth, 117, 312, 317
strategic bomber, 38, 40, 48, 57, 119–20, 213, 273
Su-7, 241
Su-22, 247
Supermarine Spitfire, 82–85, 122, 237
Super Mystere B.2, 88, 90
surveillance, 112, 231
Swordfish, 103
tactical fighter-bomber, 291
tanker, 189, 226–27
transport, 112, 164, 175–77, 179, 181, 183, 190, 192, 233, 257, 271–72, 280, 304
Tu-16 Badger, 88–89
unmanned aerial vehicle (UAV), 249, 290, 295–97, 311
VC-10, 227, 239
Wessex helicopter, 234
zeppelin, 40, 81
aircraft carrier, 59, 61–63, 101–3, 105–6, 141, 168, 170, 186, 225, 228, 236, 238, 271, 300, 305
aircraft industry, 94, 98, 120, 122–23, 125, 150, 252–53
air defense, 5, 51, 56–57, 76–77, 90, 94, 108, 110–16, 121–22, 142–44, 157, 182, 202, 205, 214, 225–26, 229, 231, 234, 236–41, 243, 245–51, 267, 280, 295, 312, 315, 318
air doctrine, 258
Air Force Reserve, 186
Air Force Satellite Communications System, 202
Air Force Space Command, 201–2, 204
Air Force Systems Command, 163
Air-Ground Operations Conference, 171
air liaison officer (ALO), 167–68
airlift, 178–86, 188–89, 191–92, 194–96, 239, 255, 280
Air Service, 46
Air Staff, 160
air superiority, 39, 58, 65–66, 75–80, 83–86, 89, 92–93, 95, 97–99, 108, 111, 115, 152, 154, 157–58, 165, 168, 171, 181, 183, 197, 235–37, 239, 245, 249–50, 253–56, 258–60, 263, 265–66, 273–74, 277, 287, 310, 315
air supremacy, 238
air tasking order (ATO), 188, 281–86, 309
Air War Plans Division-1 (AWPD-1), 119–20, 126
Air War Plans Division-42 (AWPD-42), 120
Allied Air Support Command, 155
Allied Expeditionary Air Force, 95
American Volunteer Group (Flying Tigers), 59
Ameriyya air-raid shelter, 285
Andersen AFB, Guam, 140
Anderson, Rudolph, 216
antiaircraft artillery (AAA), 49, 65, 77, 91, 93, 103–4, 108, 111–12, 121, 135–37, 141, 143–44, 147, 160, 163, 213, 216, 226, 232, 234, 240–41, 243, 245, 249–51, 295, 312, 318
Arab air forces, 88–89, 91–92
Argentina, 221–23, 225–27, 229, 231, 239–40
Argentinean air forces, 222, 226–27, 228, 236, 239
Argov, Shlomo, 243
arms control, 210–11
Army Air Corps, 39, 56, 104, 119–20, 154
Army Air Forces (AAF), 7, 15, 17, 39, 50, 59, 63–64, 72, 93–99, 119–20, 122–24, 126, 147, 158–59, 263, 275, 284, 291, 297, 315
Army Air Service, 46
Army of the Republic of Vietnam (ARVN), 139–41, 145
Army Staff College, 53
Arnold, Henry "Hap," 63, 297
Ascension Island, 227–29, 232–33, 238–39
asymmetric warfare, 277
atomic bomb, 65, 291, 315
Australia, 146, 225

Baath Party, 113
Baghdad, Iraq, 112, 285
Balkans, 103, 181, 254
Barksdale AFB, Louisiana, 112
battle-damage assessment, 170, 202
battles
    Bismarck Sea, 149–51

Britain, 59, 79, 83–85, 121, 237, 251, 253–54, 256, 274
Bulge, 17
France, 80
Kasserine Pass, 155
Kursk, 251
Midway, 146
Somme, 41
Stalingrad, 178
Verdun, 41
Bay of Pigs, 211, 213, 216
Beirut, Lebanon, 241, 248
Bekaa Valley, Lebanon, 221, 241, 243–51
Belgrade, Yugoslavia, 285
Bellows Field, Hawaii, 104
Ben-Gurion Airport, 188
Berlin, 83, 94, 124, 181, 190–92, 195–96, 210, 213, 251, 254, 258
Berlin airlift, 27, 191, 195–96
Big Week, 94, 98, 123
Bismarck Archipelago, 100
Bismarck Sea, 146, 148–49
Black Buck missions, 229–30, 238
Black Sea, 177
blitzkrieg, 79, 124, 251–54, 256, 260
bombing, 15, 79, 94, 99, 114, 120, 125–26, 136–37, 141–42, 145–46, 151, 157, 164, 203, 274, 295–96, 315
Borneo, 100
Bosnia, 285
Bremen, Germany, 122
Britain, 40, 51, 64, 78–79, 85, 108, 120, 147, 190, 213, 217
British Fighter Command, 121
British Special Air Services, 233, 238
Brown, Harold, 163
Buckley AFB, Colorado, 201
budget cuts, 53, 225, 227, 313, 316
Buenos Aires, Argentina, 230
Buff Cove, Falkland Islands, 235
Bureau of Aeronautics, 61–62
Bush, George, 109–10, 185–87

Caen, France, 95
Cairo, Egypt, 92
Cambodia, 139
Camp David peace accords, 241–42
Castro, Fidel, 211, 213
center of gravity (COG), 66–67, 267–68, 270, 275–76, 278, 292, 300
Central Intelligence Agency (CIA), 205–6, 208, 211, 213–14
centralized control, 170
Chain Home radar system, 81–82

Checkmate, 110
Cheney, Dick, 198
Chennault, Claire L., 56–59, 82, 104
Cheyenne Mountain, Colorado, 201
Chile, 229
China, 59, 100–101, 103–4, 143–46
Chinese Embassy, bombing of, 285
Chu Lai, South Vietnam, 161
Civil Reserve Air Fleet (CRAF), 184–89
civilian casualties, 110, 303
civilian morale, 274
Clark, Mark W., 167
Clay, Lucius D., 190–91
close air support (CAS), 54–56, 75–76, 85, 95, 97, 119, 133, 137–38, 151–61, 163–72, 175, 189, 204, 226, 239, 244, 246, 251, 257, 259–60, 263, 265–66, 277, 280, 287, 291, 293–94, 310
coalition, 5, 25, 108, 111–17, 184, 189, 198, 200, 202–4, 264, 266, 271–72, 279, 293–94, 307, 309, 312, 315
coercion, 26
Cold War, 23, 65–66, 99, 189, 205, 286, 290, 292, 301–2, 313
collateral damage, 51, 268, 283, 303
combat air patrol (CAP), 113, 228–29, 231, 235–39, 243, 251
combined aerospace force, 299
Combined Airlift Task Force (CALTF), 192, 194–96
Combined Bomber Offensive (CBO), 15, 120, 122, 124, 126, 259, 263, 291, 315
Combined Fleet (Japanese), 103
command of the air, 39–40, 43, 58, 75, 78, 92, 99
command and control (C^2), 20, 67, 80–82, 84, 95, 108, 113, 117, 143–44, 246, 249–50, 292–93, 304
Commando Aviacion Naval Argentina (CANA) (Argentinean naval aviation), 226–27, 229–40
compellence, 25
Coningham, Arthur, 155–59
control of the air, 51, 53–54, 58, 61, 64–65
conventional weapons, 100, 292
Coral Sea, 60, 106
Corona (satellite system), 206–10
Cuba, 208, 210–11, 213–17
Cuban missile crisis, 208

Damascus, Syria, 92, 241

Da Nang, South Vietnam, 140
Defense Advanced Research Projects Agency (DARPA), 312–13
Defense Intelligence Agency (DIA), 115–16
Defense Satellite Communications System (DSCS), 201
Defense Support Program (DSP), 198, 200, 202, 204
defensive counterair (DCA), 77, 229, 246
defensive countermeasures, 295
defensive counterspace (DCS), 77
demilitarized zone (DMZ), 139, 142
Demyansk, Soviet Union, 179–81, 255–57
de Seversky, Alexander, 63–66
deterrence, 23, 25, 31
Dhahran, Saudi Arabia, 198
Diego Garcia, 186
directed-energy weapons, 295
Discoverer satellites, 207–8
doctrine, 52, 56, 70, 88, 124, 154, 157–58, 165–66, 221, 250–52, 254, 256–60, 263–65, 275, 290, 302, 306, 311, 317
Doolittle, James, 93
Douhet, Giulio, 39–46, 48–54, 56, 58–60, 63–64, 67, 69, 72, 75, 78, 99, 310
downsizing, 189
dual technology, 316–17
Dyna-Soar, 297

early warning system, 57, 59, 112
Easter offensive, 142, 145
East Falkland, 230, 235
East Germany, 190
Egypt, 16, 86–87, 90, 241, 243, 278, 312
Egyptian Air Force (EAF), 16, 86, 88–91
Eighteenth Army (Japanese), 146
XVIII Airborne Corps, 188
Eighth Air Force, 79, 93–95, 120, 122–24, 126
Eighth Army (British), 153, 155
Eighth Army (UN), 165
VIII Fighter Command, 122
82d Airborne, 109, 186–87
Einstein, Albert, 315
Eisenhower, Dwight D., 156, 158, 206–7, 211
electronic countermeasures (ECM), 234, 241, 245–46
electronic intelligence, 229
European theater, 150, 272

expeditionary forces, 52, 235, 302, 304–6

Falkland Islands (Islas Malvinas), 221–34, 232, 235–36, 238–40
Fiebig, Martin, 178
Field Manual (FM) 100-20, *Command and Employment of Air Power*, 158–59, 165–66, 168, 263
Fifteenth Army (German), 97
Fifth Air Force, 133–38, 165, 167
51st Division (Japanese), 146, 148
Fighter Command, 83, 85
fighter-control centers, 57
1st Fighter Wing, 109
1st Marine Air Wing, 133
five-ring model, 67, 275
five-step planning, 270
Flying Tigers (see also American Volunteer Group), 104
Forrestal, James, 191
Fort Bragg, North Carolina, 186
Fort Knox, Kentucky, 57
43d Bomb Group, 148
forward air controller (FAC), 167, 170–71
forward air observers, 233
4th Air Commando Squadron (4ACS), 160
Fourth Air Force (German), 181
4080th Strategic Reconnaissance Wing, 214
France, 50, 79–80, 87, 93, 95–98, 108, 112, 120, 122, 124, 190, 252, 254, 257, 266
Freya early warning radar, 121
Fuerza Aerea Argentina (FAA) (Argentinean air force), 226–31, 233–40
Fuller, J. F. C., 15

Galland, Adolph, 84
GBU-28 penetrating bomb, 315
George, Harold L., 119
German Afrika Korps (DAK), 153, 155–57
German air force, 85, 93
German High Command, 253
Germany, 7, 15, 38, 40, 51, 59, 64–65, 79–80, 82, 85, 93–94, 97, 119–20, 122–24, 126, 147, 195, 251–52, 254, 257–58, 263, 272, 284, 293, 315
Global Positioning System (GPS), 298, 304
Golan Heights, Israel, 86
Goose Green, Falkland Islands, 226, 230, 232

331

Göring, Hermann, 79–80, 83, 178, 181
gravity bombs, 144
Great Britain, 51–52, 57, 62, 79–83, 87, 120, 122, 195, 227–28, 232
Great Scud Hunt, 202, 204
ground-controlled approach (GCA), 194
ground-controlled intercept (GCI), 115, 246–47, 249, 251
ground support, 50, 52–56, 65, 80–81, 89, 92–93, 150, 152, 157–59, 164, 166, 168, 233, 250, 254, 258, 260, 264, 290, 292–94
Guadalcanal, 146
Guam, 101, 141, 186, 192
Guanajay, Cuba, 215–16
Gulf of Taranto, 103
Gulf War, 198
gun club, 60–62, 300

Haiphong, North Vietnam, 141–44
Haleiwa Field, Hawaii, 104
Hanoi, North Vietnam, 143–44
Hansell, Haywood S., 119, 126
Hatazo, Adachi, 146, 148
Hawaii, 101, 103–4, 192
Hawaiian Air Force, 104, 108
Hawaiian Division, 104–5
Hickam AFB, Hawaii, 104–5, 107, 207
high-altitude daylight precision bombing, 56, 120, 146, 275
Hiroshima, Japan, 315
Hitler, Adolph, 79–80, 83, 86, 119, 178, 181–83, 257, 315
Ho Chi Minh Trail, 160
Hod, Mordechai, 89–90
Honolulu, Hawaii, 102
Horner, Charles, 110, 112, 118
humanitarian missions, 26–27, 175, 190, 196, 290, 318, 320
Hussein, Saddam, 108–9, 112, 114, 117, 198, 264, 292
hypersonic vehicles, 298–99, 301

Imperial Japanese Navy (IJN), 101–8
Inchon, South Korea, 133
independent air force, 42–43, 45–46, 49–50, 71–72, 291, 299
independent space force, 71, 299, 301
industrial targets, 51
industrial-web theory, 56, 99, 120, 275
information
    attack, 305, 308–9
    operations, 197, 287, 309
    resources, 305
    systems, 305, 308–9
    threats, 306
    warfare, 197, 290, 309, 317
integrated air defense systems (IADS), 241, 245, 248
intelligence, 85, 105, 112, 116, 135–36, 138, 145–46, 150, 187, 197, 209–10, 215, 236, 239, 249, 270, 274, 279, 281, 306
interdiction, 54–56, 75–76, 131–39, 141–43, 145, 149–53, 157–58, 160, 163–65, 168, 171, 189, 204, 254, 260, 263, 265–66, 277, 287, 291, 294, 310
Interdiction Plan no. 4, 134–35
International Space Station, 300
Iran, 111, 117, 198
Iraq, 20, 22, 66–67, 108, 110–14, 116–17, 187, 189, 199–200, 202, 292–94, 302
Iraqi Air Defense Command, 111
Iraqi air force, 88, 91, 111–12, 115, 117
Israel, 86–92, 115, 187–88, 198, 200, 202, 208, 221, 241, 243, 248, 251, 312
Israeli Defense Forces/Air Force (IDF/AF), 16–17, 21, 86, 88–92, 152, 241, 243–51
Israeli Defense Ministry, 202
Italian Fleet, 103
Italy, 53, 55, 57, 65, 119, 213, 217, 258, 289
Itazuke Air Base, Japan, 166

Japan, 7, 62, 65, 100–101, 106–7, 119, 150, 263
Java, 100
Johnson, Hansford T., 186
Joint Chiefs of Staff (JCS), 141, 186, 200, 285, 293
joint
    doctrine, 171, 317
    forces, 238
    operations, 317–18
    operations center (JOC), 166–67, 170–71
    planning, 54
Jordan, 16, 86, 91
Jordanian air force, 17, 88
Kari air defense, 113
Kasserine Pass, Tunisia, 153, 156, 158–59, 263
Kennedy, John F., 208, 211, 213–14, 216
Kenney, George, 146–51

Khrushchev, Nikita, 211, 213–14, 216–17
King Fahd, 109
Knox, Frank, 119
Korea, 133, 137–38, 146, 165–66, 168, 170, 302
Korean War, 165, 171, 291, 294, 319
Kosovo, Yugoslavia, 26, 279, 285
Kursk, Soviet Union, 258
Kuter, Laurence S., 119
Kuwait, 108–11, 113, 117–18, 187, 292

Lae, New Guinea, 146, 148–50
land-based airpower, 132, 148–49, 165, 235, 305, 318
Langley Field, Virginia, 56
Laos, 160
laser-guided weapons, 18, 144, 236, 285
Lebanon, 86, 241–44, 247–48, 250
LeMay, Curtis E., 160, 191–92
Libya, 292
Lockheed Corporation, 206
logistics, 93, 106, 139, 142–43, 145, 150, 153, 187–88, 228, 234–35, 239–40, 258, 265, 268, 270, 272
London, 82–85, 297
long-range bombardment, 39, 42, 46, 50
Luftwaffe, 64, 78–85, 93–99, 120–25, 156–57, 178–83, 195, 221, 237, 251–60, 266, 274, 315

MacArthur, Douglas, 145–47, 150, 165
Mahan, Alfred Thayer, 70
Malaya, 100
Mariana Islands, 60
Marine air-ground task force, 187
Marshall, George C., 104, 158
Marshall Plan, 190
master attack plan (MAP), 281, 283
Maxwell Field, Alabama, 56
McCoy AFB, Florida, 214
McNamara, Robert S., 214
Mediterranean, 103, 122, 156, 254
Mediterranean Allied Air Forces, 53
Messerschmitt, Wilhelm "Willy," 125
Midway, 60, 106
Military Airlift Command (MAC), 185–89
military objectives, 110, 264–65
missile defense system, 205
missiles, 65–66, 88, 214, 216–17, 296, 312
  AA-2 Atoll, 247
  AA-8 Aphid, 247
  AGM-45 Shrike, 229, 245–46
  AGM-65 Maverick, 246
  AGM-78 Standard, 245–46
  AIM-7F Sparrow, 247, 250
  AIM-9, 231, 250
  AIM-9L Sidewinder, 228, 230–31, 238, 247
  air-to-air (AAM), 90, 228, 247
  air launched cruise, 112
  air-to-surface, 88, 240
  Al-Abbas, 199
  Al-Hijarah, 199
  Al-Hussein, 198–99
  AM-39 Exocet, 226, 231, 234, 236, 240
  antiaircraft, 45
  antiradiation, 249–50
  antitank, 234
  ballistic, 33, 111, 207–8, 210, 213–14, 216, 292
  cruise, 113, 117, 285, 297, 313, 318
  intercontinental ballistic (ICBM), 7, 23, 72, 196, 200, 207–8, 216, 286
  intermediate-range ballistic (IRBM), 211, 213–16
  Lance, 245
  medium-range ballistic (MRBM), 211, 213–14, 216
  Patriot, 187–88, 200–202, 205
  Python 3, 247
  Roland, 226
  SA-2, 214, 245
  SA-3, 245
  SA-6, 244–45
  Scud, 113, 115–16, 187–88, 198–205
  Sea Wolf, 233
  Shafrir 2, 247
  space-to-ground, 71
  SS-4 Sandel, 216
  SS-5 Skean, 216
  submarine-launched ballistic, 200, 205, 286
  surface-to-air (SAM), 77, 111–12, 139, 141, 143–45, 205, 208, 210–11, 213–16, 226, 234, 239–41, 243, 245–51, 295, 312, 318
  surface-to-surface, 151, 198
  tactical ballistic, 133, 200, 204–5, 217, 297, 318
  Thor, 207
  Tigercat, 226
  Tomahawk, 112, 293
  TOW antitank, 248

V-1, 297
V-2, 198
Ze'ev surface-to-surface, 245
Missile Warning Center, 201
Mitchell, William "Billy," 2–3, 45–46, 48–54, 56, 58–64, 69, 72, 75, 78, 99, 103, 119–20, 148, 263
mobility, 175–76, 260, 265, 277, 287, 290, 295, 301, 304
Moffett, William A., 59–63, 72, 299
Momyer, William A., 145
morale, 43, 45, 51, 67, 93, 120, 274
Mountbatten, Louis, 150

Nagasaki, Japan, 315
Nagumo, Chuichi, 108
National Aeronautics and Space Administration, 298
national objectives, 32, 52, 70, 76, 110, 264–65, 272, 284–85, 292, 300
National Security Agency, 215
National War College, 66
naval aviation, 61–62, 103, 132, 299–300
naval blockade, 216
Netherlands, 80
Netherlands East Indies, 100
New Guinea, 145–46, 148–50
night bombing, 51, 53, 121, 144
Ninth Air Force, 93
Nixon, Richard M., 139–42, 210
No. 44 Squadron (British), 227
Normandy, France, 92, 94–99, 123
North Africa, 60, 103, 121–22, 126, 153, 155–56, 158–59, 181, 183
North American Air Defense Command, 201
North Atlantic Treaty Organization (NATO), 26
North Korea, 134–35, 165, 294
North Korean People's Army (NKPA), 133, 136, 138
North Vietnam, 141–44, 292
North Vietnamese Army (NVA), 139–45, 159, 161, 164
Norway, 81, 83
Nott, John, 225, 228
Novikov, Alexander, 256
nuclear
    deterrence, 291
    forces, 213, 286
    war, 100, 301
    weapons, 22, 27, 33, 100, 193, 205, 210, 284–86, 291–93, 309, 315, 317

biological and chemical (NBC), 20, 108, 110–11, 115–16, 198

Oahu, Hawaii, 102, 104–6, 108
offensive counterair (OCA), 77, 88, 246
offensive counterspace (OCS), 77
Office of Special Investigations, 138
Ofstie, R. A., 137
operations
    Allied Force, 26, 279, 285
    Anadyr, 213
    Argument, 123
    Babylon, 21
    Constant Guard, 140
    Deliberate Force, 285
    Desert Shield, 5, 20, 110, 112, 184–85, 188, 263, 272, 292
    Desert Storm, 5, 20, 25, 66, 112, 115–16, 184–90, 198, 202, 263, 266, 269, 272, 279, 281, 284–85, 294, 312, 315, 319
    Fall Barbarossa, 251–53, 255, 257
    Freedom Train, 141, 143–45
    Hawaii, 100–103
    Instant Thunder, 66, 110–11, 292–93
    Kanalkampf, 82
    Lien Ket I, 161
    Linebacker I, 142–45
    Overlord, 92–93, 95
    Peace for Galilee, 243
    Pocket Money, 143
    Pointblank, 93–94
    Saturate, 137–38
    Seelöwe (Sea Lion), 79–82, 86
    Strangle, 133, 135–37
    Vittles, 27, 191, 195–96
    Zitadel, 257
Ostfriesland, 49, 61, 103

Pacific Fleet, 101–3, 106–8
Pacific theater, 146, 150, 166, 271
Palestine Liberation Organization (PLO), 241–44, 248, 251
parallel attack, 66, 69, 267, 277
paralysis, 64, 66
Paris Peace Accords, 139, 145
Patrick AFB, Florida, 214
peacekeeping, 290
Pearl Harbor, 60, 101–8
Pebble Island, 233
People's Democratic Republic of Germany, 190
People's Liberation Army (PLA), 133, 135–38

People's Republic of China (PRC), 133–36, 294
Persian Gulf, 110, 116, 184–86, 188, 200–201, 284, 315
phasing of operations, 266, 277
Philippines, 100–101
planners/planning, 88–89, 92, 95, 100–102, 110–12, 114, 119, 123–24, 181, 189, 196, 221, 237–38, 240, 261, 263–66, 269–85, 291, 302, 305–6, 309, 312, 317–18
Poland, 79–80, 252, 254, 257
political objectives, 67–69, 110, 153
Port Stanley, Falkland Islands, 223–30, 233–36, 239
Powell, Colin, 293
precision attack, 26, 46, 71, 138, 292, 295
precision-guided munitions (PGM), 117, 144, 245, 249, 274, 292, 313
principles of war, 14–15, 23, 33, 36, 86
Project Harvey, 312–13
Punta Arenas, Chile, 229
Pusan, South Korea, 165–66

Rabaul, New Britain, 146, 148–50
radar cross section (RCS), 312
RAF Bomber Command, 95
RAF Fighter Command, 82–83, 85
reconnaissance, 5, 42–43, 48, 61, 76, 135, 164–65, 168, 188, 206–7, 214–16, 227–29, 236, 239, 244–45, 249, 259, 269, 277, 281, 289, 295, 297, 301
Regensburg, Germany, 123
Remedios, Cuba, 215–16
remotely piloted vehicles (RPV), 244–46, 249, 297
Republican Guard, 108, 115, 117
Republic of Korea (ROK), 133, 161
Richtofen, Wolfram von, 181–82
Ridgway, Matthew, 133
Rio Gallegos, Argentina, 230
Rio Grande, Argentina, 231
Riyadh, Saudi Arabia, 293
Rommel, Erwin, 97, 153, 155
Roosevelt, Franklin D., 119–20, 284
Royal Air Force (RAF), 3, 7, 15, 17, 50–53, 64, 79–85, 93–99, 113, 120–21, 191–92, 194, 204, 227–29, 232–34, 236–40, 251, 256
Royal Flying Corps, 50, 52–53
Royal Jordanian Air Force (RJAF), 91
Royal Saudi Air Force, 113

rules of engagement, 271
Rundstedt, Gerd von, 96

Sagua la Grande, Cuba, 214, 216
Saigon, South Vietnam, 139
San Carlos Bay, Falkland Islands, 233
San Carlos, Falkland Islands, 234–35
San Cristóbal, Cuba, 214, 216
San Julian, Argentina, 230
satellites, 3, 9, 11–13, 23, 29–32, 71, 76, 196–97, 200–201, 206–7, 210, 285, 295, 297–98, 300–301, 304, 306–8, 310
Saudi Arabia, 20, 108–10, 115, 184–89, 201, 293
Schofield Barracks, Hawaii, 104
Schwarzkopf, Norman, 110
Schweinfurt, Germany, 123
sea-based airpower, 235
Sea of Japan, 165
sea lift, 184
search and rescue, 232
Seoul, South Korea, 133
sequential attack, 266
Seventh Air Force (7AF), 142–45, 160
Seventh Army (German), 97
Seventh Fleet, 149
Seversky Aircraft Company, 63
Sharon, Ariel, 242
Shaw AFB, South Carolina, 215
ships, Argentinean
 General Belgrano, 231
 Vienticinco de Mayo, 226, 231
ships, British
 HMS *Alacrity*, 230
 HMS *Antelope*, 234
 HMS *Ardent*, 234
 HMS *Arrow*, 230
 HMS *Atlantic Conveyor*, 232, 234
 HMS *Brilliant*, 233
 HMS *Conqueror*, 231
 HMS *Conventry*, 234
 HMS *Endurance*, 225
 HMS *Fearless*, 235
 HMS *Glamorgan*, 230
 HMS *Glasgow*, 233
 HMS *Hermes*, 225, 228, 230, 232, 235
 HMS *Invincible*, 225, 228, 232, 235
 HMS *Plymouth*, 235
 HMS *Sheffield*, 231–32
 HMS *Sir Galahad*, 235
 HMS *Sir Tristram*, 235
 SS *Canberra*, 237
 SS *Queen Elizabeth II*, 237

ships, German
    Bismarck, 103
ships, US
    USS *Eisenhower*, 110
    USS *Enterprise*, 103, 105, 108
    USS *Lexington*, 62, 103, 105, 108
    USS *Missouri*, 112
    USS *San Jacinto*, 112
    USS *Saratoga*, 62, 103
    USS *Wisconsin*, 112
Sicily, 153
Sidon, Lebanon, 243–44
Sims, William, 62
Single Integrated Operation Plan (SIOP), 286
Six-Day War, 16, 86, 88, 91–92, 208, 278
Sixth Army (German), 177–78, 181–83, 257
skip bombing, 148–49
Slessor, John "Jack," 53–56, 319
Somaliland, 52
Southeast Asia, 100–101, 160, 163
Southeast Asian theater, 151
South Georgia, 224–25, 229
South Korea, 165
South Vietnam, 139–45, 159, 161, 164
South Vietnamese Air Force (VNAF), 142
Southwest Pacific Area (SWPA), 145–50
Soviet Air Defense Force, 248
Soviet air force, 88, 182–83, 221, 252, 260
Soviet doctrine, 111
Soviet Union, 27, 65, 86, 120, 133, 181, 183, 190, 198, 205–8, 210–11, 213–14, 217, 221, 247, 251–52, 254–55, 257–58, 260, 294, 301, 313
space
    access, 301
    assets, 100
    control, 70
    doctrine, 70
    forces, 36, 71–72, 77, 297–300
    operations, 196–97, 287
    planning, 264
    programs, 208, 297
    shuttle, 29, 297–98
    superiority, 75–78, 152, 260, 265, 277, 287
    surveillance, 112
    systems, 70–71, 77, 196–97, 206, 289–90, 298–99, 317, 319
    theory, 36, 69–72
    vehicles, 31, 37, 70, 289, 298

weapons, 71, 299, 301
special forces, 245, 280
special operations, 165, 265
Sputnik I, 206
Stalingrad, Soviet Union, 177–78, 180–83, 251, 254, 256–58
Stalin, Joseph, 177, 190, 196, 252
Stavka (Soviet high command), 256
Stimson, Henry, 119
strategic air campaign, 108, 110–12, 114, 116–17, 120, 124, 126, 292–94
Strategic Air Command (SAC), 142–43, 185, 189, 214, 216
strategic attack, 43, 51–54, 56, 64–66, 70, 72, 75–76, 79–81, 99–100, 103, 105–8, 111, 115–19, 124, 151–52, 154, 157, 168, 171, 205, 258–60, 263–65, 277, 280, 285, 287, 290–92, 294, 312
strategy, 56, 88, 98, 124, 251–54, 257, 260, 269–71, 276–78, 290, 306, 311, 317
Stratemeyer, George E., 165–66
Suez Canal, 103, 241
Suez War, 86
suppression of enemy air defenses (SEAD), 77, 112, 295
surprise attack, 100, 116, 256, 276, 285
surveillance, 246
Syria, 16, 86–87, 91, 241–43, 247–48, 278
Syrian Arab Air Force (SAAF), 17, 86, 88–91, 243–51
system of systems, 67

tactical air control center (TACC), 166–67, 169–70
tactical air control party (TACP), 167, 169, 171
tactical air direction center (TADC), 169
Tactical Event Reporting System, 201
Tactical School, 56
taran (Soviet ramming tactic), 255
Task Force 77 (TF77), 133, 137, 142–43, 165, 167
Tel Aviv, Israel, 188, 198
television-guided munitions, 144
terror campaign, 83, 85
Tet offensive, 139
Thailand, 140
theater campaign, 268, 270, 283
theater objectives, 273, 276, 282
3d Armored Division (Syrian), 241
transatmospheric vehicles, 298–99, 301

transporter erector launchers (TEL), 199, 202–4
Trenchard, Hugh, 50–54, 56, 61, 72, 121
Truman, Harry, 191
Tunisia, 155, 183
Tunner, William H., 194–95
Turkey, 113, 200, 213, 217
29th Tactical Reconnaissance Squadron, 215
Tyre, Lebanon, 243

Ultra, 85
United Kingdom, 222, 226–28, 243
United Nations (UN), 86–87, 108–9, 112, 116, 133, 135, 137–39, 165–66, 187, 189, 216, 222, 301
United States Air Forces in Europe (USAFE), 191–92, 194–95
United States Central Command, 110, 201–2, 204
United States Space Command, 200–202
United States Strategic Bombing Survey, 126

Vandenberg AFB, California, 207
Van Fleet, James A., 137
Vienna, Austria, 211
Vietcong, 139, 141, 159–61, 163–64
Vietnam, 139, 159–60, 162, 165, 269, 302
Vietnamization, 139–40, 142
Vietnam War, 4, 18, 20, 208, 292, 297, 312, 319
vital centers, 40, 46, 48–49, 64
Volga River, 177
Voyenno-vozdushnyye sily (VVS) (Soviet air force), 252–60

Wake Island, 101, 105
Walker, Kenneth N., 119
Warden, John, 66–69, 108, 110–11, 268, 275, 292–93
War Department, 104
War in the East, 177
war game, 285
Warsaw Pact, 208
Washington, D.C., 216
Washington Naval Limitation Treaty, 62
weapons of mass destruction, 67, 113, 115–16, 273, 292, 306
Wehrmacht, 79, 93, 182
Western Desert Air Force, 155
West Falkland, 233
West Germany, 190–91, 194
Wheeler Field, Hawaii, 104–6
Wideawake airport, Ascension Island, 227–30, 239
will of the people, 48, 50–54, 63–64, 67
Woomera, Australia, 201
World War I, 38–41, 45–46, 50–51, 62–63, 69, 81, 144, 151, 240, 289, 297, 319
World War II, 7, 15, 38–39, 44–45, 50, 53, 55, 59–60, 62–64, 72, 85, 92, 119–20, 134, 151, 154, 166, 168, 178–79, 195, 198, 205, 221, 247–48, 250–52, 256, 263, 271–72, 275, 284, 289, 291, 297, 315, 319
Wright Flyer, 289
Würzburg fire-control radar, 121

Yalu River, 133–34
Yamamoto, Isoroku, 103
Yom Kippur War, 152, 241, 245, 249, 312
Yugoslavia, 26
Yuvasov, Yevseny S., 248